NORTH CAROLINA
STATE BOARD OF COMMUNITY COLLEGES
LIBRARIES
WAKE TECHNICAL COMMUNITY COLLEGE

Controversies in CONSTITUTIONAL LAW

COLLECTIONS OF DOCUMENTS AND ARTICLES
ON MAJOR QUESTIONS OF AMERICAN LAW

PAUL FINKELMAN
GENERAL EDITOR
Virginia Polytechnic Institute and State University

A Garland Series

Contents of the Series

THE CONSTITUTION AND THE FLAG

VOLUME 1
The Flag Salute Cases

VOLUME 2
The Flag Burning Cases

PRAYER IN PUBLIC SCHOOLS AND THE CONSTITUTION, 1961-1992

VOLUME 1
Government-Sponsored Religious Activities in Public Schools and the Constitution

VOLUME 2
Moments of Silence in Public Schools and the Constitution

VOLUME 3
Protecting Religious Speech in Public Schools: The Establishment and Free Exercise Clauses in the Public Arena

GUN CONTROL AND THE CONSTITUTION
Sources and Explorations on the Second Amendment

VOLUME 1
The Courts, Congress, and the Second Amendment

VOLUME 2
Advocates and Scholars: The Modern Debate on Gun Control

VOLUME 3
Special Topics on Gun Control

THE CONSTITUTION AND THE FLAG

Volume 1
The Flag Salute Cases

Edited with an Introduction by

Michael Kent Curtis

SCHOOL OF LAW
WAKE FOREST UNIVERSITY

Garland Publishing, Inc.
New York & London
1993

Introduction copyright ©1993 Michael Kent Curtis
General Introduction copyright ©1993 Paul Finkelman
All rights reserved

Library of Congress Cataloging-in-Publication Data

The Constitution and the flag / edited by Michael Kent Curtis.
    p.   cm. — (Controversies in constitutional law)
   Contents: v. 1. The flag salute cases— v. 2. Flag burning cases.
   ISBN: 0–8153–1267–9 (alk. paper). — ISBN: 0–8153–1268–7 (alk. paper)
   1. Freedom of speech—United States—Cases. 2. Flags—Law and legislation—United States—Cases. 3. United States—Constitutional Law—Amendments—1st—Cases.   I. Curtis, Michael Kent, 1942–   II. Series.
KF4772.A7C66   1993
342.73'085—dc20
[347.30285]   92–39286
                                             CIP

Printed on acid-free, 250-year-life paper
Manufactured in the United States of America

CONTENTS

I. GENERAL INTRODUCTION vii

**II. INTRODUCTION TO THE CONSTITUTION
    AND THE FLAG** ix

Children, the Bill of Rights and the American Flag
Frank W. Grinnell 1

More About the Flag Salute Law
Frank W. Grinnell 9

More About the Flag Salute: Extracts from the Opinion of the
    Circuit Court of Appeals for the Third Circuit in Minersville
    School District v. Gobitis
Frank W. Grinnell 12

Minersville School District, Board of Education of Minersville School
District, et al. v. Gobitis et al. 16

Constitutional Law—Due Process—Freedom of Religion and
    Conscience—Compulsory Flag Salute
William F. Andersen 39

The "Reconstructed Court" and Religious Freedom:
    The Gobitis Case in Retrospect
William G. Fennell 43

Recent Restrictions Upon Religious Liberty
Victor W. Rotnem and F.G. Folsom, Jr. 61

How Questions Begot Answers in Felix Frankfurter's
    First Flag Salute Opinion
Richard Danzig 77

Civil Liberties and Democracy
Henry Steele Commager 95

Amicus Curiae Brief of the American Legion, The West Virginia
State Board of Education, etc., et al., *Appellants,* vs. Walter Barnette,
Paul Stull, and Lucy McClure, *Appellees* 99

Amicus Curiae Brief of the Committee on the Bill of Rights,
of the American Bar Association, The West Virginia State Board
of Education, etc., et al., *Appellants,* vs. Walter Barnette, Paul Stull,
and Lucy McClure, *Appellees* 123

Amicus Curiae Brief for American Civil Liberties Union,
The West Virginia State Board of Education, etc. et al.,
Defendants-Appellants, vs. Walter Barnette, Paul Stull, and
Lucy McClure, *Plaintiffs-Appellees* 149

West Virginia State Board of Education et al. v. Barnette et al. 172

The Flag-Salute Case
Thomas Reed Powell 220

Freedom of Thought and Religious Liberty Under
the Constitution
Louis B. Boudin 223

Justice Frankfurter's Opinions in the Flag Salute Cases: Blending
Logic and Psychologic in Constitutional Decisionmaking
Richard Danzig 239

The Flag Salute Cases and the First Amendment
Stephen W. Gard 289

Mrs. Susan Russo, Appellant, v. Central School District No. 1,
Towns of Rush, et al., County of Monroe, State of New York
et al., Appellees 325

Opinions of the Justices to the Governor: Supreme Judicial
Court of Massachusetts 337

Acknowledgments 343

GENERAL INTRODUCTION

This series provides teachers, scholars, and students with convenient access to the law, debates, and scholarly literature surrounding major questions of constitutional law. Each set of books—from two to four volumes—consists of four elements: an extended introduction to the problem by the editor; reprints of a few of the significant cases and briefs on the subject; Congressional testimony, and other primary documents on the problem; and the best scholarly articles on the subject. By conveniently gathering all this material in one place, each set of volumes allows users to quickly become familiar with the arguments and issues surrounding a particular constitutional controversy.

Scholars and students interested in constitutional law and public policy are often overwhelmed by the sheer amount of material published on controversial subjects. The topics in *Controversies in Constitutional Law* are timely, controversial, politically significant, and intellectually compelling. They are the issues that bring the legal academy, courts, politicians, and general public together, although not always in harmony.

Many scholars are barely able to keep up with the scholarship in their own fields. Yet, we need to learn about issues beyond our own specialties. A new course may require a quick introduction to a problem; our own research may lead us to a new issue. *Controversies in Constitutional Law* is designed to meet these needs. It will enable scholars and teachers to quickly come up to speed on the topics of each volume.

This series will also serve students at all levels of higher education. Students often encounter controversial topics without a background in how the problem developed. These volumes provide such a background. The important cases are reprinted in full; the introductions provide students with a map to the issues; the briefs, congressional testimony, and scholarly articles give convenient access to the arguments and debates.

The volumes bring together in one place a wide variety of sources and materials that are unlikely to be found in any one library. The primary documents include reported cases, briefs, testimony from legislative committee hearings, and, on occasion, executive branch publications. Few law libraries, university libraries, or public libraries will have all these materials. The secondary literature comes from the scholarly literature of law, history, political science, economics, criminology, and other relevant fields. Some of the articles are also from serious non-academic journals. All the articles and primary sources in these volumes sample a wide range of sources.

The related government publications, briefs and congressional testimony, are particularly important. Too often scholars overlook them. We tend to focus on court opinions—what the Court said. This is obviously important for understanding doctrine, but, briefs, especially amicus briefs, are also an important source of information about the larger constitutional controversy the case represents. The politics of a case is often more apparent in them than in either the oral arguments or the courts opinion. Similarly, Congressional hearings illustrate the social, philosophical, and political dimensions of these questions. These sources are an important supplement to the scholarly literature.

Our goal of limiting each collection to two to four focused volumes and our inability to secure copyright permission for some important articles forced us to make hard and judicious choices. Important articles that we could not reprint are listed in the further reading sections at the end of the author's introduction.

Controversies in Constitutional Law provides in one single place a comprehensive introduction to a topic that will satisfy most lawyers, scholars, and students. By combining cases, briefs, legislative debates and testimony from committee hearings with secondary articles, we hope to facilitate access to the problem set out in each set of volumes.

INTRODUCTION

Reading the First Amendment by the Light of the Burning Flag
— Michael Kent Curtis[1]

THE ELEPHANT AND ITS TAIL: THE FIRST AMENDMENT AND THE FLAG CASES

Two Cases about the Flag: *West Virginia Board of Education v. Barnette* **and** *Texas v. Johnson*

In 1943, in *West Virginia Board of Education v. Barnette*[2] the Supreme Court ruled that school children could not be forced to salute the flag by pledging allegiance. The Court held the forced flag salute violated a First Amendment right not to speak. Nearly half a century later, in 1989 in *Texas v. Johnson*[3] the Court overturned the conviction of a young man who had burned the flag as an act of political protest. The cases share a number of similarities. Both involve the flag. Both involve symbolism. Both turned on an interpretation of the guarantee of freedom of speech. In both the Court protected highly unpopular conduct.

Read for all they are worth, *Barnette* and *Johnson* suggest a limited area of individual intellectual autonomy, the idea of a sphere of ideas, conscience, and expression beyond the control of government. This idea assumes that, in general and with significant exceptions,[4] the advocacy of ideas we hate is beyond the power of government to suppress and the wisest and most patriotic individual expression is beyond the power of government to compel.[5] It further assumes that people have a right to make up their own minds on such matters. Such a theory is far from universally accepted and, indeed, is criticized by many.

By themselves the flag cases, and particularly the flag burning case, may seem trivial, a tiny tail to the huge elephant of free speech, free press, and freedom of religion. A central purpose of this essay is to give the reader a glimpse of the elephant itself. I do that by looking at the historical development of conceptions of individual rights and of freedom of speech and of the press, and by sketching out some of the larger legal questions the flag cases involve. In one sense the flag cases are a small part of First Amendment law. Running through them, however, are issues central to the meaning of the First Amendment. Four main themes emerge from the materials that follow.

Four Pervasive Themes
Minority Rights v. Majority Rule

First is the tension between minority rights and majority rule. Our seventeenth-century heritage of liberty was a heritage both of self-government and of individual rights beyond the power of government. The question of minority rights against majority rule has a long history, going back beyond Madison's insistence during the framing of the Bill of Rights that one of its major functions was to protect the minority from the majority.[6] A contemporary manifestation of this tension is the debate over proper judicial role. On one side are those, like Judge Robert Bork,[7] Chief Justice Rehnquist,[8] and former Attorney General Edwin Meese,[9] who criticize much judicial protection of individual rights as interfering with majority rule. On the other side are those who seek on broader or stronger judicial protection of individual rights.[10] While important, this debate obscures one of the insights that was a crucial impetus for the Bill of Rights.[11] Majority rule is a metaphor or a fiction. The people are not the same as the rulers, and the rulers may act in ways inimical to the people's—or the majority's—interest or in ways that most would disapprove if they knew all the facts.[12]

Two approaches to the tension between majority rule and individual rights appear in the differing views of Justices Jackson and Frankfurter in the flag salute cases.[13] Children who were Jehovah's Witnesses had been expelled from school because they refused to salute the flag. In this they followed the teaching of their religion that the flag salute was idolatry. Justice Jackson found a right not to salute the flag in the First Amendment's guarantee of free speech. He rejected the idea that the issue should be resolved by majority rule:

> The very purpose of a Bill of Rights was to withdraw certain subjects from the vicissitudes of political controversy, to place them beyond the reach of majorities and officials and to establish them as legal principles to be applied by the courts. One's right to life, liberty, and property, to free speech, a free press, freedom of worship and assembly, and other fundamental rights may not be submitted to vote; they depend on the outcome of no elections.[14]

Justice Frankfurter insisted the issue properly belonged in the political process:

> Except where the transgression of constitutional liberty is too plain for argument, personal freedom is best maintained—so long as the remedial

Introduction

channels of the democratic process remain open and unobstructed—when it is ingrained in a people's habits and not enforced against popular policy by the coercion of adjudicated law.... To fight out the wise use of legislative authority in the forum of public opinion and before legislative assemblies rather than to transfer such a contest to the judicial arena, serves to vindicate the self-confidence of a free people.[15]

Contemporary judges have followed a similar path. Justice Rehnquist has indicated, for example, that faced with the inevitability of mistakes courts do better to err by denying meritorious claims of constitutional right rather than by mistakenly striking down democratically enacted statutes.[16] Justice Scalia has suggested that it is better to leave protection for minority religious exercises (like Indian use of peyote in religious ceremonies) to the vagaries of the political process than to have judges weigh "the social importance of all laws against the centrality of all religious beliefs."[17]

The claims of majority rule versus minority rights easily lead to exaggeration. Those favoring a more liberal reading of guarantees of liberty do not advocate that all issues become questions of individual rights, decided by judges instead of voters. Advocates of stricter construction would still protect some rights from the political process. The broader issue of majority rule versus minority rights involves other issues—those of the scope and strength of rights.

The scope of guarantees of individual rights

Much contemporary debate about the proper role of courts focuses on the scope of individual rights and of judicial power to protect them. Similar issues arise on how broadly to read freedom of speech. Does freedom of speech and of the press include protection for anything other than explicitly political speech? Is symbolic expression, like carrying a flag or burning one as a political protest, subsumed within freedom of speech? The issue of scope is obviously related to the perceived tension between democracy and rights. If the flag salute may not be required, the majority cannot impose it. A third issue, also related to governmental power and individual rights, concerns not how broad the guarantees are, but how strong they are when they collide with other interests government wishes to pursue.

A freedom of speech and press beyond the power of government to abridge

Does the First Amendment protect any absolute values—does it protect a core of activity that the state cannot reach? The question is not whether freedom of speech and press are absolute and apply generally without limitation. Rather it is whether there are discrete areas—where the freedom of speech or the freedom of press are agreed to apply—that are simply beyond the power of government to suppress, although it may have what seem to be very good reasons for doing so.[18] The history of free-speech adjudication shows at least two very different approaches to this issue. One approach attempts, explicitly or implicitly, to identify areas of core free-speech values or broader areas where government simply may not suppress speech however weighty its reasons. A common corollary to this approach is the recognition of categories of expression such as fighting words or obscenity that are not protected as "freedom of speech."[19] The other approach is to weigh all speech—even political speech that does not advocate lawlessness, engage in libel, etc.—against the interests the state may have in suppressing it. James Madison's opposition to the Sedition Act tends toward the first—"no law abridging"—approach. Judicial and political opinion that supported suppression of political speech criticizing slavery,[20] criticizing World War I,[21] and criticizing the World War I draft[22] followed the second approach. The issue reappears in the flag-salute cases where Justice Jackson embraces the idea of a core area of free speech protection not to be balanced against governmental needs or interests.[23] In the same cases Justice Frankfurter takes the opposite approach, holding that national security needs override the asserted right of school children not to be compelled to salute the flag and to recite a political creed. Justice Frankfurter found it easier to reach his conclusion because the Witnesses were not making a political statement, were not joining the political debate. The fact that requiring the flag salute left the political processes open to opponents of the flag salute was a factor that led Justice Frankfurter to find that the right not to salute was not covered by freedom of speech. If the Witnesses had refused to salute as an act of political protest, the collision between majoritarian suppression and the role of free speech in popular government would have been more apparent.

Free speech as a part of majority rule

A fourth question raised by the discussion that follows is the relation of free speech to majority rule. If one accepts the basic theory of popular sovereignty—that the people are sovereign and that government is in some sense their agent or trustee[24]—then significant consequences follow. (Of course, the constitutional plan was designed to have government act for the public good, not simply in response to the immediate public will, which was controlled, limited, and filtered in many ways.)[25] Free speech is an essential means by which the people consult, make decisions, and select their agents or trustees. It provides alternative choices, while suppression of points of view deprives people of such choices. If the agency metaphor is taken seriously, people have a right to information about public questions and government actions. Furthermore, since free speech is essential to self-government, courts might be expected to have a positive and nurturing attitude toward it. Such an attitude would prohibit suppression by government and afford places where the people could speak and consult. In addition to its function in self-government, a second major justification for free speech is that it is an aspect of individual autonomy that deserves protection by law.[26] The two justifications can be in serious conflict. *Barnette* tends toward an autonomy rationale; *Johnson* tends to involve speech as part of the process of majority rule. These questions about the purposes of free speech and its role in the democratic process lead naturally to examining the status of free speech in the present Court, the last topic discussed in this essay.

The First Amendment and the Rehnquist Court

Even majoritarian critics of a broad judicial role might be expected to support more vigorous judicial activity in cases of speech and press. In some ways that has been so for the Rehnquist Court. Broad government suppression of speech directly and simply because it expresses hated political, literary, or scientific ideas continues to be forbidden by the Court, and the Court seems committed to continue[27] that doctrine. (At least that is so with the exception of certain expressions, for example, those that portray sex and that the Court thinks lack serious value.) The protection is crucial. It usually protects books, magazines, newspapers, radio, and television from political, literary, or scientific censorship because of the ideas they espouse.

But as the focus shifts from negative restrictions on the content of what is said to protection or facilitation of opportunities to say it, the attitude of the Court in recent years has been very different. Particularly for those activities characterized as conduct, those involving the right to speak on public property, or those bearing on the time and place and manner of speech, the Court has tended to replace strong First Amendment values with broad deference to governmental power. In these areas rules that are generally applicable and not based on point of view[28] tend to supersede interests of free speech and press.[29] In such cases, the protection of the First Amendment is being transformed from a general protection to simply, and at best, one barring discrimination.[30] Where the suppression of expression occurs as part of a broader regulatory scheme[31] that is not specifically targeted at speech or press, protection of free expression is dubious. And where may the ordinary citizen exercise broadly protected freedom of speech? The answer seems to be in a newspaper or magazine or on a television station that need not grant access[32] or in a small number of increasingly constricted[33] and often depopulated places that the Court now calls traditional public forums. These include most publicly owned streets, sidewalks, and parks.[34] In other places, even when government property is a place that could be reasonably used for free speech,[35] the broad right to speak is not protected, and indeed the government may in some settings discriminate among speakers simply based on the content of what they say.[36]

Although the Court overturned Mr. Johnson's conviction for flag burning, there is less to the decision than meets the eye, both because it applied settled First Amendment doctrine and because the impression it created of broad protection for freedom of speech is only a part of the story. More and more critics are asking how well the system of freedom of expression operates to further democratic government.[37] While the Court fairly well protects the negative right against governmental suppression of speech generally and in the shrinking public forum, these critics assert that the positive right to be heard or to hear a range of points of view is less secure. They further assert that the power of campaign contributions has produced a political system responsive to investors in politicians, not to voters. As Justice White noted wryly, the two groups are not identical.[38] But if, as a matter of First Amendment law, there was less to the flag burning decision than appeared, the political and emotional dimensions of the decision were substantial.

The *Johnson* decision and the evolution from *Barnette* to *Johnson* probably give supporters of broad free speech rights a false sense of security and satisfaction. For they wrongly infer that if burning our cherished national symbol as political protest was not punished under the statute at issue in *Johnson*, the protection of free speech is a story of steady progress and the Court must be protecting expression as never before. In one way, of course, *Texas v. Johnson* went farther than *Barnette*. *Barnette* barred compelled acts of respect for the flag. *Johnson* reversed a conviction for an act of disrespect as part of a political protest. *Barnette* did not compel the result reached in *Johnson*, but if *Barnette* had been decided the other way and had survived as a viable precedent, the outcome in *Johnson* would have been unthinkable. *Barnette* had declared that the First Amendment prohibited government enforced orthodoxy.[39] *Johnson* put that principle to a severe test, in the form of an insult to the flag that was deeply offensive to many Americans.

While it is partly true that *Johnson* represents an extension of freedom of speech, the idea needs careful qualification: because it applied settled doctrine; because of developments in other areas of First Amendment law, noted above;[40] and because of limitations inherent in the *Johnson* decision itself. *Barnette* protected the right of school children not to salute the flag, the right not to recite the political creed contained in the Pledge of Allegiance. It seems to protect a sphere of expression from governmental compulsion.

The *Johnson* decision was less expansive. It did not hold that Johnson had a right to burn the flag as an act of political protest. Instead it held that a statute *aimed at Johnson's expression in burning the flag* could not stand. Had the statute been part of a broader regulatory scheme, for example one that prohibited public burning, it would, the Court suggests, have survived.⁴¹ The distinction rests on the greater governmental power the Court thinks is needed where "conduct"⁴² is involved. (Of course speech and press typically involve some conduct.) Second, *Johnson* was at least equivocal on how absolute Gregory Johnson's right to burn the flag was. The decision left open the possibility that a more violent audience reaction might have transformed Johnson's conduct from exercise of a right to commission of a crime.⁴³

Unlike the case of the school children in *Barnette*, Gregory Johnson's flag burning was an attempt to convey a political message. One basic issue raised by the *Johnson* decision is the right to make the most fundamental criticisms of the nation, its policies, and its government. A very strong form of that principle is necessary for free institutions, but the right was slow to evolve. Punishment for making such criticisms is a type of punishment for sedition, specifically for speech critical of government and tending to spread disaffection and discontent. While history is not unequivocal, it suggests that that type of the crime of sedition is inconsistent with representative government. (The dissenters in *Johnson* insisted Johnson was not punished for his criticism, but only for the method he employed.)⁴⁴ The concept that the compelled flag salute in *Barnette* invaded a sphere of expression and conscience entitled to First Amendment protection also has significant, but not uniform, historical support.

The concept of the steady expansion of protection for speech and press is belied by history and current events. American ideas of liberty, including ideas about free speech and press, have gone through various epochs in their development. A look at these varying epochs reveals some periods of greater protection for free speech, religion, and press, and some periods of repression. History also suggests that restrictions have often seemed plausible and necessary both to officials and citizens. Punishment of flag desecrators has often been associated with more general restrictions of civil liberty. Instead of steady progress, the history of liberty suggests that guarantees are difficult to establish, easily departed from, and difficult to restore. Although leading framers of constitutional guarantees of liberty hoped that the courts would function as impenetrable bulwarks against assaults on liberty,⁴⁵ in fact the record of the courts has been mixed.

Let me try to put the issues involving the flag into a larger historical and legal mosaic. Necessarily, putting the flag cases in perspective means looking at many aspects in addition to the flag cases themselves. History has a special function here. It expands our experience and so our basis for judgement. It lets us test rules for suppression of speech—like the idea that speech that has harmful tendencies should be banned—against such earlier experience as the crusade against slavery.

Historical Background: From the Seventeenth Century to the 1930s

From the Seventeenth Century to the Bill of Rights

Ideas of representative government, religious toleration, and freedom of press and speech developed in the political and religious tumult of seventeenth-century England. As understood by some historians, the civil war of the 1640s initially was a struggle between a group of powerful landed gentry represented in Parliament and the King and his supporters.[46] As the Parliament enlisted others in the struggle, some of these people—members of the army, merchants, artisans, younger sons of the gentry families, and some members of dissenting religious sects—demanded greater religious toleration and a greater share of political power.[47] Out of the English civil war, the restoration of the Stuarts, and the Glorious Revolution of 1688, came a small group of Radical Whigs, who favored a more radical political settlement than that embraced by the ruling elite. From 1688 to about 1727 these Radical Whigs championed a number of causes: free speech and press; religious liberty, including tolerance for Jews, atheists, Unitarians, Mohammedans and by the eighteenth century even "well behaved Catholics;" separation of powers; electoral reform of Parliament including wider franchise; and the right of Englishmen, even Englishmen in the Colonies, to be ruled by laws to which they had consented.[48] As early as the 1640s, radicals had espoused the idea of fundamental rights that limited both the King and Parliament. These had included a right to criticize government and a natural right not to profess religious doctrine that one did not believe, because even professing correct doctrine was sinful in such circumstances.[49]

Though marginal in England, Radical Whigs' ideas gradually gained increased influence in America.[50] One central idea was that the people were the master and government was the servant. The people, not the legislature or government, were sovereign, and in Revolutionary America governmental power was limited by the people's instructions in a written constitution. Just as the master had the right to criticize his servant, people had the right to criticize government and public officials. Freedom of speech and press, though never fully defined, were essential to popular sovereignty.[51] These ideas were in contrast to earlier English ideas, which held that criticism of government or government officials was the crime of seditious libel; that Parliament was sovereign and its powers were unlimited; and that freedom of the press protected only the right to publish without prior governmental approval, not the right to be free from punishment after publication because of what was said.[52]

By the latter part of the eighteenth century, ideas of government limited by fundamental individual rights, including freedom of speech, of press, and of

Introduction

religion, were established in Revolutionary American state constitutions.[53] Protection of individual rights was associated with fear of abuses and corruptions of power.[54] At least some Revolutionary declarations and constitutions suggest that guarantees of liberty, including freedom of speech and press and the right to scrutinize and criticize government and its officers, were essential to protect popular sovereignty and individual rights.[55] Of course, the historical record was not uniform; it rarely is. There were also attempts to suppress criticisms aimed at government.[56]

While the federal Constitution of 1787 did protect some fundamental rights against governmental action,[57] it lacked a broad Bill of Rights. Its major explicit protections for speech and press were protection for speech in debates in Congress and the limitation of the crime of treason to waging war against the United States, or "adhering to their enemies, giving them aid and comfort."[58] Supporters of the Constitution insisted that a Bill of Rights was unnecessary. There was no need to protect freedom of speech and press, supporters said, because the Constitution gave the federal government no power over these matters. Opponents were not convinced.[59] The agreement by advocates of the Constitution to support a Bill of Rights was probably crucial to its acceptance.[60]

In the first Congress, James Madison, at first a reluctant convert to the need for a Bill of Rights,[61] sponsored and pushed through constitutional amendments. Madison had a clear view of the limits of parchment barriers against aggressive power. Still he insisted that, though not perfect, the guarantees were important. One function of a Bill of Rights was to protect the people against their governmental agents.[62] But an equally important and more difficult task was protecting the minority against the majority.[63] Madison hoped that the Bill of Rights would achieve its objective by establishing public opinion in favor of the liberties it sought to protect and by the device of judicial review. "If they are incorporated into the constitution," Madison said in Congress in 1789, "independent tribunals of justice will consider themselves in a peculiar manner the guardians of those rights; they will be an impenetrable bulwark against every assumption of power in the legislative or executive. . . . "[64] With the adoption of the American Bill of Rights, those fundamental rights became effective against the national government. Madison had also proposed protections for freedom of the press and of the rights of conscience that would limit the states as well as the federal government. That suggestion was defeated. With a few notable exceptions in the body of the original Constitution,[65] state constitutions were the only protections against state action violating fundamental rights. The federal Bill of Rights, the Supreme Court ruled in 1833, did not limit the states.[66]

The Sedition Act of 1798

Less than a decade after the adoption of the Bill of Rights, it was put to its first major test. In the Sedition Act of 1798[67] Congress acted to protect some national officials from "false, scandalous, and malicious" criticisms. The political purposes of the act were clear. It prohibited criticisms of President John Adams, but not of Vice President Thomas Jefferson, his likely opponent in the election of 1800. It would expire after the inauguration of the newly elected president. The administration targeted Jeffersonian newspaper editors and politicians and prosecuted them for what were, essentially, political criticisms of President Adams. Today it is natural to view such prosecutions with dismay. To many at the time, however, the national unity necessary to maintain a successful government seemed fragile, likely to be irreparably injured by criticisms like those made by the Sedition Act defendants. In one of the Sedition Act trials, Supreme Court Justice Chase said such criticisms were punished by all governments because they tended to destroy republican government. "If a man attempts to destroy the confidence of the people in their officers, their supreme magistrate, and their legislature, he effectually saps the government."[68] Chase's view was in accord with the law of England. "If people should not be called to account for possessing the people with an ill opinion of the government, no government can subsist," said Chief Justice Holt in 1704. "For it is very necessary for all government that the people should have a good opinion of it."[69]

While the Act was successful in the short run and upheld by the judges who heard Sedition Act cases,[70] it soon came to be viewed as an exercise in tyranny; it expired, and President Jefferson pardoned those convicted under it. From the Sedition Act until the Civil War, Congress passed no statute limiting freedom of speech or of the press.[71]

Scholars disagree on whether the Sedition Act violated the Constitution and Bill of Rights as originally understood.[72] The Act was consistent with the English idea that the freedom of the press only prohibits prior restraints on the press, not subsequent punishment for what was said, but it was generally inconsistent with practices of the American press at the time of the framing of the Bill of Rights. There had been broad exercise of press freedom in the later colonial period; suppression, often by extralegal means, of the Tory press in the Revolution; and a return to broader freedom after the Revolution. The Act was also inconsistent with ideas of popular sovereignty and free press in the Radical Whig and American tradition. In addition, the Sedition Act contradicted Federalist assurances, in the Constitutional Convention and during ratification, that the powers granted under the Constitution did not extend to the press.[73] Seen in this light, the First Amendment was a redundant safety device, like a life boat on a double-hulled ship.[74] But the framers of the state and federal guarantees of free press did not specifically explain how the inconsistencies between a broad view of free speech and press (or claims that Congress lacked power over the press) and English legal doctrine that justified suppression of sedition would be resolved. In his protest against the Sedition Act, Madison, a Republican and supporter of Jefferson, resolved the issue by concluding that the Sedition Act was inconsis-

Introduction

tent with "the right of freely examining public characters and measures, and of free communication among the people thereon, which has ever been justly deemed the only effectual guardian of every other right."[75]

From the Expiration of the Sedition Act to the Fourteenth Amendment: Slavery, Abolition, Secession, and Civil War

The libertarian conclusion that emerged from the Sedition Act prosecutions and their aftermath[76] secured basic Bill of Rights liberties from federal invasion. It left the protection of these basic liberties under state law to the states, with their own constitutions and bills of rights, where the rights were often presumed to be both cherished and safe. That conventional wisdom suffered a repeated series of shocks with the rise of militant abolitionism and of a militant pro-slavery response. Before the Civil War, in response to the crusade against slavery, Southern states and the Kansas territorial legislature suppressed fundamental rights in order to protect slavery—especially rights to free speech and press. The South became a closed society. Ministers were prosecuted for anti-slavery sermons. The *New York Tribune* was seized from the mails and burned. In the Lincoln-Douglas debates both Lincoln and Douglas recognized that Republicans could not campaign in the South. Republicans in the North circulated Hinton Helper's book attacking slavery as a campaign document. Southerners who circulated the book were prosecuted under statutes aimed at suppressing anti-slavery opinion.[77]

Slaveholders saw abolition doctrines as encouraging slave revolts. It is easy to see why. Abolitionists said slavery was kidnapping and cited the promise in the Declaration of Independence of inalienable rights for all people. Ominously, the Declaration also justified violent resistance to tyranny. While Southern states banned anti-slavery expression as tending to cause violence, Republicans insisted that state or federal laws and actions stifling anti-slavery speech violated the rights of free speech and the First Amendment. Their campaign slogan in 1856 was "free speech, free labor, free men, and Fremont."[78]

The controversy over slavery soon erupted into a debate over the nature of the American government and the meaning of its two great symbols, the flag and the Constitution. By the Fugitive Slave Act of 1850, African Americans in the North could be seized on the strength of an affidavit indicating that they were slaves. The Act denied them the right to testify on their own behalf, to jury trial, to cross-examine witnesses, or to a writ of habeas corpus before they were transported to the Southern state from which they had allegedly escaped. Once they arrived there they were presumed to be slaves because of their color.[79]

Violent resistance to the law in Boston required use of federal troops. In 1854 Anthony Burns, a recaptured escaped slave, was escorted by troops in Boston to a ship for his voyage back to slavery. Protestors lined the streets of Boston, buildings were draped in black, and American flags were hung upside down. A July 4 protest meeting again featured the American flag draped in black, hanging upside down. William Lloyd Garrison burned a copy of the Fugitive Slave Law of 1850. Then he picked up a copy of the Constitution, denounced it as "the parent of all atrocities," "a covenant with death," and "an agreement with hell," and burned it, saying, "And let the people say Amen." Many did, but there were also hisses and angry cries.[80] Most Republicans and even most abolitionists did not reject the Constitution as Garrisonians did. Instead they interpreted the American tradition as being fundamentally inconsistent with slavery.[81] Many argued that American liberty and American ideals required the inclusion of African Americans in their protections.[82]

In the secession crisis of 1861, Southern secessionists burned American flags before cheering crowds in Liberty, Mississippi, and Memphis, Tennessee.[83] The acts reflected the dominant opinion and in that circumstance, of course, there were no prosecutions. Secession and civil war sorely tested the Republican commitment to civil liberty. Some officials of the Lincoln administration had occasionally suppressed anti-administration newspapers.[84] A Union general arrested Ohio Copperhead Clement Vallandigham for making an anti-war speech. Vallandigham had denounced the Civil War as "wicked, cruel and unnecessary" and waged "for the purpose of . . . erecting a despotism . . . a war for the freedom of the blacks and the enslavement of the whites." A military commission tried him and banished him to the Confederacy. His efforts to obtain a writ of habeas corpus were denied because, as the court noted, Lincoln had suspended the writ. From his southern exile, Vallandigham made his way to Canada from which unusual location he waged his campaign for Governor of Ohio.[85]

Although he did not initiate the Vallandigham arrest and would have preferred to avoid the issue, Lincoln did support and justify it. "Must I shoot a simpleminded soldier boy," Lincoln asked, "who deserts, while I must not touch a hair of a wily agitator who induces him to desert?" The rebellion had reached the North and "under cover of 'liberty of speech'," 'liberty of press,' and '*Habeas corpus*,' [the rebels] hoped to keep on foot . . . aiders and abettors of their cause." There was no greater danger, Lincoln insisted, of such measures persisting in time of peace, than that the use of emetics during a temporary illness would continue after health was restored.[86] During the Civil War, habeas corpus was suspended and basic liberties were restricted. Prosecutions for flag desecration were part of the broader crisis of civil liberty. At least one pro-Confederate desecrator of the American flag in Union-occupied New Orleans was convicted of treason by military court and executed for the offense.[87] A civilian was arrested by the military in 1862 when he said he would not "wipe my ass with the stars and stripes."[88]

Introduction

Wartime restrictions on free speech produced protests from leading Republicans as well as Democrats. In the case of one newspaper closed by the military, Republican protests resulted in President Lincoln rescinding the order.[89] The leading historian of the subject suggests that Vallandigham's arrest was atypical and that arrests for speech, press, or association were rare.[90] Despite restrictions on civil liberty, much of the Democratic press continued its acerbic criticism of President Lincoln, describing him as a "half-witted usurper," and "the head ghoul at Washington."[91]

The Fourteenth Amendment: From a Second Bill of Rights to Judicial Counter Revolution

After winning the Civil War, Republicans faced the problems of winning the peace. In 1866 leading Republicans attempted to protect fundamental liberties, including those in the Bill of Rights, from state abridgement by proposing the Fourteenth Amendment. This assertion, though controversial, is supported by the text of the amendment, which prohibited states from abridging the privileges or immunities (or rights) of citizens of the United States or denying liberty without due process of law. The assertion is also supported by the amendment's intended function of preserving republican government and by statements of its leading supporters.[92] The Supreme Court nullified the attempt[93] and later used the amendment to provide increased protection for laissez-faire economics and for corporate power.[94] John Bingham, the principal author of Section One, later insisted that *he* had intended to protect natural persons, not corporations, but of course the Court had the last word.[95] Until the mid-1920s states seemed to be free to violate the federal Bill of Rights. Not until 1931 did the Supreme Court find state action infringing speech or press a violation of the First Amendment.[96]

Summary and Significance

What do these developments prove about burning the flag as an act of political protest? First, if flag burning is treated as symbolic speech, then by the Madison-Jefferson argument Congress would not have the power to pass a statute banning flag burning for two reasons: first, because the original Constitution did not give it power to pass laws aimed directly at speech and second, because the First Amendment forbids such laws. (Some writers have found the power to ban flag burning based on power over foreign affairs.) But whether Madison or Jefferson, and the framers of the First Amendment or modern justices would consider flag burning to be speech is, of course, a different question. If Madison and Jefferson were wrong and the First Amendment only prohibited prior restraint *and* Congress had power to pass laws aimed at speech, then a *federal* statute punishing flag burning, or any other political expression for that matter, would be constitutional. If the First Amendment forbids defining sedition to include speech critical of government and government officials, one can argue that flag burning should be protected by analogy. If the First Amendment allowed punishment for such seditious speech, then it is very hard to imagine any First Amendment problem with punishing flag burning. Finally, at least until the passage of the Fourteenth Amendment in 1868, states would have retained their power to decide whether flag burning was protected under their constitutions, without reference to the federal Constitution.

From the Fourteenth Amendment through the First World War: Freedom of Speech Without a Hard Central Core

Halter v. Nebraska,[97] the Court's first case on respect for the flag, involved its commercial use on a beer bottle label. *Halter* was a product of the era in which the Court had not yet held that the guarantees of the First Amendment limited the states. Even after it applied the Bill of Rights to the states, the Court did not find a degree of protection for commercial expression until the 1970s.[98] Halter was prosecuted for violating a Nebraska statute against commercial use of the flag. Although apparently not at issue in *Halter*, the statute also proscribed mutilation or casting contempt on the flag by word or act. While the Court did not specifically mention the First Amendment, which had not yet been held applicable to the states, Justice Harlan upheld the statute in broad language:

> [W]e cannot hold that any privilege of American citizenship or that any right of personal liberty is violated by a state enactment forbidding the flag to be used as an advertisement on a bottle of beer. . . . As the statute in question evidently had its origin in a purpose to cultivate a feeling of patriotism among the people of Nebraska, we are unwilling to adjudge that in legislating for that purpose the State . . . has infringed the constitutional right of anyone.[99]

Justice Harlan noted that the flag represented the protection of the weak from the strong, the poor from the rich, and liberty regulated by law. Indignities to the flag, Justice Harlan said, "have often been resented and sometimes punished on the spot."[100] He specifically refused to follow some state court decisions that protected commercial use of the flag under doctrines of economic liberty.[101]

From 1866 to the 1930s the Court sometimes tested federal and state laws alleged to infringe on speech and press by quite permissive standards. Only part of this permissive attitude can be explained by the failure to hold that the Fourteenth Amendment required state and local governments to obey the first. Speech or press that tended to produce bad results could be suppressed even though the speaker did not directly urge or incite commission of a crime and even though the danger might in fact be remote.[102] Some state courts tended to follow the same approach. So long as the legislature's purposes in restricting speech were rational, these courts tended to uphold them. To the

Introduction

extent they followed such an approach, courts read the relevant state or federal constitutional provisions as if there was no type of law, no category of expression, fully beyond legislative power.[103]

In addition to problems with what one could say, there was the problem of where one could say it. In 1897 the Court upheld, without reference to the "unincorporated"[104] First Amendment, a Massachusetts decision against the right of a speaker to speak in a city park.[105] Some state courts were more protective of the right to speak in public places. An Illinois court, for example, noted that such rights had been among the rights of free people since the landing of the Mayflower. Great latitude had to be allowed to public political or religious parades. It was a matter of fundamental constitutional rights.[106] Other state courts deferred to governmental decisions.[107]

Although the record of the Supreme Court was mixed, its protection of free speech and press in this period was more limited than it would later become. For example, in reviewing a contempt conviction of a newspaper editor for criticizing the state supreme court, the Court suggested, without any examination of the relevant history, that the First Amendment only protected against prior restraint of the press, not against subsequent punishment even for true criticisms.[108] State court decisions split on the right to criticize public officials, including judges.[109] Some were remarkable in their protection of free speech.[110]

Where the criticism was directed at other branches of government, the Supreme Court was more protective of free speech values. It limited contempt of Congress to acts that impaired the ability of Congress to perform its duties and found that criticism of Congress did not meet the test. It found criticism of the conduct of a member of the executive branch "a legitimate subject of statement and comment," at least in the absence of express malice.[111]

Still, also without any examination of the history of the First Amendment, the Court upheld federal convictions for attempts to interfere with the draft during World War I. The attempted interference consisted of speeches or leaflets by prominent political leaders and others. They had opposed World War I and called for political opposition to it and to the draft, but had not counseled violation of the law.[112] Memorably, Justice Holmes suggested that the First Amendment's protections shrink in wartime. The defendants' speech in the circumstances of the war created a "clear and present danger" in that it would cause "substantive evils that Congress has a right to prevent." "The most stringent protection of free speech would not protect a man in falsely shouting fire in a theatre and causing a panic."[113] The epigram's power seemed to justify punishment of those advocating political change by peaceful means. The convictions for political speech involved a fundamental question asked much later by Justice Black. May "liberties *admittedly* covered by the Bill of Rights . . . nevertheless be abridged on the ground that a superior public interest justifies the abridgment"?[114] Some contemporary scholars, including conservatives, criticized the Espionage Act decisions as inconsistent with freedom of speech and of the press, which they insisted protected "honest expression of belief as to matters resting on judgment" as well as advocacy of peaceful political change. This was so even though some converts might be further moved to engage in illegal action.[115] In construing the Espionage Act in 1917, Judge Hand had distinguished agitating against the war and draft from inciting violation of law. His approach implicitly rejected the clear and present danger test. "If one stops short of urging upon others that it is their duty or their interest to resist the law," he wrote, reading the act to avoid First Amendment problems, "it seems to me one should not be held to have attempted its violation."[116] The Court rejected such limitations.

In this World War I context, state and federal governments suppressed speech and conduct that showed disrespect for the flag. States had begun passing statutes against flag desecration in 1897. They were motivated in part by desecrations of the flag in political campaigns; political partisans burned or desecrated the flag because their opponent's advertisements were attached to it. By 1915, thirty-nine states had flag protection statutes.[117] In May 1918 the Federal Espionage Act was amended to penalize persons who "when the United States is at war shall willfully utter, print, write or publish any disloyal, profane, scurrilous or abusive language about . . . the flag of the United States. . . ."[118] The Act also prohibited abusive language about the form of government of the United States or that intended to bring it into disrepute—a classic sedition act.[119] Private citizens enforced loyalty as well. Mobs required those suspected of disloyalty to kiss the flag. One victim, E. V. Starr, refused to kiss the flag and said the flag was just cotton, paint, and marks, and "might be covered with microbes." In one of the worst World War I excesses, he was convicted of sedition in state court and sentenced to prison for not less than ten years.[120] In this period there were a number of arrests of people who made disrespectful comments about the flag.[121] Carrying the wrong sort of flag also generated prosecutions.

Some state courts upheld suppression of expression thought to have bad tendencies, including display of red flags. A Massachusetts case involved a state statute prohibiting parading with a red or black flag or with a sign carrying an inscription opposed to organized government. In a Socialist parade, Karvonen carried a red flag emblazoned in gold with the words: "Finnish Socialist Branch, Fitchburg, Mass." He was tried and convicted of violating the statute. "That this flag happens to be the usual banner of a society affiliated with a political party," the Massachusetts Supreme Judicial Court announced, was no defense. The court said that the legislature regarded a red flag "as the symbol of ideas hostile to established order, and decided that its carrying in parades would be likely to provoke turbulence. . . . "[122] The Massachusetts court used a very limited form of judicial review of the legislative judgement. Keeping public order was a

Introduction   xxv

lawful goal of the state's police power. Unless the statute "manifestly [had] no tendency" to reduce turbulence it could not be found unconstitutional. A "rational connection with the preservation of public safety" was all that was required.[123] The reasoning would have fully justified suppression of anti-slavery speech in the South before the Civil War. The idea of free speech embraced by these decisions of the World War I era seemed to lack a central core which, once identified, was protected from governmental invasion.[124]

After the war the Supreme Court continued to uphold convictions of radical speakers.[125] Justices Holmes and Brandeis began to dissent, however, seemingly giving extraordinary bite to the previously toothless clear and present danger test. They argued that advocacy of violation of the law did not justify punishing speech "where the advocacy falls short of incitement and there is nothing to indicate that the advocacy would be immediately acted on." Even then the evil threatened had to be a serious one.[126]

Lochner and Progressive Reaction

But while many courts deferred to the legislature in claims of individual rights like those in the Bill of Rights, in cases involving social and economic legislation the balancing was often done in a different manner. In 1905 in *Lochner v. New York*[127] the Court struck down a New York law that limited hours worked by bakers to sixty a week. The law was supported by substantial evidence of occupational disease related to bakers' long hours. The Court, speaking through Justice Peckham, made its own evaluation of the evidence and concluded that the law was unreasonable. "If a little unhealthfulness" could justify limiting hours, Peckham warned, there would be "no end of meddlesome interference with the rights of the individual."[128] In contrast Peckham relegated those convicted in state courts by procedures that violated commands of the national Bill of Rights to the democratic process.[129]

As the Court struck down Progressive social legislation, Progressives turned a skeptical eye on the Court's methods. The Court's invocation of "natural" or "fundamental" rights to justify decisions like the *Lochner* case led to broad questioning of the idea of "fundamental" rights. Progressives invoked the democratic process against judicial activism. In *Lochner v. New York*, Justice Holmes said, "the word liberty in the Fourteenth Amendment is perverted when it is held to prevent the natural outcome of a dominant opinion, unless it can be said that a rational and fair man necessarily would admit that the statute proposed would infringe fundamental principles as they have been understood by the traditions of our people and our law."[130] For Holmes skepticism about the idea of fundamental rights led him to turn such issues largely over to the political process. Nor did he limit his deference to economic legislation.

When Nebraska banned teaching of languages other than English, the majority of the Court found the state law violated the due process clause of the Fourteenth Amendment. The state justified the statute on the ground that teaching foreign languages would hinder learning English by students who heard only foreign languages at home. The Court did not rely on the First Amendment, not yet held applicable to the states. Instead, it insisted that teaching German was protected under the liberty of the due process clause.[131] The Court would judge whether state legislation was arbitrary and without reasonable relation to some purpose within the state's competency. Since knowledge of the German language was harmless, the legislation violated the Fourteenth Amendment.[132] Justice Holmes again dissented. "[I]t appears to me to present a question upon which men reasonably might differ and therefore I am unable to say that the Constitution of the United States prevents the experiment being tried."[133]

Writing in the *New Republic*, Professor Felix Frankfurter of Harvard Law School concluded that the cost of the power exercised by the Court in *Meyer* was "greater than its gains." Such foolish legislation would no doubt be repealed. But the Supreme Court's substantive due process decisions striking down Progressive legislation and its decisions embodying conservative values in the Constitution were "far reaching, because ever so much more durable and authoritative than even the most mischievous of repealable state legislation."[134]

The 1930s and 1940s: Stronger Protection for Free Speech

In the 1930s, before any New Deal justices joined the Court, the Court's permissive approach to governmental interferences with speech and press began to change. In 1931 the Court struck down as a prior restraint a state court injunction that prohibited further defamatory publication by a Minnesota newspaper that claimed to be exposing links between organized crime and government officials.[135] It also reversed a conviction under a California law that, as interpreted, prohibited carrying a red flag as a symbol of peaceful opposition to government.[136] By 1949 the Court required more than bad tendency to justify repression of speech; the clear and present danger test became a much tougher vehicle for protection of speech that threatened or advocated illegal conduct;[137] and the Court made a more independent and far stricter review of the state's reasons for interfering with speech or press and of the necessity for the means used. As a result, it increasingly tended to strike down governmental restrictions on speech.

Even governmental restrictions on conduct associated with speech, like leafletting, tended to fall where the state interest was not great or where the means used to advance it were broader than necessary to achieve a legitimate desired result.[138]

Introduction

The Court in the New Deal years was particularly solicitous of the free speech rights of "little people" and impecunious groups. It protected the right to speak on streets, sidewalks and parks[139] and prevented cities from prohibiting house-to-house solicitation for political and religious causes.[140]

In the process of independent judicial review of governmental suppression of speech, the 1943 *Barnette* decision was a landmark. The Court rejected a permissive "rational basis" test for state regulation of the flag salute ritual, and instead identified an area of expression beyond the power of government to control.[141] Also, and not entirely consistently, it required proof of a clear and present danger to justify interference with speech rights.[142] But the Court at first dealt with the flag salute problem in a very different way.

TESTING THE NEW LIBERTIES: THE FLAG SALUTE CASES

Gobitis: The Bill of Rights Defers to the Majority

In 1940, on the eve of America's entry into World War II, the United States Supreme Court heard the case of *Minersville School District v. Gobitis*.[143] The facts of the case were simple. The Gobitis children were Jehovah's Witnesses. Witnesses refused for religious reasons to pledge allegiance to the flag, a ceremony the local school board required of all pupils and teachers. The Gobitis children had refused to participate in their public school pledge and were expelled from school as a result.

The pledge itself had been written in the late nineteenth century by a Christian socialist.[144] The language of the pledge had undergone slight modification over the years. By 1943 it read: "I pledge allegiance to the flag of the United States of America and to the Republic for which it stands, one nation, indivisible, with liberty and justice for all." In 1892 Congress had authorized a national holiday including the pledge as a mass tribute to the flag.[145] By 1940 the pledge was, in many schools, a standard feature of the public school day. What had begun as a voluntary expression of patriotism had, in some cases, been transformed into a compulsory recital, with punishment for teachers and children who refused to participate. The flag-salute rules were designed to inculcate patriotism.[146]

The pledge was probably originally intended as a statement of aspiration, not of fact. Still the omnipresent gap between the ideal and the reality was not what troubled the Witnesses about the pledge. Their objections were theological, not political. Witnesses were a religious group. They spread their messages by street-corner witnessing and playing phonograph records and by house-to-house visits. Their aggressive proselytizing produced a number of Supreme Court decisions on freedom of speech and religion in the late 1930s and 1940s and would produce more.[147] They were critical of other organized religions (a "racket") and were intensely hostile to the Catholic Church.

Before the decision in *Gobitis,* state and federal courts had generally upheld the expulsion of Witness children who refused to salute the flag. Courts rejected the Witness claim that the flag salute was flag worship. "There is nothing in the salute or the Pledge of Allegiance which constitutes an act of idolatry, or which approaches to any religious observance," one court tartly observed.[148] The New York Court of Appeals insisted that "[s]aluting the flag in no sense is an act of worship."[149]

In *Minersville School District v. Gobitis,*[150] by a vote of 8 to 1, the Court reversed a lower court decision for Gobitis and upheld the expulsion of the Gobitis children for their conscientious refusal to salute the flag. The Court that decided *Gobitis* was a Court in transition. It had reversed many of its previous decisions, leaving most economic issues to the legislature. If legislatures had a rational basis for their decisions, which as the Court saw it they almost always did, the law would be upheld.[151] Where state decisions restricted free speech rights essential to the democratic processes, the Court engaged in a more searching examination of the statute. Many restrictions fell as a result. The Court had said it would also be more sensitive to claims of discrete and insular minorities and to claims of violations of guarantees of the Bill of Rights.[152]

Justice Frankfurter wrote for the Court. The issue was simple. Did compelling the flag salute "from a child who refuses upon sincere religious grounds" violate the Fourteenth Amendment's guarantee of liberty? Government, Frankfurter noted, could not "interfere with organized or individual expression of belief or disbelief."[153] Here, however, the children sought an exemption based on their beliefs. The flag salute was a general patriotic program and had not been directed against Witnesses. "The religious liberty which the Constitution protects has never excluded legislation of general scope not directed against doctrinal loyalties of particular sects." There was, the Court concluded, no historic warrant for concluding that the framers intended such an exemption.[154] The assertion remains controversial.[155] To buttress its conclusion, the Court cited an 1879 case upholding prosecution of Mormons for polygamy,[156] although the practice was mandated by their religion, as well as a decision refusing to exempt a college student with religious scruples against the military from a compulsory ROTC program.[157] Even if freedom of speech included the right not to speak, the Court found no exemption justified. It saw its duty to balance the state and individual interests. As the Court saw it, national unity itself was at stake. It was an interest second to none:[158]

Introduction   xxix

> The ultimate foundation of a free society is the binding tie of cohesive sentiment. Such a sentiment is fostered by all those agencies of the mind and spirit which may serve to gather up the traditions of a people, transmit them from generation to generation, and thereby create that continuity of a treasured common life which constitutes a civilized community. "We live by symbols." The flag is the symbol of our national unity. . . .[159]

The end was legitimate. It was for the school board or the state legislature to decide if the means of expelling small children with religious scruples was the best means of attaining it:[160]

> [F]or us to insist that though the ceremony may be required, exceptional immunity must be given to dissidents, is to maintain that there is *no basis* for a legislative judgement that such an exemption *might* cast doubts in the minds of the other children which would themselves weaken the effect of the exercise.[161]

As Laurent Frantz wrote in a general critique of Justice Frankfurter's balancing approach to constitutional rights, "there would seem to be no justification for putting the government's objective on one side of the scales without first requiring a demonstration that it cannot be obtained by less repressive methods. Surely the end cannot justify the means unless it requires them."[162]

The Court came perilously close to giving the legislature the same sort of essentially unreviewable power in connection with the flag salute that it gave it with reference to economic legislation. The Court twice noted that political speech remained free. The Witnesses could "fight out the wise use of legislative authority in the forum of public opinion."[163] After the decision, however, the Witnesses found themselves in literal, not metaphorical fights, not for their principles but for their lives. A wave of increased violence against the Witnesses followed the decision. The persecution did not abate until after *Gobitis* was reversed and after the Civil Rights Division of the Department of Justice weighed in on the side of the Witnesses: local United States Attorneys pointed out both the constitutional rights of the Witnesses and that state officials involved in persecution might themselves be prosecuted.[164]

How is the result in *Gobitis* to be explained? The Court balanced the interest of the government against the individual interest in liberty. It did not find that the government had invaded a sphere of free speech or religion that was simply beyond its power to regulate. It balanced government needs against claims of individual rights. But the governmental interest that loomed so large in the balance was inflated by the Court.[165] According to the Court, what was at stake was national survival. On the other hand national survival was balanced against the claim of crotchety dissidents to be exempt from laws applicable to everyone else. Once the Court chose to balance the asserted rights of the children against national security and foreclosed questioning whether compelling children was a necessary means of furthering national unity, the question was decided.[166] The comparison to *Schneider v. State*, decided shortly before *Gobitis*, is instructive.[167] In that case involving a ban on leafletting to prevent litter, the Court also recognized that the governmental interest was important. But the Court asked whether the government interest could be furthered by means, even somewhat less effective means, that would protect the government interest without infringing on free speech. The Court concluded that a ban on littering rather than on leafletting would do the trick.[168]

In his eloquent and lonely dissent in *Gobitis*, Justice Harlan Fiske Stone pointed out some shortcomings in the majority opinion. He relied both on freedom of speech and freedom of religion. He rejected the majority's deference to the legislature: "The very terms of the Bill of Rights preclude, it seems to me, any reconciliation of such compulsions with the constitutional guaranties by a legislative declaration that they are more important to the public welfare than the Bill of Rights."[169] Instead of deference to the legislature, Stone insisted on "careful scrutiny of legislative efforts" to protect individual rights.[170]

The Gobitis children did not get the benefit of such careful scrutiny or of a less restrictive means inquiry. Nor did the Court find an area of absolute protection had been invaded by the Government. Part of the reason may be doctrinal. There were cases indicating that claims of conscience did not prevail over generally applicable laws. Finally the idea that the First Amendment was about protecting political speech, which seemed not to have been restrained, made their claim seem less compelling. As we have seen, when he had argued for the adoption of a bill of rights in the House in 1789, James Madison had said that one of its key functions would be protection of the minority against the majority. Courts of justice, Madison said, would consider themselves the special guardians of those rights. Justice Frankfurter's broad deference to the legislature (or more accurately to the local school board of a small, heavily Catholic town),[171] with an exception where speech in the political process was directly restrained, undermined the function of the Bill of Rights as protection for the minority and abdicated the special role of the Court Madison had foreseen. The issue in the end is one of scope of judicial power. A court that makes all questions matters of constitutional right leaves nothing for the ordinary democratic process. A court that gives very broad deference to all legislative decisions about constitutional guarantees of individual liberty abdicates its role in the protection of liberty. The balance struck by Justice Frankfurter was strongly in favor of the state.

The *Gobitis* case was decided June 3, 1940. Between June 12 and June 20, 1940, hundreds of attacks on the Witnesses were reported to the Department of

Introduction xxxi

Justice.[172] Scholarly, religious, and press reaction to the *Gobitis* decision was decidedly negative.[173] Although the Witnesses were intensely critical of the Catholic Church, all Catholic law school law reviews, like the overwhelming number of others, were critical of the decision.[174] A powerful criticism of *Gobitis* came from Victor Rotnem, the head of the Justice Department's Civil Rights Division. In response to the Court's invocation of the importance of symbols, he noted the paradoxical symbolic effect of the decision. The symbolic power of the flag had been compromised, polluted:

> This ugly picture of the two years following the Gobitis decision is an eloquent argument in support of the minority contention of Mr. Justice Stone. The placing of symbolic exercises on a higher plane than freedom of conscience has made this symbol an instrument of oppression of a religious minority. The flag has been violated by its misuse to deny the very freedoms it is intended to represent. . . .[175]

The article noted that the Kansas Supreme Court had held expulsion of a Witness child for refusal to salute the flag violated the Kansas constitution.[176] The final footnote to this remarkable article said that a three-judge Federal District Court sitting in West Virginia had ruled against the flag salute in the case of *Barnette v. West Virginia State Board of Education*. The lower court judges had concluded that *Gobitis* was no longer good law.[177] Before the lower federal court had declined to follow Supreme Court precedent, Justices Black, Douglas, and Murphy had announced that, though they had joined in the *Gobitis* decision, they now believed it was wrongly decided.[178] The persecution of the Witnesses and the strongly negative scholarly and press reaction were probably major factors leading them to reconsider. Justice Frankfurter claimed to record a revealing exchange with Justice Douglas that took place in the fall after the decision. "Douglas said, 'Hugo will now not go with you in the Flag Salute case.' I said, 'Why, has he reread the Constitution during the summer?' Douglas replied, 'No, but he has read the papers.'"[179] One of the rare scholarly defenses of the *Gobitis* decision came from Professor Henry Steele Commanger. The majority, he concluded, had the right to experiment and in this case the legislature rather than the Court should correct mistakes.[180]

In *Gobitis* the flag salute requirement had been imposed by a local board of education which had not explained its reasons for the ritual. After *Gobitis* the West Virginia Board of Education had adopted an elaborate resolution on the salute. In language closely tracking the *Gobitis* decision, it genuflected to religious freedom; it noted that the flag salute was a general rule not aimed at religious beliefs; it noted the need for national unity as the basis of national security; it recognized the symbolic meaning of the flag; and it insisted on the importance of the salute in the formative period of a child's development.[181]

West Virginia Board of Education v. Barnette: Protection of the Minority against the Majority through a First Amendment with a Hard Central Core

Witness children expelled pursuant to the West Virginia policy confronted the Court once again with the flag salute issue. In *Barnette* the children re-litigated the question decided in *Gobitis*. The American Legion brief in *Barnette* reiterated the importance of national unity to national security:

> Government can be destroyed more quickly by assaults from within than by an attack from without. Nations have been destroyed by a breakdown in public morale. Consequently, the state through its education institutions is justified in adopting measures which will engender patriotism in the young people. . . .[182]

While the decision in *Gobitis* had inflated the flag salute into a question of national survival, Justice Jackson began his opinion in *Barnette* by limiting the issue before the Court. "The freedom asserted by these individuals does not bring them into collision with rights asserted by any other individual." The dissenting children were peaceable and orderly. There was no interference with the rights of others to participate in the ceremony. "The sole conflict is between authority and rights of the individual."[183] Nor was there any question that the state could promote patriotism. It could "require teaching by instruction and study of all in our history and in the structure and organization of government, including the guaranties of civil liberty, which tend to inspire patriotism and love of country."[184] The issue was not about ends but about means.

The state was using the flag as a symbol of "adherence to government as presently organized," Jackson wrote. "It requires the individual to communicate by word and sign his acceptance of the political ideas it thus bespeaks." The Court noted historic objections to such compelled communication, from early Christians who refused to participate in ceremonies before the statue of the emperor to William Penn's refusal to remove his hat in deference to civil authority.[185] It did not discuss the use of loyalty oaths during the American Revolution.

During the Revolution, as the campaign of George Bush for president pointed out in the controversy over the Pledge of Allegiance,[186] Congress provided that people could be summoned before a magistrate to take the oath of allegiance to the American cause. Those who refused to take the oath could be exiled.[187] In 1775 George Washington urged the new states to "fix upon some oath or affirmation of allegiance, to be tendered to all the inhabitants without exception, and to outlaw those that refuse it."[188] Still, under state statutes alternatives were often provided, as Washington's reference to affirmation suggested, for those, like Quakers, with conscientious scruples against taking oaths. North Carolina and Maryland, in deference to Quaker religious beliefs, also exempted Quakers from the requirement of removing their hats in court.[189] Of course, revolutions are different and a dubious source of precedents for other times.

The *Gobitis* decision and the parties before the Court in *Barnette* had assumed that states had a right to compel the flag salute and had framed the issue as the right of a religious minority to an exemption from the general rule. Framed in this fashion the issue was difficult because of precedent indicating no right to such exemption. Justice Jackson transformed the issue and seemed to avoid the exemption question by asking whether a ceremony "touching matters of opinion and political authority may be imposed upon the individual."[190] Instead of general power to impose the flag salute with the question of an exemption for religious dissidents based on the free exercise clause, Jackson found a general lack of such power because of the free speech guarantee.

At bottom, the *Barnette* Court rejected the ideas about compelled national unity that were the heart of *Gobitis*. The freedom "to be intellectually and spiritually diverse or even contrary" would not "disintegrate the social organization. . . . To believe that patriotism will not flourish if patriotic ceremonies are voluntary and spontaneous instead of a compulsory routine is to make an unflattering estimate of the appeal of our institutions to free minds."[191] Jackson insisted that the *Gobitis* argument based on national survival proved too much. "If validly applied to this problem, the utterance cited would resolve every issue of power in favor of those in authority and would require us to override every liberty thought to weaken or delay execution of their policies."[192]

Finally the Court in *Barnette* rejected the claim made in *Gobitis* that the Court should leave the issue of First Amendment freedoms raised in that case to "public opinion and . . . legislative assemblies rather than to transfer such a contest to the judicial arena" because all effective means of political change were left free:

> The very purpose of a Bill of Rights was to withdraw certain subjects from the vicissitudes of political controversy, to place them beyond the reach of majorities and officials and to establish them as legal principles to be applied by the courts. One's right to life, liberty, and property, to free speech, a free press, freedom of worship and assembly, and other fundamental rights may not be submitted to vote; they depend on the outcome of no elections.[193]

While the rational basis test would suffice for regulation of public utilities and the like, legislation that collided with the Fourteenth Amendment because it also collided with the first was not to be "infringed on such slender grounds."[194] Justice Jackson indicated that the Court was not following in the footsteps of *Lochner*'s broad reading of the due process clause to strike down economic legislation the Court found unreasonable. Incorporation of Bill of Rights guarantees in the Fourteenth Amendment, the Court insisted, made the command of the due process clause stronger and more specific than the clause would be without incorporation.[195] Justice Jackson concluded with a ringing statement of lack of government power to establish orthodoxy and of a First Amendment with a central core that government could not invade:

> If there is any fixed star in our constitutional constellation, it is that no official, high or petty, can prescribe what shall be orthodox in politics, nationalism, religion or other matters of opinion or force citizens to confess by word or act their faith therein. If there are any circumstances which permit an exception, they do not now occur to us.[196]

Justice Frankfurter repeated and elaborated the points he had made in *Gobitis*. He continued to attack exemptions for religious minorities from generally applicable laws. It was as if Justice Jackson, by an aikido maneuver, had stepped aside and left Justice Frankfurter lunging into space. Justice Frankfurter pointed out that the children, after engaging in the flag salute, still had the free speech right to disavow it.[197] He complained that the decision of the Court restricted the powers of democratic government; that the Court had assumed a legislative responsibility that did not belong to it; and that the Court had exalted the conscience of the minority over the conscience of the majority.[198] Finally Justice Frankfurter advocated deference to the legislature:

> Particularly in legislation affecting freedom of thought and freedom of speech much which should offend a free-spirited society is constitutional. Reliance for the most precious interests of civilization, therefore, must be found outside of their vindication in courts of law.[199]

THE 1960S: STILL GREATER PROTECTION OF FREE SPEECH

From the 1950s to the 1960s: Constitutional Rights and Free Speech Expand

In the late 1940s, with the departure of Justices Murphy and Rutledge, two of the Court's most consistent supporters of broad First Amendment rights, the character of the Court began to change. At the height of the red scare of the 1950s, the Court relaxed the clear and present danger test and upheld convictions of Communists for advocacy of forceful overthrow of the government.[200] But after further changes in personnel the Court shifted again.[201]

Introduction

The Court was moving toward broader protection for First Amendment rights. By the end of the 1960s the Court had broadly interpreted the protections the First Amendment provided against much governmental suppression of speech and press. At the same time it began to narrow the definition of those classes of speech, from obscenity[202] to libel,[203] that the state could suppress. The leading case of *New York Times v. Sullivan* severely narrowed the scope of seditious libel.[204] Factual error and defamatory content were not sufficient to strip criticism of official conduct of constitutional protection. "This is the lesson to be drawn from the great controversy over the Sedition Act of 1798 . . . which first crystallized a national awareness of the central meaning of the First Amendment."[205] Critics of the public conduct of public officials were protected from libel judgments unless their statements were intentionally false or uttered in reckless disregard of their truth.[206] Public debate, the Court insisted, "should be uninhibited, robust, and wide-open, and . . . it may well include vehement . . . attacks on government and public officials."[207]

The Court also gave broad protection for speech that earlier courts would have read as having a tendency to produce or even as advocating illegal conduct. During the Vietnam War the Georgia legislature refused to seat Julian Bond, who had been elected to that body. Bond, a pacifist, had endorsed a statement of "sympathy with and support" for the men unwilling to "respond to a military draft which would compel them to contribute their lives to United States aggression in Vietnam." He believed that people "ought not to participate in" the Vietnam war.[208] Still he later explained, he did not advocate that people break laws.[209] The Court found Bond's statements fell short of incitement to illegal conduct and were protected by "central commitment" of the First Amendment to robust and wide-open debate on public issues. The Court had traveled a long way since the decisions in *Debs*[210] and *Gilbert v. Minnesota*,[211] where anti-war speeches were found not protected by the First and Fourteenth Amendments. The contrast between the protection given to speeches and marches of the Civil Rights movement of the 1960s[212] and the fate of abolitionist expression in the pre-Civil War South is equally striking. In 1969, reversing the conviction of a Klan speaker, the Court "explained" its tough test for laws aimed at speech that advocated illegal conduct. Such speech could not be punished unless "advocacy is directed to inciting or producing imminent lawless action and is likely to produce such action."[213] In the Communist cases of the 1950s the Court had balanced the gravity of the evil of a Communist revolution, discounted by its improbability, against the claims of free speech and press.[214] By the late 1960s the Court began to look at speech advocating crime or with harmful tendencies in a different way. It asked whether the speech fit into a few narrowly defined categories of expression that could be banned.[215] If not, the Court often found the proscription of speech invalid as an invasion of core values of the First Amendment. Later in the 1980s it also subjected such proscription to an extraordinarily high level of scrutiny both of the legitimacy of the governmental interest and of whether that interest could be achieved by less restrictive means,[216] an analysis influenced by the Court's equal protection jurisprudence. The governmental interest in stifling dissent on certain subjects was treated as simply impermissible.

The Doctrinal Background for *Texas v. Johnson*: *Street, O'Brien, Spence,* and *Cohen*

The 1969 case, *Street v. New York*,[217] exemplifies the categorical process at work. There the Court considered the case of a black man who had burned his American flag on learning that James Meredith, who had integrated the University of Mississippi, had been shot. As the Court interpreted the record, Street might have been convicted either for burning the flag or for disrespectful words about it. The latter possibility, the Court insisted, violated the First Amendment. The Court considered in turn four categories of speech that could be banned and concluded that Street's speech did not fit any of them. 1. He could not be convicted for inciting others to commit unlawful acts because he had not done so. Instead he had only advocated the idea that the flag should be abandoned as a national symbol. 2. His words were not sufficiently inflammatory to constitute "fighting words"[218] and at any rate the statute under which he was convicted was not so narrowly drawn as to punish only words of that character. 3. Street's ideas could not be prohibited because they were offensive to some hearers. In addition, once again, the statute was not limited to protecting the public against shock, even if such a goal were permissible. 4. Finally, Street's words could not be punished because they showed insufficient respect for the flag. That justification was precluded by the decision in *Barnette*.[219] *United States v. O'Brien* was not implicated because the conviction could have rested on pure "speech" not "conduct." Four dissenters, including some strong supporters of First Amendment rights, found that the real issue was flag burning and that flag burning was not protected by the First Amendment.[220] Had the Court reached that issue it might well have sided with the dissent.

In *O'Brien*,[221] O'Brien had burned his draft card as a protest against the draft and war in Vietnam. The Court had upheld O'Brien's conviction for violating a statute that banned burning draft cards. The Court held that conduct that mixed speech and non-speech elements could be prohibited if the law banning the conduct met certain tests. The law had to further an important governmental interest; that interest had to be unrelated to the suppression of free expression; and the incidental restriction on alleged First Amendment interests had to be no greater than was essential to the furtherance of the governmental interest.[222] The Court concluded that maintaining the draft card was important to the functioning of the Selective Service Law. The interest in maintaining the draft card was

Introduction

not related to suppression of opinion and the means used were appropriate. Where the *O'Brien* test was applicable, the Court tested the state regulation by a quite permissive standard: the incidental restriction on alleged First Amendment freedoms must be no greater than is essential to the furtherance of the governmental interest. As Professor Ely would later suggest in a famous article on flag desecration,[223] this third part of the *O'Brien* test was construed by the Court to "require only that there be no less restrictive alternative capable of serving the state's interest *as efficiently as it is served by the regulation under attack.*"[224] But as Professor Ely noted, in almost every case involving real legislation a narrower rule was a less effective one. A ban on leafletting to prevent littering was more effective than prosecution of individual litterers. In this respect, the Court in *O'Brien* sowed the seeds of constitutional mischief that would be harvested by the Burger and Rehnquist Courts. *O'Brien* reflected a larger area where the Warren Court was uneasy. That Court was less often protective of speech, like parading, that the Court thought included a substantial element of "conduct."[225]

Although many[226] criticized the Court's conclusion in *O'Brien*, it has remained the law and indeed increasingly has been cited to justify results in freedom of expression cases. After *O'Brien*, in a case where a student wore a black armband to school to protest the war in Vietnam, the Court held that symbolic conduct could be protected as speech.[227] Protests against the war in Vietnam produced a number of flag burnings, and in 1968 Congress passed a statute prohibiting flag desecration.[228]

Could such burnings be proscribed not because of the message but because of the offense to onlookers? A case from California suggested not. In *Cohen v. California*,[229] Cohen came to a California courthouse wearing a jacket emblazoned with the slogan, "Fuck the Draft." He was convicted under a state offensive conduct statute that prohibited "behavior which has a tendency to provoke *others* to acts of violence or to in turn disturb the peace."[230] The Court noted that the conduct challenged was the act of communication. Because the statute applied throughout the state, Cohen's conviction could not be justified by the need for an especially decorous atmosphere in courthouses. Nor did Cohen's jacket fit into the categories of speech that could be banned because of the form of expression. The jacket did not meet the test of obscenity because it was not erotic. It did not meet the exception for fighting words (which if addressed to the ordinary citizen would be likely to provoke violence), because Cohen's words were not addressed to any particular person. The power of the state to prevent a speaker from intentionally provoking a group to violence was not implicated because there was no evidence of violent reaction.[231] Undifferentiated fear of violence could not justify the regulation. Finally, the Court concluded that to punish the way Cohen chose to express himself would violate fundamental First Amendment values.[232]

CALLS FOR A CONSTITUTIONAL COUNTER REVOLUTION: THE CRITICS INVOKE MAJORITARIANISM

Professor Bork's Blueprint

The Warren Court was at the center of a constitutional revolution that in many ways began in the 1930s and reached its height shortly after Chief Justice Warren retired from the Court. The calls for counter-revolution were not long in coming. In 1968 candidate Richard Nixon insisted that the Court had gone too far and promised to appoint strict constructionists to the Court. Although not clearly defined, strict construction seemed to entail a narrower construction of individual constitutional rights, particularly in the area of criminal procedure, and a broader construction of government power.[233] Put another way, the Court would, it seemed, leave a wider range of decisions to the political branches.

Advocates of strict construction, like the adherents of any philosophy, did not entirely agree on what it meant. In 1971 Professor Robert Bork, later a Circuit Judge and unsuccessful nominee to the Supreme Court, attempted to set out guidelines.[234] In many ways Professor Bork set the agenda for judicial and scholarly battles that continue to this day. Professor Bork was troubled by a recurring American problem: the tension between the role of the Supreme Court as an expounder of constitutional values and the demands of the democratic process. Because of the claims of the democratic process, he insisted, "the choice of 'fundamental values' by the Court cannot be justified."[235] The values to be enforced by the Court were only legitimate if clearly located in the document or clearly required by the processes it established. "Courts must accept any value choice the legislature makes unless it *clearly* runs contrary to a choice made in the framing of the Constitution."[236] But, alas, the meaning of many of the guarantees of individual rights in the Constitution was far from clear, and that was also true of the First Amendment. "The First Amendment," Professor Bork announced, "like the rest of the Bill of Rights, appears to have been a hastily drafted document upon which little thought was expended."[237] Nor, according to Professor Bork, should the rights in the Bill of Rights be read in light of an idea that individuals possess inherent rights.

Such claims, which had once been made for economic rights[238] were, Professor Bork announced, no more persuasive as to other individual rights. As to economic liberties, and by clear inference all other liberties as well, rhetoric about inherent individual rights was "thoroughly old hat, passé and in fact downright tiresome. . . ."[239] The "modern intellectual" judged such matters by criteria of utility, not by any idea of inherent rights.[240] Utility subjects claims of individual rights to a test of collective usefulness. The skepticism about inherent rights is by no means limited to those who characterize themselves as "conservative." What Professor Bork had to say about modern intellectuals and ideas of inherent rights was largely, but not entirely, true.[241] Professor Bork did not discuss what we should make of the fact that men like James Madison, the leading framer of the Bill of Rights, and other framers of that document and John Bingham, the leading framer of Section One of the Fourteenth Amendment, and other Fourteenth Amendment framers had believed in the idea of inherent or natural rights and thought that they were giving such rights positive law protection by virtue of constitutional provisions.[242] Nor did he discuss Madison's claim that the Bill of Rights was designed to protect the minority from the majority.

It followed from Professor Bork's ruminations that "broad areas of constitutional law ought to be reformulated."[243] Not only had decisions striking down laws fixing minimum wages or maximum hours been incorrect. So had due process decisions that struck down laws as a violation of inherent individual rights. Judge Bork's examples ranged from *Pierce v. Society of Sisters*,[244] "which set aside a statute compelling all Oregon school children to attend public [as opposed to private or parochial] schools;" to *Griswold v. Connecticut*,[245] which struck down a law that prohibited use of birth control devices by married couples. Professor Bork's article reflected a profound skepticism about courts finding and attempting to enforce constitutional values. The answer was to construe protections of rights narrowly and to leave very broad choice of values to the political, and in reality often to the bureaucratic, process.

Professor Bork also dipped the First Amendment in the acid of this values skepticism. What was left, at the end of the process, was political speech with somewhat reduced protection. The First Amendment would not protect "scientific, educational, commercial or literary expression as such."[246] In this respect, Professor Bork had a narrower view than the Continental Congress in 1774, which suggested that the importance of freedom of the press consisted, among other things, of "the advancement of truth, science, morality, and arts in general" as well as "diffusion of liberal sentiments on the administration of Government" and communication of thoughts among subjects "whereby oppressive officers are shamed or intimidated, into more honorable and just modes of conducting affairs."[247]

Professor Bork rejected the Holmes and Brandeis formulation of the clear and present danger test in favor of the majority decisions in *Gitlow v. New York*,[248] and *Whitney v. California*.[249] Where the legislature specifically targeted speech advocating illegal conduct or violent overthrow of the government it could be proscribed, according to the majority in those cases, regardless of effect or danger. In addition, Justice Edward Terry Sanford had indicated, following the *Schenck* and *Debs* cases,[250] that speech that tended to cause law breaking could also be prohibited under broader statutes aimed at conduct, where the danger was sufficient.

By suggesting that the First Amendment protected political speech, Professor Bork sounded an uncertain trumpet on issues like flag burning as political protest. In light of the repeated calls for deference to majority rule, political speech, which is essential to the democratic process, might be expected to receive the strict constructionist's most generous protection of any of the liberties in the Bill of Rights. Economic substantive due process decisions limit the range of democratic choice. Broader protection of speech and press from suppression because of the ideas expressed keeps government from narrowing political choices by putting some ideas off limits.[251] Years later in the hearings on a statute or constitutional amendment to deal with flag burning, Judge Bork concluded that the flag was a unique exception to the First Amendment.[252] That position was, at least, more protective of speech than the alternative of rewriting general principles of First Amendment law so as to ban flag burning.

Justice (now Chief Justice) Rehnquist: Skepticism about Values and Inherent Rights; Invocation of the Rights of the Majority

The skepticism about moral judgments expressed by Judge Bork was also reflected in an article written by Justice Rehnquist in 1976. "There is no conceivable way in which I can logically demonstrate, to you," the Justice wrote, "that the judgments of my conscience are superior to the judgments of your conscience..."[253] Guarantees of individual liberty are validated, the Justice explained, and "take on a form of moral goodness" because they are outcomes of the democratic political struggles, not because of inherent qualities:

> They assume a general social acceptance neither because of any intrinsic worth nor because of any unique origins in someone's ideas of natural justice, but instead simply because they have been incorporated in the constitution by the people.... It is the fact of their enactment that gives them whatever moral claim they have upon us as a society...[254]

Justice Rehnquist supported his analysis with a citation of Justice Holmes essay criticizing natural law.[255] The strict constructionists had seized the skepticism that some Progressives and others like Justice Holmes had applied to the premises of the *Lochner*[256] decision and were turning that weapon on basic non-economic rights that liberals thought should have broad protection. Justice

Introduction

Rehnquist asked to what extent "the protection of individual liberties against the state or . . . the interest of 'discrete and insular' minorities such as prisoners," should stand on "a . . . different, more favored footing" than "safeguards for businessmen threatened with ever expanding state regulation."[257] While specific guarantees could, the Justice noted, justify intervention by the Court, such guarantees were to be interpreted narrowly, as a prohibition of "specific abuses in which the [government] had engaged prior to their enactment."[258]

The Burger Court: Mixed Signals

The Burger Court broadened state power to ban "obscene" publications[259] and narrowed interpretations of criminal procedure guarantees of the Bill of Rights.[260] The Court also applied the *Barnette* decision to protect Jehovah's Witnesses who taped over the slogan "Live Free or Die" on their car license plates.[261] It cited the no coerced-speech principle in the course of protecting a utility monopoly from a state imposed rule that it carry a consumer newsletter as well as its own in its billing envelopes[262] and in protecting a newspaper from being required to grant a right of reply to those it had attacked in print.[263] It allowed some exceptions from generally applicable state laws for religious minorities,[264] a position largely reversed by the Rehnquist Court.[265] Although the Court tended to limit the public places where ordinary citizens could express their views and resisted adding other appropriate places to the list,[266] in some respects the Court was quite innovative. It interpreted the First Amendment as protecting some types of corporate expenditures designed to influence the political process and as forbidding limits on the amount of "independent" expenditures by individuals on behalf of candidates for office.[267] Critics insisted that the First Amendment was becoming a Magna Carta of economic and corporate privilege, much as the Fourteenth Amendment had been transformed in the late nineteenth and early twentieth centuries.[268]

THE LOGICAL BASIS FOR *TEXAS V. JOHNSON*

The Court and its doctrines

In spite of the intellectual counterattack against the general approach of the Warren Court, by the early 1970s the logical basis for protection of flag burning as expression was in place, and it survived into the 1980s. 1. Symbolic speech was recognized as expression. 2. Speech could not be banned simply because hearers were likely to take very serious offense and might breach the peace. Indeed speech that invited dispute and stirred people to anger was protected. 3. Expression with the tendency to provoke violence could be banned only in carefully limited circumstances. Such speech could be banned only after focusing on the actual circumstances surrounding the expression and asking whether the expression was "directed to inciting or producing imminent lawless action" and was "likely to incite or produce such action."[269] 4. The exception for fighting words would be limited to direct personal insults or invitations to fight. 5. Finally, speech that did not fit into narrowly defined exceptions to the protections of the First Amendment typically would not be prohibited because of its content. The remaining question, of course, was how acts like burning the flag fit into the *O'Brien* test.

Whatever the logic, the Court was plainly reluctant to hold that physical desecration of the flag was protected expression. On several occasions the Court avoided directly ruling on the issue.[270] In 1969, the Court did hold that words critical or disrespectful of the flag were protected speech.[271] As late as 1982 the Court refused to review the federal conviction of people who were sentenced to prison for burning a flag in Greensboro, North Carolina.[272] Before *Johnson*, most courts had held flag burning was not protected expression.[273]

Scholarly Comment, *Spence*, and Scholarly Elaboration

While most courts upheld bans on flag burning, legal commentators generally insisted that flag burning was protected speech. An article by Professor Melville Nimmer was particularly influential.[274] Professor Nimmer insisted that communicative conduct was entitled to First Amendment protection and that the line justifying regulation was the line between non-speech governmental interests and anti-speech interests. If the reason for the regulation was unrelated to the effect of the communication, then the regulation was not presumed to be a violation of First Amendment rights. For example, while an assassination of the president might be a communication, the government interest in preventing such conduct existed regardless of any whether any communication was involved. Nimmer insisted on further limitations as a means of trying to prevent suppression of speech under statutes aimed at conduct. To justify suppression, forbidden communicative conduct should materially and substantially interfere with the state's legitimate interest.[275] Although the Court would follow the first suggestion, it did not follow the second.

Professor Nimmer concluded that statutes prohibiting flag burning violated the First Amendment. The governmental interest typically advanced in support of such statutes was to preserve the flag as a symbol of national unity:

> To preserve respect for a symbol *qua* symbol is to preserve respect for the meaning expressed by the symbol. It is, then, fundamentally an interest in preserving respect for a particular idea. An act of flag desecration is a counter symbol, which may express hostility, or at least constitute a contradiction of the sanctity of the idea express by the flag symbol. A flag desecration statute is, then, in essence a governmental command that one idea (embodied in the

Introduction

flag symbol) is not to be countered by another idea (embodied in the act of flag desecration). That, of course, is precisely what the First Amendment will not permit.[276]

Translated in terms of the *O'Brien* test, protecting the symbolic value of the flag was related to the suppression of expression.

The Supreme Court followed this line of analysis in *Spence v. Washington*.[277] After the United States invaded Cambodia and students were killed by National Guardsmen in a confrontation at Kent State, Spence put a peace symbol on his American flag with removable masking tape and hung it upside down from his window. He was arrested under a statute that proscribed placing "any word, figure, mark, picture, or design" on the flag. The Court held that Spence was engaging in a form of communication. Under *Barnette* the state could not compel respect for the flag. The State of Washington argued, however, that preserving the flag as an "unalloyed symbol of our country" justified Spence's conviction.[278] The Court noted that interest "is directly related to expression in the context of activity like that undertaken" by Spence. As a result the *O'Brien* analysis was inapplicable. Spence got the benefit of a rigorous First Amendment analysis that the Court extended to expression sought to be censored on the basis of content. But the Court was cautious in its conclusion. "Given the protected character of his expression and in light of the fact that no interest the State may have in preserving the physical integrity of a privately owned flag was significantly impaired," the conviction was invalidated.[279]

In his *Flag Burning* article written the year after *Spence*, Professor Ely elaborated on the distinction made in *Spence*. If the governmental interest supporting the regulation of conduct mixed with speech *was* related to suppression of free expression, then the analysis would be switched from the *O'Brien* analysis and onto another track. There, a different and tougher form of analysis would be employed, "a categorization approach elaborated in other decisions in the Warren period. . . . "[280] In fact the Court would use a combination of categorization and a very tough "strict scrutiny" analysis.[281] Legislation would rarely survive this form of analysis.

Justice William Rehnquist, joined by Chief Justice Warren Burger and Justice Byron White, dissented in *Spence*. Not all speech was protected, Justice Rehnquist insisted, and even protected speech "may be subject to reasonable limitation when important countervailing interests are involved."[282] He cited *Halter v. Nebraska*[283] to demonstrate the state's interest. Justice Rehnquist conceded that the state could not, after *Barnette*, compel citizens to own or salute the flag or even, presumably, protect it from verbal criticism, "any more than it could punish criticisms of this country's policies or ideas:"

> But the statute in this case demands no such allegiance. Its operation does not depend on whether the flag is used for communicative or noncommunicative

purposes; upon whether a particular message is deemed commercial or political; upon whether the use of the flag is respectful or contemptuous; or upon whether any particular segment of the State's citizenry might applaud or oppose the intended message. It simply withdraws a unique national symbol as a background for communications.[284]

The Flag and Politics

In fact, of course, as the 1988 election would show again, politicians regularly do use the flag as a background for communications. Many of then Vice President Bush's television photo opportunities did exactly that. Television pictures of the candidate were superimposed on a background of one or many flags, not once but repeatedly. Nor was his rival far behind. Of course, the candidates did not physically print slogans over pictures of the flag. Others, however, had done so in the recent past. "America, love it or leave it" and later "fly it, don't burn it" were superimposed on flag bumper and window stickers. There seem to have been no prosecutions for such displays, however, even when prosecutions for people like Mr. Spence were in vogue. Prosecutions under the Alien and Sedition Acts were directed toward Jeffersonians, but not Federalists. Prosecutions under the flag statutes tended to be directed at critics of government policy, not at its supporters.

Protecting the uniqueness of the American flag as a symbol of national unity was advocated by the *Spence* dissenters to justify the conviction in that case. Could states or the federal government constitutionally ban the Confederate flag for this reason? It might be seen as contradicting the unalloyed symbolism of the American flag. To many, the Confederate flag had been divorced from its roots and no longer symbolized secession and white supremacy. It had, of course, been carried in battle against the American flag. It was the flag under which Southern troops invading Pennsylvania had seized local black people to enslave them.[285] One university had banned the display of the flag as unacceptable racist expression. The ban was held to be a violation of the First Amendment.[286] In public schools, where the protection of First Amendment rights are ever more limited, wearing the Confederate flag was occasionally banned as disruptive.[287] No general state or federal ban on the Confederate flag was attempted in the interests of protecting the American flag as a unique symbol of national unity.

In the 1988 presidential election, *Barnette* became the subject of intense political controversy. George Bush made the Pledge of Allegiance a centerpiece of his campaign. Michael Dukakis, the Democratic nominee, following an advisory opinion[288] from the state Supreme Court, had vetoed a Massachusetts law that *required* school teachers to lead students in a pledge of allegiance to the flag. Mr. Bush used the veto with devastating political effect. Mr. Bush did not discuss the protection from state compulsion of minorities with conscientious scruples. As he framed the issue it was a simple matter of patriotism. "Should public school teachers be required to lead our children in the Pledge of Allegiance?" he asked. "My opponent says no—and I say yes."[289] For his part Mr. Dukakis made no ringing defense of freedom of speech or protection for minority points of view or of teachers with conscientious scruples. He defended his action as simply following the law as laid down by the courts. In addition to the Massachusetts Court one federal court had protected from discharge a teacher who, because she did not believe America provided liberty and justice for all, refused to participate in the pledge.[290] Dukakis supporters portrayed Mr. Bush as a scofflaw. To the extent that the voters got a thoughtful discussion of the issues involved, it did not come from either presidential candidate.

In the 1930s and '40s, most courts had dismissed the idea, with something close to incredulity, that the flag salute was compelled worship of the flag.[291] Ironically, in *United States v. Eichman*,[292] the second flag burning case, the *dissenting* Justices seemed to agree that a compelled pledge of allegiance was compelled worship. Their statement on the issue may refer to Mr. Bush's successful 1988 pledge of allegiance campaign attack on Mr. Dukakis. "[T]he integrity of the symbol has been compromised," Justices Stevens, Rehnquist, O'Connor, and White lamented, "by those leaders who seem to advocate compulsory worship of the flag even by individuals whom it offends, or who seem to manipulate the symbol of national purpose into a pretext for partisan disputes about meaner ends."[293] The flag returned to the center of political controversy after the 1988 election with the 1989 decision in *Texas v. Johnson*.

TEXAS V. JOHNSON AND ITS AFTERMATH

The Decision

Gregory Johnson burned an American flag as part of a political protest during the 1984 Republican National Convention in Dallas. In *Texas v. Johnson*, the Court followed the analysis suggested by Professor Nimmer, by *Spence*, and by Professor Ely:

> We must first determine whether Johnson's burning of the flag constituted expressive conduct, permitting him to invoke the first amendment in challenging his conviction. See, *e.g.*, *Spence v. Washington*, 418 U.S. 405, 409-411 (1974). If his conduct is expressive, we next decide whether the State's regulation is related to the suppression of free expression. See, *e.g.*, *United States v. O'Brien* . . .;*Spence, supra*, at 424, n.8. If the State's regulation is not related to expression, then the less stringent standard we announced in *United States v. O'Brien* for regulations of noncommunicative conduct controls. . . . If it is, then we are outside of *O'Brien's* test and we must ask

whether this interest justifies Johnson's conviction under a more demanding standard.[294]

In the end the Court concluded that Gregory Johnson's "political expression was restricted because of the content of the message he conveyed."[295] The state had failed to prove an interest that justified punishing Johnson that was both present in the particular facts of the case and unrelated to suppression of expression.[296] Johnson's conduct simply did not fit those categories of expression—like fighting words and inciting violence—that would place it outside First Amendment protection. The Court subjected the state's interest in protecting the symbolic character of the flag to strict scrutiny, scrutiny it failed to withstand.[297] Basically the state's argument collided with two principles the Court found fundamental. First "government may not ban the expression of an idea simply because society finds the idea itself offensive or disagreeable."[298] Second, "the Government may [not] ensure that a symbol be used to express only one view of that symbol. . . ."[299]

The Dissent and the Question of a Solid Core

Four Justices dissented. The dissents explored two bases for rejection of Johnson's First Amendment claim. First they insisted that the flag was unique and that for that reason ordinary First Amendment doctrine did not apply to flag burning.[300] Whatever the merits of that approach, to the extent that the flag was treated simply as a unique exception to which no others would be added, the effect on free speech doctrine, though serious, would be limited. The second alternative, also followed by the dissent, was to recast First Amendment doctrine so that flag burning could be suppressed. Justice Rehnquist suggested, for example, that Johnson's conduct was like fighting words, deeply offensive expression that could be banned because alternative modes of expression of his message remained open. Flag burning was so inherently inflammatory that it could be suppressed.[301] Basically Justice Rehnquist insisted that the possibility of violence was sufficient to justify punishing Johnson, even without proof of danger of violence in the facts of his case. That approach, while not without support in some earlier cases,[302] seemed to resurrect the bad tendency test and was not consistent with the Court's most recent decisions on fighting words[303] or with the broad protection to the speakers choice of expression in *Cohen*.[304]

The majority did not reject the idea that hostile and violent audience reaction might justify conviction. It simply found the danger of such a reaction in the facts of Johnson's case was not sufficiently proved.[305] More basically, the approach embraced by Justice Rehnquist and even that hinted at by the majority,[306] has dangers of countenancing a heckler's veto[307] on unpopular expression, countenancing the idea that some ideas are so inflammatory that they cannot be expressed. The reasoning suggested by the Chief Justice could

Introduction

apply equally to the Klan cross burning the Court found protected in *Brandenburg*. The hint in the majority opinion that perhaps Johnson could have been punished if his audience had reacted violently seems to contradict statements by the Court in other contexts that "constitutional rights ... are not to be sacrificed or yielded to ... violence and disorder."[308] The hint is in some tension with the majority's citation of *Brandenburg*.[309] Perhaps the majority meant Johnson would be guilty only if he intended to produce a violence reaction.[310] But what if the violence is expected by the defendant, or possible, or foreseeable? The distinction made by the majority opens the possibility that Johnson's conduct, otherwise protected by the First Amendment, would lose that protection based on the actions of others. The argument for suppression of otherwise protected speech because of violent audience reaction also tends to be circular. As public reaction to the flag-salute cases shows, when the government holds the speech protected and protects the speaker, violence tends to abate.

There is danger in the idea that the speaker should be silenced because some in the audience tend to react violently to what he has to say. The speech of abolitionists in the South before the Civil War and of integrationists in the 1960s undoubtedly did tend to provoke a violent response. But the proposition urged by the Chief Justice was more limited. He sought to distinguish form of expression from content, and to ban not ideas, but only certain ways of expressing them. The danger of abuse in this approach had led the Court to define fighting words narrowly. Broader categories subject to suppression invite both suppression of political speech and politically selective use.

Second, Justice Rehnquist suggested that flag burning was inarticulate speech of low value, more effective in antagonizing than in expressing an idea.[311] One Warren Court approach to speech had been to recognize narrow and rigidly defined categories of expression (*e.g.*, libel, fighting words, obscenity) that could be banned and to resist their expansion. Indeed its work lay more in the direction of narrowing existing exceptions than in expanding them or creating new ones.[312] More recently, however, the Court has treated speech and press it sees as being of lesser value as more amenable to regulation or suppression.[313] But the Court had not yet found political speech on matters of public concern to fit within such a category because of its form. Indeed *Cohen* seems squarely to the contrary. Here again there is a danger that the power to silence inarticulate or "low value" speech would be used to silence speech the public should hear or would be used selectively on speech of which prosecutors and judges and juries (or the majority) disapprove.

In the end Justice Rehnquist returned to an idea that seems increasingly influential: that in more claims of individual liberties the Court should (with notable exceptions) defer to majority rule. Significantly, he applied this approach to flag burning as a political protest:

The cry of "no taxation without representation" animated those who revolted against the English Crown to found our Nation—the idea that those who submitted to government should have some say as to what kind of laws would be passed. Surely one of the high purposes of a democratic society is to legislate against conduct that is regarded as evil and profoundly offensive to the majority of people—whether it be murder, embezzlement, pollution, or flag burning.[314]

Politics Again

Shortly after the decision in *Johnson*, President Bush proposed a constitutional amendment designed to allow government to prohibit flag desecration. Senate and House hearings on the subject featured testimony from many distinguished constitutional scholars. Opponents of the amendment, including many scholars, usually advocated a statutory prohibition of flag burning instead of a constitutional amendment, or at least insisted that a statute would probably be found constitutional.[315] They feared that the amendment would make possible discrimination based on point of view among those who used the flag for political expression. William Barr, of the Department of Justice, said that those who, for example, hung the flag upside down as a protest against government policy could be punished by statutes authorized by the proposed amendment.[316] So there was more to the proposed ban on physical desecration than was at first apparent. After the experience of Governor Dukakis, many politicians believed that failure to support some measure to protect the flag was political suicide. In the end the statute passed, the constitutional amendment was defeated, and the Flag Protection Act of 1990 was later held a violation of the First Amendment.[317] After that decision the Congress again refused to pass the proposed amendment. The failure of the constitutional amendment represented congressional and public unwillingness to restrict the coverage of the First Amendment in order to punish those who desecrate the flag.

TEXAS V. JOHNSON TODAY: CONTINUITY AND CHANGE

Johnson Reaffirmed and Explained: From Flag Burning to Cross Burning

To skeptics it seemed that the rule of *Texas v. Johnson* would have a short constitutional life. The case had been decided by a five-four vote and two of the five, Justices Brennan and Marshall soon retired from the Court. In fact,

Introduction

however, in *R.A.V. v. St. Paul*[318] both the majority and the concurring Justices cited *Texas v. Johnson* with apparent approval. R.A.V., a juvenile, identified only by his initials, had burned a cross on the lawn of a black family in St. Paul. The ordinance under which R.A.V. was prosecuted prohibited disorderly conduct, defined as placing on public or private property objects, including a burning cross or Nazi swastika, "which one knows or has reasonable ground to know arouses anger or alarm or resentment in others on the basis of race, color, creed, religion or gender...." All parties and all Justices conceded that R.A.V.'s conduct could be punished under a properly drawn ordinance or statute. The question was whether the ordinance under which R.A.V. was convicted met the requirements of the First Amendment.

All the Justices agreed that it did not,[319] but they did not agree on why it didn't. There were two main approaches. In an opinion by Justice Scalia, the majority assumed, for purposes of its decision, that the Minnesota definition of fighting words was consistent with the First Amendment. That assumption allowed the majority to confront what it understood to be the more troubling aspect of the ordinance. The majority held the ordinance void because, as it read the ordinance, it took a class of speech that could be punished—fighting words—and divided it into the permissible and the proscribable, based on the state's approval or disapproval of the underlying message. The majority thought this division violated the First Amendment because it discriminated among messages based on content and points of view.[320] Justice Scalia's examples were intended to clarify the point. States could ban obscene publications he noted, but not only those that criticized governmental policy. Under the St. Paul ordinance, according to Justice Scalia's majority opinion, "[o]ne could hold up a sign saying, for example, that all 'anti-Catholic bigots' are misbegotten; but not that all 'papists' are, for that would insult and provoke violence 'on the basis of religion.'"[321] The example is curious, because it does not seem to involve fighting words. For one thing the words are not directed at individuals. If a statute could reach such signs consistent with the First Amendment, then the protection against suppression of speech as "fighting words" may be less stringent than it previously seemed.[322] Justice Scalia did not give us the context in which his hypothetical sign holders acted. Did they hold their anti-Catholic signs up at a nativist political rally where the crowd included a number of Catholics or in the front yard of a Catholic family?

Justice Scalia's opinion, citing the flag-burning decision, insisted that *R.A.V.* was really not the first time the Court had applied its rules against content and viewpoint discrimination within a class of expression that could be totally banned under a proper statute. At any rate here, at some length, is what Justice Scalia had to say:

Introduction

The first amendment generally prevents government from proscribing speech
. . . or even expressive conduct, see, *e.g., Texas v. Johnson* . . . because of
disapproval of the ideas expressed. Content-based regulations are presumptively invalid. [H]owever our society . . . has permitted restrictions upon the
content of speech in a few limited areas which are "of such slight social value
as a step to truth that any benefit that may be derived from them is clearly
outweighed by the social interest in order and morality." [E.g., obscenity,
defamation, and fighting words.]. . . . [T]hese areas of speech can consistently
with the first amendment be regulated because of their constitutionally
proscribable content (obscenity, defamation, etc.)—[but] they may [not] be
made the vehicles for content discrimination unrelated to their distinctively
proscribable content. Thus the government may proscribe libel; but it may
not make the further content discrimination of proscribing *only* libel critical
of government. . . . The proposition that a particular instance of speech can be
proscribable on the basis of one feature (e.g., obscenity) but not on the basis
of another (e.g., opposition to the city government) is commonplace. . . . We
have long held, for example, that nonverbal expressive activity can be
banned because of the action it entails, but not because of the ideas it
expresses—so that burning a flag in violation of an ordinance against outdoor
fires could be punishable, whereas burning a flag in violation of an ordinance
against dishonoring the flag could not. See *Johnson* . . . [323]

Applying his analysis to the St. Paul ordinance, Justice Scalia concluded that the
St. Paul ordinance violated the First Amendment because it discriminated both
on the basis of content and point of view:

[e]ven as narrowly construed by the Minnesota Supreme Court, the ordinance is facially unconstitutional. Although the phrase in the ordinance,
"arouses anger, alarm or resentment in others," has been limited by the
Minnesota Supreme Court's construction to reach only those symbols or
displays that amount to "fighting words," the remaining . . . terms make clear
that the ordinance applies only to "fighting words" that insult, or provoke
violence, "on the basis of race, color, creed, religion or gender." Displays
containing abusive invective, no matter how vicious or severe, are permissible unless they are addressed to one of the specified disfavored topics. Those
who wish to use "fighting words" in connection with other ideas—to
express hostility, for example, on the basis of political affiliation, union
membership, or homosexuality—are not covered. The first amendment
does not permit St. Paul to impose special prohibitions on those speakers
who express views on disfavored subjects.[324]

The concurring Justices denied the assumption that the ordinance as construed
by the Minnesota Supreme Court covered only speech that could be prohibited. They said the St. Paul ordinance, as construed, *was* limited to words that by

Introduction

their very nature inflicted injuries but, they insisted, the Minnesota Court was vague as to what injuries qualified. The concurring justices concluded that hurt feelings, offense, and resentment would qualify as the necessary injury under the Minnesota statute.[325] As a result they held the ordinance went beyond those fighting words that could be suppressed under applicable precedent, including *Texas v. Johnson*,[326] *Street v. New York*,[327] and *Cohen v. California*.[328] These cases had held that the fact that expressive activity causes hurt feelings, offense, or resentment does not render the expression unprotected. Since it covered both protected and proscribable speech, these Justices would strike down the ordinance in the interest of sheltering the protected speech they thought the ordinance reached.[329]

Political Speech in the 1990s: Protection, Deference, and the Shrinking Forum

The flag-burning cases were explained and reaffirmed by *R.A.V.* Three large issues are involved: the rule against content discrimination as a central First Amendment value; the danger that the Court may confuse the part with the whole and use the anti-discrimination rule to justify *restrictions* of the more nearly absolute protections of the First Amendment; and finally the issue of postive First Amendment rights like those involved in the public forum. What the cases say, and do not say, tell us much about the Court's view of the First Amendment. First, *Johnson* and *R.A.V.* reaffirm the anti-discrimination component of the First Amendment as a central protection for political speech. They recognize that suppressing political expression because of content or point of view violates a crucial First Amendment value. But if that is the text of *Johnson* as explained by *R.A.V.*, other issues lurk below the surface of recent decisions. The Court sometimes seems to hint that the First Amendment is merely an anti-discrimination amendment vulnerable to general, non-discriminatory laws not aimed specifically at speech. While *R.A.V.* shows that the Court is very unlikely to endorse the most extreme form of this idea, the idea may still be moving First Amendment law in an unfortunate direction. Another issue is raised by *R.A.V.* and *Johnson*, one the cases do not discuss, but that should enter the discussion. For if a central meaning of the First Amendment is protection for political messages because speech is central to democracy, what must we think of a system that is closing channels of communication available to the less affluent, and, still worse, providing us with a poltical system responsive to investors in politicians, not voters? The smoke and heat of the decision in *Johnson* tend to obscure these questions, but to fail to consider them is to have a radically incomplete picture of the system of freedom of expression. The last two issues—a First Amendment limited to equal protection and shrinking or inadequate positive rights to speak—deserve more detailed consideration.

A First Amendment reduced to equal protection?

Literally and centrally the First Amendment prohibits the legislature from passing laws that "abridge" freedom of speech or press or the right to assemble peaceably.[330] The Court has recognized historical and categorical exceptions to freedom of speech and of the press—*e.g.*, libel, obscenity, fighting words. Still laws that are aimed directly at suppressing speech or press not within one of these narrow exceptions and solely because of what is said are the clearest examples of what the legislature has been instructed by the First Amendment to avoid.[331] But laws aimed directly at suppressing speech because of point of view are not the only threats to First Amendment freedoms.

By invoking generally applicable laws to overcome certain claims of free speech or free religion, the Court defers value judgments to the political process and avoids what it sees as the pitfalls of judicial activism. Laws that are aimed at conduct and apply generally have been both held and said to overcome claims to First Amendment protection: they have superceded claims of freedom of religion by Indians whose sacred use of peyote in their religious rituals was prohibited by a generally applicable state law;[332] have been said to be sufficient to overcome claims of freedom of speech of flag burners who violate a generally applicable law banning public burning;[333] and in the view of Justice Scalia, they overcome First Amendment claims of a nude dancer whose dance before a group of consenting adults is prosecuted as a violation of a generally applicable state law against public nudity.[334] To support invoking the generally applicable state law rule in the nude dancing case, Justice Scalia cited Justice Frankfurter's opinion in *Minersville School District v. Gobitis*.[335] By deferring to generally applicable laws, the Court is able to scrutinize some claims of free speech and press by a much more permissive standard. If the state law challenged in the case of the nude dancer or the Indian religious group applies formally to all and has an important[336] or perhaps rational[337] purpose unrelated to suppressing expression, it survives. The advantage of this approach is that it seems to preclude the Court from choosing which symbolic expressions or religious exercises will be protected from general laws as speech or religion and which will not. The *R.A.V.* case is a closely related phenomenon. The ordinance in that case failed because it lacked general applicability—because the Court thought it discriminated among message senders based on their underlying ideas. The problem could be cured simply by passing a broader statute aimed at suppressing fighting words and omitting the limitation to messages related to race, religion, or gender.

The Court's developing romance with generally applicable laws that override First Amendment claims could lead to a First Amendment without a hard central core. Some very repressive laws can be designed as laws that are aimed at "conduct" and are not specifically targeted at speech because of a disfavored

Introduction

viewpoint. The government has a valid and important interest in preventing conduct that interferes with recruiting for the armed services. A law prohibiting such activities is general, does not target a point of view, and is aimed at conduct. If anti-war speeches that do not advocate lawlessness nevertheless move some listeners to interfere with recruiting, and if such generally applicable laws reach speech and supersede First Amendment claims, then anti-war speeches could be suppressed. Flag burning as political protest or advocacy of integration could be banned under a generally applicable law aimed at conduct that tended to produce violence. Of course, such ideas are inconsistent with existing precedent.[338] In spite of hints that the Court is flirting with such a theory, most clearly in symbolic speech cases, it almost surely will, and certainly should, reject it.

The tort rule against intentional infliction of emotional distress is a generally applicable rule of law not specifically aimed at speech. Still when *Hustler* magazine lampooned preacher-public figure Jerry Falwell, the Court held Falwell could not recover for the tort of intentional infliction without meeting First Amendment standards—showing a false statement of fact made with knowledge of falsity or reckless disregard of whether it was true or false.[339] The First Amendment fenced in a generally applicable rule not targeted at speech—as indeed it must. But in *Texas v. Johnson*, the Court hinted at a different approach. One state interest in suppressing flag burning was the interest in preventing a violent reaction. *Johnson* finessed the issue by finding insufficiently specific proof of the danger of a violent reaction in the narrow facts of that case. Johnson had argued that since the violent reaction was based on the content of his message, that fact connected the state's interest to the suppression of expression in an impermissible way. The Court responded in a footnote suggesting that the state's desire to prevent violent audience reaction might not be impermissibly related to suppression of expression.[340]

The Court has not been presented squarely with the question, but a footnote in *R.A.V.* suggests that otherwise protected speech is not to be suppressed because of reaction to the message it conveys.[341] The insight should apply whether the symbols used to express the idea are words or other symbols such as a flag burned as political protest or a flag to which a peace sign is attached. Flag burning as a political protest, putting a peace sign on a flag, posting signs, and handing out leaflets are all "activities of special First Amendment significance."[342] Sensitive understanding of that fact should lead to recognizing the importance of the system of freedom of expression when such speech is threatened by generally applicable laws.

While the Court is unlikely to embrace the most extreme claims for the leveling power of generally applicable laws, its infatuation with anti-discrimination analysis as the major component of First Amendment law may lead it to other mischief. Specifically its equal protection analysis may lull the Court into tolerating broader categorical exceptions to First Amendment freedoms. Justice Scalia's examples of "fighting words" in *R.A.V.* ("All Papists are misbegotten") may indicate diminished absolute protection against suppression of speech as fighting words. In return he provides increased relative protection against discrimination. Another example of reduced absolute protection against suppression based on content could be renewed constitutional acceptance of group libel.

In one of its curious aspects, the *R.A.V.* opinion notes that libel is not protected speech or press. To support its citation to libel as unprotected, the Court cites the group libel case of *Beauharnais v. Illinois*,[343] like *Minersville* an opinion by Justice Frankfurter. Beauharnais had circulated a petition to the city counsel opposing open housing because of the alleged criminal propensities of African Americans. In doing so he violated a state statute that prohibited falsely attributing crime or lack of virtue to any racial or religious group. Over the dissent of four members including the strong protest of Justice Black, the Court upheld his conviction. The First Amendment exception for libel could be extended to libel of groups, and the exception could be used to punish political speech. Some courts and scholars had assumed that *Beauharnais*, like *Minersville*, belonged in the dustbin of history.[344]

After *R.A.V.* the particular form of the *Beauharnais* statute should not stand, because it only prohibited ascribing lack of virtue based on race or religion. It failed the *R.A.V.* test of generality. If the citation to *Beauharnais* indicates approval of the concept of group libel laws (as perhaps it does *not*), then the state simply needs a general statute, one that prohibits falsely ascribing lack of virtue to members of *any* group. Instead of absolute protection against group libel laws, we would have relative protection against discrimination based on point of view.

To be sure, relative protection decreases the likelihood of enactment. As Justice Jackson noted in reference to the *equal protection* clause, "nothing opens the door to arbitrary action so effectively as to allow . . . officials to pick and choose only a few to whom they will apply legislation and thus to escape the political retribution that might be visited upon them if larger numbers were affected."[345] But if passed, a general group libel law is far worse, affecting speech aimed at capitalists, workers, those who run multi-national corporations, men, and women, to name only a few. The result would put the courts in the business of evaluating the truth or falsity of much political speech or worse. Although seemingly neutral, such a rule protects the status quo. Both feminists and their opponents, or in an earlier era both abolitionists and slave holders, would be equally affected by the rule. But silencing advocates of change, as well as supporters of the status quo, tends to protect the status quo. Nor is it likely that broader statutes will be applied in a neutral fashion. Broader laws tend to be selectively enforced against unpopular people and causes. We need a First

Introduction

Amendment to protect us against the times when attempts to silence opposition are at their height.³⁴⁶ For that reason shrinking the absolute protections of the First Amendment is unwise, even if accompanied by expanding relative or equality protections. It is unwise for the captain of the Titanic to dispense with the life boats because the ship has a double hull. The decision in *United States v. O'Brien*, relied on in *Texas v. Johnson*, is an attempt to deal with the speech-conduct conundrum. But it is a decidedly ambiguous tool for the protection of expression. If the Court concludes that a regulation of conduct is related to the suppression of expression, or perhaps more narrowly the suppression of certain points of view, then strict First Amendment principles apply. That is the good news. But if the Court concludes that the purpose of the regulation is more general and is not aimed at suppression, then the Court applies tests that governmental action virtually never fails.³⁴⁷ The statute stands even though the result is to suppress speech or press. Put another way, the only time *O'Brien* provides vigorous protection for expression is when *O'Brien* switches back to traditional First Amendment analysis. The Court has expanded the use of the weak *O'Brien* tests to new areas. In the case of banning candidates' signs on public utility poles, the fact that viewpoint discrimination was not involved seemed sufficient to convince the Court to apply the *O'Brien* tests that the government almost never fails.³⁴⁸ In *Seattle Times v. Rhinehart*,³⁴⁹ the Court cited standards like those in *O'Brien* and concluded that no heightened First Amendment scrutiny was required for court orders requiring confidentiality for information obtained in pre-trial discovery. By such orders information about defective products and environmental hazards has been hidden from other litigants, from the public, and even from governmental regulators.

Application of *O'Brien* analysis to a an increasing variety of First Amendment problems, and similar recent developments in First Amendment law, make the anti-discrimination principle of *Johnson* narrower than it first appears. To the extent that the Court categorizes the First Amendment claim as arising in a non-traditional public forum, rules against content or viewpoint discrimination are attenuated or abandoned. When the Court limits or refuses to expand those areas like streets and parks where ordinary citizens have full First Amendment rights, it limits the scope of the *Johnson* rule. If you and others are unable to speak in a place at all, as far as that place is concerned, you will derive little comfort from the fact that if you could speak there, government could not discriminate against you because of your message.

Reduction of positive rights to freedom of speech and the incredibile shrinking forum

The Jehovah's Witnesses provoked many of the free speech cases decided by the New Deal Court. They helped establish the right to distribute literature,³⁵⁰ to go door-to-door and speak to people at their homes,[351] to sell their literature door-to-door without paying a tax for the privilege of canvassing,[352] and the right not to be restrained from such activity by the unbridled discretion of public officials.[353] The rights were not only negative, but positive. The rights survived generally applicable laws that were not specially designed to suppress speech because of its point of view. The Witnesses were granted the right to use some governmental property—streets and parks—for free speech and free religion. They were protected against taxes on the privilege of going door-to-door that other merchants, not exercising First Amendment rights, were required to pay.[354] Such rights hardly equal ownership of a television network, but, as the Court noted, they were basic to the poorly financed causes of little people. In the 1960s many courts found public forum rights in public bus advertisement slots, in transportation terminals, and similar public places.[355]

More recently the Court has been remarkably insensitive to such concerns. It upheld a ban on political but not commercial advertisements on a city bus system,[356] upheld barring a presidential candidate from making speeches in areas of a military base open to the pubic — although presidents made speeches in such locations on other bases,[357] upheld a ban on putting unstamped matter in mailboxes,[358] upheld a ban on sale of literature on a public sidewalk outside a post office,[359] upheld a ban on placing political posters on pubic utility poles on public streets,[360] and held an airport terminal not to be a public forum.[361] Although it has continued to consider streets and parks public forums where suppression of speech will be more vigorously prohibited, in other (non-traditional public forum) locations a rational basis for suppression is typically sufficient. By classifying such places as non-public forums the Court has allowed discrimination based on content[362] and sometimes, it seems, based on viewpoint.[363]

In cases involving speech even in traditional public forums the Court has relaxed its standards for judging claims that First Amendment rights have been violated. At one time the Court tended to insist that regulations of speech be accomplished by the least restrictive means. So, for example, the ban on handbilling was struck down because the less restrictive alternative of prosecuting litterers was available. Recently, however, the Court has indicated that challenged measures involving time, place, and manner limits on speech need only be "narrowly tailored" to accomplish their objective, a requirement satisfied in this context if the "regulation promotes a substantial governmental interest that would be achieved less effectively absent the regulation."[364] The Court is using the *O'Brien* standard to judge restrictions on speech in the public forum. But the ban on handbilling in *Schneider* was more effective than pursuing myriad individual litterers. Professor Ely suggested that "[b]ringing the handbill and kindred cases into line with *O'Brien* would go a long way toward eviscerating the first amendment."[365] If so, the evisceration is well under way.

Introduction lvii

The way the Court has dealt with the complex questions of wealth, corporate wealth, and politics has been in contrast to its approach to securing opportunities for expression for poorly financed causes of little people.[366]

CONCLUSION

Critics of flag burning are often correct. In recent years at least, flag burning typically is more effective at antagonizing than persuading. There is a sort of media version of Gresham's law by which images of protestors burning American flags supplant and disqualify more thoughtful criticisms. At least until the right seemed to be recognized and protected, the response to flag burning was often violent.[367] Flag burning in contemporary America has negative persuasive power and offends the sensitivities of most, including those who have made great sacrifices for the ideals the flag represents. Such gratuitous offense for so little purpose is stupid. But for those who think the First Amendment has a solid core, that political speech is part of it, and that politically motivated burning of one's own flag is political speech, suppressing flag burning as political protest is simply not a constitutionally available option.

A First Amendment with a solid core leaves unregulated some political speech that does cause significant pain and distress and that advocates evil ideas. How is one to answer the suggestion that those facts justify suppression? One of the most interesting ideas in the massive literature on flag burning is Calvin Massey's suggestion that societies, like individuals, achieve transformation not by repression of their darker side but by acknowledging it and by dialogue with it.[368] An example is the controversy about students who wore Confederate flag patches to school. Schools that responded by encouraging student dialogue aimed at developing an understanding of what the Confederate flag meant to those who wore it and what it meant to black students, and coupled the dialogue with discussion of guarantees of liberty, probably did more for improved race relations than those that simply responded with repression.[369]

The symbolic value of the flag is important, and as Justice Frankfurter said, we live by symbols. But expelling school children who refuse to salute the flag because of religious conviction or jailing political protestors who tape a peace sign to the flag or those who verbally criticize the flag and even those who burn the flag is also powerfully symbolic. The symbolism of these actions undermines the symbolism of liberty that the flag stands for. Any rule of law that in fact suppresses political speech or that operates to let some claim the symbolism of the flag ("We support our troops") and deny it to others ("Peace Now") is a rule that undermines the meaning of the flag. It may not be fair to judge laws and judicial decisions on flag burning by the company they keep. Still, punishment for flag desecration often has been associated with much broader repression or attempted repression of speech and press. In Communist nations recently, flag desecration was associated with democratic revolutions.

The great contribution of Justice Jackson's decision in *West Virginia Board of Education v. Barnette* was that in clear, forceful and non-technical language it explained the deeper meaning of free speech in the flag-salute controversy. One measure of the unfortunate distance traveled by First Amendment law over the last few years is to compare the simplicity of *Barnette* to the complexity of *R.A.V.*[370]

A crucial function of decisions about the First Amendment is to provide guidance for the public at large, for city councils, for legislatures, for prosecutors and city attorneys, and for trial judges. Doctrines that are so technical and subtle that they are difficult to understand, even for law professors who devote extraordinary time to studying them, perform that function poorly. Part of the problem may be related to the decline in the belief in the ability of courts to find and articulate basic values. Part may be a crumbling consensus on First Amendment values. Part may involve unwillingness candidly to admit that doctrine is being changed. At any rate, the new First Amendment is driven by extraordinary attention to highly complex and formalistic rules, rules whose very complexity seems to divert the Court, the public, and advocates from the purposes such rules are designed to achieve. By rejecting censorship based on content where speech does not fall into previously established categories it finds justify suppression, the Court protects core First Amendment values and tells legislatures clearly what they may not do. Such a clear bright line rule applied without regard to the justice's reaction to the particular expression is an essential part of protecting freedom of speech. To the considerable extent the Court has adhered to such values, it has protected most speech and press in a very significant way. How well its commitment will hold in the face of a true crisis is a question only the future can answer. The right to be free from governmental suppression because of point of view is precious and important. But a fully working system of free expression requires that people, rich and poor, have access to opportunities for expression and that speech not be suppressed by general rules designed for otherwise valid purposes. The New Deal Court in fact gave speech special protections and required governmental action—maintaining a public forum—that facilitated speech. The approach of the present Court to these issues has been a disaster. It is insensitive to concerns that an open society must require more than formal equality. The poor as well as the rich may make unlimited contributions to "independent" political action committees and the rich as well as the poor are precluded from collecting funds for political causes in front of the post office or in airport terminals. The laws are generally applicable and do not on their face discriminate based on viewpoint. But the First Amendment should guarantee more than that.

Introduction   lix

NOTES

1. B.A. University of the South, J.D. University of North Carolina, M.A. The University of Chicago, Associate Professor of Law, Wake Forest University School of Law. I wish to thank Peter Buddock, Betsy Jones, Michael Driver, and Kurt Seeber for research assistance. Professors J. Wilson Parker, David Logan, Ronald Wright, Akhil Amar, David Rabban, Michael Gerhardt and William Van Alstyne read earlier drafts of the paper and made helpful suggestions. The shortcomings are my own.

2. 319 U.S. 624 (1943). The decision was handed down on flag day.

3. 491 U.S. 397 (1989).

4. *See, e.g.*, Miller v. California, 413 U.S. 15 (1973) (obscenity); Paris Adult Theatre v. Slaton, 413 U.S. 49 (1973) (obscenity); Brandenburg v. Ohio, 395 U.S. 444 (1969) (incitement to imminent lawless action likely to produce such action.) The fact that the exceptions exist does not, of course, necessarily indicate that such exceptions should exist.

5. Stephen Gard, "The Flag Salute Cases and the First Amendment," 31 *Clev. St. L. Rev.* 419, 421-425 (1982) [hereafter "The Flag Salute Cases"].

6. 2 Bernard Schwartz, *The Bill Of Rights: A Documentary History* 616 (Madison to Jefferson), 1025, 1029 (Madison in the first Congress) (1971) [hereafter Schwartz, *The Bill Of Rights*].

7. Robert H. Bork, *The Tempting Of America: The Political Seduction Of The Law* (1990) [hereafter *The Tempting Of America*].

8. William Rehnquist, "The Notion of a Living Constitution," 54 *Tex. L. Rev.* 693 (1976); William Rehnquist, "Government by Cliché," 45 *Mo. L. Rev.* 379 (1980).

9. Edwin Meese, "Address before the A.B.A." (July 9, 1985).

10. *See, e.g.*, Ronald Dworkin, *Taking Rights Seriously* (1977). Bruce Ackerman, *We The People: Foundations* (1991); Suzanna Sherry, "The Framers' Unwritten Constitution" 54 U. *Chi. L. Rev.* 1127 (1987).

11. Edmund Morgan, *Inventing The People: The Rise Of Popular Sovereignty In England And America* 282-85 (1988) [hereafter Morgan, *Inventing The People*]; Michael Kent Curtis, "In Pursuit of Liberty: The Levellers and the American Bill of Rights" 359, 387 (1991) [hereafter "The Levellers"]; Alan Craig Houston, *Algernon Sidney And The Republican Heritage In England And America* 264-65 (1991) [hereafter Houston, *Sidney*].

12. *See* United States v. Stanley, 483 U.S. 669 (1987) (soldier fraudulently induced to participate and used like lab animal for dubious LSD experiment denied constitutional tort recovery for injury government secretly imposed on him).

13. West Va. Bd. of Educ. v. Barnette, 319 U.S. 624, 638 (Jackson, J.) and 662, 666 (Frankfurter, J., *dissenting*).

14. 319 U.S. at 638 (1943).
15. Minersville School Dist. v. Gobitis, 310 U.S. 586, 599-600, (1940) (Frankfurter, J.).
16. Furman v. Georgia, 408 U.S. 238, 468 (1972) (Rehnquist, J., *dissenting*).
17. Employment Division, Dep't of Human Resources v. Smith, 494 U.S. 872, 890 (1990). Justice Jackson and a slim majority of the New Deal Court agreed and took the same position on claims of free exercise of religion. *See In re* Summers, 325 U.S. 561 (1945) (Reed, J.) The Court upheld a state decision denying a law license to a conscientious objector to military service.
18. Laurent Frantz, "The First Amendment in the Balance," 71 *Yale L.J.* 1424, 1430-32 (1962) [hereafter "The First Amendment in the Balance"]; Hugo Black, "The Bill of Rights," 35 *N.Y.U. L. Rev.* 865, 867 (1960).
19. *See, e.g.*, Chaplinsky v. New Hampshire, 315 U.S. 568 (1942), Miller v. California, Brandenburg v. Ohio, 395 U.S. 444 (1969). Recognition of the categories and their usefulness does not, of course, imply approval of all the categories chosen or of their definition.
20. *Cf.*, State v. Worth, 52 N.C. (7 Jones) 488, 492 (1860). The opinion does not explicitly mention either guarantees of free speech or press.
21. Debs v. United States, 249 U.S. 211 (1919); Gilbert v. Minnesota, 254 U.S. 325 (1920).
22. Schenck v. United States, 249 U.S. 47 (1919).
23. "The Flag Salute Cases," 31 *Clev. St. L. Rev.* at 421-30.
24. Federalists tended to emphasize popular sovereignty, not agency. The antifederalist recognition that popular sovereignty is a fiction or a metaphor was an important impetus for a federal bill of rights. Morgan, *Inventing The People*, at 282 (1988) *Alexander Hamilton, James Madison, John Jay, The Federalist*, No. 22 at 146, No . 49 339 (Jacob Cooke, ed. 1961) [hereafter *The Federalist*.]
25. *Id.* On ideas of agency *see* Akhil Amar, "The Bill of Rights as a Constitution," 100 *Yale L.J.* 1131, 1204-05 (1991), *Compare* Leveller ideas of government as a trust, Richard Overton, *An Appeal* (1647) reprinted in Wolfe, ed. *Leveller Manifestoes* 157, 162 *with* John Locke, *An Essay Concerning The True Original, Extent, And End Of Civil Government (Second Treatise On Civil Government)* (1690, 1694) in Ernest Barker, ed., *Social Contract* 87 (1960).
26. For a discussion of theories of justification for free speech, *see* David Logan, "Tort Law and the Central Meaning of the First Amendment," 51 *U. Pitt. L. Rev.* 493, 530-34 (1990).
27. R.A.V. v. St. Paul, 112 S.Ct. 2538 (1992).
28. Discrimination based on "content" bans discussions of entire topics. For example, government might ban discussion of abortion. Discrimination based on point of view involves suppression of one view point (*e.g.*, that of supporters of abortion) but not another (that of opponents of abortion).

Introduction lxi

29. *Cf.* also, R.A.V. v. City of St. Paul, 112 S. Ct. 2538 (1992). In that case the Court struck down a city ordinance aimed at only unprotected "fighting words" because of perceived discrimination based on the underlying point of view. Fighting words based on race, religion, or gender were proscribed, but not those based on, for example, sexual orientation.

30. *Compare* Employment Div., Dep't. of Human Resources of Oregon v. Smith, 494 U.S. 872 (1990)—prohibition of use of peyote in Indian religious rite *with* Barnes v. Glen Theatre, 111 S. Ct. 2456 (1991) (ban of public nudity applied to prohibit nude dancing in a bar), U.S. v. Kokinda 497 U.S. 723(1990) (sidewalk in front of post office building not a public forum where free speech activities are permitted as a right), and Ward v. Rock Against Racism 491 U.S. 781 (1989) (standards for judging restriction of speech in the public forum relaxed and further limitations on the public forum hinted at); Nadine Strossen, "Free Speech Jurisprudence of the Rehnquist Court," 1192 *Free Speech Yearbook* 86.

31. *Compare* Employment Div., Dep't. of Human Resources of Oregon v. Smith, 494 U.S. 872 (1990) (prohibition of use of peyote in Indian religious rite) *with* Barnes v. Glen Theatre, 111 S. Ct. 2456 (1991) (ban of public nudity applied to prohibit nude dancing in a bar).

32. *See, e.g.*, Miami Herald Pub. Co. v. Tornillo, 418 U.S. 241 (1974) (holding Florida right of reply statute to be unconstitutional).

33. City Council v. Taxpayers for Vincent, 466 U.S. 789 (1984); U.S. v. Kokinda, 497 U.S. 720 (1990).

34. *Id.*

35. City Council v. Taxpayers for Vincent, 466 U.S. 789, (1984).

36. Perry Educ. Ass'n. v. Perry Local Educators' Association, 460 U.S. 37 (1983). The Court upheld access to teachers' mailboxes for a union representing the teachers, but not its rival. The Court said the difference was based not on content but on status.

37. *See, e.g.*, William Greider, *Who Will Tell The People: The Betrayal Of American Democracy* (1992); Mark Hertsgaard, *On Bended Knee: The Press And The Reagan Presidency* (1988); Ben H. Bagdikain, *The Media Monopoly* (1987); Mark A. Graber, *Transforming Free Speech* (1991); "The Public Mind, With Bill Moyers," Shows 1-4, Nov. 8, 15, 22, and 29 1989, Journal Graphics Inc.

38. F.E.C. v. National Conservative Political Action Comm. 470 U.S. 480 (1985) (White J. *dissenting*).

39. 319 U.S. 624 (1943).

40. *See, e.g.*, U.S. v. Kokinda 497 U.S. 720 (1990) (sidewalk in front of post office building not a public forum where soliciting funds is permitted); Ward v. Rock Against Racism 491 U.S. 781 (1989) (standards for judging restriction of speech in public forum relaxed); Nadine Strossen, "Free Speech Jurisprudence of the Rehnquist Court," 1992 *Free Speech Year Book* 86.

41. R.A.V. v. St. Paul, 112 S. Ct. 2538 (1992).

42. The Court often relies on the speech-conduct distinction, distinguishing between pure speech and actions associated with it, like picketing, that also involve conduct more susceptible to regulation. Commentators have criticized the distinction between "speech" and "conduct" as having "less determinate content than is sometimes supposed. All communication ...involves conduct. Moreover, if the expression involves talk it may be noisy; if written, it may become litter." Lawrence Tribe, *American Constitutional Law*, 825-27 (1988), [hereafter Tribe, *Constitutional Law*].

43. Texas v. Johnson, 491 U.S. 397, 407-08 n.4 (1989).

44. Texas v. Johnson, 491 U.S. at 397.

45. 2 Schwartz, *The Bill Of Rights* 1031 (Madison).

46. For a discussion of controversies among historians of seventeenth-century England, *see* Lawrence Stone, "The Revolution over the Revolution" (book review) XXXIX, No. 11, *N.Y. Rev. of Books* 47 (June 11, 1992).

47. *See, e.g.*, "The Levellers," 8 *Const. Comm.* 359 (1991); Morgan, *Inventing The People* 55-77; Derek Hirst, *Authority And Conflict, England 1603-1658* 271-79 (1986).

48. David Mayer, "The English Radical Whig Origins of American Constitutionalism," 70 *Wash. U. L.Q.* 131, 162-63 (1991) [hereafter "English Radical Whig Origins"]; David Rabban, "The Ahistorical Historian: Leonard Levy on Freedom of Expression in Early American History," 37 *Stan. L. Rev.* 795, 823 (1985) [hereafter "Levy on Freedom of Expression"]; 1 John Trenchard and Thomas Gordon, *Cato's Letters* 101 (6th ed. 1755, Da Capo Press Reprint 1971 (hereafter Trenchard, *Cato*).

49. Richard Overton, *A Remonstrance Of Many Thousand Citizens*, (1646) in Don Wolfe, *Leveller Manifestoes Of The Puritan Revolution* 157, 162 (1944), hereafter Wolfe (ed.), *Leveller Manifestoes*; Richard Overton, *To . . . The Commons Of England . . .* (1649), *id.* at 326-29.

50. "Levy on Freedom of Expression," 37 *Stan. L. Rev.* 795.

51. 1 Trenchard, *Cato* at 100-103; "Levy on Freedom of Expression," 37 *Stan. L. Rev.* at 806-16. At first most seventeenth- and eighteenth-century radicals limited "the people" entitled to political power to those with some degree of economic independence, a definition that could include small artisans and small farmers, but not servants or those accepting alms or women, or children. The limitation reflected, in part, fear of the corrupting power of wealth and, in part of cultural assumptions. Houston, *Sidney* 207.

52. 4 William Blackstone, *Commentaries On The Laws Of England* 151-52 (1769); "Levy on Freedom of Expression," 37 *Stan. L. Rev.* at 828-29; "English Radical Whigs Origins," 70 *Wash. U. L.Q.* at 196-207.

53. 1 Bernard Schwartz, *The Bill Of Rights*, at 231-379.

Introduction

lxiii

54. *Id.* at 222. (Address to Inhabitants of Quebec, 1774).
55. *See id.* at 223; Pennsylvania Constitution of 1776, 266 at XII, 273 at § 35; *see* 268 at § 13.
56. Leonard Levy, *The Emergence Of A Free Press* 286-319 (1985).
57. *U.S. Const.* Art. I, §9 (habeas corpus; prohibition on bill of attainder or ex post facto law; Art. III, §2 (criminal jury trial); Art. III, §3 (limited definition of treason.)
58. *U.S. Const.* Art. I, sec. 6 and Art. III, §3. William T. Mayton, "Seditious Libel and the Lost Guarantee of A Freedom of Expression," 84 *Col. L. Rev.* 91, 97-119 (1984).
59. *See, e.g., James Madison, Notes Of Debates In The Federal Convention Of 1787* 640 (Adrienne Koch, ed., 1966). (Sherman saying that protection of freedom of the press was "unnecessary. The power of Congress does not extend to the Press."); *The Federalist* no. 84, at 579 (Jacob Cooke, ed. 1961) (Hamilton); Schwartz, *The Bill Of Rights At 1034* (Jackson, in debate on Bill of Rights in the House saying the press was in no danger because "There is no power given to Congress to regulate this subject as they can commerce...."); William Van Alstyne, "Book Review," 99 *Harv. L. Rev.* 1089 (1986).
60. The story is told in Bernard Schwartz, *The Great Rights Of Mankind: A History Of The American Bill Of Rights* 119-159 (1977). Federalists, first in Massachusetts, then more fully in Virginia and other states, agreed to recommend amendments securing additional rights as a device to deflate opposition to the Constitution in state conventions that were called to ratify it.
61. Paul Finkelman, "A Reluctant Paternity: James Madison and the Bill of Rights," 1990 *Sup. Ct. Rev.* 301, 302-303 (1990).
62. Schwartz, *The Bill Of Rights*, at 617, 615-17 (Madison to Jefferson, Oct. 17, 1788); Akhil Amar, "The Bill of Rights as a Constitution," 100 *Yale L.J.* 1131 (1991).
63. Schwartz, *The Bill Of Rights* at 616; 1025, 1029 (Madison proposing a Bill of Rights in Congress. Paul Finkelman, "The First Ten Amendments as a Declaration of Rights," 16 *S. Ill. U. L.J.* 351 (1992).
64. Schwartz, *The Bill Of Rights* at 1031.
65. *U.S. Const.* Art. I, § 10; Art. IV, secs. 2 and 4.
66. Barron v. Baltimore, 32 U.S. (7 Pet.) 243 (1833).
67. 1 Stat. 596 (1798).
68. United States v. Thomas Cooper, 25 Fed. Cas. 631, at 639.
69. Rex v. Tuchin, quoted in James Fitzgerald Stephen, *History Of The Criminal Law In England* 318 (Reprint 1973) (1883).
70. *See, e.g.*, United States v. Cooper, 25 Fed.Cas. 631 (C.C.D.Pa. 1800); United States v. Callender, 25 Fed.Cas. 239 (C.C.D.Va. 1800); United States v. Lyon, 15 Fed.Cas 1183 (C.C.D.Vt. 1798).

71. Michael Gibson, "The Supreme Court and Freedom of Expression from 1791 to 1917," 55 *Fordham L. Rev* 263, 271 (1986), hereafter "Freedom of Expression: 1791 to 1917"].

72. *See, e.g.*, Leonard Levy, *The Emergence Of A Free Press* (1985); "Levy on Freedom of Expression," 37 *Stan. L. Rev.* 795; William T. Mayton, "Seditious Libel and the Lost Guarantee of A Freedom of Expression," 84 *Col. L. Rev.* 91 (1984).

73. "Levy on Freedom of Expression," 37 *Stan. L. Rev.* at 795.

74. Randy E. Barnette, "Reconceiving The Ninth Amendment," 74 *Cornell L. Rev.* 1, 23-24 (1988). For origins of the press clause and their bearing on sedition, *see* David Anderson, "The Origins of the Press Clause," 30 *U.C.L.A. L. Rev.* 455 (1983).

75. "Virginia Resolutions," December 21, 1798 in 1 Melvin Urofsky, ed., *Documents Of American Constitutional And Legal History* 160 (1989) [hereafter *Urofsky Documents*].

76. United States v. Hudson, 11 U.S. (7 Cranch) 32 (1812) (no federal common law of crimes and therefore no common law power over seditious libel). *See* Gary Rowe, "The Sound of Silence: United States v. Hudson & Goodwin, The Jeffersonian Ascendency, and the Abolition of Federal Common Law Crimes," 101 *Yale L. J.* 919 (1992).

77. Michael Kent Curtis, *No State Shall Abridge: The Fourteenth Amendment And The Bill Of Rights* 30-33 (2d Ed. 1987) [hereafter Curtis, *No State Shall Abridge*].

78. *Id.*

79. *See* Stanley Campbell, *The Slave Catchers* 32-46 (1968); Thomas Morris, *Free Men All*, 130-47 (1974); Fugitive Slave Act, Chapter 60, §§ 1-10, 9 Stat. 462 (1850); James M. McPherson, *Battle Cry Of Freedom: The Civil War Era*, 80 (1988) [hereafter McPherson, *Battle Cry Of Freedom*].

80. *Id.* at 119-120; Phillip S. Paludan, *A Covenant With Death: The Constitution, Law, And Equality In The Civil War Era*, 2-3 (1975).

81. 2 *Collected Works Of Abraham Lincoln* 405-406 (R. Blaser, ed., 1953); Curtis, *No State Shall Abridge*, at 42-46.

82. The women's rights movement followed essentially the same strategy in attacking discrimination against women. Seneca Falls Declaration of Sentiments and Resolutions (1848) in *Urofsky Documents*, at 337.

83. Robert Justin Goldstein, "The Great 1989-1990 Flag Flap: An Historical, Political, and Legal Analysis," 45 *U. Miami L. Rev.* 19, 37 (1990) [hereafter "The Great Flag Flap"].

84. Curtis, *No State Shall Abridge*, at 40.

85. McPherson, *Battle Cry Of Freedom*, at 597-98.

86. *Id.* at 598-99. After the war was over the Supreme Court ruled that military trial of a civilian in a non-war zone where the civil courts were operating was unconstitutional. Ex Parte Milligan, 71 U.S. 2 (1866).

Introduction

87. "The Great 1989-90 Flag Flap," 45 *U. Miami L. Rev.* 19, 37 (1990).
88. Mark Neely, Jr., *The Fate Of Liberty, Abraham Lincoln And Civil Liberties* 64 (1991) [hereafter Neely, *The Fate Of Liberty*].
89. Curtis, *No State Shall Abridge*, at 40. See Neely, *The Fate Of Liberty* 188-92.
90. Neely, *The Fate Of Liberty* 138.
91. "Freedom of Expression from 1791 to 1917," 44 *Fordham L. Rev.* at 271, n. 28.
92. William Crosskey, "Charles Fairman, 'Legislative History,' and the Constitutional Limits on State Authority," 22 *U. Chi. L. Rev.* 1 (1954); Michael Kent Curtis, "Further Adventures of the Nine Lived Cat: A Response to Mr. Berger on Incorporation of the Bill of Rights," 42 *Ohio St. L.J.* 89, 91-93 (1982); Akhil Amar, "The Bill of Rights and the Fourteenth Amendment," 101 *Yale L.J.* 1193 (1992). *But see* William Nelson, *The Fourteenth Amendment* (1988); Raoul Berger, *The Fourteenth Amendment And The Bill Of Rights* (1989).
93. Slaughter House Cases, 83 U.S. (16 Wall.) 36 (1872); United States v. Cruikshank, 92 U.S. (2 Otto) 542 (1875).
94. *See, e.g.*, Santa Clara County v. Southern Pac. Ry. Co., 118 U.S. 394 (1886) (corporations are persons under the due process clause); Lochner v. New York, 198 U.S. 45 (1905) (60-hour week for bakers struck down under the due process clause).
95. Erving Beauregard, "John A. Bingham and the Fourteenth Amendment," 40 *The Historian* 67, 69 (1987).
96. Stromberg v. California, 283 U.S. 359 (1931); Near v. Minnesota, 283 U.S. 697 (1931).
97. 205 U.S. 34 (1907).
98. *See, e.g.*, Virginia State Board of Pharmacy v. Virginia Citizens Consumer Council, 425 U.S. 748 (1976).
99. 205 U.S. at 42-43.
100. *Id.* at 41.
101. *Id.* at 44-45.
102. Fox v. Washington, 236 U.S. 273, 276-277 (1915) (newspaper article urging nudists to boycott the prudes who encouraged their prosecution held to have the bad tendency to encourage indecent exposure); Patterson v. Colorado 205 U.S. 454 (1907) (criticisms of state supreme courts had the bad tendency to interfere with the administration of justice).
103. "The First Amendment in the Balance," 71 *Yale L.J.* 1424, 1430.
104. The "incorporation" doctrine refers to requirements that states obey guarantees of the Bill of Rights. The idea seems to be that guarantees are incorporated by reference.
105. Davis v. Massachusetts, 167 U.S. 43 (1897).

106. Rich v. City of Naperville, 42 Ill. App. 222, 223-24 (1891); *In re* Frazee, 30 N.W. 72, 75-76 (Mich. 1886); David Rabban, "The First Amendment in its Forgotten Years," 90 *Yale L.J.* 514 (1981).

107. Fitts v. Atlanta, 49 S.E. 793 (Ga. 1905). *Ex parte* Thomas, 102 P. 19, 20 (Cal. Dist. Ct. App. 1909).

108. Patterson v. Colorado, 205 U.S. 454, 462 (1907). Holmes did suggest courts were amenable to criticism once the case was final, presumably a limitation on the law of contempt. 205 U.S. at 462. For a thought-provoking discussion of the facts of Patterson, see. L. A. Scot. Powe, Jr., *The Fourth Estate And The Constitution: Freedom Of The Press In America* 1-7 (1991). For state cases limiting contempt power *see, e.g.*, Storey v. Illinois, 79 Ill. 45, 48-53 (1875); Gibson, "Freedom of Expression from 1791 to 1917," 55 *Fordham L. Rev.* 263, 285 n.141. For other discussions of the history of the First Amendment *see* David Rabban, "The First Amendment in Its Forgotten Years," 90 *Yale L.J.* 514 (1981) (taking a bleaker view of the Court and the First Amendment in its early years) [hereafter "The First Amendment in Its Forgotten Years"] and David Yassky, "Eras of the First Amendment," 91 *Col. L. Rev.* 1699 (1991).

109. "Freedom of Expression From 1791 to 1917," 55 *Fordham L. Rev.* 263, 285 n.141.

110. Coleman v. MacLennan, 98 P. 281 (Kan. 1908).

111. Marshall v. Gordon, 243 U.S. 521 (1917); Gandia v. Pettingill, 222 U.S. 452, 457 (1912); "Freedom of Expression: 1791 to 1917," 55 *Fordham L. Rev.* at 283.

112. Schenck v. United States, 249 U.S. 47 (1919); Debs v. United States, 249 U.S. 211 (1919).

113. Schenck v. United States, 249 U.S. 47, 52 (1919).

114. Hugo Black, "The Bill of Rights," 35 *N.Y.U. L. Rev.* 865, 867 (1960); "The First Amendment In The Balance," 71 *Yale L.J.* at 1432.

115. Walter Nelles, *Espionage Act Cases* 77-78, 80 (1918); Mark Graber, *Transforming Free Speech* 38-41 (1991); Ernest Freund, "The Debs Case and Freedom of Speech," *The New Republic*, May 13, 1919, at 13, reprinted in 40 *U. Chi. L. Rev.* 239 (1973).

116. Masses Publishing Co. v. Patten, 244 F. 535, 540 (1917).

117. "The Great Flag Flap," 45 *U. Miami L. Rev.* at 38.

118. David T. Prosser, "Desecration of the American Flag," 3 *Ind. Legal F.* 159 (1969) [hereafter "Desecration of The American Flag"].

119. Tribe, *Constitutional Law* 842 n.10.

120. *Id.* at 165-66. *See Ex Parte* Starr, 263 F. 145 (D., Mont. 1920).

121. "Desecration of the American Flag," 3 *Ind. Legal F.*, at 160-68.

122. Commonwealth v. Karvonen, 106 N.E. 556, 557 (Mass. 1914).

123. 106 N.E. at 557.
124. "The First Amendment in the Balance," 71 *Yale L.J.*, at 1437.
125. *See, e.g.*, Gitlow v. New York, 268 U.S. 652 (1925).
126. 247 U.S. 357, 372, Brandeis, *concurring*.
127. 198 U.S. 45 (1905).
128. Richard Skolnik, "Rufus Peckham," in *3 Justices Of The United States Supreme Court* 1697 (Leon Friedman And Fred Israel, eds., 1969).
129. Maxwell v. Dow, 176 U.S. 581, 604–05 (1900).
130. Lochner v. New York, 198 U.S. 45, 76 (1905) (Holmes, J. *dissenting*).
131. Meyer v. Nebraska, 262 U.S. 390, 399 (1922).
132. 262 U.S. at 403.
133. 262 U.S. at 412 (Holmes, J. *dissenting*).
134. Felix Frankfurter, "Can the Supreme Court Guarantee Toleration," 43 *New Republic* 85 (1925), cited in William G. Fennell, "The 'Reconstructed Court' and Religious Freedom: The Gobitis Case in Retrospect," 19 *N.Y.U. L. Rev.* 31, 45 (1941).
135. Near v. Minnesota, 283 U.S. 697 (1931). For a short and lively account of the case *see* Fred Friendly, *The Minnesota Rag: The Dramatic Story Of The Landmark Supreme Court That Gave New Meaning To Freedom Of The Press* (1981).
136. Stromberg v. California, 283 U.S. 359 (1931).
137. *See* Cantwell v. Connecticut, 310 U.S. 296 (1940); Terminiello v. Chicago, 337 U.S. 1 (1949).
138. Schneider v. State, 308 U.S. 147 (1939).
139. *Id*.
140. Martin v. City of Struthers, 319 U.S. 141 (1943).
141. "The Flag Salute Cases," 31 *Clev. St. L. Rev.* at 421–25.
142. West Virginia Board of Education v. Barnette, 319 U.S. 624, 639 (1943). To the extent that protection for a category of speech is absolute, legislation directly abridging it and aimed specifically at the speech would not seem permissible even though the danger in a particular case was great and imminent. A law aimed at certain types of behavior would involve different questions.
143. 310 U.S. 586 (1940).
144. Sidney Blumenthal, *Pledging Allegiance: The Last Campaign Of The Cold War* 263 (1990), [hereafter Blumenthal, *Pledging Allegiance*].
145. David Manwaring, *Render Unto Caesar: The Flag Salute Controversy* 2 (1962), [hereafter Manwaring, *Render Unto Caesar*].

146. *Id.* at 4. At the same time Massachusetts required the flag salute it also required a loyalty oath from all public and private school teachers. *Id.* For a contemporary criticism of both laws *see* George Gardner and Charles Post, "The Constitutional Questions Raised by the Flag Salute and Teachers' Oath Acts in Massachusetts," XVI *B.U.L.R.* 803 (1936).

147. Richard Hough, "The Jehovah's Witnesses Cases in Retrospect," 6 *West. Pol. Q.* 78 (1953); E. Waite, "The Debt of Constitutional Law to Jehovah's Witnesses," 28 *Minn. L. Rev.* 209 (1944). *See* Wooley v. Maynard, 430 U.S. 705 (1977).

148. Nicholls v. Lynn, 7 N.E.2d 577, 580 (Mass. 1937).

149. People ex rel. Fish v. Sandstrom, 18 N.E.2d 840, 842 (N.Y. 1939).

150. 310 U.S. 586 (1940).

151. United States v. Carolene Products Co., 304 U.S. 144, 152 (1938).

152. *Id.* at 153 n. 4. *See* Richard Danzig, "Justice Frankfurter's Opinions in the Flag Salute Cases: Blending Logic and Psychologic in Constitutional Decisionmaking," 36 *Stan. L. Rev.* 675, 686-89 (1984) [hereafter "Frankfurter's Opinions"].

153. 310 U.S. at 592-93.

154. 310 U.S. at 593.

155. Michael McConnell, "The Origins and Historical Understanding of Free Exercise of Religion," 103 *Harv. L. Rev.* 1409 (1990).

156. Reynolds v. United States, 98 U.S. 145 (1878).

157. Hamilton v. University of California, 293 U.S. 245 (1934).

158. 310 U.S. at 595-96.

159. 310 U.S. at 596.

160. 310 U.S. at 596-98.

161. 310 U.S. at 599-600 (emphasis added).

162. "The First Amendment in the Balance," 71 *Yale L.J.* at 1439.

163. 310 U.S. at 600. For scholarly support for deference by the Judiciary, *see* James B. Thayer, "The Origin and Scope of the American Doctrine of Constitutional Law," 7 *Harv. L. Rev.* 129 (1893).

164. Manwaring, *Render Unto Caesar* at 180-81, 186.

165. Richard Danzig, "How Questions Begot Answers in Felix Frankfurter's First Flag Salute Opinion," 1977 *S. Ct. Rev.* 257, 261-63 (1978), [hereafter, "How Questions Begot Answers"].

166. "The Flag Salute Cases," 31 *Clev. St. L. Rev.* at 430.

167. "How Questions Begot Answers," 1977 *S. Ct. Rev.* at 266.

168. Schneider v. State, 308 U.S. 147 (1939).

Introduction   lxix

169. Minersville School Dist. v. Gobitis, 310 U.S. 605 (1940).

170. 310 U.S. at 606.

171. Manwaring, *Render Unto Caesar*, at 81.

172. Victor W. Rotnem and F. G. Folsom, Jr., "Recent Restrictions Upon Religious Liberty," 36 *Am. Pol. Sci. Rev.* 1053, 1061 (1942)[hereafter "Recent Restrictions"].

173. Manwaring, *Render Unto Caesar*, at 148-62.

174. Manwaring, *Render Unto Caesar*, at 155.

175. "Recent Restrictions," 36 *Am. Pol. Sci. Rev.* at 1063 n. 30.

176. *Id.* at 1063 n. 30.

177. *Id.* at 1068 n. 38.

178. Jones v. Opelika, 316 U.S. 584, 623 (1942) (Justices Black, Douglas, and Murphy, J.J., *dissenting*).

179. "Frankfurter's Opinions," 36 *Stan. L. Rev.* at 723 n. 135.

180. Henry Commanger, "Civil Liberties and Democracy," 42 *Scholastic* 13 (1943).

181. Cited in Brief for the American Legion, Amicus Curiae, West Virginia Board of Education v. Barnette, 319 U.S. 624 (1943) [hereafter "Legion Brief"].

182. "Legion Brief" at 18.

183. West Va. Bd. of Educ. v. Barnette 319 U.S. 624, 630 (1943).

184. 319 U.S. at 631 n. 11.

185. *Id.* at 633.

186. Linda Greenhouse, "Patriotism and the Pledge: Symbolism, More Than Precedent, Is the Issue in The Bush and Dukakis Clash," *N.Y. Times*, Aug. 27, 1988, § 1, at 1.

187. George K. Gardner and Charles Post, "The Constitutional Questions Raised by the Flag Salute and Teachers' Oath Acts in Massachusetts," XVI *B.U.L. Rev.* 803, 812, 822 (1936). Gardner and Post note that the Massachusetts Constitution continued in force existing laws of the province "such parts only excepted as are repugnant to the rights and liberties continued in this constitution." They note that the Massachusetts Bill of Rights prohibited legislative declarations of treason although such acts had passed during the Revolution. They also note that the Revolution eliminated the usual test of citizenship by birth and presumably justified a means of determining citizenship. *Id.* at 822.

188. Harold Hyman, *To Try Men's Souls: Loyalty Tests In American History* 85 (1959); Sanford Levinson, "Constituting Communities Through Words that Bind: Reflections on Loyalty Oaths," 84 *Mich. L. Rev.* 1440, 1149-50 (1986).

189. McConnell, "Origins of Free Exercise," 103 *Harv. L. Rev.* at 1471.

190. 319 U.S. at 636.
191. 319 U.S. at 641.
192. 319 U.S. at 636.
193. 319 U.S. at 638.
194. 319 U.S. at 639.
195. 319 U.S. at 640.
196. 319 U.S. at 642.
197. 319 U.S. at 664.
198. 319 U.S. at 662–63, 666.
199. 319 U.S. at 670–71.
200. Dennis v. United States, 341 U.S. 494 (1951).
201. Scales v. United States, 367 U.S. 203 (1961); Noto v. United States, 367 U.S. 290 (1961); Aptheker v. Secretary of State, 378 U.S. 500 (1964).
202. Memoirs v. Massachusetts, 398 U.S. 413 (1966).
203. New York Times Co. v. Sullivan, 376 U.S. 254 (1964).
204. 376 U.S. 254.
205. 376 U.S. at 273.
206. 376 U.S. at 279–80.
207. 376 U.S. at 270.
208. Bond v. Floyd, 385 U.S. 116, 120, 122 (1966).
209. 385 U.S. at 134.
210. Thomas Emerson, "Freedom of Expression in Wartime," 116 *U. Pa. L. Rev.* 975, 988 (1968). *See also* United States v. Spock, 416 F.2d 165 (1st Cir. 1969).
211. 254 U.S. 325 (1920).
212. Edwards v. South Carolina, 372 U.S. 229 (1963).
213. Brandenburg v. Ohio, 395 U.S. 444, 447 (1969).
214. Dennis v. United States, 384 U.S. 855, (1966).
215. John Hart Ely, "Flag Desecration: A Case Study in the Roles of Categorying and Balancing in First Amendment Analysis," 88 *Harv. L. Rev.* 1482 (1975) [hereafter "Flag Desecration"].
216. Perry Education Assn. v. Perry Local Educators' Assn., 460 U.S. 37, 45 (1983) citing Carey v. Brown, 447 U.S. 455, 461 (1980) which applied an equal protection standard. *See* Simon & Schuster v. New York Crime Victims Bd., 112 S.Ct. 501, 513 (1992) (Kennedy J. *concurring* and protesting use of equal protection standards to evaluate fully-protected speech).

Introduction lxxi

217. 394 U.S. 576 (1969).
218. 394 U.S. at 591-92.
219. 394 U.S. at 593.
220. 394 U.S. at 596.
221. 391 U.S. 367 (1968).
222. United States v. O'Brien, 391 U.S. 367, 377 (1968).
223. "Flag Desecration," 88 *Harv. L. Rev.* at 1482.
224. *Id.* at 1484-855.
225. *See, e.g.*, Cox v. Louisiana, 379 U.S. 536, 538-43 (1965) Harry Kalven, *The Negro And The First Amendment* 173-214 (1965).
226. *See, e.g.*, Dean Alfange, "Free Speech and Symbolic Conduct: The Draft Card Burning Case," 1968 *S. Ct. Rev.* 1.
227. Tinker v. Des Moines Indep. Comm. Dist., 393 U.S. 503 (1969).
228. 18 U.S.C. § 700(b) (1968).
229. 403 U.S. 15 (1971).
230. 403 U.S. at 17 (emphasis added).
231. 403 U.S. at 20.
232. 403 U.S. at 26.
233. Aaron Singer, ed., *Campaign Speeches Of American Presidential Candidates 1928-1972* 361 (1976).
234. Robert H. Bork, "Neutral Principles and Some First Amendment Problems," 47 *Ind. L.J.* 1 (1971) [hereafter "Neutral Principles"].
235. *Id.* at 8.
236. *Id.* at 10-11 (emphasis added).
237. *Id.* at 22.
238. *See, e.g.*, Lochner v. New York, 198 U.S. 45 (1905).
239. "Neutral Principles," 47 *Ind. L.J.* at 18.
240. *Id.* at 18.
241. Cass R. Sunstein, "Beyond the Republican Revival," 97 *Yale L.J.* 1539, 1579 (1988). The idea of pre-political natural or inherent rights in the view of Professor Sunstein led to the abuses of the Lochner era. *See also* Mark Tushnet, "An Essay on Rights," 62 *Tex. L. Rev.* 1363 (1984).
242. Schwartz, *The Bill Of Rights* at 1029 (Madison on the Bill of Rights in relation to natural rights); *e.g.*, *No State Shall Abridge*, at 87 (Bingham).
243. "Neutral Principles," 47 *Ind. L.J.* at 11.

244. 268 U.S. 510 (1925). Judge Bork later suggested that *Pierce* could be justified under the guarantee of free speech and religion. *The Tempting Of America*, at 48–49.
245. 381 U.S. 479 (1965).
246. "Neutral Principles," 47 *Ind. L.J.* at 28.
247. 1 Schwartz, *The Bill Of Rights* at 223 (Address to Inhabitants of Quebec).
248. 268 U.S. 652 (1925).
249. 274 U.S. 357 (1927).
250. Gitlow v. New York, 268 U.S. 652 (1925).
251. "The First Amendment in the Balance," 74 *Yale L.J.* 1424 (1962).
252. *Hearings On Measures To Protect The Physical Integrity Of The American Flag*, S. Hrg. 101-355, *Senate Judiciary Committee* 99 (1989).
253. William Rehnquist, "A Living Constitution," 54 *Tex. L. Rev.* 693 (1976).
254. *Id.* at 704.
255. *Id.* at 704–05.
256. Lochner v. New York, 198 U.S. 45 (1905).
257. William Rehnquist, "A Living Constitution," 54 *Tex. L. Rev.* 693 (1976).
258. *Id.*
259. Miller v. California, 413 U.S. 15 (1973).
260. Apodoca v. Oregon, 406 U.S. 404 (1972)—allowing state non-unanimous jury verdict; United States v. Leon, 468 U.S. 897 (1984).
261. Wooley v. Maynard, 430 U.S. 705 (1977).
262. Consolidated Edison Co. v. Public Service Comm'n, 447 U.S. 530 (1980).
263. Miami Herald Pub. Co. v. Tornillo, 418 U.S. 241 (1974).
264. Wisconsin v. Yoder, 406 U.S. 205 (1972) (exempting the Amish from compulsory school attendance laws).
265. *See* Employment Division, Dep't of Human Resources v. Smith, 494 U.S. 872, 890 (1990).
266. *E.g.*, Lehman v. City of Shaker Heights, 418 U.S. 298 (1974).
267. First National Bank of Boston v. Bellotti, 435 U.S. 765 (1978); Buckley v. Valeo, 424 U.S. 1 (1976).
268. Mark Tushnet, "An Essay on Rights," 62 *Tex. L. Rev.* 1363, 1386-87 (1984).
269. Brandenburg v. Ohio, 395 U.S. 444, 447 (1969).
270. Street v. New York, 394 U.S. 576 (1969) (conviction of flag burner overturned because it might have been based on critical words about the flag that were

Introduction

lxxiii

constitutionally protected); People v. Cowgill, 274 Ca. App. 2d 923, 78 Cal. Rptr. 853 (App. Dept. Super. Ct. 1969), appeal dismissed, 396 U.S. 371 (1972) (conviction for wearing flag made into a vest as an attractive and appropriate Election Day gesture); Smith v. Gougen, 415 U.S. 566 (1974) (flag desecration statute found unconstitutionally vague as applied to young man who wore a flag patch on the seat of his pants).

271. Street v. New York, 394 U.S. 576 (1969).

272. Kime v. United States, 459 U.S. 949 (1982) (Brennan, J. *dissenting* from denial of certiorari). A defendant in that case was represented by a then law partner of the author of this piece.

273. *E.g.*, United States v. Crosson, 462 F.2d 96 (9th Cir. 1972); Monroe v. State, 295 S.E.2d 512 (Ga. 1982); for the opposite result, *see* Monroe v. State Court of Fulton County, 739 F.2d 1984 (1984).

274. Melville Nimmer, "The Meaning of Symbolic Speech Under the First Amendment," 21 *U.C.L.A. L. Rev.* 29 (1972) [hereafter "Symbolic Speech"].

275. *Id.* at 43.

276. *Id.* at 57.

277. 418 U.S. 405 (1974).

278. 418 U.S. at 412.

279. 418 U.S. 415.

280. "Flag Desecration," 88 *Harv. L. Rev.* at 1484

281. Texas v. Johnson, 491 U.S. at 407-411. Strict scrutiny is the most rigorous critical review the Court applies to governmental action. It focuses on whether the governmental purposes are legitimate and whether the purposes could be achieved by less restrictive means that would not interfere with constitutional rights. Typically, when the Court applies strict scrutiny, the statute is found unconstitutional.

282. 418 U.S. at 417, Rehnquist, J. *dissenting*.

283. 207 U.S. 34 (1907) cited at 418 U.S. at 418-20.

284. 418 U.S. at 422-23.

285. McPherson, *Battle Cry Of Freedom*, at 649.

286. Doe v. Univ. of Michigan, 721 F. Supp. 852 (E.D. Mich. 1989).

287. Nat Hentoff, "The Boy With a Confederate Flag on His Back," *Village Voice*, July 5, 1988, at 31.

288. "Opinions of the Justices to the Governor," 363 N.E.2d 251 (1977).

289. Blumenthal, *Pledging Allegiance* 262-63.

290. Russo v. Central Sch. Dist., 469 F.2d 623 (2d Cir. 1972).

291. Nicholls v. Lynn, 7 N.E.2d 577 (Mass. 1937) People ex rel. Fish v. Sandstrom, 18 N.E.2d 840 (N.Y. 1939).

292. 490 U.S. 310, 323 (1990) (Stevens, Rehnquist, White, and O'Connor, J., *dissenting*).

293. *Id.*

294. 491 U.S. at 403.

295. 491 U.S. at 412.

296. Kent Greenwalt, "O'er The Land of the Free: Flag Burning As Speech," 37 *U.C.L.A. L. Rev.*, 925, 936 (1990) [hereafter "Flag Burning As Speech"].

297. 491 U.S. at 412.

298. 491 U.S. at 414.

299. 491 U.S. at 417.

300. 491 U.S. at 442, (Rehnquist, J., *dissenting*); M. Tushnet, "The Flag Burning Episode: An Essay on the Constitution," 61 *U. Colo. L. Rev.* 39, 44 (1990).

301. 491 U.S. at 430-31.

302. *Compare* Feiner v New York, 340 U.S. 315 (1951) *with* Chaplinsky v. New Hampshire, 315 U.S. 568 (1942).

303. *See* Houston v. Hill, 482 U.S. 451 (1987).

304. Cohen v. California, 403 U.S. 15 (1971).

305. Texas v. Johnson, 491 U.S. at 407, n. 4 and at 408-10. *See also* "Flag Burning As Speech," 37 *U.C.L.A. L. Rev.* 925, 934.

306. 491 U.S. at 407, n. 4.

307. Harry Kalven, *The Negro And The First Amendment* 140-45 (1965).

308. Cooper v. Aaron, 358 U.S. 1, 16 (1958); Frantz, "The First Amendment in the Balance," 71 *Yale L.J.* at 1438.

309. Brandenburg v. Ohio, 395 U.S. 444, 447 (1969) (burning cross at political rally coupled with reference to revenge held to be not sufficient to justify sedition conviction so that a statute that permitted conviction in those circumstances was unconstitutional). In connection with its citation to Brandenburg the Court also stressed that the mere possibility of violent reaction was not sufficient to justify a conviction. Texas v. Johnson, 491 U.S. 397, 409 (1989).

310. *Compare* the citation to Brandenburg in Texas v. Johnson, 491 U.S. 397, 409 (1989) *with* the *caveat* at 491 U.S. 397, 407 n.8. Does a violent reaction one expects or should reasonably foresee but does not desire mean one's conduct is "directed" to producing violence?

311. 491 U.S. at 432.

312. *See, e.g.*, Memoirs v. Massachusetts, 383 U.S. 413 (1966) (plurality opinion) reversing obscenity finding in connection with Fanny Hill; New York Times v.

Introduction   lxxv

 Sullivan, 376 U.S. 254 (1964), restric1ting application of libel laws in cases of public officials.

313. Young v. American Mini Theaters, Inc., 427 U.S. 50 (1976) (plurality opinion) (sexually explicit but not obscene expression); FCC v. Pacificia Foundation, 438 U.S. 726 (1978) (radio monologue containing seven dirty words; City of Renton v. Playtime Theatres, Inc., 475 U.S. 41 (1986) (zoning "adult" movie theatres virtually out of the city).

314. 491 U.S. at 435.

315. *Hearings on Measure to Protect the Physical Integrity of the Flag: Hearing Before the Committee of the Judiciary United States Senate*, 101st Congress, 1st sess. 140-81 (Professor Lawrence Tribe) 187-234 (Professor Geoffrey Stone) 536-557 (Professor Walter Dellinger) (1990) [hereafter "Hearings"].

316. *Id*. at 150, 170. William Van Alstyne, "Freedom of Speech and the Flag Anti-Desecration Amendment: Antinomies of Constitutional Choice" in *Free Speech Year Book* 96, 101 N. 18 (1991).

317. United States v. Eichman, 496 U.S. 310 (1990).

318. 112 S. Ct. 2538, 2542 (Majority Opinion), 2559 (White, J. Blackmon, T. and O'Connor, T., *concurring*) (1992).

319. R.A.V. v. City of St. Paul, 112 S. Ct. 2538 (1992).

320. R.A.V. v. City of St. Paul, 112 S. Ct. 2538, 2547-48 (1992).

321. 112 S. Ct. at 2548.

322. *See* 112 S. Ct. at 2547-48.

323. 112 S. Ct. at 2543-45.

324. 112 S. Ct. at 2547.

325. 112 S. Ct. at 2560-61 (White, J., *concurring*).

326. 491 U.S. 404, 414 (1989).

327. 394 U.S. 576, 592 (1969). *See also* Terminiello v. Chicago, 337 U.S. 1 (1949).

328. 403 U.S. 15, 20 (1971).

329. For some years the Court had suggested such "overbroad" statutes should be struck down so they would not inhibit people from exercising their right to engage in protected speech. For example, a statute banning speech that aroused anger would be overbroad. It could include not only face-to-face epithets likely to produce an immediate breach of the peace (fighting words the Court holds the states can ban) but also advocacy of socialism (something the state could not prohibit consistent with the First Amendment.) The legislature could always enact a narrower statute that reached only unprotected conduct.

330. Hans A. Linde, "'Clear and Present Danger' Reexamined: Dissonance in the Brandenburg Concerto," 22 *Stan. L. Rev.* 1163, 1174 (1970).

331. *Id.*

332. Employment Div., Dep't. of Human Resources v. Smith, 110 S. Ct. 1595 (1990).

333. Texas v. Johnson, 491 U.S. 397 (1989).

334. Barnes v. Glen Theatre, Inc., 112 S. Ct. 2456, 2465-67 (1991).

335. *Id.* at 2467 (Scalia, J., *concurring*).

336. *Id.*

337. *Id.* Justice Scalia suggested that in effect his approach was not so different from the *O'Brien* analysis embraced by the majority. *Cf. also,* Cohen v. Cowels Media Co., 111 S.Ct. 2513 (1991).

338. *E.g.*, Brandendenburg v. Ohio, 395 U.S. 444 (1969).

339. Hustler Magazine v. Falwell, 485 U.S. 46 (1988). In Hustler, the Court applied to Falwell's intentional infliction claim the standard articulated in New York Times v. Sullivan, 376 U.S. 254 (1964).

340. 491 U.S. at 408, n.4: "This view has found some favor in the lower courts. *See* Monroe v. State Court of Fulton County, 739 F.2d 568, 574-75 (CA 11 1984). Johnson's theory may overread [First Amendment protection in this situation] insofar as it suggests that a desire to prevent a violent audience reaction is 'related to expression' in the same way that a desire to prevent an audience from being offended is 'related to expression.' Because we find that the State's interest in preventing breaches of the peace is not implicated on these facts, however, we need not venture further into this area."

341. 112 S.Ct. 2538 at 2549 n.7.

342. Tribe, *Constitutional Law* 830.

343. 343 U.S. 250 (1950); R.A.V. v. City of St. Paul, 112 S. Ct. 2538, 2543 (1992).

344. Collin v. Smith, 578 F.2d 1197, 1205 (7th Cir. 1978); American Booksellers Assn. Inc. v. Hudnut, 771 F.2d 323, 331 at n. 3 (7th Cir. 1985), *aff'd* 475 U.S. 1001 (1986).

345. Railway Express Agency v. New York, 336 U.S. 106, 112 (1949) (Jackson, J., *concurring*).

346. *See* Vincent Blasi, "The Pathological Perspective and the First Amendment," 85 *Colum. L. Rev.* 449 (1985). Others have noted the sometimes paradoxical effect of the equality rationale. *See* Geoffrey Stone, "Content Regulation and the First Amendment," 25 *Wm. & Mary L. Rev.* 189, 205 (1983); Carey v. Brown, 447 U.S. 455, 475 (Rehnquist, J. *dissenting*.)

347. "Flag Burning As Speech," 37 *U.C.L.A. L. Rev.* at 931; Werhan, "The O'Briening of Free Speech," 19 *Ariz. St. L.J.* at 645.

348. City Council v. Taxpayers for Vincent, 466 U.S. 789, 808-10 (1984).

349. 467 U.S. 20 (1984).

350. Schneider v. State, 308 U.S. 147, 163 (1939).

351. Martin v. City of Struthers, 318 U.S. 413 (1943).

352. Murdock v. Pennsylvania, 319 U.S. 105 (1943); Follett v. Town of McCormick, 321 U.S. 573 (1944).

353. Lovell v. City of Griffin, 303 U.S. 444 (1938); Schneider v. State, 308 U.S. 147 (1939).

354. Murdock v. Pennsylvania, 319 U.S. 105 (1943); Follet v. Town of McCormick, 321 U.S. 573 (1944).

355. Michael Kent Curtis, "Ads on Busses," 46 *N.C. L. Rev.* 900 (1968).

356. Lehman v. City of Shaker Heights, 418 U.S. 298 (1974).

357. Greer v. Spock, 424 U.S. 828 (1976).

358. United States Postal Service v. Council of Greenburgh Civic Assns., 453 U.S. 114 (1981).

359. United States v. Kokinda, 497 U.S. 720 (1990).

360. City of Los Angeles v. Taxpayers for Vincent, 466 U.S. 789 (1983).

361. International Society for Krishna Consciousness v. Lee, 112 S.Ct. 2701, 2706 (1992). A closely divided Court permitted leafletting but not solicitation of funds. Lee v. International Society for Krishna Consciousness, 112 S.Ct. 2709 (1992).

362. Lehman v. City of Shaker Heights, 418 U.S. 298, 301 (1974).

363. Perry Educ. Assn. v. Perry Local Educators' Assn., 460 U.S. 37 (1983).

364. Ward v. Rock Against Racism, 109 S. Ct. 2757, 2758 (1989).

365. "Flag Desecration," 88 *Harv. L. Rev.* at 1487.

366. *E.g.*, Buckley v. Valeo, 424 U.S. 1 (1976) (Congress may not limit political expenditures by "independent" political action committees); First National Bank of Boston v. Bellotti, 435 U.S. 765 (1978) (prohibition on corporate spending on ballot measures held unconstitutional); *but see* Austin v. Michigan Chamber of Commerce, 110 S.Ct. 1391 (1990) (five-to-four): (prohibition on independent corporate spending to elect or defeat candidates upheld).

367. David Prosser, "Desecration of the American Flag," 3 *Ind. Leg. For.* at 216-219.

368. Calvin Massey, "Pure Symbols and the First Amendment," 17 *Hast. Const. L. Q.* 369, 375-76 (1990).

369. Nat Hentoff, "The Boy With a Confederate Flag on His Back," *Village Voice*, July 5, 1988, at 31.

370. *See* Lackland H. Bloome, Jr., "Barnette and Johnson, A Tale of Two Opinions," 75 *Iowa L. Rev.* 417 (1990).

CHILDREN, THE BILL OF RIGHTS AND THE AMERICAN FLAG.

On the water gate of the World's Fair in Chicago in 1893 appeared the late President Eliot's much quoted inscription,

"Toleration in religion, the best fruit of the last four centuries".

In 1928, in the case of *Glaser* v. *Congregation Kehillath Israel* (263 Mass. 435 at p. 437), Chief Justice Rugg, speaking for a unanimous court, referred to the "great guaranties of religious liberty and equality before the law of all religions" and described them as follows,

> "Freedom to worship the Supreme Being 'in the manner and season most agreeable to the dictates of his own conscience,' 'provided he doth not disturb the public peace, or obstruct others in their religious worship,' is secured by art. 2 of the Declaration of Rights of the Constitution of this Commonwealth. By art. 11 of the Amendments to the Constitution further provision is made for the security of religious freedom, concluding with the mandate that 'all religious sects and denominations, demeaning themselves peaceably, and as good citizens of the commonwealth, shall be equally under the protection of the law; and no subordination of any one sect or denomination to another shall ever be established by law.'
> By art. 46 of the Amendments, 'No law shall be passed prohibiting the free exercise of religion.'"

Some years ago, a statue of Anne Hutchinson, banished to Rhode Island for her religious views, about 300 years ago, was erected in front of the Massachusetts State House and, in 1936, by Chapter 11 of the Resolves of that year, the Massachusetts Legislature "revoked" the sentence of "expulsion" of Roger Williams to Rhode Island in 1636.

For generations the principle of toleration has been reflected in our law allowing persons who have religious scruples about taking an "oath" to "affirm" without swearing. The Nation has recognized and protected the religious beliefs of "conscientious objectors" in connection with military service.

In 1935, by Chapter 258 of that year, the legislature provided that in each school "under the control of the school committees," each teacher shall cause the pupils under his charge to salute the flag and recite in unison with him at opening exercises at least once each week the "Pledge of Allegience to the flag." Failure for two weeks to cause the pupils so to do subjects *the teacher* to a criminal penalty.

(1)

As pointed out by Chief Justice Rugg, however (in *Nichols* v. *Mayor,* etc., of Lynn, 1937 Adv. Sheets, 537), the statute "established no penalty for a disobedient pupil" but is directed to the school committee and the teacher.

Shortly after the passage of the statute a child in Lynn, eight years of age, who, with his parents, was of a religious group known as "Jehovah's Witnesses", quietly refused to take part in the ceremony of saluting the flag on the ground that it was contrary to his religious belief. A member of "Jehovah's Witnesses," as stated by the court "through the literal reading of the Bible and especially of the first two Commandments as found in Exodus XX, believes that he "must express reverence to God alone and not to the flag, which is not the symbol of God". "According to his belief, a salutation is equivalent to an act of reverence or adoration or idolatry and in violation of the Commandments of scripture."

The child was excluded from the school and in a proceeding to reinstate the child in school, the court, *without questioning the genuine nature of the belief of the child and his parent,* decided that the salute and pledge required by the statutes "has nothing to do with religion"; that it was merely education in patriotic appreciation of our form of government and, therefore, the statute was constitutional, and the expulsion of the child from school did not invade the rights of the child.

A similar decision was rendered by a Federal Court of three judges in Massachusetts, on January 4th, 1939, in regard to three children belonging to the same religious sect who were excluded from a public school in Deerfield (See *Johnson* v. *Town of Deerfield,* 25 Fed. Supp. 918) and this judgment was affirmed, but without a reasoned opinion, by the Supreme Court of the United States on April 17th, 1939. This seems rather curious in view of the vigorous opinion of Judge Maris of the Federal District Court for the Eastern District of Pennsylvania, who refused to follow our Massachusetts Court and other courts because he considered that . . .

> "they overlooked the fundamental principle of religious liberty . . . namely that no man even if he be a school director or a judge is empowered to censor another's religious convictions or set bounds to the areas of human conduct in which those convictions should be permitted to control his actions, *unless compelled to do so by an overriding public necessity which properly requires the exercise of the police power.*"*

---

* *Gobitis* v. *Minersville School Dist.*, 21 Fed. Supp. 271.

He found no prejudice to the public safety in a quiet, conscientious refusal for religious reasons, to salute the flag. On the contrary, he said,

"Our beloved flag, the emblem of religious liberty, apparently has been used as an instrument to impose a religious test as a condition of receiving the benefits of public education. And this has been done without any compelling necessity of public safety or welfare. We may well recall that William Penn, the founder of Pennsylvania, was expelled from Oxford University for his refusal for conscience sake to comply with regulations not essentially dissimilar, and suffered more than once imprisonment in England because of his religious convictions. . . . In these days when religious intolerance is again rearing its ugly head in other parts of the world it is of the utmost importance that the liberties guaranteed to our citizens by the fundamental law be preserved from all encroachment."

Nevertheless, it appears to be settled in Massachusetts, for the present at least, that a child may be excluded from the public schools solely for conscientious objections to the flag *salute*, however respectful and devoted he and his parents may be to the flag and all that it stands for, including religious liberty.

In an interesting discussion in a recent legal periodical appear the following passages,

"Each court upholding the salute has declared that the act of saluting could not possibly be a religious observance. . . . In this . . . objective determination that a certain act can not have religious significance lies the danger to religious freedom." The Supreme Court of the United States "has defined religion as one's views of his relations to his Creator and to the obligations which they impose of reverence for his being and character and of obedience to his will. Thus, unless the constitutional guaranties are inflexible, only the individual seems qualified to determine whether certain acts interfere with the 'free exercise' of that 'view'. Judicial inquiry would seem proper only to determine the character of the opposition. Once the sincerity and religious nature of the objection have been discovered, the courts should recognize that the salute may restrict religious liberty and frankly face the question whether it may nevertheless be compelled." *Har. Law Rev.* for June, 1938, 1418.

The end is not yet, and the serious problem of statutory construction and constitutional rights is now before the courts in connection with more drastic attempts to "compel" the children.

As pointed out by Chief Justice Rugg in 1937, "the public obligation to provide for general education" is imposed by Chapter

5, § 2 of the Massachusetts Constitution, and for many years it has been provided that children between the ages of seven and sixteen, with certain exceptions not material to this discussion, shall attend the public school and it is the duty of the parents and the school committee to enforce such attendance unless the child is being educated in some adequate private school approved by the committee, but it is expressly provided by General Laws, Chapter 76, § 1 that the school committees "shall not withhold such approval on account of religious teaching."

In an article in "Law Notes" for April, 1939, by Thomas G. Booth, it is stated that,

> "Because of their religious scruples as against saluting the flag, children have been expelled from public schools in twelve states. In some instances they have been brutally whipped, threatened with terms in reformatories, and otherwise mistreated. . . .
>
> 'The salute of the flag,' said Judge Lehman (in the New York case of *People* v. *Sandstrom*) 'is a gesture of love and respect—fine when there is real love and respect back of the gesture. The flag is dishonored by a salute by a child in reluctant and terrified obedience to a command of secular authority which clashes with the dictates of conscience. The flag "cherished by all our hearts" should not be soiled by the tears of a little child. The Constitution does not permit, and the legislature never intended, that the flag should be so soiled and dishonored.' "

Following the decision of the Federal Courts in Massachusetts in the Deerfield case, the three children were, not only excluded from school, but were summoned to the District Court in Greenfield on charge of being "habitual school offenders", under a statute passed many years before the compulsory flag salute was ever thought of, and in spite of the statement by Chief Justice Rugg already quoted from the Lynn case that the flag salute statute "established no penalty for a disobedient pupil".

At the hearing before the judge of the District Court, the judge, as we understand, although expressing reluctance, committed the children to a training school, which we understand to be a sort of reform school for delinquent children. This decision has, we understand, been appealed to the Superior Court and the appeal is likely to come up soon. Meanwhile, the children are at liberty, but subject, of course, to the commitment overhanging them.

The questions of law which must arise as a result of this judicial order that three young children between the ages of seven and twelve shall be torn from their home and parents, and placed in a county institution because of their religious belief are of such importance that they should be more generally understood by the public and thought about by the legal profession on both sides of the bench. There seem to be two distinct questions of law. First, can the old statute providing that,

> "A child under sixteen persistently violating reasonable regulations of the school he attends, or otherwise persistently misbehaving therein, so as to render himself a fit subject for exclusion therefrom, shall be deemed an habitual school offender, and unless placed on probation . . . may . . . be committed to a county training school,"

be legally interpreted to extend to the flag salute statute which the Supreme Judicial Court has expressly stated "established no penalty" for a child who failed to salute for religious reasons? This is a question of statutory construction. The second question is whether the persistent offender statute, if it is construed to include the later flag salute requirement, can be constitutionally applied not only to exclude the children from the schools and their opportunity for education, but to take them from their parents and force them into an institution of a reformatory character. This second question is one of constitutional law as to religious liberty and the rights of the child under the Bill of Rights. Incidental to this second question, there arises the practical question of commonsense as to what happens after they are forced into the training school? Do they require them to salute the flag there, and, if the children refuse for the same religious reasons, what happens then? Do they thrash them, or deprive them of food, or what form of altruistic brutality is applied?

As to the first question, the Supreme Court of the United States has said that there is a "cardinal rule of construction that where the language of an act will bear two interpretations equally obvious, that one which is clearly in accordance with the provisions of the constitution is to be preferred." (*Knights Templars Indemnity Co. v. Jarman,* 187 U. S. 197 at p. 205.) Under this rule, it would seem that the persistent school offender act should not be interpreted to include flag salute cases when there was no other form of "misbehavior" involved and the refusal to salute was because of religious belief genuinely held. All the modern literature and philosophy of juvenile courts and considerate treatment of children supports this view.

But if the courts should hold that the persistent offender statute does apply to these flag salute cases, even though the flag salute statute specifies no penalty for the child, then the courts must face squarely the honest belief of the children and their parents in the religious aspect of the salute and decide whether there is any reasonable danger to the public safety or welfare which can justify the exercise of the police power to the extent of overriding genuine religious beliefs and forcing young children away from their homes into public disciplinary institutions, with all that such institutions involve, as a matter of commonsense, in their influence for good *or evil* on the individual child. The question can not be avoided by simply denying what these people genuinely believe. The objections raised to the so-called "child labor" or "child control" amendment should not be forgotten when the question of "power" is considered.

In connection with a grave issue of this kind, it is well to remember that one of the earliest important decisions of the Supreme Judicial Court, after the adoption of the Massachusetts constitution in 1780, was the decision (by Justices Sargeant, David Sewall and James Sullivan in 1781, sustained in 1783 by the full court, then consisting of Chief Justice Cushing and Justices Sargeant, Sewall and Sumner), that slavery was inconsistent with the first article of the Bill of Rights. This decision was rendered while slave auctions were being advertised in Massachusetts and the legislature had taken no action in the matter.

Under the reasoning of the opinion of the court in *Weems* v. *U. S.*, 217 U. S. at pp. 372–373, the question may also arise whether taking a child from its home because of conscientious belief and placing it in a state institution is a "cruel and unusual punishment" in violation of the 26th Article of the Massachusetts Bill of Rights. Also the salute requirement does not apply to children in private schools.

James Madison once said,

> "In framing a government which is to be administered by men over men, the great difficulty lies in this; you must first enable the government to control the governed, and in the next place oblige it to control itself."

The question in these cases seems to be whether government through its three branches, or any of them, will "control itself" in the presence of, and in the treatment of, a child.

We believe the statute should be changed to protect genuinely conscientious children but, whatever the law may be decided to mean, we respectfully suggest that the governor exercise the pardoning power in every such case of a *genuinely* conscientious child.

The interference with religion involved in the suppression of Mormonism was based on the danger to public morality. The vaccination cases are based on danger to public health. What threatened public danger is there from the sect of "Jehovah's Witnesses" which justifies the exercise of the police power upon them?

In a recent letter to the press appears the following statement,
". . . the religion which believes that saluting an emperor's statue is idolatry is not harmful. Many Christians were thrown to the beasts for that. Now we have a religion which believes that saluting the flag, emblem of the sovereign people, is idolatry. We ought to deal kindly with its zealots. Probably they would express their loyalty in some other way not contrary to their religion, and yet explicit enough to make it safe to stop persecuting them." *

FRANK W. GRINNELL.

* The position of parents, who are members of the sect, is an awkward one. They are required to provide education for their children—they are supposed to have the right to train their children in their own religion and to have them at home. If they cannot afford a private school and the children are excluded from the public schools because of their religious belief, what are they to do?

MORE ABOUT THE FLAG SALUTE LAW.

The April-June number of the QUARTERLY contained an extended discussion of the legal aspects, constitutional and statutory, of the compulsory flag salute statute and the "persistent school offender" statute, under which three children between the ages of seven and twelve years have, not only been excluded from a public school, but have been ordered by a district court to be taken from their home and placed in a "county training school" for a quiet refusal to make the flag salute because they have been taught at home that the flag salute is a form of idolatry in violation of the Second Commandment in the twentieth chapter of Exodus. It was stated in the press that the order of the District Court was sustained in the Superior Court and that the questions of law are on their way to the Supreme Judicial Court.

One or two aspects of the legal problem, briefly referred to in that article, deserve a little fuller treatment in order to bring the whole problem into better perspective.

It was pointed out that the statutory "salute" requirement does not apply to children in private schools. It applies only to children in public schools "under the control of the school committees". Private schools require the approval of the school committees, but the statute provides that those committees "shall not withhold such approval on account of religious teachings," G. L. Chap. 76, § 1. Accordingly, if the religious group, describing themselves as "Jehovah's Witnesses", should establish a private school, in which the children were taught that a salute to the flag violated the Second Commandment, the compulsory salute requirement would not seem to apply to that school.

As no child seems compelled by law in any private school in Massachusetts, to-day, to violate his or her conscience in this matter, the result is that the liberty of conscience depends upon the question whether the parents are rich enough to send their children to private schools. This practical discrimination on a cash basis, which exists in fact although it does not appear on the face of the statute, is, nevertheless, pertinent to the question of religious freedom, which surely includes liberty of conscience in obedience to religious belief. There is no such discrimination in the vaccination cases (See G. L. Chap. 111, § 183).

It was suggested in the article referred to that under the reasoning of the opinion in *Weems* v. *U. S.*, 217 U. S. at pp. 372–373, the question might arise whether taking a child from its home because of religious belief and placing it in a "county training school" does not violate the twenty-sixth article of the Massachusetts Bill of Rights, which prohibits "cruel and unusual punishment." We are not familiar with the different county training schools in Massachusetts, but they are obviously "reformatory" institutions, and in considering the constitutionality of a commitment of children between the ages of seven and twelve to such an institution, instead of their own homes, solely on the ground of a

(1)

genuine act of conscience, "the undercurrents of deterioration" which face the individual children in such institutions, as a matter of commonsense, should not be forgotten. In this connection, the recent little book entitled, "Youth in the Toils," by Harrison and Grant, published about a year ago by Macmillan Company, should be read. A brief review of it appeared in the QUARTERLY for January-April, 1938, pp. 42-43.

An abbreviation of the article, already referred to, was published in the *Boston Herald* and in the *Springfield Republican* in June. We received various interesting letters in consequence and the following quotation appeared in one of them:

> "I have searched Church History and I find that the issue arose in the reign of Trajan, whose persecutions of the Christians were . . . as resisting the effort of government to compel them to an action against their conscience—to pour out the libation to the bust of Caesar."

Referring to the many cases against the Quaker refusal to take an oath in the reign of Charles I, Cromwell, Charles II the letter continues:

> "The Declarations of Charles II, James and William and Mary, and the Acts of Parliament finally gave them their freedom. These cases are closely parallel to those against Jehovah's Witnesses. Literally thousands of Quakers went to jail.
>
> "In missionary lands the same question frequently arises. It is acute now in Korea. Although in Japan the government is not pressing the matter, in Korea, a conquered country, a determined effort is being made to compel the Christians, particularly school children, to go with the Shintoists to the Shinto shrine, called in this case Jinja, and make the Shinto bow. *Government* is trying to *compel* people to act against their consciences."

Ever since 1780 the Massachusetts constitution has allowed Quakers to "make affirmation" instead of taking an oath (see Chap. VI, Art. I and Art. VI of the Amendments). This, of course, is a recognition of the right of religious conscience.

Another person, with experience as a former school teacher, writes that,

> "Experience taught me that the flag salute became only a gabbled form, one more item in the daily dozen of public school gestures. Moreover, it put all the emphasis on the flag, not on the country."

This writer also expressed the view that if the teacher, or some one connected with the school, quietly explained to the children, in such a way that they could understand it, what the country has done for them, that the children would be willing to express appreciation in some manner resembling the "affirmation" of a Quaker and avoiding all questions of religious conscience. The education of the child in the appreciation of what our republican institutions mean lies in an explanation which the child understands rather than in the repetition of a required formula which disturbs the child.

As suggested in the previous article the pardoning power might well be exercised in cases of *genuinely* conscientious children if it becomes necessary, after all legal proceedings are concluded, in order to prevent their being regarded as religious martyrs.

F. W. GRINNELL.

MORE ABOUT THE FLAG SALUTE.

EXTRACTS FROM THE OPINION OF THE CIRCUIT COURT OF APPEALS FOR THE THIRD CIRCUIT IN MINERSVILLE SCHOOL DISTRICT *v.* GOBITIS.

The QUARTERLY for April–June, and for July–September, contained discussions of the requirement of the flag salute, not only as a condition of a child's right to attend the public school, but as a compulsory requirement for violation of which a conscientious child might be sent to a reform school because of religious belief. The opinion was expressed that such a requirement was a violation of the right to religious liberty, and it was suggested that the flag salute statutes and ordinances should be changed to comply with the constitution, and that any conscientious child who was taken from home and placed in a county training school, for such a reason, should be protected by the governor, through his exercise of the pardoning power, in order to avoid making religious martyrs of children. In the first article, the opinion of Judge Maris of the District Court for the Eastern District of Pennsylvania was referred to. He refused to follow the Massachusetts Courts and other courts, and decided that the school authorities in Minersville, Pennsylvania, had no right to exclude a child from school because of a refusal, on religious grounds, to salute the flag. This case of *Minersville School District* v. *Gobitis* was carried to the Circuit Court of Appeals, which unanimously affirmed the decision of Judge Maris in an extended opinion by Circuit Judge Clarke, on November 10th, 1939. Judge Clarke said:

"Eighteen big states have seen fit to exert their power over a small number of little children . . . The method of exercise has sometimes been by their representatives in solemn conclave assembled and sometimes, as here, by an administrative agency (school board). The matter of exercise is in that field where, above all, or so we had supposed, power must yield to principle. In other words, the area of action is within the aura of conscience . . .

"The appellees, a little girl of thirteen and a little boy of twelve, refused to salute the flag . . . They stood in respectful silence while the other children submitted to the requirement and were dealt with accordingly by being expelled. The reason for their refusal raises the constitutional issue of this appeal. They and their parents are members of a group (we avoid for the present more definite characterization) known as Russellites, or, more colloquially, Earnest Bible Students, and Jehovah's Witnesses.

The defendant school board admits that this group 'sincerely and honestly believe that the act of saluting a flag contravenes the law of God' in that it constitutes a bowing down to a graven image.

"The so-called flag salute or regulation first appeared in Kansas in 1907. The idea, without benefit of sanctions, seems to have originated with an employee of the magazine, *The Youth's Companion*. It was first put in practice at the National Public School Celebration on October 21, 1892, pamphlet, The Youth's Companion Flag Pledge . . . The voluntary character of the ceremonial act soon disappeared into law and litigation." . . .

Judge Clarke then quotes from the 14th chapter of the volume by Col. Moss entitled, "The Flag of the United States, Its History and Symbolism," as follows:

"Another form that false patriotism frequently takes is so-called 'Flag-worship'—blind and excessive adulation of the Flag as an emblem or image,—superpunctiliousness and meticulosity in displaying and saluting the Flag—without intelligent and sincere understanding and appreciation of the ideals and institutions it symbolizes. 'This, of course, is but a form of idolatry—a sort of glorified idolatry', so to speak."

The court rules that the free exercise of religion is within the same principle of protection which was recently applied by the Supreme Court of the United States, *in the Hague Case in New Jersey*, to protect the right of free speech and assembly. The court says:

"Many of the considerations there validated apply here and we need not repeat them. There are others that have even greater cogency. They can be summed up thus. A man may die for the right to express his opinion. He has died or suffered worse than death for the right to worship according to his conscience. That is implicit in the definitions of religion we have cited, in the long history of the struggle for religious liberty before the law, and in the utterances of our statesmen."

After extended quotations on the subject of religion and religious freedom, the opinion concludes as follows:

"We conclude with two examples from the history of the 'small sects' of Pennsylvania's early days. The state was colonized and founded by William Penn. He came to the new country because his refusal to subordinate religious scruples to educational coercion led to his expulsion from Oxford University in the old. Document by John Aubrey (now in the Bodleian Library).

"George Washington, the almost universal character of whose wisdom always freshly surprises, a century later wrote a letter to the descendants of those whom William Penn brought with him. In it General Washington said:

" 'Government being, among other purposes, instituted to protect the persons and consciences of men from oppression it certainly is the duty of rulers, not only to abstain from it themselves, but according to their stations to prevent it in others.

" 'I assure you very explicitly, that in my opinion the conscientious scruples of all men should be treated with great delicacy and tenderness; and it is my wish and desire, that the laws may always be as extensively accommodated to them, as a due regard to the protection and essential interests of the nation may justify and permit.' Writings of George Washington (Sparks Ed. Vol. 12, pp. 168–169), Letter to the Religious Society Called Quakers, October, 1789.

"The appellant School Board has failed to 'treat the conscientious scruples' of all children with that 'great delicacy and tenderness'. We agree with the father of our country that they should and we concur with the learned District Court in saying that they must.

"The decree of the District Court is affirmed."

While protecting the children the court says in the course of the opinion "One might note that the sect does not appear to practice the tolerance that it now asks for these young members of its flock."

MINERSVILLE SCHOOL DISTRICT, BOARD OF EDUCATION OF MINERSVILLE SCHOOL DISTRICT, ET AL. v. GOBITIS ET AL.

CERTIORARI TO THE CIRCUIT COURT OF APPEALS FOR THE THIRD CIRCUIT.

No. 690. Argued April 25, 1940.—Decided June 3, 1940.

1. A state regulation requiring that pupils in the public schools, on pain of expulsion, participate in a daily ceremony of saluting the national flag, whilst reciting in unison a pledge of allegiance to it "and to the Republic for which it stands; one Nation indivisible, with liberty and justice for all"—*held* within the scope of legislative power, and consistent with the Fourteenth Amendment, as applied to children brought up in, and entertaining, a conscientious religious belief that such obeisance to the flag is forbidden by the Bible and that the Bible, as the Word of God, is the supreme authority. P. 591.
2. Religious convictions do not relieve the individual from obedience to an otherwise valid general law not aimed at the promotion or restriction of religious beliefs. P. 594.
3. So far as the Federal Constitution is concerned, it is within the province of the legislatures and school authorities of the several States to adopt appropriate means to evoke and foster a sentiment of national unity among the children in the public schools. P. 597.
4. This Court can not exercise censorship over the conviction of legislatures that a particular program or exercise will best promote in the minds of children who attend the common schools an attachment to the institutions of their country, nor overrule the local judgment against granting exemptions from observance of such a program. P. 598.

108 F. 2d 683, reversed.

CERTIORARI, 309 U. S. 645, to review the affirmance of a decree (24 F. Supp. 271; opinion, 21 F. Supp. 581) which perpetually enjoined the above-named School District, the members of its board of education, and its superintendent of public schools, from continuing to enforce an order expelling from the public schools certain minors (suing in this case by their father as next friend) and from

Argument for Petitioners.

requiring them to salute the national flag as a condition to their right to attend.

Mr. Joseph W. Henderson, with whom *Messrs. John B. McGurl, Thomas F. Mount,* and *George M. Brodhead, Jr.* were on the brief, for petitioners.

The resolution of the School Board requiring pupils to salute the flag was lawfully adopted, and the expulsion of the children was within its power and authority.

The expulsion of the children did not violate any right under the Constitution of the United States. *Leoles* v. *Landers,* 302 U. S. 656; *Hering* v. *State Board of Education,* 303 U. S. 624; *Gabrielli* v. *Knickerbocker,* 306 U. S. 621; *Johnson* v. *Deerfield,* 306 U. S. 621; *Johnson* v. *Deerfield,* 307 U. S. 650; *Leoles* v. *Landers,* 184 Ga. 580; *Hering* v. *State Board of Education,* 118 N. J. L. 566; *Gabrielli* v. *Knickerbocker,* 12 Cal. 2d 85; *Johnson* v. *Deerfield,* 25 F. Supp. 918; *People* v. *Sandstrom,* 279 N. Y. 523; *Nicholls* v. *Mayor,* 7 N. E. 2d 577; *Hamilton* v. *Regents,* 293 U. S. 245; *Coale* v. *Pearson,* 290 U. S. 597; *Reynolds* v. *United States,* 98 U. S. 145; *Davis* v. *Beason,* 133 U. S. 333; *Jacobson* v. *Massachusetts,* 197 U. S. 11; *Selective Draft Law Cases,* 245 U. S. 366; *Shapiro* v. *Lyle,* 30 F. 2d 971; *United States* v. *MacIntosh,* 283 U. S. 605, 625.

The expulsion of the children did not violate any right under the Constitution of Pennsylvania. *Commonwealth* v. *Lesher,* 17 S. & R. (Pa.) 155, 160; *Wilkes-Barre* v. *Garabed,* 11 Pa. Super. 355, 366; *Commonwealth* v. *Herr,* 229 Pa. 132, 141; *Stevenson* v. *Hanyon,* 7 Pa. Dist. Rep. 585; *Pittsburgh* v. *Ruffner,* 134 Pa. Super. 192, 198; *Oaths of Allegiance in Public Schools,* 25 Pa. Dist. & County Rep. 8.

The refusal of the children to salute the national flag at school exercises because they believed that to do so would violate the written law of Almighty God as contained in the Bible was not founded on a religious belief. *Davis* v. *Beason,* 133 U. S. 333, 342.

The act of saluting the flag has no bearing on what a pupil may think of his Creator or what are his relations to his Creator. Nor is a pupil required to exhibit his religious sentiments in a particular "form of worship" when saluting the flag, because the ceremony is not, by any stretch of the imagination, a "form of worship." Like the study of history or civics or the doing of any other act which might make a pupil more patriotic as well as teach him or her "loyalty to the State and National Government," the salute has no religious implications. *Nicholls* v. *Mayor*, 7 N. E. 2d 577, 580; *Leoles* v. *Landers*, 184 Ga. 580, 587; *Peoples* v. *Sandstrom*, 279 N. Y. 523, 529.

The commandments of Jehovah, as set forth in the Bible, do not prohibit the saluting of a national flag but on the contrary approve of that practice.

The act of saluting the flag is only one of many ways in which a citizen may evidence his respect for the Government. Every citizen stands at attention, and the men remove their hats, when the national anthem is played; yet such action can not be called a religious ceremony. The same respect is shown the American flag when it passes in a parade; yet that is not a religious rite.

Though members of Jehovah's Witnesses endeavor to extend religious implications to a ceremony purely patriotic in design, they do not accord to others the religious freedom which they demand for themselves, claiming that there is no limit to which they may go when they think they are worshipping God. *Cantwell* v. *Connecticut*, 126 Conn. 1; 310 U. S. 296.

The act of saluting the flag does not prevent a pupil, no matter what his religious belief may be, from acknowledging the spiritual sovereignty of Almighty God by rendering to God the things which are God's. *Hardwick* v. *Board of School Trustees*, 54 Cal. App. 696, 712.

Messrs. Joseph F. Rutherford and *George K. Gardner* argued the cause, and with the former *Mr. Hayden Covington* was on the brief, for respondents.

Arguments for Respondents.

The rule compelling respondents to participate in the ceremony of saluting the flag and the act of its School Board in expelling them because they refrained, violate their rights guaranteed by Art. I, § 3, of the Constitution of Pennsylvania and the Fourteenth Amendment of the Constitution of the United States.

The vital question is: Shall the creature man be free to exercise his conscientious belief in God and his obedience to the law of Almighty God, the Creator, or shall the creature man be compelled to obey the law or rule of the State, which law of the State, as the creature conscientiously believes, is in direct conflict with the law of Almighty God?

This Court has repeatedly held that the individual alone is privileged to determine what he shall or shall not believe. The law, therefore, does not attempt to settle differences of creeds and confessions, or to say that any point or doctrine is too absurd to be believed. That rule was laid down more than one hundred years ago by the Pennsylvania courts in *Schriber* v. *Rapp,* 5 Watts 351, 363.

As early as 1784 a like question was before the House of Delegates of the State of Virginia. Mr. Jefferson prepared a Bill: "For establishing religious freedom." After defining religious freedom and reciting "that to suffer the civil magistrate to intrude his powers into the field of opinion, and to restrain the profession or propagation of principles on supposition of their ill tendency, is a dangerous fallacy which at once destroys all religious liberty," it is declared "that it is time enough for the rightful purposes of civil government for its officers to interfere when principles break out into overt acts against peace and good order." See *Reynolds* v. *United States,* 98 U. S. 145, 162.

Will any court attempt to say that respondents mistakenly believe what is set forth in the twentieth chapter of Exodus in the Bible? The belief of respondents is not based upon conjecture or a myth. Respondents' belief is based strictly upon the Bible. The minor respondents from their infancy have been taught by their father to rely upon the Bible.

The saluting of the flag of any earthly government by a person who has covenanted to do the will of God is a form of religion and constitutes idolatry.

The modern-day compulsory flag saluting as a daily exercise or ceremony in the public schools is clearly an experiment. The nation has existed for more than a century without any such enforced rule. To expel children from school and deny them the opportunity of an education because they refuse to violate their conscience, is wrong and is cruel and unusual punishment. "No cruel experiment on any living creature shall be permitted in any public school of this Commonwealth." 24 Purdon's Pa. Stat. Ann. § 1554.

"The greatest dangers to liberty lurk in insidious encroachment by men of zeal, well meaning, but without understanding." Mr. Justice Brandeis, in *Olmstead* v. *United States,* 277 U. S. 479. See *Associated Press* v. *National Labor Relations Board,* 301 U. S. 103, 141.

The rule certainly abridges the privileges of the respondents and deprives them of liberty and property without due process of law. Cf. *Pierce* v. *Society of Sisters,* 268 U. S. 510, 534–535

Petitioners claim that the purpose of saluting the flag is to "Instill in the children patriotism and love of country." But why limit that compulsory rule to teachers and pupils of the public schools? Why not require that same ceremony in all the schools? Why not apply the same rule to all officials of the Nation and State, from the President and the members of Congress down to the very least and humblest citizen? The general answer would be that the enforcement of such a rule is ridiculous and nonsensical. Chap. 14, "Patriotism of the Flag," Moss, *The Flag of the United States, Its History and Symbolism,* pp. 85–86.

By leave of Court, briefs of *amici curiae* were filed on behalf of the Committee on the Bill of Rights, of the American Bar Association, consisting of *Messrs. Douglas Arant, Zechariah Chafee, Jr., Grenville Clark, Osmer C. Fitts, Lloyd K. Garrison, George I. Haight, Monte M. Lemann, Ross L. Malone, Jr., Burton W. Musser, Joseph A. Padway*, and *Charles P. Taft;* and by *Messrs. George K. Gardner, Arthur Garfield Hays, Osmond K. Fraenkel, William G. Fennell, Jerome M. Britchey*, and *Alexander H. Frey*, on behalf of the American Civil Liberties Union,—urging affirmance.

MR. JUSTICE FRANKFURTER delivered the opinion of the Court.

A grave responsibility confronts this Court whenever in course of litigation it must reconcile the conflicting claims of liberty and authority. But when the liberty invoked is liberty of conscience, and the authority is authority to safeguard the nation's fellowship, judicial conscience is put to its severest test. Of such a nature is the present controversy.

Lillian Gobitis, aged twelve, and her brother William, aged ten, were expelled from the public schools of Minersville, Pennsylvania, for refusing to salute the national flag as part of a daily school exercise. The local Board of Education required both teachers and pupils to participate in this ceremony. The ceremony is a familiar one. The right hand is placed on the breast and the following pledge recited in unison: "I pledge allegiance to my flag, and to the Republic for which it stands; one nation indivisible, with liberty and justice for all." While the words are spoken, teachers and pupils extend their right hands in salute to the flag. The Gobitis family are affiliated with "Jehovah's Witnesses," for whom the Bible as the Word of God is the supreme authority. The children had been brought up conscientiously to believe that such a gesture of respect for the flag was forbidden by command of Scripture.[1]

The Gobitis children were of an age for which Pennsylvania makes school attendance compulsory. Thus they were denied a free education, and their parents had to put them into private schools. To be relieved of the financial burden thereby entailed, their father, on behalf of the children and in his own behalf, brought this suit. He sought to enjoin the authorities from continuing to exact participation in the flag-salute ceremony as a condition of his children's attendance at the Minersville school. After trial of the issues, Judge Maris gave relief in the District Court, 24 F. Supp. 271, on the basis of a thoughtful opinion at a preliminary stage of the litigation, 21 F. Supp. 581; his decree was affirmed by the Circuit Court of Appeals, 108 F. 2d 683. Since this decision ran counter to several *per curiam* dispositions of this Court,[2] we granted *certiorari* to give the matter full reconsideration. 309 U. S. 645. By their able submissions, the Committee on the Bill of Rights of the American Bar Association and the American Civil Liberties Union, as friends of the Court, have helped us to our conclusion.

We must decide whether the requirement of participation in such a ceremony, exacted from a child who refuses

---

[1] Reliance is especially placed on the following verses from Chapter 20 of Exodus:

"3. Thou shalt have no other gods before me.

"4. Thou shalt not make unto thee any graven image, or any likeness of any thing that is in heaven above, or that is in the earth beneath, or that is in the water under the earth:

"5. Thou shalt not bow down thyself to them, nor serve them: . . ."

[2] *Leoles* v. *Landers*, 302 U. S. 656; *Hering* v. *State Board of Education*, 303 U. S. 624; *Gabrielli* v. *Knickerbocker*, 306 U. S. 621; *Johnson* v. *Deerfield*, 306 U. S. 621; 307 U. S. 650. Compare *New York* v. *Sandstrom*, 279 N. Y. 523; 18 N. E. 2d 840; *Nicholls* v. *Mayor and School Committee of Lynn*, 7 N. E. 2d 577 (Mass.).

upon sincere religious grounds, infringes without due process of law the liberty guaranteed by the Fourteenth Amendment.

Centuries of strife over the erection of particular dogmas as exclusive or all-comprehending faiths led to the inclusion of a guarantee for religious freedom in the Bill of Rights. The First Amendment, and the Fourteenth through its absorption of the First, sought to guard against repetition of those bitter religious struggles by prohibiting the establishment of a state religion and by securing to every sect the free exercise of its faith. So pervasive is the acceptance of this precious right that its scope is brought into question, as here, only when the conscience of individuals collides with the felt necessities of society.

Certainly the affirmative pursuit of one's convictions about the ultimate mystery of the universe and man's relation to it is placed beyond the reach of law. Government may not interfere with organized or individual expression of belief or disbelief. Propagation of belief—or even of disbelief—in the supernatural is protected, whether in church or chapel, mosque or synagogue, tabernacle or meeting-house. Likewise the Constitution assures generous immunity to the individual from imposition of penalties for offending, in the course of his own religious activities, the religious views of others, be they a minority or those who are dominant in government. *Cantwell* v. *Connecticut, ante,* p. 296.

But the manifold character of man's relations may bring his conception of religious duty into conflict with the secular interests of his fellow-men. When does the constitutional guarantee compel exemption from doing what society thinks necessary for the promotion of some great common end, or from a penalty for conduct which appears dangerous to the general good? To state the problem is to recall the truth that no single principle can answer all of life's complexities. The right to freedom of religious belief, however dissident and however obnoxious to the cherished beliefs of others—even of a majority—is itself the denial of an absolute. But to affirm that the freedom to follow conscience has itself no limits in the life of a society would deny that very plurality of principles which, as a matter of history, underlies protection of religious toleration. Compare Mr. Justice Holmes in *Hudson Water Co.* v. *McCarter,* 209 U. S. 349, 355. Our present task, then, as so often the case with courts, is to reconcile two rights in order to prevent either from destroying the other. But, because in safeguarding conscience we are dealing with interests so subtle and so dear, every possible leeway should be given to the claims of religious faith.

In the judicial enforcement of religious freedom we are concerned with a historic concept. See Mr. Justice Cardozo in *Hamilton* v. *Regents,* 293 U. S. at 265. The religious liberty which the Constitution protects has never excluded legislation of general scope not directed against doctrinal loyalties of particular sects. Judicial nullification of legislation cannot be justified by attributing to the framers of the Bill of Rights views for which there is no historic warrant. Conscientious scruples have not, in the course of the long struggle for religious toleration, relieved the individual from obedience to a general law not aimed at the promotion or restriction of religious beliefs.[3] The mere possession of religious convictions

---

[3] Compare II Writings of Thomas Jefferson (Ford ed.) p. 102; 3 Letters and Other Writings of James Madison, pp. 274, 307–308; 1 Rhode Island Colonial Records, pp. 378–80; 2 *Id.* pp. 5–6; Wiener, Roger Williams' Contribution to Modern Thought, 28 Rhode Island Historical Society Collections, No. 1; Ernst, The Political Thought of Roger Williams, chap. VII; W. K. Jordan, The Development of Religious Toleration in England, *passim.* See *Commonwealth* v. *Herr,* 229 Pa. 132; 78 A. 68.

which contradict the relevant concerns of a political society does not relieve the citizen from the discharge of political responsibilities. The necessity for this adjustment has again and again been recognized. In a number of situations the exertion of political authority has been sustained, while basic considerations of religious freedom have been left inviolate. *Reynolds* v. *United States,* 98 U. S. 145; *Davis* v. *Beason,* 133 U. S. 333; *Selective Draft Law Cases,* 245 U. S. 366; *Hamilton* v. *Regents,* 293 U. S. 245. In all these cases the general laws in question, upheld in their application to those who refused obedience from religious conviction, were manifestations of specific powers of government deemed by the legislature essential to secure and maintain that orderly, tranquil, and free society without which religious toleration itself is unattainable. Nor does the freedom of speech assured by Due Process move in a more absolute circle of immunity than that enjoyed by religious freedom. Even if it were assumed that freedom of speech goes beyond the historic concept of full opportunity to utter and to disseminate views, however heretical or offensive to dominant opinion, and includes freedom from conveying what may be deemed an implied but rejected affirmation, the question remains whether school children, like the Gobitis children, must be excused from conduct required of all the other children in the promotion of national cohesion. We are dealing with an interest inferior to none in the hierarchy of legal values. National unity is the basis of national security. To deny the legislature the right to select appropriate means for its attainment presents a totally different order of problem from that of the propriety of subordinating the possible ugliness of littered streets to the free expression of opinion through distribution of handbills. Compare *Schneider* v. *State,* 308 U. S. 147.

Situations like the present are phases of the profoundest problem confronting a democracy—the problem which Lincoln cast in memorable dilemma: "Must a government of necessity be too *strong* for the liberties of its people, or too *weak* to maintain its own existence?" No mere textual reading or logical talisman can solve the dilemma. And when the issue demands judicial determination, it is not the personal notion of judges of what wise adjustment requires which must prevail.

Unlike the instances we have cited, the case before us is not concerned with an exertion of legislative power for the promotion of some specific need or interest of secular society—the protection of the family, the promotion of health, the common defense, the raising of public revenues to defray the cost of government. But all these specific activities of government presuppose the existence of an organized political society. The ultimate foundation of a free society is the binding tie of cohesive sentiment. Such a sentiment is fostered by all those agencies of the mind and spirit which may serve to gather up the traditions of a people, transmit them from generation to generation, and thereby create that continuity of a treasured common life which constitutes a civilization. "We live by symbols." The flag is the symbol of our national unity, transcending all internal differences, however large, within the framework of the Constitution. This Court has had occasion to say that ". . . the flag is the symbol of the Nation's power, the emblem of freedom in its truest, best sense. . . . it signifies government resting on the consent of the governed; liberty regulated by law; the protection of the weak against the strong; security against the exercise of arbitrary power; and absolute safety for free institutions against foreign aggression." *Halter* v. *Nebraska,* 205 U. S. 34, 43. And see

United States v. *Gettysburg Electric Ry. Co.,* 160 U. S. 668.[4]

The case before us must be viewed as though the legislature of Pennsylvania had itself formally directed the flag-salute for the children of Minersville; had made no exemption for children whose parents were possessed of conscientious scruples like those of the Gobitis family; and had indicated its belief in the desirable ends to be secured by having its public school children share a common experience at those periods of development when their minds are supposedly receptive to its assimilation, by an exercise appropriate in time and place and setting, and one designed to evoke in them appreciation of the nation's hopes and dreams, its sufferings and sacrifices. The precise issue, then, for us to decide is whether the legislatures of the various states and the authorities in a thousand counties and school districts of this country are barred from determining the appropriateness of various means to evoke that unifying sentiment without which there can ultimately be no liberties, civil or religious.[5] To stigmatize legislative judgment in providing for this universal gesture of respect for the symbol of our national life in the setting of the common school as a lawless inroad on that freedom of conscience which the Constitution protects, would amount to no less than the pronouncement of pedagogical and psychological dogma in a field where courts possess no marked and certainly no

---

[4] For the origin and history of the American flag, see 8 Journals of the Continental Congress, p. 464; 22 *Id.,* pp. 338–40; Annals of Congress, 15th Cong., 1st Sess., Vol. 1, pp. 566 *et seq.; Id.,* Vol. 2, pp. 1458 *et seq.*

[5] Compare Balfour, Introduction to Bagehot's English Constitution, p. XXII; Santayana, Character and Opinion in the United States, pp. 110–11.

controlling competence. The influences which help toward a common feeling for the common country are manifold. Some may seem harsh and others no doubt are foolish. Surely, however, the end is legitimate. And the effective means for its attainment are still so uncertain and so unauthenticated by science as to preclude us from putting the widely prevalent belief in flag-saluting beyond the pale of legislative power. It mocks reason and denies our whole history to find in the allowance of a requirement to salute our flag on fitting occasions the seeds of sanction for obeisance to a leader.

The wisdom of training children in patriotic impulses by those compulsions which necessarily pervade so much of the educational process is not for our independent judgment. Even were we convinced of the folly of such a measure, such belief would be no proof of its unconstitutionality. For ourselves, we might be tempted to say that the deepest patriotism is best engendered by giving unfettered scope to the most crochety beliefs. Perhaps it is best, even from the standpoint of those interests which ordinances like the one under review seek to promote, to give to the least popular sect leave from conformities like those here in issue. But the courtroom is not the arena for debating issues of educational policy. It is not our province to choose among competing considerations in the subtle process of securing effective loyalty to the traditional ideals of democracy, while respecting at the same time individual idiosyncracies among a people so diversified in racial origins and religious allegiances. So to hold would in effect make us the school board for the country. That authority has not been given to this Court, nor should we assume it.

We are dealing here with the formative period in the development of citizenship. Great diversity of psychological and ethical opinion exists among us concerning the best way to train children for their place in society. Because of these differences and because of reluctance to permit a single, iron-cast system of education to be imposed upon a nation compounded of so many strains, we have held that, even though public education is one of our most cherished democratic institutions, the Bill of Rights bars a state from compelling all children to attend the public schools. *Pierce* v. *Society of Sisters*, 268 U. S. 510. But it is a very different thing for this Court to exercise censorship over the conviction of legislatures that a particular program or exercise will best promote in the minds of children who attend the common schools an attachment to the institutions of their country.

What the school authorities are really asserting is the right to awaken in the child's mind considerations as to the significance of the flag contrary to those implanted by the parent. In such an attempt the state is normally at a disadvantage in competing with the parent's authority, so long—and this is the vital aspect of religious toleration—as parents are unmolested in their right to counteract by their own persuasiveness the wisdom and rightness of those loyalties which the state's educational system is seeking to promote. Except where the transgression of constitutional liberty is too plain for argument, personal freedom is best maintained—so long as the remedial channels of the democratic process remain open and unobstructed [6]—when it is ingrained in a people's habits and not enforced against popular policy by the coercion of adjudicated law. That the flag-salute is an allowable portion of a school program for those who do not invoke conscientious scruples is surely not debatable. But for us to insist that, though the ceremony may be required, exceptional immunity must be

---

[6] In cases like *Fiske* v. *Kansas*, 274 U. S. 380; *De Jonge* v. *Oregon*, 299 U. S. 353; *Lovell* v. *Griffin*, 303 U. S. 444; *Hague* v. *C. I. O.*, 307 U. S. 496, and *Schneider* v. *State*, 308 U. S. 147, the Court was concerned with restrictions cutting off appropriate means through which, in a free society, the processes of popular rule may effectively function.

given to dissidents, is to maintain that there is no basis for a legislative judgment that such an exemption might introduce elements of difficulty into the school discipline, might cast doubts in the minds of the other children which would themselves weaken the effect of the exercise.

The preciousness of the family relation, the authority and independence which give dignity to parenthood, indeed the enjoyment of all freedom, presuppose the kind of ordered society which is summarized by our flag. A society which is dedicated to the preservation of these ultimate values of civilization may in self-protection utilize the educational process for inculcating those almost unconscious feelings which bind men together in a comprehending loyalty, whatever may be their lesser differences and difficulties. That is to say, the process may be utilized so long as men's right to believe as they please, to win others to their way of belief, and their right to assemble in their chosen places of worship for the devotional ceremonies of their faith, are all fully respected.

Judicial review, itself a limitation on popular government, is a fundamental part of our constitutional scheme. But to the legislature no less than to courts is committed the guardianship of deeply-cherished liberties. See *Missouri, K. & T. Ry. Co.* v. *May,* 194 U. S. 267, 270. Where all the effective means of inducing political changes are left free from interference, education in the abandonment of foolish legislation is itself a training in liberty. To fight out the wise use of legislative authority in the forum of public opinion and before legislative assemblies rather than to transfer such a contest to the judicial arena, serves to vindicate the self-confidence of a free people.[7]

Reversed.

---

[7] It is to be noted that the Congress has not entered the field of legislation here under consideration.

Mr. Justice McReynolds concurs in the result.

Mr. Justice Stone, dissenting:

I think the judgment below should be affirmed.

Two youths, now fifteen and sixteen years of age, are by the judgment of this Court held liable to expulsion from the public schools and to denial of all publicly supported educational privileges because of their refusal to yield to the compulsion of a law which commands their participation in a school ceremony contrary to their religious convictions. They and their father are citizens and have not exhibited by any action or statement of opinion, any disloyalty to the Government of the United States. They are ready and willing to obey all its laws which do not conflict with what they sincerely believe to be the higher commandments of God. It is not doubted that these convictions are religious, that they are genuine, or that the refusal to yield to the compulsion of the law is in good faith and with all sincerity. It would be a denial of their faith as well as the teachings of most religions to say that children of their age could not have religious convictions.

The law which is thus sustained is unique in the history of Anglo-American legislation. It does more than suppress freedom of speech and more than prohibit the free exercise of religion, which concededly are forbidden by the First Amendment and are violations of the liberty guaranteed by the Fourteenth. For by this law the state seeks to coerce these children to express a sentiment which, as they interpret it, they do not entertain, and which violates their deepest religious convictions. It is not denied that such compulsion is a prohibited infringement of personal liberty, freedom of speech and religion, guaranteed by the Bill of Rights, except in so far as it may be justified and supported as a proper exercise of the state's power over public education. Since the state, in competition with parents, may through teaching in the public schools indoctrinate the minds of the young, it is said that in aid of its undertaking to inspire loyalty and devotion to constituted authority and the flag which symbolizes it, it may coerce the pupil to make affirmation contrary to his belief and in violation of his religious faith. And, finally, it is said that since the Minersville School Board and others are of the opinion that the country will be better served by conformity than by the observance of religious liberty which the Constitution prescribes, the courts are not free to pass judgment on the Board's choice.

Concededly the constitutional guaranties of personal liberty are not always absolutes. Government has a right to survive and powers conferred upon it are not necessarily set at naught by the express prohibitions of the Bill of Rights. It may make war and raise armies. To that end it may compel citizens to give military service, *Selective Draft Law Cases,* 245 U. S. 366, and subject them to military training despite their religious objections. *Hamilton* v. *Regents,* 293 U. S. 245. It may suppress religious practices dangerous to morals, and presumably those also which are inimical to public safety, health and good order. *Davis* v. *Beason,* 133 U. S. 333. But it is a long step, and one which I am unable to take, to the position that government may, as a supposed educational measure and as a means of disciplining the young, compel public affirmations which violate their religious conscience.

The very fact that we have constitutional guaranties of civil liberties and the specificity of their command where freedom of speech and of religion are concerned require some accommodation of the powers which government normally exercises, when no question of civil liberty is involved, to the constitutional demand that those liberties be protected against the action of government itself. The state concededly has power to require and control the education of its citizens, but it cannot by a general law compelling attendance at public schools preclude attendance at a private school adequate in its instruction, where the parent seeks to secure for the child the benefits of religious instruction not provided by the public school. *Pierce* v. *Society of Sisters,* 268 U. S. 510. And only recently we have held that the state's authority to control its public streets by generally applicable regulations is not an absolute to which free speech must yield, and cannot be made the medium of its suppression, *Hague* v. *Committee for Industrial Organization,* 307 U. S. 496, 514, *et seq.,* any more than can its authority to penalize littering of the streets by a general law be used to suppress the distribution of handbills as a means of communicating ideas to their recipients. *Schneider* v. *State,* 308 U. S. 147.

In these cases it was pointed out that where there are competing demands of the interests of government and of liberty under the Constitution, and where the performance of governmental functions is brought into conflict with specific constitutional restrictions, there must, when that is possible, be reasonable accommodation between them so as to preserve the essentials of both and that it is the function of courts to determine whether such accommodation is reasonably possible. In the cases just mentioned the Court was of opinion that there were ways enough to secure the legitimate state end without infringing the asserted immunity, or that the inconvenience caused by the inability to secure that end satisfactorily through other means, did not outweigh freedom of speech or religion. So here, even if we believe that such compulsions will contribute to national unity, there are other ways to teach loyalty and patriotism which are the sources of national unity, than by compelling the pupil to affirm that which he does not believe and by commanding a form of affirmance which violates his religious convictions. Without recourse to such compulsion the state is free to compel attendance at school and require teaching by instruction and study of all in our history and in the structure and organization of our government, including the guaranties of civil liberty which tend to inspire patriotism and love of country. I cannot say that government here is deprived of any interest or function which it is entitled to maintain at the expense of the protection of civil liberties by requiring it to resort to the alternatives which do not coerce an affirmation of belief.

The guaranties of civil liberty are but guaranties of freedom of the human mind and spirit and of reasonable freedom and opportunity to express them. They presuppose the right of the individual to hold such opinions as he will and to give them reasonably free expression, and his freedom, and that of the state as well, to teach and persuade others by the communication of ideas. The very essence of the liberty which they guaranty is the freedom of the individual from compulsion as to what he shall think and what he shall say, at least where the compulsion is to bear false witness to his religion. If these guaranties are to have any meaning they must, I think, be deemed to withhold from the state any authority to compel belief or the expression of it where that expression violates religious convictions, whatever may be the legislative view of the desirability of such compulsion.

History teaches us that there have been but few infringements of personal liberty by the state which have not been justified, as they are here, in the name of righteousness and the public good, and few which have not been directed, as they are now, at politically helpless minorities. The framers were not unaware that under the system which they created most governmental cur-

STONE, J., dissenting.

tailments of personal liberty would have the support of a legislative judgment that the public interest would be better served by its curtailment than by its constitutional protection. I cannot conceive that in prescribing, as limitations upon the powers of government, the freedom of the mind and spirit secured by the explicit guaranties of freedom of speech and religion, they intended or rightly could have left any latitude for a legislative judgment that the compulsory expression of belief which violates religious convictions would better serve the public interest than their protection. The Constitution may well elicit expressions of loyalty to it and to the government which it created, but it does not command such expressions or otherwise give any indication that compulsory expressions of loyalty play any such part in our scheme of government as to override the constitutional protection of freedom of speech and religion. And while such expressions of loyalty, when voluntarily given, may promote national unity, it is quite another matter to say that their compulsory expression by children in violation of their own and their parents' religious convictions can be regarded as playing so important a part in our national unity as to leave school boards free to exact it despite the constitutional guarantee of freedom of religion. The very terms of the Bill of Rights preclude, it seems to me, any reconciliation of such compulsions with the constitutional guaranties by a legislative declaration that they are more important to the public welfare than the Bill of Rights.

But even if this view be rejected and it is considered that there is some scope for the determination by legislatures whether the citizen shall be compelled to give public expression of such sentiments contrary to his religion, I am not persuaded that we should refrain from passing upon the legislative judgment "as long as the remedial channels of the democratic process remain open and unobstructed." This seems to me no less than the surrender of the constitutional protection of the liberty of small minorities to the popular will. We have previously pointed to the importance of a searching judicial inquiry into the legislative judgment in situations where prejudice against discrete and insular minorities may tend to curtail the operation of those political processes ordinarily to be relied on to protect minorities. See *United States v. Carolene Products Co.*, 304 U. S. 144, 152, note 4. And until now we have not hesitated similarly to scrutinize legislation restricting the civil liberty of racial and religious minorities although no political process was affected. *Meyer* v. *Nebraska*, 262 U. S. 390; *Pierce* v. *Society of Sisters, supra; Farrington* v. *Tokushige*, 273 U. S. 284. Here we have such a small minority entertaining in good faith a religious belief, which is such a departure from the usual course of human conduct, that most persons are disposed to regard it with little toleration or concern. In such circumstances careful scrutiny of legislative efforts to secure conformity of belief and opinion by a compulsory affirmation of the desired belief, is especially needful if civil rights are to receive any protection. Tested by this standard, I am not prepared to say that the right of this small and helpless minority, including children having a strong religious conviction, whether they understand its nature or not, to refrain from an expression obnoxious to their religion, is to be overborne by the interest of the state in maintaining discipline in the schools.

The Constitution expresses more than the conviction of the people that democratic processes must be preserved at all costs. It is also an expression of faith and a command that freedom of mind and spirit must be preserved, which government must obey, if it is to adhere to that justice and moderation without which no free government can exist. For this reason it would seem that legislation which operates to repress the religious freedom of small minorities, which is admittedly within the scope of the protection of the Bill of Rights, must at least be subject to the same judicial scrutiny as legislation which we have recently held to infringe the constitutional liberty of religious and racial minorities.

With such scrutiny I cannot say that the inconveniences which may attend some sensible adjustment of school discipline in order that the religious convictions of these children may be spared, presents a problem so momentous or pressing as to outweigh the freedom from compulsory violation of religious faith which has been thought worthy of constitutional protection.

CONSTITUTIONAL LAW — DUE PROCESS — FREEDOM OF RELIGION AND CONSCIENCE — COMPULSORY FLAG SALUTE — The minor plaintiffs, aged twelve and thirteen, had been excluded from the public school because of repeated refusal to salute the national flag and recite the pledge of allegiance in accordance with an authorized order of the school board. They sought an injunction in the federal district court against such prohibition, alleging that the order violated the Fourteenth Amendment as an infringement on the free exercise of religion in that their beliefs forbade the revering of anything but God. The injunction was granted [1] and the decree was affirmed by the circuit court of appeals.[2] A writ of certiorari was granted by the Supreme Court. *Held*, that it was within the power of the state to promote the national unity as symbolized by the flag, and that reasonable means chosen to achieve this end would not be considered a violation of the freedom of religion and conscience which is protected against state action by the Fourteenth Amendment. Justice Stone dissented on the ground that since other methods consistent with individual liberty were available for promoting patriotism and national unity, the Court should invalidate the requirement of a flag salute as an unjustifiable infringement upon freedom of conscience. *Minersville School District v. Gobitis*, (U. S. 1940) 60 S. Ct. 1010.

The rising tide of nationalism during the past few years has resulted in much legislation, not the least of which has been the extremely controversial flag

---

[9] For criticisms of the various doctrines upon which non-liability has been based, see Zollman, "Damage Liability of Charitable Institutions," 19 MICH. L. REV. 395 (1921); Smith, "The Tort Liability of Charitable Institutions," 12 CONN. B. J. 214 (1938); 33 ILL. L. REV. 601 (1939); 12 ST. JOHNS L. REV. 99 (1937).

[10] 12 R. I. 411 (1879).

[11] 14 A. L. R. 572 at 573 (1921).

[1] Gobitis v. Minersville School District, (D. C. Pa. 1937) 21 F. Supp. 581.

[2] Minersville School District v. Gobitis, (C. C. A. 3d, 1939) 108 F. (2d) 683.

salute measures.[3] Jehovah's Witnesses, a small sect, have tested the validity of these measures at every opportunity, since their literal interpretation of the Bible has resulted in the religious belief that the practice of saluting the flag contravenes the law of God in that it constitutes a bowing down to a graven image.[4] Most of the state courts faced with this question have dismissed it lightly on the assumption that saluting the flag could have no religious connotation and necessarily could not collide with any constitutional guarantee of religious freedom.[5] In the principal case the Supreme Court recognized that freedom of conscience and of individual religious beliefs are included among the fundamental liberties

---

[3] They have evoked considerable comment: 34 MICH. L. REV. 1237 (1936); 36 MICH. L. REV. 485 (1938); 51 HARV. L. REV. 1418 (1938); 23 MINN. L. REV. 247 (1939); 27 GEO. L. J. 231 (1938); 18 ORE. L. REV. 122 (1938); 23 IOWA L. REV. 424 (1938); 2 UNIV. PITT. L. REV. 206 (1936); 4 UNIV. PITT. L. REV. 243 (1938); 86 UNIV. PA. L. REV. 431 (1938); 12 TEMPLE L. Q. 513 (1938); 23 CORN. L. Q. 582 (1938); Gardner and Post, "The Constitutional Questions Raised by the Flag Salute and Teachers' Oath Acts in Massachusetts," 16 BOST. UNIV. L. REV. 802 (1936); Clark, "The Limits of Free Expression," 73 U. S. L. REV. 392 (1939); 6 KAN. CITY L. REV. 217 (1938); 14 NOTRE DAME LAWY. 115 (1938); 8 GEO. WASH. L. REV. 1094 (1940); 24 MASS. L. Q., Nos. 2, 3, 4 (1939). These comments are in great part critical of the positions taken by the state courts in upholding the legislation.

[4] Book of Exodus, chapter 20, verses 3-5: "Thou shalt have no other gods before me. Thou shalt not make unto thee any graven image, or any likeness of any thing that is in heaven above, or that is in the earth beneath, or that is in the water under the earth. Thou shalt not bow down thyself to them, nor serve them, for I the Lord thy God am a jealous God."

[5] Hering v. State Board of Education, 117 N. J. L. 455, 189 A. 629 (1937), affd. per curiam, 118 N. J. L. 566, 194 A. 177 (1938), appeal dismissed per curiam 303 U. S. 624, 58 S. Ct. 752 (1938); Leoles v. Landers, 184 Ga. 580, 192 S. E. 218 (1937), appeal dismissed per curiam, 302 U. S. 656, 58 S. Ct. 364 (1937); Nicholls v. Mayor, 297 Mass. 65, 7 N. E. (2d) 577 (1937); State ex rel. Bleich v. Board of Public Instruction, 139 Fla. 43, 190 So. 815 (1939); Johnson v. Town of Deerfield, (D. C. Mass. 1939) 25 F. Supp. 918, affd. per curiam, 306 U. S. 621, 59 S. Ct. 791 (1939); People v. Sandstrom, 279 N. Y. 523, 18 N. E. (2d) 840 (1939); Gabrielli v. Knickerbocker, 12 Cal. (2d) 85, 82 P. (2d) 391 (1938), appeal dismissed and certiorari denied, 306 U. S. 621, 59 S. Ct. 786 (1939). These decisions were based on two misconceptions, first, that a person's religion and its obligations should be determined objectively, and second, that the decision of the Supreme Court in Hamilton v. Regents of University of California, 293 U. S. 245, 55 S. Ct. 197 (1936), was authority for their position. On this second point, see 24 MASS. L. Q., Nos. 2, 3, 4, (1939), indicating that it is one thing to condition entrance to college upon an act violating religious freedom and still another to so condition attendance at free public schools (with possible criminal liability of the parent and reform school for the child). On the first point, freedom to choose one's own religion, one's relations to his Maker and the obligations thereof, is basic to religious freedom. To allow a public officer to determine whether those convictions are religious is to sound the death knell of religious liberty. Prior decisions of the Court have recognized the subjective element of religious convictions. See Watson v. Jones, 13 Wall. (80 U. S.) 679 (1871); Reynolds v. United States, 98 U. S. 145 (1878); Davis v. Beason, 133 U. S. 333, 10 S. Ct. 299 (1890); Cantwell v. Connecticut, 310 U. S. 296, 60 S. Ct. 900 (1940).

protected by the due process clause. Earlier it had been held that the freedom of religion expressly secured against federal aggression by the First Amendment was not by implication included in the Fourteenth Amendment as a limitation on state action,[6] but a line of decisions culminating in *Cantwell v. Connecticut*[7] reversed that view.[8] Freedom of religion has been defined by the Court as absolute freedom of belief and thought and freedom of exercise of those beliefs and thoughts subject to regulation for the protection of society.[9] In the name of protection of society, legislation has been upheld prohibiting affirmative religious acts and practices that affected mental and physical health,[10] or that offended public ethics and morals.[11] Nor has it been doubted that politically organized society in furnishing a program of self-defense may disregard the scruples of a conscientious objector.[12] In the principal case the development of sentiment in favor of national cohesion and unity was considered to be sufficient to override the claim to freedom of conscience. But is it desirable to allow the liberties, usually considered to be basic in our political system, to be brushed aside so easily?[13] It is true that in questioning the means used by the legislature to reach an admittedly legitimate end the court must necessarily weigh factors of policy and formulate an opinion on matters extralegal in nature, i.e., matters which the members of the court are presumably no more competent to pass upon than other intelligent persons.[14] It is precisely on this issue, the scope of judicial

---

[6] Brunswick-Balke-Collander Co. v. Evans, (D. C. Ore. 1916) 228 F. 991; People ex rel. v. Board of Education, 245 Ill. 334, 92 N. E. 251 (1910).

[7] 310 U. S. 296, 60 S. Ct. 900 (1940).

[8] Meyer v. Nebraska, 262 U. S. 390, 43 S. Ct. 625 (1923); Pierce v. Society of Sisters, 268 U. S. 510, 45 S. Ct. 571 (1925); Stromberg v. California, 283 U. S. 359, 51 S. Ct. 532 (1931); Hamilton v. Regents of University of California, 293 U. S. 245, 55 S. Ct. 197 (1936); Cantwell v. Connecticut, 310 U. S. 296, 60 S. Ct. 900 (1940).

[9] Cantwell v. Connecticut, 310 U. S. 296, 60 S. Ct. 900 (1940).

[10] People v. Pierson, 176 N. Y. 201, 68 N. E. 243 (1903); State v. Verbon, 167 Wash. 140, 8 P. (2d) 1083 (1932); Vonnegut v. Baum, 206 Ind. 172, 188 N. E. 677 (1934); Knowles v. United States, (C. C. A. 8th, 1909) 170 F. 409; Delk v. Commonwealth, 166 Ky. 39, 178 S. W. 1129 (1915); New v. United States, (C. C. A. 9th, 1917) 245 F. 710.

[11] Reynolds v. United States, 98 U. S. 145 (1878); Davis v. Beason, 133 U. S. 333, 10 S. Ct. 299 (1890); Updegraph v. Commonwealth, 11 S. & R. (Pa.) 394 (1824).

[12] United States v. Mackintosh, 283 U. S. 605, 51 S. Ct. 570 (1931); Hamilton v. Regents of University of California, 293 U. S. 245, 55 S. Ct. 197 (1936). A good many problems here were avoided by exempting conscientious objectors from the draft laws.

[13] It has been suggested that since this nation has long been free from religious persecution it has perhaps become uninterested in the rights of minorities. 18 Ore. L. Rev. 122 at 128 (1938).

[14] They must determine whether the end justifies the use of the particular means —simply a matter of individual opinion based on the sum total of a person's experience colored by his basic philosophy of living. See Biklé, "Judicial Determination of Questions of Fact Affecting the Constitutional Validity of Legislative Action," 38 Harv. L. Rev. 6 (1924).

review, that the present Court split, the majority being of the opinion that in questionable cases personal freedom could best be maintained by the democratic process as long as the remedial channels of that process functioned.[15] Justice Stone thought that such an approach would result in a complete surrender of constitutional protection of minorities to the popular will. The required flag salute would seem to be of little efficacy when applied to persons sincerely believing it to be a sinful act,[16] and it is extremely doubtful whether it is desirable even when applied to children having no such beliefs.[17] It is premature to conclude that the Court has succumbed to a spirit of superpatriotism.[18] If individual liberties are something more than the by-product of a democratic process,[19] if in fact they have an intrinsic value worthy of protection, it is difficult to justify a decision which subordinates a fundamental liberty to a legislative program of questionable worth.[20]

William F. Andersen

---

[15] Thereby distinguishing liberty of exercise of religion from liberty of speech, press and assemblage in that the latter are indispensable to the remedial channels of the democratic process. Compare Hague v. Committee for Industrial Organization, 307 U. S. 496, 59 S. Ct. 954 (1939); Schneider v. State, 308 U. S. 147, 60 S. Ct. 146 (1939); Thornhill v. Alabama, (U. S. 1940) 60 S. Ct. 736.

[16] See Shinn v. Barrow, (Tex. Civ. App. 1938) 121 S. W. (2d) 450. Judge Clark, Minersville School District v. Gobitis, (C. C. A. 3rd, 1939) 108 F. (2d) 683 at 691, quoting from Hensley, "The Constitutional Aspects of Compulsory Pledges of Allegiance and Salutes to the American Flag," THE LAWYER, November, 1939, p. 5 at 10, stated: "There is a psychological futility in compelling a child to salute the flag when that impinges on his or her religious tenets; such compulsion generates resentment, and is calculated to produce a precisely antithetical result to that which was planned by the authors of the flag-saluting ceremony." See also Judge Lehman's concurring opinion in People v. Sandstrom, 279 N. Y. 523 at 533, 18 N. E. (2d) 840 (1939), where it is suggested that the flag is soiled and dishonored by such compulsion when against the dictates of conscience.

[17] Minersville School District v. Gobitis, (C. C. A. 3rd, 1939) 108 F. (2d) 683 at 692.

[18] As was suggested in 35 TIME, No. 24, p. 22 (June 10, 1940).

[19] See note 15, supra.

[20] See the dissenting opinion of Chief Justice Hughes in United States v. Mackintosh, 283 U. S. 605, 51 S. Ct. 570 (1931).

THE "RECONSTRUCTED COURT" AND RELIGIOUS FREEDOM: THE GOBITIS CASE IN RETROSPECT

WILLIAM G. FENNELL

THE appointment of Justice Stone to be Chief Justice of the United States Supreme Court brings to mind numerous decisions indicative of his liberal philosophy. Of these none deserves a higher place than his dissenting opinion in the *Compulsory Flag Salute* case.[1]

The majority opinion by Justice Frankfurter and Justice Stone's dissent in that case present an opportunity to study the conflicting attitudes of two eminent jurists—both reputedly "liberals"—on the question of the "accommodation" between the constitutional guarantee of religious freedom and the expanding doctrine of the police power, and the scope of judicial review of state legislation affecting civil liberties. No other recent case affords a better opportunity to study the approach of what one might call the "liberal democratic" jurist and the "liberal constitutionalist" jurist to the problem of conflict between rights of conscience and the proper demands of the state. The liberal democrat puts complete trust in the majority popular will to correct foolish legislation which violates the constitutional liberties of the first ten Amendments, and would reduce the participation of the Supreme Court in the process of correcting such legislation to keeping open the means by which undesirable legislation may be repealed, such as: the right to vote, to disseminate information, to organize politically, and to assemble. The liberal constitutionalist, however, while placing no less importance upon keeping these channels for correcting legislation open, nevertheless recognizes the important role which the Supreme Court has under the Constitution of scrutinizing even more searchingly legislation which comes within the specific prohibitions of the first ten Amendments, especially legislation vio-

---

WILLIAM G. FENNELL, B.A., 1930, LL.B., 1933, Yale University, is a member of the New York Bar and contributor to various legal periodicals.

[1] Minersville School District v. Gobitis, 310 U. S. 586, 601, 60 Sup. Ct. 1010, 1017 (1940).

lating constitutional rights of national, racial, or religious minorities. As a protagonist of the "liberal democratic" point of view, Justice Frankfurter has nowhere stated it better than in the majority decision in the *Gobitis* case:

> "Judicial review, itself a limitation on popular government, is a fundamental part of our constitutional scheme. But to the legislature no less than to the courts is committed the guardianship of deeply-cherished liberties. . . . Where all the effective means of inducing political changes are left free from interference, education in the abandonment of foolish legislation is itself a training in liberty. To fight out the wise use of legislative authority in the forum of public opinion and before legislative assemblies rather than to transfer such a contest to the judicial arena, serves to vindicate the self-confidence of a free people."[2]

And Justice Stone's statement in his dissenting opinion is a clear exposition of the opposing point of view:

> "The Constitution expresses more than the conviction of the people that democratic processes must be preserved at all costs. It is also an expression of faith and a command that freedom of mind and spirit must be preserved, which government must obey, if it is to adhere to that justice and moderation without which no free government can exist. For this reason it would seem that legislation which operates to repress religious freedom of small minorities, which is admittedly within the scope of the protection of the Bill of Rights, must at least be subject to the same judicial scrutiny as legislation which we have recently held to infringe the constitutional liberty of religious and racial minorities."[3]

The significance for religious freedom in this difference of high opinion cannot be overestimated. The *Gobitis* decision is one of the very few decisions of the Supreme Court involving religious freedom[4] although religious freedom antedates freedom of speech

---

[2] *Id.* at 600, 60 Sup. Ct. at 1015-1016.
[3] *Id.* at 606-607, 60 Sup. Ct. at 1018.
[4] The other cases are: Cantwell v. Connecticut, 310 U. S. 296, 60 Sup. Ct. 900 (1940); Hamilton v. Regents, 293 U. S. 245, 55 Sup. Ct. 197 (1934); Davis v. Beason, 133 U. S. 333, 10 Sup. Ct. 299 (1890).

and of the press.⁵ The majority opinion, however, makes a distinction between the rights guaranteed by the first ten Amendments: those which afford popular means for "inducing political changes", such as freedom of speech, of the press, and of assembly, on the one hand; and freedom of religion, of belief, and of conscience on the other. It admits that a stricter view of the presumption of constitutionality should prevail in cases involving the former; but that in cases involving the latter, the Court will not pass upon the means employed by the legislature directed to an object within its competence even though religious liberty may thereby be infringed. In other words, the remedy for such "foolish legislation" as the compulsory flag salute law, a law compelling attendance of all children at public schools, or one prohibiting the teaching of a particular language lies with the legislature and not the courts. This doctrine is important enough to warrant examination of the case in which it arose. It seems to imply that the popular majority may with immunity from court interference impose legislation which violates the constitutional rights of the minority—except in the limited sphere where freedom of expression, by the press, speech, or assembly are involved.⁶ It ignores the fact that the Constitution has heretofore been considered a limitation on majority will translated into governmental action.⁷ It gives inevitably a wide sweep of power to the party obtaining a majority at the polls; permits the majority to enact "foolish legislation" which may suppress constitutional rights of a minority and says in effect to the affected minority: "Your remedy is at the next election. We will not hold this legislation unconstitutional, even though it comes within the prohibitions of the First Amendment. We will keep you free to assemble, to publish, and to speak; and if we do that you have no cause to complain." Such a doctrine is fraught with dan-

---

⁵Warren, *The New Liberty under the Fourteenth Amendment* (1926) 39 HARV. L. REV. 431, 461.
⁶Note Stone's criticism in his dissenting opinion in the *Gobitis* case, 310 U. S. at 605-606, 60 Sup. Ct. at 1017-1018.
⁷*See* Speech of former Chief Justice Hughes (then Secretary of State and President of the American Bar Association) in Westminster Hall, London, in August, 1924, reprinted (1941) 27 A. B. A. J. 416, 418; Albertsworth, *The New Constitutionalism* (1940) 26 A. B. A. J. 865.

ger to any political, religious, or racial minority, and as such it is dangerous to our democracy. The fact also that it is bottomed upon a distinction of doubtful validity between the several constitutional guarantees is itself an invitation to further whittling away of those very rights by means of which "foolish legislation" may be corrected.

The case, in which this novel constitutional doctrine was enunciated, involved the belief, peculiar to the religious sect of Jehovah's Witnesses, that saluting the flag is an idolatrous practice—one of the beliefs which have brought this sect into frequent collisions with the law since 1935.[8] At least four other cases involving the validity of compulsory flag saluting laws reached the Supreme Court before the *Gobitis* case; and in each, the Court by a *per curiam* opinion refused on jurisdictional grounds to hear argument.[9] It was not until the Circuit Court of Appeals for the Third Circuit[10] had upheld the District Court[11] in granting an injunction to Walter Gobitis, a member of Jehovah's Witnesses, enjoining the School Board of the Minersville School District in Pennsylvania from exacting participation in the flag salute ceremony as a condition of his children's attendance at school, that the Supreme Court could no longer avoid a decision on the question and granted certiorari.[12] Until the *Gobitis* case there had thus been no full presentation by briefs and oral argument to the Supreme Court of an

[8]In addition to the *Gobitis* case in the Supreme Court, see Cantwell v. Connecticut, 310 U. S. 296, 60 Sup. Ct. 900 (1940); Schneider v. New Jersey, 308 U. S. 147, 60 Sup. Ct. 147 (1939); Lovell v. City of Griffin, 303 U. S. 444, 58 Sup. Ct. 666 (1938); and a recent case in the Tenth Circuit, Oney v. Oklahoma City, 120 F. (2d) 861 (C. C. A. 10th, 1941); for discussion of other instances, see THE PERSECUTION OF JEHOVAH'S WITNESSES; AMERICAN CIVIL LIBERTIES UNION, LIBERTY'S NATIONAL EMERGENCY (1941) 27-30. For popular discussions of Jehovah's Witnesses, see series by Logan in New York Post, July 15, 16, 17, and 18, 1940; High, *Armageddon, Inc.*, SAT. EVE. POST, Sept. 14, 1940, pp. 18-19; Southworth *Jehovah's 50,000 Witnesses*, (1940) 151 THE NATION 110-112.

[9]Leoles v. Landers, 302 U. S. 656, 58 Sup. Ct. 364 (1937); Hering v. State Board of Education, 303 U. S. 624, 58 Sup. Ct. 748 (1938); Gabrielli v. Knickerbocker, 306 U. S. 621, 59 Sup. Ct. 786 (1939); Johnson v. Town of Deerfield, 306 U. S. 621, 59 Sup. Ct. 791 (1939), *rehearing denied*, 307 U. S. 650, 59 Sup. Ct. 832 (1939).

[10]Minersville School District v. Gobitis, 108 F. (2d) 683 (C. C. A. 3rd, 1939).

[11]Gobitis v. Minersville School District, 24 F. Supp. 271 (E. D. Pa. 1939).

[12]The holding of the Third Circuit in the *Gobitis* case conflicted with the holdings of state and federal courts against Jehovah's Witnesses in the cases cited in note 9 *supra*.

important issue involving a conflict of the rights of conscience and the power of the State.[13]

The Gobitis children, on refusing to salute the flag on religious grounds, were expelled from school, and their father brought the injunction suit in which he was successful in the District Court. In the argument before the Supreme Court, he was supported by briefs filed by the Committee on the Bill of Rights of the American Bar Association[14] and by the American Civil Liberties Union. It was argued against the law in these briefs, *inter alia,* that so far as the children were concerned, the flag salute must be regarded as a religious ritual; that there was no public need for the compulsory flag salute sufficient to justify the overriding of the religious scruples of the children; that even if it be deemed to serve a public need, there are other and better ways of accomplishing the same purpose without infringing the religious convictions of the children; that entirely aside from the religious aspect, it is an infringement of individual liberty and that it could not be sustained as a valid exercise of the state's police power.

To the astonishment of many,[15] Justice Frankfurter, long identified as a "liberal", rejected all of these arguments, and speaking for himself and five of the other justices, upheld the compulsory flag salute law. Justice McReynolds merely concurred in the result, but Justice Stone in his dissenting opinion characterized the law sustained by the majority opinion as "unique in the history

[13]The refusal to hear argument in Johnson v. Town of Deerfield, 306 U. S. 621, 59 Sup. Ct. 791 (1939), cited *supra* note 9, was severely criticised by Professor Hart of the Harvard Law School, *The Business of the Supreme Court at the October Terms 1937 and 1938* (1940) 53 HARV. L. REV. 579, 604-605. In a general criticism of *per curiam* opinions he points out that a question of fundamental constitutional rights was disposed of *per curiam* in *Johnson v. Town of Deerfield,* the decision relying upon two other *per curiam* opinions.

[14]*Annual Report of A. B. A. Committee on Bill of Rights* (1940) 1 BILL OF RIG. REV. 47.

[15]See, for example, the editorials, *Reaction to the Flag Salute Decision,* St. Louis Post-Dispatch, June 13, 1940; *On Religious Freedom,* New York Sun, June 6, 1941; *Harlan Fiske Stone,* New York World-Telegram, June 13, 1941; *Religious Freedom* (1940) 102 NEW REPUB. 852-855. The comment of Dean Christian Gauss of Princeton is interesting: "When liberal democratic nationalists, like Felix Frankfurter, write these decisions, we may well ask whether Americanism has not already progressed to an ungodly stage. Earlier democrats like Jefferson, who probably was the first man to use the word Americanism, would not have agreed with our 'liberalized' court of today." New York Herald Tribune, July 21, 1940, "Books".

of Anglo-American legislation",[16] and vigorously condemned the holding and the reasoning upon which it was based for surrendering "the constitutional protection of the liberty of small minorities to the popular will."[17]

The decision in the *Gobitis* case was the more surprising because exactly two weeks before, the Court had rendered a decision[18] of the utmost importance defining the extent of religious freedom under the First Amendment. This case had also involved Jehovah's Witnesses, two members of which had been arrested in the City of New Haven for soliciting funds for religious purposes without first obtaining a permit from the secretary of the public welfare council, who, before issuing the permit, must have found that the "cause" was a religious one; and for playing a phonograph record of anti-Catholic speeches of their leader, "Judge" Rutherford, in a predominantly Catholic neighborhood, the latter activity being alleged as a breach of the peace. Convictions were reversed on both counts on the ground that the religious liberty of the defendants had been violated, first, by the statute, which required a permit (which might be refused) after a determination by a public official that the cause was a religious one; and, second, by extending the common law offense of breach of the peace to cover their conduct, which had not been marked by violence, in attempting to gain converts. To reach this conclusion, the Court held that the religious liberty guaranteed against infringement by Congress by the First Amendment was by reason of the Fourteenth Amendment a limitation upon the states also.[19]

The importance of the *Cantwell* decision is great, since it marked the first time in the Supreme Court's existence when it

[16] Instant case at 601, 60 Sup. Ct. at 1016.
[17] *Id.* at 606, 60 Sup. Ct. 1018.
[18] Cantwell v. Connecticut, 310 U. S. 296, 60 Sup. Ct. 900 (1940).
[19] This is in accord with the trend of decisions since New York v. Gitlow, 268 U. S. 652, 45 Sup. Ct. 625 (1925); Near v. Minnesota, 283 U. S. 697, 51 Sup. Ct. 625 (1931); Stromberg v. California, 283 U. S. 359, 51 Sup. Ct. 532 (1931); Powell v. Alabama, 287 U. S. 45, 53 Sup. Ct. 55 (1932); Grosjean v. American Press Co., 297 U. S. 233, 56 Sup. Ct. 444 (1936); Herndon v. Lowry, 301 U. S. 242, 57 Sup. Ct. 677 (1937); Palko v. Connecticut, 302 U. S. 319, 58 Sup. Ct. 149 (1937); De Jonge v. Oregon, 299 U. S. 353, 57 Sup. Ct. 255 (1937). For prior development and criticism of the doctrine, see Warren, *The New Liberty under the Fourteenth Amendment* (1926) 39 HARV. L. REV. 431.

definitely held that the Fourteenth Amendment protected from state interference the religious freedom guaranteed by the First.[20] Religious freedom under the Fourteenth Amendment, the Court held (Justice Roberts speaking for a unanimous bench),[21] embraced two concepts: The freedom to believe and the freedom to act upon belief. The first, comprehending freedom of conscience and to adhere to such religious organization or form of worship as one may choose, is absolute and cannot be restricted by law; but in the nature of things the second cannot be absolute, and remains subject to regulation for the protection of society. However, this power must be so exercised as not unduly to infringe the protected freedom. The soundness of this holding is evident. If religious freedom means only freedom to believe and does not comprehend freedom to act upon belief as well, it is an absurdity. Without such an implementation of belief, religious freedom becomes a meaningless term. As former Chief Justice Hughes, dissenting in the *Macintosh* case, said: "The essence of religion is belief in a relation to God involving duties superior to those arising from any human relation."[22]

It was against this background of a two-week old precedent, strongly supporting religious liberty from state interference, that Justice Frankfurter spoke for the Court's majority in the *Gobitis* case; and held that a school regulation compelling children to salute the flag against their admitted conscientious and religious scruples was constitutional; and by implication that it did not fall within the narrow ambit of rights which the Court (under his doctrine of judicial review) should be zealous to protect. The very proximity of the *Cantwell* and *Gobitis* decisions serves to whet the interest of the jurist as to why the *Gobitis* case was decided as it was.

A cynic might rationalize the result as an example of a case which had the misfortune to be argued and decided in the tense atmosphere of mingled fear and patriotism that precluded active

---

[20]The assumption in Hamilton v. Regents, 293 U. S. 245, 265, 55 Sup. Ct. 197, 205 (1934), cited *supra* note 4, was dictum only.
[21]Cantwell v. Connecticut, 310 U. S. at 303-304, 60 Sup. Ct. at 903.
[22]United States v. Macintosh, 283 U. S. 605, 633-4, 51 Sup. Ct. 570, 573 (1930).

and feverish defense efforts in the Spring of 1940. The case must, however, be taken as another manifestation of the "new constitutionalism", so ably described by Professor Albertsworth[23] as an indication of the extreme view—that in matters of policy the legislature is supreme.

It must be admitted that the Court was faced with the perplexing and age-old problem of deciding whether, where the right of the state to promote national unity collides with the right of an individual to act upon his religious beliefs, the one or the other should prevail. While admitting that the compulsory flag salute law violated the freedom of children and their parents to act upon their religious beliefs, Justice Frankfurter justified this infringement upon the ground that, since freedom to act upon religious belief is not absolute, it may be regulated by the state under the police power for the promotion of a specific need or interest of secular society—consequently, that while the enforcement of the law under the circumstances was a deprivation of liberty, it was with due process of law.[24] It will be recalled that the Court two weeks earlier in the *Cantwell* case had also said that the right to act upon religious belief was subject to regulation for the protection of society, but had added significantly that the power to regulate must be so exercised as not unduly to infringe the protected freedom.[25] This limitation seems to have been all but forgotten by the majority in the *Gobitis* case. It justifies Professor Hamilton's criticism that Justice Frankfurter "discovered, though he piled up words to hide it, that religious liberty is a local question."[26]

The far-reaching effect of this precedent in expanding the doctrine of the police power and in subjecting the constitutional guarantee of religious freedom (and by implication the other "freedoms" not directly related to effecting political change) to the vagaries of local legislatures cannot be over-estimated. The Court, in the *Gobitis* decision, expanded the bounds of the police power far be-

---

[23] Albertsworth, *The New Constitutionalism, supra* note 7.
[24] Instant case at 594, 60 Sup. Ct. at 1019.
[25] See note 20 *supra*.
[26] Hamilton and Braden, *The Supreme Court Today* (1940) 103 NEW REPUB. 178, 180.

yond its admitted objectives for the protection of public health, safety, and morals. By including as an objective of the police power the promotion of "national cohesion" and "national unity,"[27] the Court pushed the boundary of the police power to a point where the states are held to have the power to require compulsory acts of its citizens even though religious liberty may be infringed. The only requirement is that the legislation promote national unity or cohesion. Legislation with such a purpose, in other words, is due process. But it should not be overlooked that the opinion goes a step farther and concludes that state legislatures alone have the power to determine the appropriateness of the means used to promote national unity.[28] As Justice Stone describing the majority holding in his dissent said:

> ". . . it is said that since the Minersville School Board and others are of the opinion that the country will be better served by conformity than by the observance of religious liberty which the Constitution prescribes, the courts are not free to pass judgment on the Board's choice."[29]

Emphasis is placed in the majority opinion upon the state's exclusive interest in education:

> "But the courtroom is not the arena for debating issues of educational policy."[30] "To deny the legislature the right to select the appropriate means for its attainment (*i.e.*, "national cohesive sentiment") presents a totally different order of problem from that of the propriety of subordinating the possible ugliness of littered streets to the free expression of opinion through distributing handbills."[31]

It is that which Justice Frankfurter defines as "the precise issue,"[32] and to it Justice Stone interposes his doctrine of "accommodation":[33] the fact that we have constitutional guarantees re-

---

[27]Instant case at 596-7, 60 Sup. Ct. at 1013-1014; *cf.* Chief Judge Crane's opinion in People v. Sandstrom, 279 N. Y. 525, 18 N. E. (2d) 841 (1939). *See* (1940) 18 N. Y. U. L. Q. Rev. 124.
[28]Instant case at 598, 60 Sup. Ct. at 1014-1015.
[29]*Id.* at 602, 60 Sup. Ct. at 1016-1017.
[30]*Id.* at 598, 60 Sup. Ct. at 1014-1015.
[31]*Id.* at 595, 60 Sup. Ct. at 1013. Parenthetical remark by author.
[32]*Id.* at 597, 60 Sup. Ct. at 1014.
[33]*Id.* at 603, 60 Sup. Ct. at 1017.

quires *accommodation* of the powers which government normally exercises, when no question of civil liberties is involved, to the constitutional demand that those liberties be protected against the action of *government itself*. He argues that there are other ways to promote education and to inculcate patriotism than by infringing the constitutional immunity. It is interesting that former Chief Justice Hughes in his dissent in the *Macintosh* case advanced somewhat the same idea in a statement often-quoted:

> "The battle for religious liberty has been fought and won with respect to religious beliefs and practices, which are not in conflict with good order, upon the very ground of the supremacy of conscience within its proper field. What that field is, under our system of government, presents in part a question of constitutional law and also, in part, one of legislative policy in avoiding unnecessary clashes with the dictates of conscience."[34]

The avoidance of unnecessary clashes—the accommodation of the normal powers of government to the constitutional demand that religious liberty be protected is the essence of the entire question.

We have thus far considered the decision from the constitutional standpoint; but it is even less satisfactory from a practical one. A statesmanlike[35] utterance on a question of constitutional rights should at least suggest a solution. This the majority apparently attempted as follows:

> "What the school authorities are really asserting is the right to awaken in the child's mind considerations as to the significance of the flag contrary to those implanted by the parent. In such an attempt the state is normally at a disadvantage in competing with the parent's authority, so long— and this is the vital aspect of religious toleration—as parents are unmolested in their right to counteract by their own persuasiveness the wisdom and rightness of those loyalties which

[34] United States v. Macintosh, 283 U. S. 605, 634, 51 Sup. Ct. 570, 578-579 (1930), cited *supra* note 21.

[35] "If the statesman is bound to be, in the practical discharge of his duties, a conscientious jurist, the jurist must, in his work of examination and testing, always keep in mind the point of view of the statesman," VON HOLST, CONSTITUTIONAL LAW OF THE UNITED STATES OF AMERICA (Auth. ed. 1887) 3. See COTTON, THE CONSTITUTIONAL DECISIONS OF JOHN MARSHALL (1905) *vii*.

the state's educational system is seeking to promote."[36]

But the fallacy in this is that if the school authorities were only asserting the right *to educate* the child in love of country and patriotism, even if the state's instruction were diametrically opposed to the parents' teaching at home, there could be no quarrel with the majority's opinion, and it might justly be said that the parents' right to direct the upbringing of their children was protected. But by the compulsory flag salute law, the state seeks *to compel* the child to do an act which it has been taught at home is wrong. Thus the competitive process visualized by the majority opinion is illusory—the parents are, by the state's right *to compel,* put at a distinct disadvantage.

There can be no denying that the decision left "rights and duties" of parents and children in a complete chaos. They are left in this dilemma: If the objecting parent cannot afford to send his child to private school, he may, on the one hand, permit his child to yield to the state's compulsion (in short, renounce his religious freedom); or on the other, stand by his convictions and face the possibility of criminal prosecution. One practical solution, urged upon the Court on brief,[37] but rejected by the majority, which is suggested by a seventy-five year old Massachusetts precedent,[38] and which is in accord with our democratic traditions of religious liberty and avoiding unnecessary clashes with the dictates of conscience, is this: Permit the objecting children to stand respectfully by, while the salute is being given by the other children.[39] But the majority felt[40] that to make any such suggestion would be substituting the Court's judgment for the School Board's on a determination of the best *means* of inculcating patriotism in the schools. That the means adopted by the School Board might violate constitutional guarantees seemingly did not bother the majority. Jus-

[36]Instant case at 599; 60 Sup. Ct. at 1015.
[37]Brief for American Civil Liberties Union, Amicus Curiae, p. 13.
[38]Spiller v. Inhabitants of Woburn, 12 Allen, 127 (Mass. 1866).
[39]Note the action of Probate Judge Arthur E. Moore of Rochester, Minnesota, in securing agreement of school officials and Jehovah's Witnesses to pledging allegiance to "United States of America" omitting all reference to the flag, reported (1941) 77 SURVEY MIDMONTHLY 64.
[40]Instant case at 598-599, 60 Sup. Ct. at 1014-1015.

tice Stone alone of all the justices contended that there was no latitude for a legislative judgment that the compulsory expression of belief which violates religious convictions would better serve the public interest than their protection.[41]

The unfortunate effects of the decision during the past year are now a matter of public record.[42] That there have been patriotic zealots who have construed the majority decision to permit the taking of children from their parents to send them to reformatories as delinquent children is indicated by the cases.[43] Local school boards, construing (perhaps too literally) the broad grants of power implied by the *Gobitis* decision, have suspended children from school for failing to salute, and have later prosecuted them as delinquents. It is, however, a tribute to the democratic character of our courts that so far no higher state court has held that failure to comply with the compulsory flag salute law constitutes juvenile delinquency.[44]

In the case of *New Hampshire v. Lefebvre*,[45] two children were suspended from school in Nashua for failing to salute. Since the parents were too poor to send the children to private school, they were given instruction at home. Not long after, the school board filed a complaint against the parents charging that the children were delinquents. The municipal court found that they were delinquent for not attending school and ordered that they be committed to the State Industrial School. Appeal was taken to the Superior Court but neither the municipal judge nor the Superior Court would grant suspension of the order of commitment pending appeal.

---

[41]*Id.* at 605, 60 Sup. Ct. at 1017-1018.
[42]From May to October, 1940, it has been claimed there were 335 cases of mob violence in 44 states involving 1,448 persons, see AMERICAN CIVIL LIBERTIES UNION, LIBERTY'S NATIONAL EMERGENCY (1941) 27; THE PERSECUTION OF JEHOVAH'S WITNESSES, *op. cit. supra* note 8.
[43]State v. Lefebvre, 20 A. (2d) 185 (N. H. 1941); *In re* Reed, 28 N. Y. S. (2d) 92 (App. Div. 4th Dept. 1941).
[44]See *The Gobitis Case in Retrospect* (1941) 1 BILL OF RIG. REV. 267: ". . . the courts have shrunk from so barbaric a result." In the light of Justice Frankfurter's statement about the "abandonment of foolish legislation" it is interesting to note that in the past year what relief against the compulsory flag salute law has been obtained has come from the courts, not legislatures. No legislature has repealed a compulsory flag salute law during that time.
[45]20 A. (2d) 185 (N. H. 1941).

Upon transfer of the case to the Supreme Court of New Hampshire, however, the latter court released the children pending a final decision. The decision of the Supreme Court, reversing the holding of the lower courts, deserves more publicity than it has received, and illustrates the reluctance of the courts to follow the *Gobitis* decision to its logical conclusion. The Court said in part:

> "If the order appealed from is executed, these three children and their parents will be visited with the breaking up of the family, an institution of primary value in our social life. The reason . . . would be no more than the conscientious acts of the children, based upon the religious teachings of their parents. . . .
>
> "It would be one thing to say that the Legislature intended to permit school authorities to prescribe ceremonial forms for such teaching, and to exclude from public school privileges those children who decline, for whatever motive to conform. But in view of the sacredness in which the state has always held freedom of religious conscience, it is impossible for us to attribute to the Legislature an intent to authorize the breaking up of family life for no other reason than because some of its members have conscientious religious scruples not shared by the majority of the community, at least provided those scruples are exercised in good faith . . . not tinged with immorality or marked with damage to the rights of others."[46]

A similar conclusion was reached by the Appellate Division of the New York Supreme Court.[47]

It is true that the *Gobitis* decision did not deal with the specific question which faced the Court in the *Lefebvre* case. It is to be hoped that should a case involving such a point reach the Supreme Court the *Gobitis* case may be distinguished.[48] And yet such a holding would be logically difficult in view of the broad language of the *Gobitis* decision.

The other branch of the *Gobitis* decision worthy of study is that alluded to at the outset of this article, namely, the limitation which the decision places upon the Court's power to review cases

---

[46]*Id.* at 187.
[47]*In re* Reed, 28 N. Y. S. (2d) 185 (App. Div. 4th Dept. 1941).
[48]See *The Gobitis Case in Retrospect, supra* note 44.

involving legislation violative of rights guaranteed by the Bill of Rights. The difference of opinion between Justices Frankfurter and Stone arises from views apparently long held by each. Justice Stone for example had taken occasion in 1937,[49] in an illuminating footnote[50] to a decision, to analyze quite carefully his own theory of the scope of judicial review, and the extent of the presumption of constitutionality in cases where state legislation *prima facie* fell athwart prohibitions of the Bill of Rights. In the *Carolene Products* case,[51] he argued that "a narrower scope for the presumption of constitutionality" should prevail when legislation, *prima facie* within specific prohibitions of the first ten amendments to the Constitution, is before the Court. In partial agreement with Justice Frankfurter's views as later expressed in the *Gobitis* decision, he argued that legislation restricting political processes which can ordinarily be expected to bring about repeal of undesirable legislation should be subjected to a more exacting judicial scrutiny. But, and here we find the nub of his disagreement with Justice Frankfurter, Justice Stone implied that the same considerations, requiring a more exacting scrutiny, enter into the review of statutes directed at particular religious, national, and racial minorities, and he posed the question which his own dissenting opinion in the *Gobitis* case goes far to answer:

> ". . . whether prejudice against discrete and insular minorities may be a special condition, which tends seriously to curtail the operation of those political processes ordinarily to be relied upon to protect minorities, and which may call for a correspondingly more searching judicial inquiry."[52]

It seems apparent from the *Gobitis* decision that Justice Frankfurter limits the "doctrine of more exacting judicial scrutiny" to

---

[49] United States v. Carolene Products Co., 304 U. S. 144, 58 Sup. Ct. 778 (1938).
[50] *Id.* at 152-153, 58 Sup. Ct. at 783-784.
[51] There was a curious split amongst the Justices in this case: Chief Justice Hughes and Justices Brandeis and Roberts concurred with Justice Stone in his "footnote". Justice Black concurred in all of the opinion except the part containing the "footnote". Justice Butler wrote a separate opinion, Justice McReynolds dissented, and Justices Cardozo and Reed took no part in the case. Thus Justice Stone's "footnote" represented "minority doctrine".
[52] United States v. Carolene Products Co., 304 U. S. 144, 153, 58 Sup. Ct. 778, 784 (1938).

legislation violating freedom of speech, press, or assembly, but in respect to other legislation (including legislation which on its face violates religious liberty) he would apply the broadest presumption of constitutionality. In failing to recognize Justice Stone's corollary that religious prejudice may tend to curtail the ordinary judicial processes and call for greater judicial scrutiny, Justice Frankfurter was following views long held by him. In 1925 in an opinion of Justice McReynolds the Supreme Court unanimously held unconstitutional a law of the State of Oregon which required that all children attend public schools.[53] Justice (then Professor) Frankfurter criticized this decision and a decision in another case[54] which arose out of the hysteria of the First World War holding unconstitutional a Nebraska law which prohibited the teaching of German in the public schools, saying:

> "For ourselves we regard the cost of this power of the Supreme Court on the whole as greater than its gains. After all, the hysteria and chauvinism that forbade the teaching of German in Nebraska schools may subside, and with its subsidence bring repeal of the silly measure; the narrow margin by which the Oregon law was carried in 1922 may, with invigorated effort on the part of the liberal forces, result in its repeal, at least by a narrow margin. But when the Supreme Court strikes down legislation directed against trade unions, or enshrines the labor injunction into the Constitution, or denies to women in industry the meager protection of minimum wage legislation, we are faced with action more far-reaching, because ever so much more durable and authoritative than even the most mischievous of repealable state legislation."[55]

It would seem from the above statement that Professor Frankfurter's objection was directed not merely to the scope which judicial review of state legislation should take but to the power of the Supreme Court to hold such legislation unconstitutional. Furthermore one gathers from the above statement that the reasons behind it were primarily pragmatic and grew out of opposition to decisions

[53]Pierce v. Society of Sisters, 268 U. S. 510, 45 Sup. Ct. 571 (1924).
[54]Meyer v. Nebraska, 262 U. S. 390, 43 Sup. Ct. 625 (1922).
[55]*Can the Supreme Court Guarantee Toleration?* (1925) 43 NEW REPUB. 85. This article is now contained in Justice Frankfurter's book LAW AND POLITICS (1939).

which had held unconstitutional social and labor legislation. But whatever the reasons, or the precise point of the objection, it should not be overlooked that the law which the Supreme Court held unconstitutional was directed at destroying (and if it had been upheld by the Supreme Court and not soon repealed by the legislature or the people, would most certainly have destroyed) all Catholic parochial schools, as well as other private schools, in the State of Oregon. Moreover the possibility that, in a period when the Ku Klux Klan was a popular and expanding movement, the law might have been copied in other states should not be ignored. It is plain that the law violated religious freedom—the freedom to educate a child in the school of a certain religious group if the parents so desire. By Justice Stone's test,[56] the law should have been, and was, subjected by the Court to "a more careful judicial scrutiny", the usual presumption of constitutionality was given "narrower scope", and after such scrutiny was held unconstitutional unanimously. By Justice Frankfurter's test as enunciated in the *Gobitis* case, however, the presumption should have been broadly applied, and the legislation upheld as the act of a popular majority, who might, in the future, obtain increased "training in liberty" by "education in the abandonment of this foolish legislation". But consider where such a disposition of the Oregon School Law case would have left Catholic parochial and private schools, to say nothing of parents and children who desired to send their children to such schools rather than to public schools. Such schools would have been compelled to close; Catholic and other children would have been compelled to attend public schools. Their only solace would have been that they might enjoy the privilege of agitating in favor of repeal of the "foolish legislation".

Observing the chaotic situation in which the *Gobitis* decision left the practical problem, and imagining the equally chaotic situation which would have been created had the Oregon School Law been upheld—situations which recall another unstatesmanlike opinion in the *Dred Scott* case[57]—the doctrine, that the people and not

---

[56]See notes 49 and 50 *supra*.
[57]Dred Scott v. Sandford, 19 How. 393 (U. S. 1856).

the Supreme Court should correct legislation which violates the Bill of Rights, seems unfortunate practically and unjustified constitutionally. To exercise care in seeing that no legislation is permitted to stand which threatens the processes whereby political changes may ordinarily be effected is necessary, but alone it is not enough. Anyone who has attempted to secure the enactment of a sane divorce law in New York, or anyone who has attempted to secure the repeal of the "Jim Crow" laws in any of our Southern states will no doubt have found that while all the effective means of inducing political change have been open to him, he will not have obtained his objective. It is in such situations where prejudice against minorities curtails the operation of ordinary political processes that the Supreme Court has a duty to scrutinize even more carefully legislation which violates the rights of religious or racial minorities.

If the Bill of Rights is to mean anything, it must be a limitation upon state legislatures as well as upon the national government. To this end the Supreme Court must discharge its inherent responsibility under our constitutional system[58] and scrutinize even more exactingly legislation which upon its face falls within the prohibitions of the first ten Amendments. If the "reconstructed court" (to use Justice Frankfurter's own phrase in another case)[59] continues to adhere in cases involving religious liberty to the doctrine of the majority in the *Gobitis* case, the scope of the state police power will be immeasurably enhanced and religious liberty will be at the mercy of shifting political majorities. It is to the lasting credit of the new Chief Justice that he comprehended that the Constitution expresses more than the conviction that democratic processes must be preserved at all costs; it is also an expression of faith and a command *which government itself must obey* that freedom of mind and spirit must be preserved. This is the very "genius" of American constitutional democracy.[60] But it is a fundamental which the "new constitutionalism" seems in danger of

---

[58]"The Supreme Court is the real arbiter of our liberties." WHIPPLE, OUR ANCIENT LIBERTIES (1927) 140.
[59]Graves v. O'Keefe, 306 U. S. 466, 487, 59 Sup. Ct. 595, 602 (1939).
[60]See note 7 *supra*.

forgetting. It is of the same cloth as the English doctrine stemming from Magna Carta that there are certain rights of Englishmen which even the Crown may not suppress. It is this which distinguishes ours from other democracies which have ended in dictatorships by means of *majority* usurpation of power, the suppression of minorities and finally the corruption of government itself by a dictator or a one-party system.

Any attempt by judicial dogma to weaken the position of the Supreme Court in our constitutional system must be condemned. Any doctrine which tends to remove religious freedom and other constitutional liberties from the Court's protection and to make them subject to the "popular will", by broad presumptions of constitutionality or by failure to scrutinize even more exactingly legislation which falls within the prohibitions of the first ten Amendments, is dangerous to the survival of our "ancient liberties".[61]

It is because the *Gobitis* case enunciated such a doctrine in respect to freedom of religious belief and practice that it deserves far greater examination and understanding than it has received during its first year as a precedent.[62]

[61]*Cf.* WHIPPLE, *op. cit. supra* note 57.
[62]See *The Gobitis Case in Retrospect, supra* note 43; Cushman, *Constitutional Law 1939-1940* (1941) 35 AM. POL. SCI. REV. 250, 269.

RECENT RESTRICTIONS UPON RELIGIOUS LIBERTY

VICTOR W. ROTNEM AND F. G. FOLSOM, JR.

U. S. Department of Justice

Within the last five years, the Supreme Court of the United States has added decisions of greater importance to the case law of religious freedom than had been accumulated in all the years since the adoption of the Bill of Rights. The importance of two of these recent decisions rests upon the subordination of freedom of action based on sectarian beliefs to the restrictions of society as a whole. In one of the two cases, the law of society was a board of education order that school children participate in the flag salute exercise on pain of expulsion from the public schools;[1] in the other, it was peddlers' license tax ordinances.[2] Because neither of these decisions has been accepted as a firmly rooted precedent, it will be well to examine them in the light of the history of the federally secured right of religious freedom and in the light of the immediate public reactions to them.

A considerable proportion of the early emigration to the thirteen original colonies was undoubtedly due to a desire to escape religious persecution in England and on the Continent. Those colonists, however, were as insistent that their own particular form of religion be adhered to as their oppressors had been. The story of Roger Williams, who was expelled from the colony of Massachusetts because of his non-conformist views and who established the colony of Rhode Island as a sanctuary of religious tolerance, and that of Ann Hutchinson, who also was exiled from the Bay Colony for a like reason, are monuments to the intolerance of the Puritans.

But by the time of the adoption of the Constitution, the principle of religious freedom which Roger Williams so stoutly advocated and put into practice in Rhode Island had gained such headway that its omission from the law of the land was at once protested; and, significantly, the first tenet of the so-called Bill of Rights was a cure of that want: "Congress shall make no law respecting an establishment of religion, or prohibiting the free exercise thereof, ..."

It will be observed that this declaration is an inhibition only on the federal government. It does not prevent the states from doing

---
[1] Minersville District v. Gobitis, 310 U.S. 586 (1940).
[2] Jones v. Opelika, 316 U.S. 584 (1942).

1053

the things thus prohibited to the Congress.[3] The amendment embodies the principle of the separation of church and state. In the words of the Supreme Court, it was designed to allow everyone under the jurisdiction of the United States to entertain such notions respecting his relation to his Maker and the duties they impose as may be approved by his judgment and conscience, and to exhibit his sentiments in such form of worship as he may think proper, not injurious to the rights of others, and to prohibit legislation for the support of any religious tenets or the modes of worship of any sect.[4]

The right to think as one wishes regarding religion can scarcely be doubted; the question which today seems to prompt the action of the secular authorities is the right to practice religious dictates. The rule in this regard is old and sound. It is, briefly, that there is a right to practice any religious principle and teach any religious doctrine which does not, as above indicated, injure the personal rights of others, nor offend the laws established by society for peace and morality.[5] The example that at once comes to mind as illustrating the overreaching and abuse of religious freedom is the practice of polygamy by the Mormons. This practice conflicted with the bigamy laws of the territory of Utah, and it was held that no religious conviction supporting it could excuse a breach of the law.[6]

In one such case, the Reynolds case, the Supreme Court quoted the highly significant preamble of "An Act Establishing Religious Freedom" drafted by Thomas Jefferson for the state of Virginia: "That to suffer the civil magistrate to intrude his powers into the field of opinion, and to restrain the profession or propagation of principles on the opposition of their ill tendency, is a dangerous fallacy which at once destroys all religious liberty...." It was time enough, the Act declared, to invoke the powers of civil government when the practice of opinions resulted in overt breaches of peace and good order.

In keeping with these principles, the federal courts have refused to review a decision of an ecclesiastical tribunal on religious matters.[7] Nor would they question a will creating an endowment for a

[3] Permoli v. New Orleans, 3 How. 589, 609 (1845).
[4] Davis v. Beason, 133 U.S. 333, 342 (1890).
[5] Watson v. Jones, 13 Wall. 679 (1871).
[6] Reynolds v. United States, 98 U.S. 145 (1878); Davis v. Beason, 133 U.S. 333 (1890). [7] Watson v. Jones, 13 Wall, 679 (1871).

school and providing that no religion be taught there, nor any cleric be allowed on the grounds.[8] On the other hand, a prosecution of persons pretending to occult powers as a part of a scheme to use the mails to defraud is no violation of the First Amendment.[9]

The Fourteenth Amendment has now become recognized as a bulwark against state infringement of the same religious liberties which the First Amendment secured from federal interference.[10] Religious freedom is so elementary to the concept of ordered "liberty" that it must be said to be within the meaning of that term in the Fourteenth Amendment,[11] which reads, in pertinent parts, as follows: " . . . nor shall any state deprive any person of . . . liberty, . . . , without due process of law, . . ." The liberty of religion protected from state interference by this amendment includes the absolute right of any person to entertain whatever views regarding religion his conscience may dictate, and the right to exercise those beliefs in such ceremonies and practices as do not conflict with the laws of society for peace and good morals. Any invasion by a state of the right to believe as one sees fit would undoubtedly be considered arbitrary, and hence violative of due process; and so would a state infringement of the right to exercise those religious beliefs unless such exercise conflicted with the secular laws regarding peace and good morals.

This brief review brings us to a consideration of the cases decided by the Supreme Court in the last five years. A small religious sect or society known as Jehovah's Witnesses has served as the guinea pig for all the important cases in this period.

The Jehovah's Witnesses are the followers of the religious doctrines formulated by the late pastor, Charles T. Russell. Russell was born in Pittsburgh in 1852 and was brought up in the Presbyterian faith. At the age of sixteen, he decided that the then existing schools of religious thought were wrong, and he built up a religion of his own, centered around calculations as to the second coming of Christ and the battle of Armageddon. His followers, formerly

---

[8] Vidal et al. v. Girard's Executor, 2 How., 43 U.S. 126 (1844).

[9] New v. United States, 245 Fed. 710 (1917). See also "Criminal Aspects of Fortune-Telling," *Moody's Monthly*, July, 1942, by Pvt. I. H. Rubenstein. Rubenstein was prompted to write this article by the increase of fortune-tellers as an incident of the present war.   [10] See Hamilton v. Regents, 293 U.S. 245 (1934).

[11] See Palko v. Connecticut, 302 U.S. 319 (1937). It should be noted that most state constitutions already contain provisions similar to those of the First Amendment of the federal constitution.

known as "Russellites" but adopting the name "Jehovah's Witnesses" in 1931, believe that their highest function is to disseminate their interpretations of the Bible and their religious beliefs. To accomplish this purpose, a non-profit, non-stock corporation was founded in 1884 under the laws of Pennsylvania, and now known as the Watch Tower Bible and Tract Society. The corporation owns printing plants located in Brooklyn, New York, Berne (Switzerland), and other places, and these plants are devoted to the printing of books, magazines, and pamphlets embodying the Witnesses' beliefs. The corporation also supplies Witnesses with phonographs, public address cars, and recorded explanations of the contents of the large volume of printed matter. Armed with the Society's publications and with the portable phonographs, individual Witnesses carry out their conviction that they must spread the gospel as they see it by street corner and door-to-door distribution of the books and bulletins.

Publications of the Society contain highly contentious teachings. They attack all institutionalized churches and sects as things of Satan. The members decry any form of religious ceremony and, in this connection, they refuse to salute the flag because they believe that that practice runs counter to the commandment that they should not bow down to any "graven image."[12] The Society teaches "that we are not of this world" and discourages Witnesses from participation in politics or the support of war. Each Witness claims to be a minister of the gospel.[13]

These beliefs have occasioned intense animosity in every state of the Union, and the virulent attacks on institutionalized religion, particularly the Catholic church, are highly offensive to many people. Small town officials are flooded with protests on those days when the "witnessing" activities are being carried on. As a result, peddling and solicitation ordinances have been applied as a restraining mechanism. The religious convictions against the flag

[12] The Jehovah's Witnesses' position somewhat resembles that of the early Christians who were martyred for rejecting the symbols of the self-deified Roman emperors. The resemblance is incomplete, however, because the flag has no parallel religious significance.

[13] This claim has been advanced before local boards of the Selective Service System as the basis for demands by individual Witnesses for draft exemption under Section 5(d) of the Selective Training and Service System Act of 1940. In Opinion No. 14, Vol. III, National Headquarters Selective Service System, it was recognized that those Jehovah's Witnesses who devoted their full time to the Society's activities were in a position to be considered by local boards as ministers of the gospel.

salute and against military service have aroused the ire of patriotic groups such as veterans' organizations, and this has occasioned further protests and often mob violence. In those communities where local or state law requires that children in public schools salute the flag, numerous school children adhering to the Jehovah's Witnesses' belief have been expelled for refusing to do so.

In due course, these questions have come before the Supreme Court. The first of the decisions, in 1938, involved an ordinance of the city of Griffin, Georgia, making it a nuisance to distribute literature such as leaflets and handbooks within the city limits without first obtaining permission of the city manager.[14] The defendant, Alma Lovell, a Jehovah's Witness, was convicted because she distributed Watch Tower and Bible Tract Society literature without seeking a permit. In holding the Griffin ordinance unconstitutional, the federal Supreme Court invoked the free speech and free press guarantees of the Fourteenth Amendment, stating that the local law was void on its face because it forbade every sort of distribution except such as the city manager saw fit to allow. The significance of this opinion to religious freedom was the tacit and not much disputed acknowledgment that free religious expression is protected by the Constitution's free speech and free press guarantees.

The next case extended the above rule to an Irvington, New Jersey, ordinance requiring canvassers and peddlers to register with the chief of police and secure a permit from him.[15] The provision which allowed the chief of police to refuse a permit, if he determined that the applicant's character was not good or his canvassing project not free from fraud, was held to give the local officer too great a discretion in deciding for himself what ideas were good or bad. The "free speech" involved was again free religious speech.

In Cantwell v. Connecticut, the defendant Witnesses ignored a state law requiring that before persons might solicit money for a religious cause they must first apply to the secretary of the local public welfare council, who was charged with the responsibility of providing a certificate if he found the cause to be a religious one.[16] This, the Supreme Court ruled, unconstitutionally authorized the

[14] Lovell v. Griffin, 303 U.S. 444 (1938).
[15] Schneider v. Irvington, 308 U.S. 147 (1939).
[16] 310 U.S. 296 (1940).

secretary of the public welfare council to censor religion. The necessity that he pass upon the question of what was or was not a religious cause was a prior restraint on the freedom of religion. It was conceded that if fraud occurred under the guise of religion, it could be punished, and again if a general system of regulation of solicitation were established without any religious test, and not unreasonably burdening solicitation, it would be valid.

Cantwell not only had been convicted of soliciting without the required certificate, but he was also convicted on a charge of inciting a breach of peace. His street-corner phonograph recital had attacked institutionalized religions and had aroused the ire of a Catholic audience. The Court said that even though the expression of this view of religion might be very offensive to some, yet no conviction could be predicated upon it, because the right of freedom of expression protected it.

These three cases were favorable to the Jehovah's Witnesses with regard to their right to distribute religious literature, to solicit funds, and to present peaceably their unorthodox views. The Cantwell case reiterated the well established rule that the right to think and believe what one wishes about religion is absolute, while the right to act and speak in accordance with those views is subject to limitation in the interest of peace and good order. Cantwell's demeanor had been courteous. He might not have fared so well had it been otherwise. In 1942, in Chaplinsky v. New Hampshire, the Court considered the case of an over-zealous Witness convicted under a New Hampshire statute against the public use of abusive language against others. The defendant had called a police officer a "damned Fascist" and "a god-damned racketeer." The Court did not think this an exercise of religion, since the statements contributed nothing to the exposition of the defendant's ideas. The so-called "fighting words" were held not to be under the protection of the Constitution 315 U.S. 568 (1942).[17]

---

[17] The objection is often made that one religious sect should not be protected by constitutional guarantees when its members verbally abuse other religions. A test of this view came under a New Jersey statute which made it a misdemeanor to make statements in the hearing of two or more persons which incite or advocate hatred against any group on the ground of race or religion. In a case involving German-American Bund antisemitic utterances, the New Jersey supreme court held this statute so vague that it conflicted with the free-speech and religious-freedom guarantees of the Fourteenth Amendment. State v. Klapprott, 127 N.J.L. 395 (1941). Jehovah's Witnesses had been prosecuted under this same statute. But see Cantwell

In a case arising in New Hampshire, the Supreme Court upheld a state statute prohibiting street parades without a special license.[18] A group of Jehovah's Witnesses had marched in a line carrying signs along a busy intersection in the city of Manchester on a Saturday night. The act, as limited by state decisions to apply only to formation marches in a public thoroughfare, was ruled to be a reasonable police measure; freedom of assembly and of expression giving way slightly to public convenience. These decisions resulted in no discussion or public reaction of any moment, and appear to have been generally accepted as sound.

The two decisions mentioned at the outset remain to be considered. One was in 1940 and the other in 1942. The earlier was Minersville District v. Gobitis, 310 U.S. 586 (1940). The school board of the Minersville school district made a ruling that all children attending the public schools of the district should give the flag salute at the opening of the school day. The children of Walter Gobitis attended those schools, being, however, Jehovah's Witnesses, and as such holding the religious conviction that to salute the flag was to disobey the commandment of the Bible against obeisance to a graven image. They were expelled; and Gobitis applied to the federal district court for an injunction against enforcement of the expulsion order.

On December 1, 1937, Federal District Judge Maris denied the defendant school district's motion to dismiss the injunction suit.[19] He said public officials should not question the religious basis of a sincere refusal to act when public safety, health, or morals, or personal or property rights, were not prejudiced by such refusal; the refusal to salute the flag because of religious convictions did not involve such dangers. It was pointed out that the effect of the ruling of the school board was to make the flag, which is a symbol of religious liberty, a means of imposing a religious test as a condition of receiving the benefits of public education. Later, Judge

---

v. Connecticut, 310 U.S. 296, 309, and 310 (1940), discussed above, in which the federal Supreme Court indicated that the free speech guarantees of the First and Fourteenth Amendments did not protect statements so profane, indecent, or abusive to the person of a listener as to amount to a breach of peace.

[18] Cox v. New Hampshire, 312 U.S. 569 (1941). And compare Leiby v. Manchester, 117 F. (2d) 661, holding that the distributors of literature and periodicals must comply with an ordinance requiring buttons to be secured from the superintendent of schools, who had no discretion to refuse them. Cert. den. 313 U.S. 562 (1941).   [19] 21 F. Supp. 581, E.D. Pa.

Maris granted the requested injunction against the enforcement of the "salute or be expelled" order of the school board.[20] It may be noted parenthetically here that in the years 1937 and 1938 the Department of Justice received exactly three letters concerning the Jehovah's Witnesses; the following year, 1939, apparently as a result of American reactions to the spreading conflict in Europe, numerous complaints were made to the Department regarding attacks upon the Witnesses.

On March 4, 1940, the United States Circuit Court of Appeals for the Third Circuit sustained the Gobitis injunction in a cogent opinion.[21] The Court noted that the conflict boiled down to a question of whether the flag-salute requirement was such a rule of society for safety and good morals as must take precedence over liberty of conscience. It observed that the Minersville school board rule imposed, not a prohibition upon action, but rather a command to do an act, and concluded that it was not of sufficient moment as a device for instilling respect for country to outweigh freedom of religious conscience. If invoked, it was held, the rule denied the religious freedom on which is based a great measure of the respect due this nation and its flag.

But both lower courts were reversed in the federal Supreme Court on June 3, 1940.[22] Mr. Justice Frankfurter, speaking for the eight-to-one majority of the Court, acknowledged the question as being one of balancing a rule of political society against considerations of religious freedom. His conclusion, however, ran contrary to that of the circuit court. The necessity for cohesive patriotic sentiments was felt to be more important than the non-conformist religious views of the Witnesses. Said the majority:

"Our present task then, . . . is to reconcile two rights in order to prevent either from destroying the other. . . . National unity is the basis of national security. . . The precise issue, then, for us to decide is whether the legislatures of the various states and the authorities in a thousand counties and school districts of this country are barred from determining the appropriateness of various means to evoke that unifying sentiment without which there can ultimately be no liberties, civil or religious. . .

---

[20] 24 F. Supp. 271, E.D. Pa., June 18, 1938.   [21] 108 Fed. (2d) 683.

[22] The Supreme Court had on four previous occasions upheld flag salute regulations in *per curiam* decisions: Leoles v. Landers *et al.*, 302 U.S. 656 (1937); Hering v. State Board of Education, 303 U.S. 624 (1938); Gabrielli v. Knickerbocker, 306 U.S. 621 (1939); and Johnson v. Deerfield, 306 U.S. 621 (1939), rehearing denied, 307 U.S. 650 (1939).

So to hold would in effect make us the school board for the country. That authority has not been given to this Court, nor should we assume it."

The Court then declined to question the choice by the school board of the flag exercise as an appropriate means to instill patriotic sentiment.

Admittedly, there are difficult questions involved here. Before attempting to suggest a solution, it will be well to review the effect of the decision.

Between June 12 and June 20, 1940, hundreds of attacks upon the Witnesses were reported to the Department of Justice. Several were of such violence that it was deemed advisable to have the Federal Bureau of Investigation look into them. At Kennebunk, Maine, the Kingdom Hall was burned. At Rockville, Maryland, the police assisted a mob in dispersing a Bible meeting. At Litchfield, Illinois, practically the entire town mobbed a company of some sixty Witnesses who were canvassing it, and it was necessary to call on the state troopers to protect the members of the sect. Several Witnesses were charged with riotous conspiracy at Connersville, Indiana, their attorney was mobbed, and he and several other Witnesses who had attended the arraignment were beaten and driven out of town. At Jackson, Mississippi, members of a veterans' organization, led by an individual claiming the rank of major, forcibly removed a number of Witnesses and their trailer homes from the town.

Three instances of such vigilantism led by state or municipal officers caused the Department of Justice to seek indictments against the officers for violation of the Civil Rights Act.[23] Jehovah's Witnesses conventions in July, 1940, were held in twenty cities in some fifteen states. At the urgent request of the Department of Justice, through the United States attorneys, local law enforcement officers were induced to give these conventions adequate protection, so that no violence attended. In this connection, it should be noted also that persecution of the Witnesses is peculiarly a small town and rural community phenomenon, whereas the conventions were held in larger cities.

[23] Sec. 52, T. 18, U.S.C. The respective grand juries refused to indict. Then an information was filed in the worst of the three assaults in which a chief of police and deputy sheriff had forced a group of Jehovah's Witnesses to drink large doses of castor oil and had paraded the victims through the streets of Richwood, West Virginia, tied together with police department rope. The trial of this outrage resulted in a speedy conviction.

In the two years following the decision, the files of the Department of Justice reflect an uninterrupted record of violence and persecution of the Witnesses. Almost without exception, the flag and the flag salute can be found as the percussion cap that sets off these acts.

Attempts have been made to prosecute school children who had been expelled under "salute or be expelled" regulations on the ground that such children were incorrigible delinquents.[24] The parents have been prosecuted for failure to make their children attend school.[25] In Oklahoma, a group of Witness children, expelled from the Woods county public schools for refusal to salute the flag, were being tutored by an ex-school teacher in her home. She now has been convicted of failing to require the flag salute in her private classes, although she had formulated a different exercise, consisting of a pledge of allegiance to God and country and expressing respect for the flag.[26]

Attempts have been made to enforce ordinances requiring the flag salute as a condition precedent to the right to distribute literature.[27] Mississippi has enacted a statute, allegedly prompted by the stand of the Jehovah's Witnesses against the flag salute, making it a crime to distribute printed matter calculated to encourage disloyalty to the United States.[28] Numerous Witnesses have been indicted under this act because they distributed literature explaining the sect's opposition to the flag salute.[29] The flag has been used in a manner bordering on immorality by mobs which have baited groups of Jehovah's Witnesses throughout the country. Mayoralty courts and justice of peace courts in nearly every state in the Union

[24] *In re* Lefebvre, 20 Atl. 2nd, 185. *In re* Jones, 24 N.Y. Supp. 2nd, 10 (1940).

[25] *In re* La Trecchia, N.J. Sup. Ct. decided June 30, 1942, holding that the parents cannot be fined when the school board expels their children for refusing to salute the flag; West Virginia v. Mercante, C. Ct. Hancock Co., W.Va., June 1, 1942, to the same effect; and see the following pending cases: South Dakota v. Davis and wife, Sup. Ct. S.D.; Arizona v. Davis, Sup. Ct. Ariz.; Partian v. Oklahoma, Okla. Crim. Ct. of Appeals; Pendley v. Oklahoma, Okla. Crim. Ct. of Appeals; Pendley v. Oklahoma, Okla. Crim. Ct. of Appeals. Cf. People v. Sandstrom, 279 N.Y. 523 (1939).

[26] Carter-Mort v. Oklahoma, pending upon appeal, Okla. Crim. Ct. of Appeals.

[27] Kennedy et al. v. City of Moscow, Dist. Ct. Idaho. 39 F. Supp. 26 (1941). Reid et al. v. Brookville et al., Dist. Ct., W.D. Pa., decided May 2, 1941.

[28] H.R. 689 (Mo.) Regular Legislative Session, 1942.

[29] One of these cases, Mississippi v. Mills and Wife, is now pending on appeal in the Miss. Sup. Ct.

have entertained evidence relative to the refusal of the Witnesses to compromise their religious convictions about the flag as an excuse to convict them on charges of breach of the peace, inciting to riot, violation of peddling ordinances, and other misdemeanors. Few such convictions, however, have been honored on appeal to courts of record.

This ugly picture of the two years following the Gobitis decision is an eloquent argument in support of the minority contention of Mr. Justice Stone. The placing of symbolic exercises on a higher plane than freedom of conscience has made this symbol an instrument of oppression of a religious minority. The flag has been violated by its misuse to deny the very freedoms it is intended to represent—the freedoms which themselves best engender a healthy "cohesive" respect for national institutions. In short, public health, safety, and morals have not been fortified by the compulsory flag salute laws. Indeed, the result has been quite the contrary.

It seems probable that a reversal of that ruling would profoundly enhance respect for the flag.[30] The vigor of constitutional guarantees such as religious freedom, on which respect for flag and country must depend, stems from their ever renewed public recognition and observance. How much more effective an instrument of patriotic education it would be if the flag salute itself were made a practical daily exercise of a fundamental liberty, a liberty which is one of the four great freedoms for which this nation is now fighting!

Perhaps, however, Congress has by-passed the constitutional issue here involved and supplied a statutory solution. On June 22, 1942, Public Law No. 623, codifying the rules and customs regarding the use of and respect due the flag of the United States, became law. Section 7 of that act reads as follows:

"That the pledge of allegiance to the flag, 'I pledge allegiance to the flag of the United States of America and to the Republic for which it stands, one Nation indivisible, with liberty and justice for all,' be rendered by standing with the right hand over the heart; extending the hand, palm upward, toward the flag at the words 'to the flag' and holding this position until the end, when the hand drops to the side. However, civilians will always show full respect to the flag when the pledge is given by merely standing at attention, men removing the headdress. Persons in uniform shall render the military salute."

[30] In the most recent case, the supreme court of Kansas has held that the refusal to salute the flag could not under the Kansas constitution be a ground for expelling a pupil from the Kansas public schools. Kansas v. Smith, decided July 10, 1942.

This measure was sponsored by the American Legion, and to that organization must go the credit for the statesmanship reflected in the recognition of "respect" as the most universally acceptable and tolerant word to be used in connection with the flag.

Observe that full respect is all that is called for from civilians. Such respect may be shown merely by standing at attention. It is submitted that this law of Congress lays down a federal standard with regard to a matter which is primarily a concern of the national government, and therefore state and local regulations demanding a different standard of performance must give way entirely, or at least be made to conform. Speaking more concretely, a school board order respecting flag salute exercises should not now be permitted to exact more of the pupil with religious scruples against the flag salute than that he should stand at attention while the exercise is being conducted. Full respect will thus be shown as measured by the paramount federal law, and the Jehovah's Witnesses have again and again affirmed that they respect the flag and the principles which it represents. The Department of Justice has been assured that the Witnesses have no objection to standing at attention during the flag salute exercise. Finally, it is worthy of note that in the case next to be discussed three members of the majority of the Court in the Gobitis case have gratuitously acknowledged that the flag salute ruling was wrongly decided.[31]

This brings us to a consideration of the most recent religious freedom opinion of the Supreme Court, which involved variously a book and magazine peddler's licensing ordinance of the city of Opelika, Alabama,[32] a peddler's licensing ordinance of the city of

[31] Mr. Justice Black, Mr. Justice Douglas, and Mr. Justice Murphy joined in the following remarks, Jones v. Opelika, etc., decided June 8, 1942: "The opinion of the Court sanctions a device which in our opinion suppresses or tends to suppress the free exercise of a religion practiced by a minority group. This is but another step in the direction which Minersville School District v. Gobitis, 310 U.S. 586, took against the same religious minority and is a logical extension of the principles upon which that decision rested. Since we joined in the opinion in the Gobitis case, we think this is an appropriate occasion to state that we now believe that it was also wrongly decided. Certainly our democratic form of government functioning under the historic Bill of Rights has a high responsibility to accommodate itself to the religious views of minorities, however unpopular and unorthodox those views may be. The First Amendment does not put the right freely to exercise religion in a subordinate position. We fear, however, that the opinions in this and in the Gobitis case do exactly that."

[32] The amount of the tax was $10 per annum, $5 for transient book agents.

Fort Smith, Arkansas,[33] and a similar ordinance of the city of Casa Grande, Arizona.[34] Each ordinance exacted a tax of varying amounts as a condition precedent to the right to peddle, and in each case Jehovah's Witnesses had been convicted of offending these ordinances by distributing religious literature, asking and receiving in return a "contribution" usually of a sum fixed as the price of the particular piece of literature.

The Supreme Court, by a five to four majority, ruled that sales of religious literature by the Witnesses were more commercial than religious transactions, and therefore such transactions could properly be subjected to a non-discriminatory privilege tax.

In a dissent filed by Chief Justice Stone, it is pointed out that the license fees were straight taxes and were no part of any reasonable regulatory scheme, that the tax measures were enacted for ordinary business enterprises, while the Witnesses' activity was religious and their money transactions in the nature of solicitation. He concluded that such taxes were a prior restraint upon the defendants' religious activities, and hence offended the religious freedom guarantees of the Fourteenth Amendment:

" . . . It seems fairly obvious that if the present taxes, laid in small communities upon peripatetic religious propagandists, are to be sustained, a way has been found for the effective suppression of speech and press and religion despite constitutional guarantees. The very taxes now before us are better adapted to that end than were the stamp taxes which so successfully curtailed the dissemination of ideas by eighteenth-century newspapers and pamphleteers, and which were a moving cause of the American Revolution. See Collett, *History of the Taxes on Knowledge*, vol. 1, c. 1; May, *Constitutional History of England*, 7th ed., vol. 2, p. 245; Hanson, *Government and the Press, 1695–1763*, pp. 7–14; Morison, *The English Newspaper, 1622–1932*, pp. 83–88; Grosjean v. American Press Co. supra, 245–49. Vivid recollections of the effect of those taxes on the freedom of the press survived to inspire the adoption of the First Amendment."

In a separate dissent, Mr. Justice Murphy emphasizes that the purpose of the activity in question was not commercial, but was rather dissemination of religious views. The burden of the tax was, therefore, directly upon freedom of speech, of the press, and of religion.

[33] The amount of the tax was $25 per month, $10 per week, or $2.50 per day.
[34] The amount of the tax was $25 per quarter-year.

This decision caused an immediate reaction in the press. The majority of the editorials examined expressed dissatisfaction with the result reached.[35] The minority opinions were lauded. While this reaction can be in part attributed to the fear that freedom of the press was unfavorably involved, it nevertheless was heartening to observe that so unpopular a minority sect as Jehovah's Witnesses found so many ready champions to defend its constitutional rights. Some papers gave the opinion straight reporting treatment, some editorialized on the continuation of split opinions in the high court, and a very few sided with the majority.[36]

Too little time has passed for any possible trend occasioned by the license tax decision to be accurately reflected in the Department of Justice files, but already letters have been received requesting copies of the opinion for information as a basis for drafting peddlers' licensing ordinances for the avowed purpose of putting a stop to Jehovah's Witnesses' activities. The thought is present that most communities will at once resort to this expedient. If this occurs, the fears of the dissenting Justices that such legislation is oppressive will appear to be justified.

The following comments are offered in an effort to pin down the problem, which is likely to become lost in rhetorical references to the Constitution. The gist of the majority opinion is found in the following sentence: "But it is because we view these sales as partaking more of commercial than religious or educational transactions that we find the ordinances, as here presented, valid."

This is an assumption which it will be well to consider in the light of the following facts, pro and con: *Pro:* (1) Transfer of books or other literature, and a fixed payment in return, having the ap-

---

[35] *Age Herald*, Birmingham, Ala., June 11, 1942; *Courier*, Evansville, Ind., June 11, 1942; *Free Press*, Burlington, Vt., June 10, 1942; *Journal-Transcript*, Peoria, Ill., June 11, 1942; *Times-Dispatch*, Richmond, Va., June 12, 1942; *Herald*, Hutchinson, Kan., June 11, 1942; *News and Courier*, Charleston, S. C., June 12, 1942; *Virginian-Pilot*, Norfolk, Va., June 12, 1942; *Enterprise*, Beaumont, Tex., July 5, 1942; *Journal-Times*, Racine, Wis., June 11, 1942; *Times-Herald*, Washington, D. C., June 12, 1942; *State Gazette*, Trenton, N. J., June 11, 1942; *Tribune*, Lewiston, Ida., June 11, 1942; *Democrat*, Johnstown, Pa., June 15, 1942; *Post-Dispatch*, St. Louis, Mo., June 12, 1942; *Journal of Commerce*, Chicago, Ill., June 15, 1942; *Dispatch*, Roswell, N. Mex., June 11, 1942. And see the editorials in *Newsweek*, June 29, 1942, Vol. 19, No. 26, p. 68, and *Time*, June 22, 1942, Vol. 39, No. 25, pp. 55, 56.

[36] *Herald-News*, Passaic, N. J., June 11, 1942. Admittedly, this footnote and footnote 29 represent the sampling method. But observe that on the basis of these samples the ratio is 19 to 1.

pearance of a sale; (2) Witnesses who devote their full time to their missionary work receive expense money.[37] *Con:* (1) The admitted non-profit nature of the transaction; (2) The undisputed fact that the articles involved were religious and a means of evangelizing; (3) The distributors are professed ministers of their religion and do not profit personally; (4) The funds collected are devoted to the support of the religious movement; (5) The probable fact that the purchaser views his payment of money as nothing more than a contribution.

If this is an honest tabulation, the religious character of the transaction is supported by the numerically preponderant facts. The weight to be assigned to each fact is conjectural, but no part of the money transaction can be divorced from its religious aspect. The distribution of the literature is an exercise of religion, just as is a Sunday sermon. The money received goes to the support of that exercise. By the exaction of a tax, that exercise of religion is burdened, and to the extent that it is, the freedom of religion defined in the First Amendment and protected by the Fourteenth Amendment is inescapably abridged.

The conclusion is that the majority of the Court drew a line between commercial and religious transactions, but did not make sufficiently clear the basis for drawing it. There seems to be reason for arguing that the line should not have been drawn in favor of the commercial taxable aspect when the transaction was fundamentally dissemination of religious beliefs, the distributor being a minister or evangelist without personal gain, and when the money received is directly sustaining of the means of religious expression. Were the distributor or salesman to peddle primarily for personal profit, he might well be taxed for the privilege of distributing even religious tracts. Again, if the articles sold were not religious treatises, though sold for the profit of a religious organization, a tax on the seller would not appear to abridge any exercise of religion. In each such instance, the profit motive, or the non-religious nature of the articles dispensed, would divorce the religious from the commercial aspect of the otherwise equivocal "sales."

Admittedly, the balancing of the conflicting religious and social interests in both the flag salute case and the license tax cases is a delicate and difficult problem. The foregoing discussion has attempted to attack this problem in the light of the nation-wide pic-

[37] Cf. Opinion No. 14, Vol. III, National Headquarters Selective Service System.

ture which has been peculiarly available to the writers through the files of the Department of Justice. Should these issues again be presented to the Supreme Court, as it seems inevitable they will be, it is hoped that the reflections here expressed will be thrown in the balance.[38]

[38] A motion has been made for a rehearing of Jones v. Opelika, etc., decided June 8, 1942. A petition for *certiorari* has been filed in the Supreme Court in a somewhat similar license tax case arising in the District of Columbia, Busey v. Dist. of Columbia, decided April 15, 1942, in the U. S. Court of Appeals for the District of Columbia.

On October 6, 1942, a three-judge court sitting in the District Court of the United States for the Southern District of West Virginia in the case of Walter Barnette *et al.* v. West Virginia State Board of Education granted an injunction against the State Board prohibiting enforcement of the flag salute requirement in the public schools of West Virginia in cases where school children have religious scruples against participating in the salute. The court felt that the authority of the Gobitis case had been so impaired by the change of heart of three members of the Supreme Court who had joined in the majority opinion that it was no longer a binding precedent. An order permitting the defendant, State Board, to appeal was entered by District Judge Ben Moore October 30, 1942.

RICHARD DANZIG

HOW QUESTIONS BEGOT ANSWERS IN FELIX FRANKFURTER'S FIRST FLAG SALUTE OPINION

Lawyers who draft briefs, bureaucrats who compose issue papers, and surveyors assessing popular opinion all know that the way they pose questions powerfully affects—if it does not determine—the answers they will receive. Appellate judges know, or ought to know, that a lawyer's shrewdness, imagination, and forensic skill will be as much manifested in an articulation of the "questions presented" in a case as it will be in the arguments advanced about the resolution of those questions. The wise judge also knows that at the stage of opinion writing, the advantage of framing the questions passes to the bench. Probably no other factor operates so strongly in favor of securing approval for an opinion of the courts as the willingness of readers to accept the question put by the opinion writer.

Richard Danzig is Associate Professor of Law, Stanford University.

AUTHOR'S NOTE: Parts of this essay are drawn from a larger work on the *Flag Salute* cases and *Martin v. Struthers*. Portions of that larger work have been presented at Stanford, Harvard, Yale, and The University of Chicago Law Schools. These portions have been supported by grants from the American Bar Foundation and the Rockefeller Foundation. I am grateful for the assistance. Beyond this, the contributions of Jay Casper, Fred Konefsky, and Jan Vetter to the larger project have been so substantial that I think they must be specifically reflected even in this short essay. I owe particular thanks to them.

© 1978 by The University of Chicago. All rights reserved.
0-226-46429-6/78/1977-9000$01.58

The first of my propositions here is that the opinions of Justice Frankfurter often benefited from his understanding this fact. I offer two pairs of cases by way of illustration. In both *Wolf v. Colorado*[1] and *Rochin v. California*,[2] the petitioners contended that their state criminal convictions were constitutionally infirm because they rested on evidence which had been illegally obtained. In *Wolf*, Justice Frankfurter sided with the state; in *Rochin*, with the petitioner. He did not do this by invoking different constitutional doctrines. Nor did he contrast the facts to which the constitutional standard was applied.[3] Justice Frankfurter produced contradictory opinions in these cases by a technique that might be called "differential focusing." He directed attention to different questions in each case. In *Wolf* he focused on remedies. Was it compatible with basic notions of "ordered liberty" to restrict Wolf to a tort suit as the method of redressing the effects of an illegal search? In *Rochin* the focus was on rights. The question Justice Frankfurter saw in the case was whether the challenged search itself was so repelling as to be contrary to the concept of "ordered liberty." Presumably Rochin, too, could invoke the remedy of a tort suit. But this point was ignored.

A similar ploy characterizes my second pair of examples, *Francis v. Resweber*[4] and *Solesbee v. Balkcom*,[5] two cases roughly contemporaneous to *Wolf*. The lawyers for Willie Francis argued that it was contrary to basic notions of "ordered liberty" to attempt again to electrocute him after a first electrocution had miscarried. Justice Frankfurter focused only on the remedy. He did not ask whether a second electrocution attempt would be contrary to "ordered liberty." Instead he put a more beguiling question. Did it contravene fundamental notions of liberty to leave this question to the decision of a state governor? It did not. Three years later Solesbee's lawyers pressed the claim that it contravened the Constitution to execute an insane man. Justice Frankfurter agreed. He did not ask

---

[1] 338 U.S. 25 (1949).

[2] 342 U.S. 165 (1952).

[3] To the contrary, the facts in *Wolf* were stated in so scanty a fashion that it is only by consulting the record and briefs that one can determine the nature and circumstances of the search in question.

[4] 329 U.S. 459 (1947).

[5] 339 U.S. 9 (1950).

whether it was adequate to leave such a matter to the decision of a state governor who might grant a reprieve. Instead he focused on the right. Did an insane person have a constitutional right not to be executed? With the question phrased in this manner, Justice Frankfurter decided for the petitioner.

The tendency to ask a question about remedies in some cases and about rights in others is so frequently exhibited in Justice Frankfurter's opinions that differential focusing might fairly be said to be a process central to the functioning of his jurisprudence. When he was self-abnegating about the use of judicial power he tended to focus on remedy. He would build an argument for restraint in the use of federal constitutional power by noting the existence of alternative remedies by resort to the common law, to legislation, or to the executive authority. Conversely, when moved to intervene and exercise judicial power, Justice Frankfurter would phrase the issue at hand in terms of rights.

In this essay, rather than dwell on this point, however, I should like to make some observations stemming from the fact that "differential focusing" is part of a larger phenomenon. It is an aspect of asking questions, and Justice Frankfurter had other modes of asking questions that are worthy of attention. I propose here to examine in some detail one of these other modes but in the context of a single case. I call this technique "inflation" and show how it not only shaped an important opinion, but served to dispose of a precedent that might otherwise have undermined that opinion. Beyond this, by a detailed review of a single case, I hope to cast some light on a larger problem: Why was it that Justice Frankfurter's questions were frequently loaded? I suggest that contemporary circumstances were very important factors in the case discussed here, and that it was at the point of question framing that these factors were most readily absorbed in the Justice's opinion. In general, I suggest, the technique of loading questions, whether by means of inflation or by differential focusing, permits simultaneous deference to two conflicting but greatly valued imperatives. It gives play to a judge's sense of what is right and necessary in the everyday world, while it preserves the purity of an opinion's legal logic. The judge refrains from smuggling things personal and expedient into the analysis. Instead, they are made part of the premise from which the analysis proceeds.

I

In June of 1940, in *Minersville School District v. Gobitis*,[6] the Supreme Court of the United States held by a vote of eight to one that it was constitutionally tolerable to expel children of Jehovah's Witnesses from public schools if they refuse to salute the flag. Felix Frankfurter wrote the majority opinion; Harlan Fiske Stone wrote the lone dissent. Near the beginning of his opinion, Justice Frankfurter sketched the facts of the case in the barest detail:[7]

> Lillian Gobitis, aged twelve, and her brother William, aged ten, were expelled from the public schools of Minersville, Pennsylvania, for refusing to salute the national flag as part of a daily school exercise. . . . The Gobitis family are affiliated with "Jehovah's Witnesses," for whom the Bible as the Word of God is the supreme authority.

He then went through a series of permutations of statements of the issue. First the Justice said: "We must decide whether the requirement of participation in such a ceremony, exacted from a child who refuses upon sincere religious grounds, infringes without due process of law the liberty guaranteed by the Fourteenth Amendment."[8] Shortly thereafter, the question was put again in a somewhat different form:[9] "When does the constitutional guarantee [of free exercise of religion] compel exemption from doing what society thinks necessary for the promotion of some great common end, or from a penalty for conduct which appears dangerous to the general good?" Two pages later the question recurred: "the question remains whether school children, like the Gobitis children, must be excused from conduct required of all the other children in the promotion of national cohesion."[10]

Finally, in a fourth version, Justice Frankfurter articulated "the question" of the case in its ultimate form:[11]

> The case before us must be viewed as though the legislature of Pennsylvania had itself formally directed the flag-salute for the children of Minersville; [and] had made no exemption for children whose parents were possessed of conscientious scru-

---

[6] 310 U.S. 586 (1940).
[7] *Id.* at 591.
[8] *Id.* at 592–93.
[9] *Id.* at 593.
[10] *Id.* at 595.
[11] *Id.* at 597.

ples like those of the Gobitis family.... The precise issue, then, for us to decide is whether the legislatures of the various states and the authorities in a thousand counties and school districts of this country are barred from determining the appropriateness of various means to evoke that unifying sentiment without which there can ultimately be no liberties, civil or religious.

Thus phrased, Justice Frankfurter was sure of the resolution of the issue in the case. The Court, he said, should not "stigmatize legislative judgment in providing for this universal gesture of respect for the symbol of our national life . . . ,"[12] and it ought not to "exercise censorship over the conviction of legislatures that a particular program or exercise will best promote in the minds of children who attend the common schools an attachment to the institutions of their country."[13] To exempt children on grounds of religion, the Court would have to "maintain that there is no basis for a legislative judgment"[14] that they ought not to be exempted. Since exemption of some might undermine the program for all, there was a basis for the legislative judgment, and the claim of unconstitutionality had to fail.

II

At crucial points in its analysis this opinion was dependent on acts of "inflation." The magnitude of the inflation is most apparent when one realizes that, though Justice Frankfurter spoke of "stigmatiz[ing]" the "legislative judgment" and of "exercis[ing] censorship over the conviction of legislatures," in fact no decision to mandate a flag salute had ever been made by the Pennsylvania legislature, much less had that legislature ever considered whether religious scruples might warrant exemption from a general requirement. The state legislature had merely established school districts, set procedures for electing school boards, and specified subjects these boards might require. Beginning in 1919, that authority explicitly extended to supervising work in "civics, including loyalty to the State and National Government."[15]

---

[12] *Ibid.* [13] *Id.* at 599. [14] *Id.* at 600.

[15] 1921 Pa. Laws 983. For this information, as well as for the details of events in Minersville, I have relied on MANWARING, RENDER UNTO CAESAR 76, 81 ff. (1962), and on STEVENS, SALUTE 32 ff (1973), both of whom interviewed participants in the town, on the school board, and in the litigation.

When the Gobitis children refused to conform, no statute or regulation, not even one of the Minersville School District, required them to salute. A pledge of allegiance occurred in the Minersville school merely by custom; no regulation mandated it. The Gobitis's insubordination" provoked the school board to inquire of the State Department of Public Instruction whether it could coerce a salute. A Department opinion declared that it could. At this time, also, the state attorney-general ruled to the same effect. The Minersville Board then met and established a salute requirement. "Immediately following this vote,"[16] the school superintendent rose and declared the Gobitis children expelled.

It required a substantial inflation for Justice Frankfurter to draw from the events in the small town of Minersville, in Schuylkill County, Pennsylvania, an assertion that the "case before us must be viewed as though the legislature of Pennsylvania had itself formally directed the flag-salute."[17] Yet more inflation was required to replace the Minersville school board by "the legislatures of the various states and the authorities in a thousand counties and school districts,"[18] and to argue that the Court should not strike down the salute requirement because to do so would be to "exercise censorship over the conviction of legislatures that a particular program or exercise will best promote in the minds of children who attend the common schools an attachment to the institutions of their country."[19] By stating, working, reworking, and then again reworking the question in the case, Justice Frankfurter eventually brought the matter to a point where the decision pivoted on an inflated rather than a real concern. The question became not how the *ex post facto* act of a single small-town school board was to be assessed against the challenge of the Gobitis children, but whether the "conviction" of countless "legislatures" was to be honored.

An argument could have been made to justify this act of inflation. It might have been said that any effort to distinguish between a school board and a legislative judgment would chill the tendency of legislatures to delegate decisions to agencies. Surely President Roosevelt's Justices did not want to discourage such delegation. Moreover, they might well have wanted to foreclose any thought of federal

---

[16] Manwaring, note 15 *supra*, at 83. Stevens, note 15 *supra*, at 34, says "Minutes after the vote [the Superintendent] expelled the Witnesses' Children."

[17] 310 U.S. at 597.   [18] *Ibid.*   [19] *Id.* at 599.

courts piercing the veil of state relationships by passing on such a delicate intrastate question as whether a school board had the authority to do as it did.[20]

But the doctrine underlying this approach was not debated. The logic behind Justice Frankfurter's policy of judicial deference, and thus restraint, was open to challenge. It had to be premised at least in part on notions about legislatures: their representativeness, their responsiveness, and their capacity for making constitutional judgments. Were the same notions equally relevant to the decision of the Minersville School Board? This question was never asked because the question that was asked masked the issue.

Authority lay directly at hand that could have been used to support a holding that judgments of the legislature were unique in their claim to deference, and that challenged actions which could not be directly traced to legislative intent should be reviewed without the benefit of a favorable presumption. In the very month that *Gobitis* was being written, Justice Roberts had advanced this thought for a unanimous Court in *Cantwell v. Connecticut*.[21] There, one count of the conviction of a Jehovah's Witness for playing a virulently anti-Catholic phonograph record on a street corner rested on "the common law offense of inciting a breach of the peace."[22] Justice Roberts held that the Court would not defer to the state interest in criminalizing such conduct "in the absence of a statute narrowly drawn to define and punish specific conduct."[23] In words whose logic could have been made relevant to *Gobitis*, Justice Roberts said:[24]

---

[20] There was even precedent at hand which proscribed such inquiry in a case involving an economic regulation. In Pacific States Co. v. White, 296 U.S. 176 (1935), Justice Brandeis, for a unanimous Court, upheld an order of Oregon's Department of Agriculture. There it was "urged that this rebuttable presumption of the existence of a state of facts sufficient to justify the exertion of the police power attaches only to acts of legislature; and that where the regulation is the act of an administrative body, no such presumption exists, so that the burden of proving the justifying facts is upon him who seeks to sustain the validity of the regulation." *Id*. at 185. To this, Justice Brandeis replied: "The question of law may, of course, always be raised whether the legislature had power to delegate the authority exerted. Compare *Panama Refining Co. v. Ryan*, 293 U.S. 388 and *A.L.A. Schechter Poultry Corp. v. United States*, 295 U.S. 495. But where the regulation is within the scope of authority legally delegated, the presumption of the existence of facts justifying its specific exercise attaches alike to statutes, to municipal ordinances, and to orders of administrative bodies." *Id*. at 186.

[21] 310 U.S. 296 (1940).

[22] *Id*. at 300.

[23] *Id*. at 311.

[24] *Id*. at 307–08.

Conviction on the fifth count was not pursuant to a statute evincing a legislative judgment that street discussion of religious affairs, because of its tendency to provoke disorder, should be regulated, or a judgment that the playing of a phonograph on the streets should in the interest of comfort or privacy be limited or prevented. Violation of an Act exhibiting such a legislative judgment and narrowly drawn to prevent the supposed evil, would pose a question differing from that we must here answer. Such a declaration of the State's policy would weigh heavily in any challenge of the law as infringing constitutional limitations. Here, however, the judgment is based on a common law concept of the most general and undefined nature.

Justice Frankfurter, however, avoided *Cantwell* and the whole of the issue of the appropriate deference to be given the state action by the way in which he phrased the question before him. In declaring that in this case he weighed a legislative judgment against an individual right, he advanced a proposition for which he cited neither authority nor reason. But because the proposition was buried in the phrasing of the question it garnered no attention from either the dissent or from the numerous critics of the opinion.

III

There was another precedent besides *Cantwell v. Connecticut* which Justice Frankfurter had to overcome in order to reach the result in *Gobitis*. *Schneider v. State*,[25] decided by nearly a unanimous Court earlier that very Term, ran counter to the simple rationality test Frankfurter advanced in *Gobitis*. In *Schneider* the Court held that four cities' undeniably rational statutes that prohibited leafletting because it tended to lead to littering were consitutionally invalid as invasions of the rights of free speech. In an opinion which Frankfurter joined, Justice Roberts put the Court on the record this way:[26]

> We are of opinion that the purpose to keep the streets clean and of good appearance is insufficient to justify an ordinance which prohibits a person rightfully on a public street from handing literature to one willing to receive it. Any burden imposed upon the city authorities in cleaning and caring for the streets as an indirect consequence of such distribution re-

---

[25] 308 U.S. 147 (1939).   [26] *Id.* at 162.

sults from the constitutional protection of the freedom of speech and press. This constitutional protection does not deprive a city of all power to prevent street littering. There are obvious methods of preventing littering. Amongst these is the punishment of those who actually throw papers on the streets.

Here is how Frankfurter distinguished *Schneider* in *Gobitis*:[27]

> We are dealing with an interest inferior to none in the hierarchy of legal values. National unity is the basis of national security. To deny the legislature the right to select appropriate means for its attainment presents a totally different order of problem from that of the propriety of subordinating the possible ugliness of littered streets to the free expression of opinion through distribution of handbills. Compare *Schneider* v. *State*, 308 U.S. 147.

Frankfurter put this view yet more clearly in a private letter to Justice Stone:[28]

> It is not a case where conformity is exacted for something you and I regard as foolish—namely a gesture of respect for the symbol of our national being—even though we deem it foolish to exact it from Jehovah's Witnesses. It is not a case, for instance, of compelling children to partake in a school dance or other scholastic exercise that may run counter to this or that faith.

On its own terms, this view was indisputable. "National security" indeed might so commonly be thought to rank higher than the public interest in avoiding littering, that any judge at all alive to the world would think *Gobitis* a different case from *Schneider*. But such an analysis compared incommensurate concerns. "National security" was not self-evidently at stake in *Gobitis*. One might as well say that "public health" was at issue in *Schneider* and argue, as Frankfurter once argued in defense of a statute, "Health is the foundation of the state."[29]

---

[27] 310 U.S. at 595.

[28] Frankfurter to Stone, 27 May 1940. The original of this letter may be found in the Stone Papers, Library of Congress, Box 65, File 690. Copies are extant in the Frankfurter Papers, Library of Congress, Box 105, File 2197, and in the Murphy Papers (University of Michigan, Ann Arbor), Box 60, File 690.

[29] Adkins v. Children's Hospital, 261 U.S. 525 (1923), Brief for the Appellants, at 1053.

On their face, the government actions questioned in *Gobitis* and *Schneider* prescribed flag saluting and proscribed littering. If judges and other observers saw larger issues at play it was through individual acts of inflation. The facts presented by these controversies were like flaccid balloons waiting to be pumped up by those who interested themselves in the matter. The size the cases would reach when full blown, the heights of abstraction to which they would be lifted, would be determined by the heat of the principles with which they were injected and by the energy and intensity with which Justices pumped them.

What Felix Frankfurter was doing in comparing *Schneider* and *Gobitis* was to take the former case in its uninflated, flaccidly factual state and compare it with a fully inflated *Gobitis*. There is no reason to believe that the comparison was duplicitous. Rather, it seems simply that for Frankfurter, the state interest in *Schneider* consistently appeared limp—nothing in his thought or experience gave it buoyancy. In contrast, he invested the flag-salute controversy with issues of such great intensity that for him it always loomed full blown.

When acts of inflation precede and determine much of the logic of an opinion, when, as I have suggested, such acts obfuscate issues and swap relevant precedent, then it is imperative for an analysis of an opinion to inquire into the causes of inflation. Toward this end, I would suggest that Felix Frankfurter was encouraged in his inflation of *Gobitis* by his present and past concerns. *Gobitis* was written against the backdrop of his perceptions of the need to mobilize America for war and of the psychological problems in doing so. Harold Ickes recorded this sense of Felix Frankfurter on the eve of the announcement of *Gobitis*:[30]

> The discussion at Archibald MacLeish's on Sunday night [the *Gobitis* decision was announced on Monday morning] ran until well after twelve o'clock, I hear, with Felix Frankfurter holding the center of the stage. Apparently there was a good deal of feeling between Bob Jackson and Felix. The latter is really not rational these days on the European situation.

To Frankfurter it was apparent that America would have to fight Germany. But in May of 1940 Americans were neither united

---

[30] 3 THE SECRET DIARY OF HAROLD ICKES 199 (1954).

nor prepared to fight. As Frankfurter put it to the President in a suggestive metaphor, it was necessary that the country be "taken to school"[31] and educated about the struggle ahead. His input into a Roosevelt speech the following autumn was largely devoted to "emphasizing that the indispensable defenses—those without which tanks and flames even are of no avail—are the defenses of the mind . . . [I]f recent history teaches us anything, it is that those who are hostile to the democratic way of life count most on disorganizing the moral forces of democracy."[32]

"Mobilization" in every sense of the word was an intense and pervasive concern for Frankfurter while he wrote *Gobitis*. On May 3, he brought with him to lunch at the White House with the President his former mentor, Henry Stimson, once Secretary of State and Secretary of War. Stimson's diary records that the three "talked quite openly . . . about a number of confidential foreign policy developments."[33] Frankfurter left some hint of his mood by recording his gratitude to Roosevelt as thanks for "taking me out of my marble prison."[34]

In March, 1939, Hitler had swallowed Czechoslovakia; in September he had moved into Poland. The Russians had invaded Finland in December of that year. On April 9, 1940, sixteen days before *Gobitis* was argued, the supposedly "phony" wars of the North had become more chillingly real as the Germans stormed and quickly subdued Denmark and Norway. On the tenth of May, as Frankfurter was assembling his opinion, Luxembourg, Holland, and Bel-

---

[31] Quoted in FREEDMAN, ROOSEVELT AND FRANKFURTER: THEIR CORRESPONDENCE, 1928–1945 512 (1967). See also Frankfurter to Stimson, 27 June 1940, Frankfurter Papers, Library of Congress, Box 104, File "Stimson Correspondence" (appearance before a Senate Committee should be made "a first rate opportunity for educating the American people to an understanding of what national defense really means . . . an informed and vigorous public opinion is indispensable to the realization of an effective program of national defense").

[32] Frankfurter to Sam Rosenman, 7 Oct. 1940, Frankfurter Papers, Library of Congress, Box 246, File 4329. (The carbon is unsigned, but clearly from Frankfurter.)

[33] Stimson Diary, Henry L. Stimson Papers, Library Wf Congress.

[34] Frankfurter to Roosevelt, 3 May 1940, reprinted in FREEDMAN, note 31 *supra*, at 521. See also JOHNSON, THE BATTLE AGAINST ISOLATION 72 (1944), quoting a letter from Frankfurter to William Allen White which "came on May 26, 1940": "The bench is partly prison; but not even the stuffiest notions of propriety preclude my expressing my gratitude to you for mobilizing our opinion so that our action may become effective in the challenge that mad brute force is hurling against the accumulated gains—oh! so painfully accumulated—of civilization."

gium were invaded.[35] That night Roosevelt delivered "one of the greatest speeches of his career,"[36] saying, among other things, that if the "dictator states" were successful in dominating Europe, "they will, we know down in our hearts, enlarge their wild dream to encompass every human being and every mile of the earth's surface."[37] Frankfurter immediately telegraphed the President, "Our gratitude for . . . [you] at your best."[38]

The month was studded with bad news from Europe, militant Roosevelt speeches, and highly evocative letters from Frankfurter to the President. On May 16 the Justice sat in the House of Representatives as the President spoke. An hour later he wrote:[39]

> These are days when one realizes the importance of things unseen, and is sure of things not susceptible of ordinary proof. . . . [You inspire] all who are determined that the precious achievements of man's spiritual nature shall not perish from the earth. . . .
> Your message was just right. You can count on Lincoln's "common people."

On May 26, a day after another presidential speech, Frankfurter summed up the feelings of the moment and the month:[40]

> Dear Frank—
> This is Sunday morning and I humbly believe that not the most pious church attendant has his thought more outside himself and on the ultimate destiny of mankind than I have this forenoon here in my study. It is in that mood that I am venturing to break in on you. My one excuse is that I cannot resist doing so.
> You don't have to be told what thoughts you stirred in me yesterday morning about our country and your relation to it at this juncture. And these thoughts have been with me for all these weeks—hardly anything else has been.

---

[35] On the events of this period and the reaction to them in Washington, see LANGER & GLEASON, THE CHALLENGE TO ISOLATION, 1937–1940 (1952), esp. pp. 436–96.

[36] The judgment is Max Freedman's note 31 *supra*, at 521.

[37] *Ibid.*

[38] Frankfurter to Roosevelt, 10 May 1940. *Id.* at 522.

[39] Frankfurter to Roosevelt, 16 May 1940. *Ibid.*

[40] Frankfurter to Roosevelt, 26 May 1940. *Id.* at 523.

Indeed, since Frankfurter sent a carefully worded five-page confidential letter about *Gobitis* to Stone on Monday, May 27, it seems highly likely that the work on which his war thoughts intruded, as he sat in his study that Sunday morning, was his flag salute opinion. Writing to Stone as "his thought . . . [was] outside himself and on the ultimate destiny of mankind," Frankfurter clearly made the link between his judicial and his extrajudicial lives, between his correspondence with the President and his correspondence with Stone:[41]

> For time and circumstances are surely not irrelevant in resolving . . . this particular case. . . . I had so many talks with Holmes about his espionage opinions and he always recognized that he had a right to take into account the things that he did take into account when he wrote Debs and the others [during the spring of 1919] and the different emphasis he gave the matter in the Abrams case [in the fall of 1919].

Frankfurter was not merely reflecting abstractly on war-related questions at the time he wrote these words. The letter of May 26 urged Roosevelt to solicit the resignation of his cabinet so that a new cabinet especially committed to and suited for the war effort could be formed.[42] In pressing this suggestion, Frankfurter reflected a plan he had evolved around this time with a law school classmate and close friend, Grenville Clark. Their aim was to replace the incompetent and uncommitted Secretary of War, Woodring, with someone more capable and inclined toward preparedness. By the end of the month, during a lunch in Frankfurter's Supreme Court chambers, Frankfurter and Clark agreed on a candidate: Henry Stimson.[43]

---

[41] Frankfurter to Stone, 28 May 1940, note 27 *supra*.

[42] Frankfurter to Roosevelt, 26 May 1940, in FREEDMAN, note 31 *supra*, at 523.

[43] SPENCER, A HISTORY OF THE SELECTIVE TRAINING AND SERVICE ACT OF 1940 (Ph.D. Diss. Harvard University 1951). Spencer, drawing on separate interviews with Clark and Frankfurter, says that, at this luncheon, "[T]hey pondered several possibilities . . . but in a matter of minutes they suddenly seized by common consent on the perfect candidate: Henry L. Stimson." *Id.* at 113. Freedman, writing while apparently unaware of Spencer's thesis and with no apparent authority for a contrary conclusion, dates Frankfurter's campaign for Stimson at least as far back as the May 3 White House luncheon. FREEDMAN, note 31 *supra*, at 521. A letter from Clark to McGeorge Bundy, detailing these events as background for Bundy's biography of Stimson, supports Spencer's view. See Clark to Bundy, 18 July 1947 in Frankfurter Papers, Library of Congress, Box 44, File 789 (copy).

On June 1, the day that *Gobitis* was handed down, Frankfurter visited the President and urged Stimson's candidacy on him.[44] On June 20 the Frankfurter-Clark idea was implemented. Stimson was appointed Secretary of War and Judge Patterson, a former law partner of Clark's and a protege of Frankfurter's,[45] was named Assistant Secretary of War.[46]

Simultaneously, over the period beginning in late May, Frankfurter privately reviewed and encouraged a plan devised by Clark and others to have the United States conduct its first peacetime draft. During the following September this plan also matured. Despite an initial total lack of support from professional politicians, Congress passed and the President signed the Selective Service Act.[47]

The natural—one is tempted to say inevitable—overlap between Frankfurter's war-related concerns and his thinking about the flag salute case was probably enhanced by a fact which may seem surprising to one who focuses only on Justice Frankfurter's passionate assertions about the dispassionate, insulated nature of the judicial process. The Justice's partner in these lobbying efforts, Grenville Clark, was not only an old friend and preparedness activist, but was a former legal associate of FDR's and the man who had introduced Roosevelt to Frankfurter.[48] He was also the leading signer and the responsible principal behind an American Bar Association Committee on the Bill of Rights amicus brief in support of the Witnesses in *Gobitis*. He had organized the committee, suggested the brief, and then supervised its drafting.[49]

Efforts to prepare the country for war and efforts at writing the

---

[44] SPENCER, note 43 *supra*, at 115 ff. (Spencer's account of the conversation is based on an interview with Frankfurter.) See also Frankfurter to Roosevelt, 4 June 1940, reprinted in FREEDMAN, note 31 *supra*, at 524, recapitulating arguments for Stimson and Patterson.

[45] Frankfurter to Patterson, 5 July 1932: "You will always remain my prize baby student—favorite editor-in-chief of the *Law Review*...." Quoted in BAKER, FELIX FRANKFURTER 240 (1969).

[46] In his placement of Patterson as Stimson's second, Frankfurter replicated a service he had performed for Stimson several decades earlier when Stimson was Secretary of State and needed advice on the appointment of an undersecretary. At that time Frankfurter's nominee was Joseph P. Cotton.

[47] See, generally, SPENCER, note 43 *supra*.

[48] BAKER, note 45 *supra*, at 24.

[49] "Most of the actual writing seems to have been done by the Chairman, Grenville Clark," MANWARING, note 15 *supra*, at 126, citing a letter to this effect from Walter Fennell, an ACLU lawyer active in the case.

salute opinion involved some of the same people and many of the same days. The psychological effect of this conjunction of people and events was to abet an inflated perception of the state's interests in *Gobitis*. It was as if the littering question in *Schneider* had arisen in the midst of an epidemic endangering the health of a nation, and as though a chief (albeit behind the scenes) medical officer was called on to write the opinion in that case.[50]

Nor were assessments of the relevant variables in *Gobitis* conducted only against the backdrop of contemporary events. Frankfurter saw the judicial role in this crisis in the context of his impressions of the judicial role in prior crises.[51] During the Great Depression, legislative action had been paralyzed by judicial reaction. Even before that, indeed for the whole of his adult lifetime, Felix Frankfurter had seen the Supreme Court cut down legislative initiatives dealing with what he viewed as pressing problems. As an academic, as a publicist,[52] and as a litigator[53] he had bitterly fought this tendency toward legislative emasculation by constitutionalization. He was not about to succumb to it now.

Here an argument advanced by the Witnesses was probably counterproductive. The Witnesses' lawyer attacked the salute requirement as an ill-advised experiment, indeed a "cruel experiment":[54]

> The modern-day compulsory flag saluting as a daily exercise or ceremony in the public schools is clearly an experiment. The nation has existed for more than a century without any such enforced rule or even the thought thereof.

[50] "I should think you historians fail, as much as you fail in anything, in recapturing that impalpable thing, what was in the air." FELIX FRANKFURTER REMINISCES 57 (Phillips, ed., 1960).

[51] In this, as in other respects, Frankfurter was not unique in his thoughts. See, *e.g.*, JACKSON, THE STRUGGLE FOR JUDICIAL SUPREMACY xv (1941): "The preservation of democracy on this continent may well depend on an effective government through which it may function. If we are now able to organize our economy effectively to support national defense against totalitarianism, it will be because it no longer can be slowed up by the obstacles to effective government which were interposed in the path of our national defense against depression."

[52] See, most notably, for example, Frankfurter's unsigned editorial, *Can The Supreme Court Guarantee Toleration?*, in KURLAND, ED., FELIX FRANKFURTER ON THE SUPREME COURT 175 (1970), decrying the fact that the "inclination of a single Justice, the tip of his mind—or his fears—determines the opportunity of a much-needed social experiment to survive, or frustrates, at least for a long time, intelligent attempt to deal with a social evil."

[53] See Brief for the Appellants, note 29 *supra*, at lxvi.

[54] Brief for the Respondents, p. 20.

This could not but have struck sparks from Justice Frankfurter. He seemed determined to make the *Gobitis* case—even if it was marginal to the war effort—an occasion for giving a clear signal to legislatures that their attempts to prepare the nation for war would not be hampered as efforts at dealing with past problems had been. Though the message came through in the opinion, the motive, and the context which generated it, were more starkly revealed in private correspondence. I return to the letter Frankfurter wrote to Stone, and quote from it more fully:[55]

> . . . it seems to me that we do not trench on an undebatable territory of libertarian immunity to permit the school authorities a judgment as to the effect of this exemption in the particular setting of our time and circumstances.
> For time and circumstances are surely not irrelevant considerations in resolving the conflicts that we do have to resolve in this particular case. Contingencies that may determine the fate of the constitutionality of a rent act (Chastleton Corp v Sinclair 264 US 543) may also be operative in the adjustment between legislatively allowable pursuit of national security and the right to stand on individual idiosyncracies.
> . . . I had many talks with Holmes about his espionage opinions and he always recognized that he had a right to take into account the things that he did take into account when he wrote Debs and others, and the different emphasis he gave the matter in the Abrams case.
> After all, despite some of the jurisprudential "realists" a decision decides not merely the particular case. Just as *Adkins v. Children's Hospital* had consequences not merely as to the minimum wage laws but in its radiations and in its psychological effects, so this case would have a tail of implications as to legislative power that is certainly debatable and might easily be invoked far beyond the size of the immediate kite.
> . . .

Frankfurter's reference to the *Adkins* case underscores two causes of his acts of inflation in this case. At one level *Adkins* stood for the debilitating effects Frankfurter saw as "radiations" from an adverse decision on the constitutionality of a particular statute.[56]

---

[55] Frankfurter to Stone, 27 May 1940, note 28 *supra*.

[56] See also FELIX FRANKFURTER REMINISCES, note 50 *supra*, at 103-4: "[S]econdly, a decision like the Adkins decision doesn't merely bring about the result in that case, but has very serious inhibiting influences on kindred legislation. . . . [A]ny other social

There, by striking down a women's minimum wage law, an activist Court had chilled progressive initiatives throughout the country. *Adkins* was an especially significant example of paralyzing negativism, because it was in sustaining this precedent and thus striking down a New York minimum wage law that the Court, in Frankfurter's judgment, reached its nadir during the New Deal years,[57] and it was in reversing *Adkins*, in *West Coast Hotel v. Parrish*,[58] that the Court began its climb back to respectability through restraint.

At another level the citation to *Adkins* reinforced the earlier reference to *Chastleton*. For in *Adkins* counsel attempted, through the medium of an 1106-page, heavily factual "Brandeis brief," to show that contemporary circumstances justified the questioned legislative action. But in *Adkins*, as contrasted with *Chastleton* (which a year later also dealt with a District of Columbia statute), the Court refused to consider anything other than juridical fact.[59] Reasoning from that vantage point, Justice Sutherland, for the majority, concluded that the Nineteenth Amendment and collateral "great changes" in the status of women brought "contractual, political and civil" inequalities between men and women, "almost, if not quite, to the vanishing point."[60] Thus, in the opinion of the Court, a legislature had no basis for specially regulating the wages of women.

---

legislation would encounter the argument that it's unconstitutional within the principle, or the meaning, or implication of the Adkins case. And so, while there might be only one bomb, as it were, the radiation from it did lethal damage to kindred legislation." On Frankfurter's largely futile efforts to limit "radiation" from *Adkins*, see Vose, *The National Consumers' League and the Brandeis Brief*, 1 MIDWEST J. POL. SCI. 267, 275, 281-82 (1957).

[57] Morehead v. New York ex rel. Tipaldo, 298 U.S. 587 (1936). And in the judgment of more objective observers as well, see JACOBS, LAW WRITERS AND THE COURTS 95 (1954): "With the decision in the *Adkins* case the apparent trend away from substantive due process, from liberty of contract, and from laissez faire was abruptly halted. In a very real sense the majority opinion delivered by Justice Sutherland . . . constitutes the high-water mark in the application of laissez faire principles by the Supreme Court."

[58] 300 U.S. 379 (1937).

[59] "We have also been furnished with a large number of printed opinions approving the policy of the minimum wage, and our own reading has disclosed a large number to the contrary. These are all proper enough for the consideration of the lawmaking bodies, since their tendency is to establish the desirability or undesirability of the legislation; but they reflect no legitimate light upon the question of its validity, and that is what we are called upon to decide." 261 U.S. at 559-60.

[60] 261 U.S. at 553.

The force of the recollection of this case at the time of *Gobitis* had to be great for Felix Frankfurter. For the counsel who wrote the "Brandeis brief" in *Adkins* and who argued that "On all these questions we appeal from 'judgment by speculation' to 'judgment by experience,' "[61] and who lost the case, was Frankfurter himself. The assertion of the relevance of circumstances was no thought of the moment inspired by the events of 1940. It was part and parcel of the complex attitude which Frankfurter brought to the *Gobitis* case.

IV

This essay is not intended as a complete analysis of the content or causes of Felix Frankfurter's position in the first flag salute case. Such an analysis needs to dwell, among other things, on Frankfurter's own assimilation as an immigrant Jew into American life and the relationship between that experience and the issues provoked by the conduct and the arguments of the Jehovah's Witnesses. The point here is a modest one which puts this complex of issues aside. It is that significant concepts were smuggled into the *Gobitis* opinion by the act of inflating one side of the question at hand. The question in *Gobitis* was made to seem different in kind from the question in *Schneider*, and it was made to pivot on a question of deference to a legislative judgment which had never been made. Though Justice Stone dissented from Frankfurter's opinion and a great Associate Justice later wrote an opinion reversing the holding in this case, though a generation of academics and others have criticized Justice Frankfurter's performance, the inflation in the *Gobitis* opinion has been largely unnoticed. In this, as in other cases, readers and writers of judicial opinions would do well to focus more on the questions asked before turning to the intellectual operation which generates the answers given.[62] As the point has been put in quite another context, "In our ends shall be our beginnings."

---

[61] Brief for the Appellants, note 29 *supra*, at lxvi; 261 U.S. at 535.

[62] I have tried to do this in the larger work described in the author's note at the beginning of this essay.

Civil Liberties and Democracy

By Henry Steele Commager

It is almost three years, now, since the Supreme Court held that a school board might legally require all children to salute the American flag, and that the religious scruples of some children did not justify an exception in their case. Now the question is coming before the Court again, and there is a good deal of speculation about the outcome of the new case.

This problem of the flag salute and the reluctant children seems—on the face of it—a minor one, a tempest in a teapot, as it were. But as in so many cases of this kind, it raises issues of profound importance—issues that go to the very fundamentals of our whole constitutional system, our whole way of life.

It raises the question, first, of religious liberty and the meaning of the guarantee in our Bill of Rights. It raises, next, the question of the right of the state to require, in the interests of national unity and patriotism, conformity to certain rules and practices. It raises, further, the question of the role of the Court in interpreting these conflicting rights and claims. And it raises, finally, the whole question of the reconciliation, in our system, of liberty and authority.

Right of the Majority

A good deal of nonsense has been written about this case and the issues involved. Conservatives have tried to make the whole thing a question of patriotism—in time of war—as if the Republic would totter on its foundations if a few school children refrained, for conscience's sake, from going through a particular ceremony. Liberals have painted the Supreme Court as an engine of despotism, and have conjured up bogeys of fascism and nazism. Most of those who have talked or written about the matter seem to have missed the point in the whole thing. That point can be put quite simply: does the majority have the right, within the wide arena of political power, to try its own experiments, even to make its own mistakes?

Let it be said, at once, that the school board requirement of compulsory flag salute presents no clear-cut issue of legality. The very fact that the courts differed on it should indicate that. No state may "deprive any person...of liberty...without due process of law"—and this has been interpreted to mean that no state may prohibit the "free exercise" of religion.

On the other hand, the state, through its local agencies, controls public education. Is the requirement that all children in public schools salute the flag a proper educational device? Is it a violation of the religious liberty of those who have religious scruples about this ceremony? How far may the legislature go in fitting the public educational scheme to its notions of what is desirable or necessary? How far should it go in yielding to alleged religious scruples?

Between Two Extremes

These are not easy questions—not nearly so easy as either conservatives or liberals would have us think. Much is to be said for the right of the legislature to control the educational program of its public schools, and if the legislature honestly believes that saluting the flag will make for a greater degree of national unity, it should, perhaps, be indulged in that belief. Much is to be said, too, for yielding as far as is possible to religious scruples, no matter how absurd they may seem to ordinary people.

Yet there are obviously limits at both ends. We would not think it proper— or legal—for a legislature to require, for example, that all students in public schools be educated to Catholicism, or to Methodism. Nor would we, on the other hand, be inclined to give way to an alleged religious scruple against any reading or writing. We should say, in the first instance, that the legislature was going too far—was violating religious freedom. We would say, in the second, that no one could refuse to have his children educated on the plea that his religion didn't permit education—that is a specious plea.

The flag salute requirement lies somewhere between these extremes. Something is to be said for it as an experiment in education. Something is to be said, too, for the religious scruples of the children involved. It is not, in short, a clear-cut case.

Democracy Learns From Experience

Then comes the real question: who is to decide? This is really the question to which the Court addressed itself. The Court—speaking through Mr. Justice Frankfurter—did not approve of this flag salute requirement. Indeed, it expressed grave misgivings about this requirement. But it did say, is this a judicial question or is it a legislative question? Mr. Frankfurter put this well:

For ourselves, we might be tempted to say that the deepest patriotism is engendered by giving unfettered scope to the most crotchety beliefs...But the courtroom is not the arena for debating issues of educational policy ... So to hold would in effect make us the school-board for the country. That authority has not been given in this Court, nor should we assume it.

This seems to me to be the common sense of the matter. The compulsory flag salute is an experiment. It is probably a mistaken experiment. It will probably do more harm than good. But what is the proper remedy for a mistaken experiment? Is it to rush to the Court and ask the Court to nullify the misguided law? Or is it rather to allow public opinion to come around to the point where it recognizes the mistake and asks the legislature to repeal the law?

Has not the majority, in a democratic system, the right to make experiments, even to make mistakes? And can we not trust our legislature to correct their mistakes? Is there, indeed, any hope for democracy if it is to depend, always, on correction from the judiciary? Is not the surest guarantee of democracy the fact that it can and does learn from experience?

IN THE

Supreme Court of the United States

OCTOBER TERM, 1942

No. 591

THE WEST VIRGINIA STATE BOARD OF
EDUCATION, etc., et al.,
Appellants,

vs.

WALTER BARNETTE, PAUL STULL and
LUCY McCLURE,
Appellees.

BRIEF OF THE AMERICAN LEGION, Amicus Curiae

AUTHORITY OF THE AMERICAN LEGION TO FILE BRIEF AS AMICUS CURIAE IN THIS CAUSE

The American Legion, as Amicus Curiae, filed with the Clerk of this Court the written consent of the parties to this Cause, authorizing it to file a Brief as Amicus Curiae herein as required by Section 9 of Rule 27 of this Court.

OPINIONS BELOW

The opinions of the court below are reported in 47 Fed. Supp. (Adv.), page 251.

JURISDICTION

A statement as to jurisdiction has been filed and separately printed, pursuant to Rule 12, Paragraph 1 of this

Court. Jurisdiction is invoked under Section 380, Title 28, U. S. C. A. Probable jurisdiction was noted January 4, 1943 (R. 62).

STATEMENT OF THE CASE

This is an appeal from the judgment of the United States District Court for the Southern District of West Virginia rendered by a three-judge court convened under the provisions of Section 266, amended, of the Judicial Code (28 U. S. C. A. 380). The suit involves the constitutionality of a regulation or order promulgated by the West Virginia State Board of Education under the provisions of Section 5, Article 2, Chapter 18 of the Code of West Virginia, 1931 (Appendix A), and subject to the provisions of Section 5-a, Article 8, Chapter 18 of the Code of West Virginia, as last amended (Appendix A-1), and Section 9, Article 2, Chapter 18 of the Code of West Virginia, as amended by Chapter 38, Acts of the Legislature, 1941 (Appendix A-2). The regulation of the Board (Appendix B) requires children and teachers in the public schools to salute the American flag and provides that such salute become a regular part of the program of activities in the public schools, with the further provision that refusal to salute the flag be regarded as an act of insubordination to "be dealt with accordingly." Section 5-a, Article 8, Chapter 18 of the Code of West Virginia, as amended (Appendix A-1), provides, among other things, that failure of a child to comply with the established regulations of the State Board of Education shall result in refusal of further admission of the child to school until such regulations are complied with.

Suit was instituted August 19, 1942, in the District Court of the United States for the Southern District of West Virginia by three persons belonging to the sect known as "Jehovah's Witnesses," the parents of children attending the public schools of West Virginia, against the Board of Education of the State of West Virginia; claiming Federal jurisdiction because the regulation or order of the Board was a denial of religious liberty and was violative of rights which the First Amendment to the Federal Constitution protected against impairment by the Federal Government, and which the Fourteenth Amendment thereof protected against impairment by the states (R. 16); and further claiming jurisdiction in equity because of the absence of an adequate remedy at law (R. 15). The suit was brought by plaintiffs (appellees) in behalf of themselves, their children and all other persons in the State of West Virginia in like situation. The purpose of the suit was to secure an injunction restraining the West Virginia Board of Educaton (appellants) from enforcing against them an order or regulation requiring children in the public schools to salute the American flag (R. 1-16). The case was heard on application of appellees for an interlocutory injunction, but the parties to the suit agreed that it be submitted for a final decree on the bill of complaint and the motion of appellants to dismiss the bill.

Appellants moved to dismiss the bill on the grounds that the regulation of the Board was a proper exercise of power vested in it by the Legislature of the State of West Virginia; that under the doctrine of the case of *Minersville School District* v. *Gobitis,* 310 U. S. 586, the salute of the flag required by it could not be held to be a violation of religious rights of plaintiffs; and that the bill presented no substantial Federal question arising under the Constitution of the United States and involved no substantial Federal question because of the decision of this Court in the case of *Minersville School District* v. *Gobitis,* which decision had not been modified or overruled, and because there was no act of the Congress of the United States which undertook or purported to legislate with respect to the nature of the allegations contained in the complaint (R. 43-45).

It was and is the contention of appellees that to salute the flag, as required by the regulation of the Board, would do violence to the commands of Almighty God, according to Chapter 20 of the Book of Exodus (R. 3).

4

Disposition of Case by Trial Court

The court below determined that the regulation of the Board of Education, insofar as it required a salute to the flag from school children who have conscientious religious scruples against giving such salute, is violative of the rights of religious liberty guaranteed by the Fourteenth Amendment against infringement by the state; that plaintiffs were entitled to an injunction restraining the Board of Education, its agents and employees and all teachers in the schools of the state from requiring plaintiffs' children, or the children of other persons for whom the suit was brought and having religious scruples against giving the flag salute, to give such salute or from expelling them from school for failure to give the salute (R. 47-48).

Findings of Fact

Inasmuch as the case was submitted for decision upon the allegations of the bill of complaint and the averments of the motion to dismiss the same, the District Court summarized certain facts appearing therefrom. The court

> 1. That this is a suit to protect rights and privileges guaranteed by the 14th Amendment to the Constitution of the United States and the matter in controversy exceeds the sum or value of $3,000.00.
>
> 2. That plaintiffs are citizens of West Virginia and have children who attend the public schools of that state.
>
> 3. That plaintiffs and their children are members of a sect known as "Jehovah's Witnesses" and, as such, have conscientious scruples based on religious grounds against saluting the flag of the United States or any other national flag.

4. That the defendant, the West Virginia State Board of Education, has adopted a regulation requiring children in the public schools of the state to salute the flag of the United States and providing for their expulsion from school upon failure to give such salute.

5. That because of their conscientious scruples based on religious belief, plaintiffs and their children will not comply with the regulation of the Board of Education requiring the flag salute, and that the Board of Education unless restrained will expel plaintiffs' children from school for failure to comply therewith.

6. That, upon the expulsion of plaintiffs' children from school, they will be deprived of the benefit of education in the public schools to which they are entitled under the laws of West Virginia, and plaintiffs will have to pay to have them educated in private schools or be subject to prosecution under the compulsory education law of West Virginia for failure to send them to schools.

7. That this suit is brought by plaintiffs in behalf of themselves and all other persons similarly situated with respect to the enforcement of the regulation of the Board of Education.

Final Judgment

The court below in its final decree of October 6, 1942, awarded a permanent injunction restraining and inhibiting appellants from requiring the children of appellees, or any other children having religious scruples against such action, to salute the flag of the United States or any other flag, or from expelling such children from the public schools of the state for failure to salute it, as prayed for in plaintiffs' bill of complaint (R. 45-46).

SPECIFICATION OF ERRORS RELIED UPON

The American Legion as Amicus Curiae will rely upon the assignment of errors filed with the petition for appeal (R. 57) as constituting also the points stated to be relied upon (R. 60):

1. The Court erred in overruling defendants' motion to dismiss plaintiffs' complaint for want of jurisdiction.

2. The Court erred in holding, as a conclusion of law, that the regulation of the West Virginia State Board of Education, in so far as it requires a flag salute from school children who have conscientious scruples based on grounds of religion against giving such salute, is violative of the rights of religious liberty guaranteed by the 14th Amendment against infringement by the states.

3. The Court erred in holding, as a conclusion of law, that plaintiffs are entitled to an injunction restraining the State Board of Education, its agents and employees, and all teachers in the schools of the state from requiring plaintiffs' children or the children of other persons for whom the suit is brought, having religious scruples against giving the flag salute, to give such salute or from expelling them from school for failure to give same.

4. The Court erred in awarding the permanent injunction prayed for in the plaintiffs' bill.

5. The decision of the Court is counter to a decision of the Supreme Court of the United States handed down on June 3, 1940, in the case of *Minersville School District, Board of Education of Minersville School District, et al., Petitioners, v. Walter Gobitis, Indivilually, and Lillian Gobitis and William Gobitis, Minors, by Walter Gobitis, Their Next Friend*, reported in 310 U. S. 586, 84

Law. ed. 1375, which said decision has in no manner been overruled or modified.

SUMMARY OF ARGUMENT

I

The appellants' motion to dismiss the Bill of Complaint should be sustained as no substantial Federal question is involved.

> *Ex parte Poresky,* 290 U. S. 30, 32;
> *Louisville & Nashville Railroad Company* v. *Garrett,* 231 U. S. 298;
> *Utley* v. *City of St. Petersburg,* 292 U. S. 106;
> *Leoles* v. *Landers,* 302 U. S. 656;
> *Hering* v. *State Board of Education,* 303 U. S. 624;
> *Minersville School District, et al.* v. *Gobitis,* 310 U. S. 586, 594, 595.

II

House Joint Resolution 303 (Appendix C) does not supersede the Flag Salute Regulation adopted by appellants.

> House Joint Resolution 303, Public Law 623, 77th Congress (second session), passed and approved June 22, 1942 (Appendix C).
> *Barnette et al.* v. *The West Virginia State Board of Education,* 47 Federal Supp. 251, 255.

III

The regulation adopted by the West Virginia State Board of Education adheres to the principles enunciated by this Court and in no respect departs from or attempts to enlarge upon those principles.

> *Minersville School District, et al.* v. *Gobitis,* 310 U. S. 586;
> *Halter* v. *Nebraska,* 205 U. S. 34, 42, 43.

IV

The regulation of the West Virginia State Board of Education was designed to promote national security without which the free exercise of religious beliefs would ultimately fail.

> *Halter* v. *Nebraska*, 205 U. S. 34, 35;
> *Hamilton* v. *University of California*, 293 U. S. 245, 266, 268;
> *Minersville School District, et al.* v. *Gobitis*, 310 U. S. 586, 593.

V.

The Salute to the Flag and the Pledge of Allegiance as required by the regulation of the State of West Virginia Board of Education is not a religious rite and therefore not in conflict with the exercise of the religious views of the appellees.

> *People ex rel. Fish* v. *Sandstrom*, 279 N. Y. 523-529, 530;
> *Bleich* v. *Board of Public Instruction*, 139 Fla. 43-45, 190 So. 815.

ARGUMENT

I.

The Appellants' Motion to Dismiss the Bill of Complaint Should be Sustained as no Substantial Federal Question is Involved

The bill of complaint in this case alleges that the regulation promulgated by appellants requiring a salute to the Flag and the statutes of West Virginia pursuant to which such regulation was adopted violate the First and Fourteenth Amendments to the Constitution of the United States. Whether a substantial Federal question

9

is presented must be determined from a consideration of the allegations contained in the bill of complaint. *Ex parte Poresky,* 290 U. S. 30. In this case the court made the following observation:

> "* * * The question may be plainly unsubstantial, either because it is 'obviously without merit' or because 'its unsoundness so clearly results from the previous decisions of this court as to foreclose the subject and leave no room for the inference that the question sought to be raised can be the subject of controversy.' * * *"

Ex parte Poresky, 290 U. S. 30, 32.

In the further case of *Louisville & Nashville Railroad Company v. Garrett,* 231 U. S. 298, it was held that unless the Federal question is substantial, the jurisdiction fails.

In the case of *Utley v. City of St. Petersburg, Florida,* 292 U. S. 106, the court laid down the principle that no substantial Federal question forming a basis for review by this court was presented by the contention of invasion of a constitutional right where such question had been settled by previous decision of this court.

In the case of *Leoles* v. *Landers,* 302 U. S. 656, the validity of a regulation of the School Board of Atlanta, Georgia, requiring all pupils attending public schools to participate in certain patriotic exercises, including an individual salute to the Flag by each pupil, was involved. In the further case of *Hering* v. *State Board of Education,* 303 U. S. 624, the validity of a statute of New Jersey providing that every Board of Education should require the pupils to salute the Flag and repeat the Pledge of Allegiance every school day, was in question. In each of these cases substantially the same constitutional question presented in the instant case was involved, and in each case this court dismissed the appeal for the want of a substantial Federal question.

In the case of *Minersville School District, et al* v. *Gobitis*, 310 U. S. 586, 594, 505, which is the last expression of this court on the question presented in the bill of complaint, the court in an exhaustive opinion determined the question in controversy herein in the following language.

" * * * The religious liberty which the Constitution protects has never excluded legislation of general scope not directed against doctrinal loyalties of particular sects. Judicial nullification of legislation cannot be justified by attributing to the framers of the Bill of Rights views for which there is no historic warrant. Conscientious scruples have not, in the course of the long struggle for religious toleration, relieved the individual from obedience to a general law not aimed at the promotion or restriction of religious beliefs. The mere possession of religious convictions which contradict the relevant concerns of a political society does not relieve the citizen from the discharge of political responsibilities. The necessity for this adjustment has again and again been recognized. In a number of situations the exertion of political authority has been sustained, while basic considerations of religious freedom have been left inviolate. Reynolds v. United States, 98 U. S. 145, 25 L. ed. 244; Davis v. Beason, 133 U. S. 333, 33 L. ed. 637, 10 S. Ct. 299; Selective Draft Law Cases (Arver v. United States), 245 U. S. 366, 62 L. ed. 349, 38 S. Ct. 159, L. R. A. 1918C 361, Ann. Cas. 1918B 856; Hamilton v. University of California, 293 U. S. 245, 79 L. ed. 343, 55 S. Ct. 197. In all these cases the general laws in question, upheld in their application to those who refused obedience from religious conviction, were manifestations of specific powers of government deemed by the legis-

11

lature essential to secure and maintain that orderly, tranquil, and free society without which religious toleration itself is unattainable. * * *''

This case discusses and decides every substantial point raised by the appellees in their bill of complaint and expressly holds that a requirement that children attending public schools participate in a ceremony requiring a salute to the Flag and the Pledge of Allegiance does not infringe upon the due-process of law clause of the Constitution of the United States in its guarantee of religious liberties under the Fourteenth Amendment.

II

House Joint Resolution 303 (Appendix C) Does Not Supersede the Flag Salute Regulation Adopted by Appellants

The appellees in their bill of complaint have advanced the contention that House Joint Resolution 303, Public Law 623, 77th Congress (2nd session) approved June 22nd, 1942 (Appendix C) supersedes Section 5, Article 2, Chapter 18 (Appendix A); Section 5A, Article 8, Chapter 18 (Appendix A-1), Section 9, Article 2, Chapter 18 (Appendix A-2) of the Code of West Virginia, 1931, as amended, and the regulation of the West Virginia State Board of Education (Appendix B) promulgated pursuant thereto. (Record—Pages 11 and 12.)

The court below disposed of this question in the following language:

"We are not impressed by the argument that the powers of the School Board are limited by reason of the passage of the joint resolution of June 22nd, 1942, pertaining to the use and display of the flag.''

> *Barnette et al.* v. *The West Virginia State Board of Education,* 47 Federal Supp. 251, 255.

We believe this is a sound conclusion. A careful examination of that resolution discloses that it was adopted merely for the purpose of codifying and emphasizing existing rules and customs pertaining to the display and use of the Flag of the United States of America and the resolution does not attempt to establish any new rules or customs not already recognized as being in existence. It is not mandatory and does not attempt to outline a course of conduct to be observed by children attending public schools as it only codifies customs and rules for proper respect to the Flag when it is being hoisted or lowered, or when it is passing in a parade or in a review. Section 5 of the Act is as follows:

> "That during the ceremony of hoisting or lowering the flag or when the flag is passing in a parade or in a review, all persons present should face the flag, stand at attention, and salute. Those present in uniform should render the right-hand salute. When not in uniform, men should remove the headdress with the right hand holding it at the left shoulder, the hand being over the heart. Men without hats merely stand at attention. Women should salute by placing the right hand over the heart. The salute to the flag in the moving column should be rendered at the moment the flag passes." (Appendix C.)

We do not believe that this resolution was intended to carry the force or effect given it by the appellees and that it in no way conflicts with the West Virginia statutes or the regulation of the West Virginia State Board of Education in question.

III

The Regulation Adopted by the West Virginia State Board of Education Adheres to the Principles Enunciated by This Court and in no Respect Departs from or Attempts to Enlarge Upon Those Principles

The preamble of the regulation of the West Virginia State Board of Education, reads in part as follows:

"WHEREAS, The West Virginia State Board of Education honors the broad principle that one's convictions about the ultimate mystery of the universe and man's relation to it is placed beyond the reach of law; that the propagation of belief is protected whether in church or chapel, mosque or synagogue, tabernacle or meeting house; that the Constitutions of the United States and of the State of West Virginia assure generous immunity to the individual from imposition of penalty for offending, in the course of his own religious activities, the religious views of others, be they a minority or those who are dominant in the government, but

WHEREAS, The West Virginia State Board of Education recognizes that the manifold character of man's relations may bring his conception of religious duty into conflict with the secular interests of his fellowman; that conscientious scruples have not in the course of the long struggle for religious toleration relieved the individual from obedience to the general law not aimed at the promotion or restriction of the religious beliefs; that the mere possession of convictions which contradict the relevant concerns of political society does not relieve the citizen from the discharge of political responsibility, and

14

>WHEREAS, The West Virginia State Board of Education holds that national unity is the basis of national security; that the flag of our Nation is the symbol of our National Unity transcending all internal differences, however large within the framework of the Constitutions; that the Flag is the symbol of the Nation's power; the emblem of freedom in its truest, best sense; that it signifies government resting on the consent of the governed, liberty regulated by law, protection of the weak against the strong, security against the exercise of arbitrary power, and absolute safety for free institutions against foreign aggression, and
>
>WHEREAS, The West Virginia State Board of Education maintains that the public schools, established by the legislature of the State of West Virginia under the authority of the Constitution of the State of West Virginia and supported by taxes imposed by legally constituted measures, are dealing with the formative period in the development in citizenship that the Flag is an allowable portion of the program of schools thus publicly supported." * * *

The regulation, of which the foregoing excerpt is a part, was adopted June 9th, 1942. Apparently, the purposes to be effected by such regulation were primarily based on the sound fundamental principles laid down in the case of *Minersville School District, et al.* v. *Gobitis*, 310 U. S. 586, decided by this court June 3rd, 1940. A careful comparison of said regulation with the opinion expressed by the court in the above case clearly discloses that the West Virginia State Board of Education had directly in mind the promotion of national unity and solidarity, both of which are recognized as proper functions of the state in said opinion. The language employed in said regulation in many respects is taken verbatim from said opinion. The object to be accomplished thereby is expressly approved in said case.

The right of a state to strengthen patriotism and the love of country among its people by legislation encouraging respect for the flag has long been recognized. In the case of *Halter* v. *Nebraska,* 205 U. S. 34, the court made the following comment:
at pages 42 and 43 of said opinion made the following comment:

"So, a state may exert its power to strengthen the bonds of the Union, and therefore, to that end, may encourage patriotism and love of country among its people. When, by its legislation, the state encourages a feeling of patriotism towards the nation, it necessarily encourages a like feeling towards the state. One who loves the Union will love the state in which he resides, and love both of the common country and of the state will diminish in proportion as respect for the flag is weakened. Therefore a state will be wanting in care for the well-being of its people if it ignores the fact that they regard the flag as a symbol of their country's power and prestige, and will be impatient if any open disrespect is shown towards it. * * * * * that to every true American the flag is the symbol of the nation's power,—the emblem of freedom in its truest, best sense. It is not extravagant to say that to all lovers of the country it signifies government resting on the consent of the governed; liberty regulated by law; the protection of the weak against the strong; security against the exercise of arbitrary power; and absolute safety for free institutions against foreign aggression. As the statute in question evidently had its origin in a purpose to cultivate a feeling of patriotism among the people of Nebraska, we are unwilling to adjudge that in legislation for that purpose the state erred in duty or has infringed the constitutional right of anyone. On the contrary, it may reasonably be affirmed that a duty rests upon each state in every legal way to encourage its people to love the Union with which the state is indissolubly connected.''

Thus the duty of strengthening the bonds of the Union is not alone a Federal function, but must be shared by each state and its citizens if the ultimate in national unity is to be attained. The West Virginia State Board of Education in adopting the regulation in question was not attempting to set up a state religion, nor was it attempting to abridge the right of individual citizens to the free exercise of their personal religious belief. The purpose was entirely different; it was not restrictive, but affirmative in character, the promotion of national unity. The results to be obtained in nowise transcended or indicated a trend in excess of the principles enunciated by this court in the case of *Halter* v. *Nebraska*, 205 U. S. 34 and *Minersville School District, et al* v. *Gobitis*, 310 U. S. 586. We realize that possibly in times of great national emergency, prejudiced majorities might seize upon expressions made by this court, to advance their cause against helpless minorities and attempt to place a construction on such expressions which was never intended. When such practices occur, we are content to rest the judgment of such action with the sound discretion of this court. The regulation in question, however, is neither an attempted departure from, nor extension of the principles announced by the court. It is merely the exercise of a function adopted in conformance therewith for the promotion of a great common end, national cohesion. It is not designed to establish or restrict religious beliefs, but for the advancement of ''an interest inferior to none in the hierarchy of legal values.'' As stated by the court in the case of *Minersville School District, et al.* v. *Gobitis*, 310 U. S. 586-595, to-wit:

"National unity is the basis of national security. To deny the legislature the right to select appropriate means for its attainment presents a totally different order of problem from that of the propriety of subordinating the possible ugliness of littered streets to the free expression of opinion through distribution of handbills. Compare Schneider v. Irvington, 308 U. S. 147, ante, 155, 60 S. Ct. 146."

Doubtless, thousands of communities have adopted the salute to the Flag and the Pledge of Allegiance as a part of the training in the school room since the decision in *Minersville School District et al. v. Gobitis*, 310 U. S. 586 and this expression of patriotism has now become an accepted movement in the formative period of the child's education for the development of future citizenship. It would be going very far to say that the regulation in question had no reasonable connection with the common good and was not promotive of a sound public policy or that it did not strengthen national security without the preservation of which the very rights for which the appellees contend would ultimately be destroyed.

IV

The Regulation of the West Virginia State Board of Education was Designed to Promote National Security Without Which the Free Exercise of Religious Beliefs Would Ultimately Fail

The Regulation of the West Virginia State Board of Education (Appendix B) was designed to promote national security. The exercise of this function by a state is recognized in the case of *Minersville School District v. Gobitis*, 310 U. S. 586, 596 in the following language:

"Unlike the instances we have cited, the case before us is not concerned with an exertion of the legislative power for the promotion of some specific need or interest of secular society—the protection of the family, the promotion of health, the common defense, the raising of public revenues to defray the cost of government. But all these specific activities of government presuppose the existence of an organized political society. The ultimate foundation of a free society is the binding tie of cohesive sentiment. Such a sentiment is fostered by all those agencies of the mind and spirit which may serve to gather up the traditions of a people, transmit them from generation to generation, and thereby create that continuity of a treasured common life which constitutes a civilization."

The events which have transpired in our national life since the rendition of this decision have demonstrated that an adequate national defense is not alone concerned with armies and navies and matters distinctly military in character, but includes as well, the moral strength or public opinion of its citizens. This is vital to the maintenance of national security. Government can be destroyed more quickly by assaults from within than by attack from without. Nations have been destroyed by a break down in the public morale. Consequently, the state through its educational institutions is justified in adopting measures which will engender patriotism in the young people, who will represent the succeeding generations, for the great task of preserving the foundations upon which freedom of religious expression is founded. The paramount issue in the United States within the past two years has been national unity against forces which, if they were successful, would destroy the liberties upon which freedom of religion is based. This issue has permeated our entire structure from the National Government down to the smallest community.

The individual citizen has been impressed with the fact that his duty in this respect is of prime importance. The movement has no element of hysterics, but is predicated on the sound premise that the national conscience must be made aware of the necessity for national cohesion if we are to have national security. A state is not required to wait until the danger to public welfare is imminent, but may adopt sound measures to correct an evil in its inception. The regulation in question is not a war-time measure, but quite the contrary. It was designed to promote through educational means a better citizenship for the future and thus guarantee national security for succeeding generations.

It cannot be said that this regulation does not promote the common good in view of the fact that during the past few years we have witnessed the fall of many nations composed of liberty-loving people because their national security was not adequate.

The legislative body of a state has the right to establish and promote a sound public policy under the Tenth Amendment to the Constitution, and the courts have been slow in restricting the exercise of this right excepting in cases where some other right equally precious has been at stake.

> *Halter* v. *Nebraska,* 205 U. S. 34, 35;
> *Hamilton* v. *University of California,* 293 U. S. 245, 266;
> *Minersville School District* v. *Gobitis,* 310 U. S. 586, 593.

In the case of *Hamilton* v. *University of California,* 293 U. S. 245, Associate Justice Cardoza in a concurring opinion at page 266 of that decision made the following comment in this connection:

> "This may be condemned by some as unwise or illiberal or unfair when there is violence to conscientious scruples, either religious or merely

ethical. More must be shown to set the ordinance at naught. In controversies of this order courts do not concern themselves with matters of legislative policy, unrelated to privileges or liberties secured by the organic law.''

The freedom to follow conscience is a relative right, and while it may be exercised freely when not in conflict with some other right equally as well recognized, yet it must give way to the superior authority of a free people to adopt legislative policies which have for their ultimate purpose the very preservation of such right.

In discussing this right of the individual, Associate Justice Cardoza in the above cited case of *Hamilton* v. *University of California*, 293 U. S. 245, at page 268 stated as follows:

"The right of private judgment has never yet been so exalted above the powers and the compulsion of the agencies of government. One who is a martyr to a principle—which may turn out in the end to be a delusion or an error—does not prove by his martyrdom that he has kept within the law."

V

The Salute to the Flag and the Pledge of Allegiance as Required by the Regulation of the State of West Virginia Board of Education is not a Religious Rite and Therefore not in Conflict with the Exercise of the Religious Views of the Appellees

The salute to the Flag and the Pledge of Allegiance required of the school children under the regulation adopted by the West Virginia State Board of Education (Appendix B) is not a requirement pertaining to religion. The salute to the Flag by the placing of the right hand upon the breast is an act of respect of the highest order to the symbol of freedom. It in no way conflicts with the individual's freedom to worship Jehovah and was never intended to conflict therewith. It merely recognizes that the Flag represents the freedom upon which religious liberty rests—one of the most beloved rights yet developed by a political society. This salute does not engender in the mind of the individual the thought that the Flag is an image to be worshiped, or that it is a part of a religious rite. To assume such a position would be an admission that human emotions involving acts of respect and devotion all fall in the same category, and yet human experience teaches that this is not true. The devotion to Jehovah is as distinguishable from an act of respect towards the Flag as the love which a man bears to a devoted wife is different from the devotion he bears to his children. Nor is the Pledge of Allegiance a restriction upon the appellees exercise of their religious beliefs. A pledge is a promise (see Webster's New International Dictionary, Second Edition) as distinguished from an oath which might be termed a declaration invoking the Supreme Power. If the term ''promise'' is substituted for the word ''pledge'' in respect to the Pledge of Allegiance, it would read as follows:

> ''I promise allegiance to the Flag of the United States of America and to the Republic for which it stands; one nation indivisible, with Liberty and Justice for all.''

Thus, the individual making this pledge merely promises allegiance to the symbol of freedom and to the Republic which has exalted that freedom under which religious liberties are protected. It is a pledge of support to a political system which has established the right to worship Jehovah as the individual conscience dictates. The distinction is clearly pointed out in the recent cases of: *People ex rel. Fish* v. *Sandstrom,* 279 N. Y. 523, 529,

530; *Bleich* v. *Board of Public Instruction,* 139 Fla. 43, 45, 190 So. 815. Consequently, the salute to the Flag and the Pledge of Allegiance are promotive of the appellees rights and not restrictive, as they contend. A construction should be given to this ceremony in keeping with its intended purposes and in accord with the end to be accomplished.

VI

Legion's Position

The American Legion is interested in the preservation and promotion of national security, yet also believes in the preservation and protection of individual religious freedom as given by the First and Fourteenth Amendments to the Constitution and that this right should always be given freedom of expression except where it may conflict with the rightful exercise of that authority under which such freedom was created and through which it is protected.

The Preamble to the Legion's Constitution is prefaced with the clause: "For God and Country we associate ourselves together for the following purposes." The Preamble contains the following precepts

> "To uphold and defend the Constitution of the United States of America; to maintain law and order; to foster and perpetuate a one hundred per cent Americanism; to preserve the memories and incidents of our association in the Great War; to inculcate a sense of individual obligation to the community, state and nation; to combat the autocracy of both the classes and the masses; to make right the master of might; to promote peace and good will on earth; to safeguard and transmit to posterity the principles of Justice, Freedom and Democracy; to consecrate and sanctify our comradeship by our devotion to mutual helpfulness."

Our organization is composed of more than one million members who fought abroad and served at home in the last War in order to preserve and perpetuate our national security, upon which all of the freedoms which the individual citizen enjoys, is predicated. We therefore believe that when this security is involved it should be given prime consideration. Consequently, we feel that the regulaton in question, being promotive of national security, should be upheld.

VII

CONCLUSIONS

It is respectfully submitted:

(1) That appellants' motion to dismiss the bill of complaint should be sustained.

(2) That the flag salute regulation promulgated by appellants and the statutes of West Virginia affording a basis in law therefor, does not violate any of the provisions of the Constitution of the United States.

(3) That this Court in well-considered decisions has determined all of the questions raised in this case adversely to the contentions of appellees.

(4) That neither the West Virginia statutes nor the regulation of appellants complained of by appellees has been superseded by any act of the Congress of the United States.

(5) That the judgment appealed from should be reversed.

Respectfully submitted,

RALPH B. GREGG,
National Judge Advocate and General Counsel for The American Legion, Amicus Curiae.

Supreme Court of the United States

No. 591　　　　　　　　　　　　October Term, 1942

THE WEST VIRGINIA STATE BOARD OF EDUCATION, etc., et al.,

Appellants,

vs.

WALTER BARNETTE, PAUL STULL, AND LUCY McCLURE,

Appellees.

BRIEF OF THE COMMITTEE ON THE BILL OF RIGHTS, OF THE AMERICAN BAR ASSOCIATION, AS FRIENDS OF THE COURT.

Preliminary Statement.

This brief is filed by the Committee on the Bill of Rights, of the American Bar Association, as friends of the Court.[1] This Committee was permitted to intervene in the same capacity in Minersville School District v. Gobitis, 310 U.S. 586 (1940), which involved similar issues of the constitutionality of the compulsory flag salute for children in the public schools. The Committee appears with due authority from the American Bar Association, given in the manner described in our brief in the Gobitis case, to which we beg leave to refer. The consent of counsel for the parties has also been given.

The Gobitis case related to the constitutionality of a regulation of the Minersville School District in Pennsylvania estab-

---

[1] The membership of the Committee is as follows: Douglas Arant, Chairman (Alabama); Julius Birge (Indiana); George L. Buist (South Carolina); William D. Campbell (California); Zechariah Chafee, Jr. (Massachusetts); L. Stanley Ford (New Jersey); Abe Fortas (District of Columbia); George I. Haight (Illinois); H. Austin Hauxhurst (Ohio); Monte M. Lemann (Louisiana); Alvin Richards (Oklahoma); Earl F. Morris (Ohio); Burton W. Musser (Utah); Basil O'Connor (New York). George L. Buist does not join in this brief.

lishing the compulsory flag salute. The brief filed by this Committee opposed its constitutionality. The majority of the Court upheld the regulation. The present Chief Justice filed a dissenting opinion, contending that there had been an unconstitutional denial of religious liberty.

The case at bar concerns the constitutionality of a resolution of the West Virginia Board of Education, adopted January 9, 1942, requiring all pupils in the West Virginia public schools to participate regularly in a salute of the flag; and saying a refusal so to salute shall be regarded as an act of insubordination and dealt with accordingly. This means that the child will be excluded from school until he complies, and that his parents are liable to prosecution for his absence.[2]

This suit was brought in the United States District Court to enjoin the enforcement of the resolution by the Board of Education and other defendants. The plaintiffs are three members of an unincorporated religious body called Jehovah's witnesses, with children of compulsory school age, and they sue for the benefit of their own children and for all other Jehovah's witnesses in West Virginia who are similarly situated and their children, said to aggregate many hundreds. They state that all Jehovah's witnesses sincerely believe that the act of participating in the flag-saluting ceremony violates the Biblical Commandment against bowing down to graven images. The facts, as found by the trial court,[3] are that the plaintiffs and their children have conscientious scruples based on religious grounds against saluting the flag; that because of such scruples the children will not comply with the regulation of the Board of Education and will be expelled from school; and that the children will thus be deprived of public school education, and the plaintiffs will either have to pay to have them educated in private schools or be subject to prosecution under the compulsory education law of West Virginia for failure to send them to school.

The plaintiffs claim that they are thus deprived of the "liberty" guaranteed to them by the Fourteenth Amendment,

---

[2] W. Va. Code (1931) Chap. 18, Art. 8, as amended by Acts of Legis. (1941) c. 32.
[3] Record, p. 47.

which includes religious liberty guaranteed by the First Amendment. They say the resolution of the Board of Education on January 9, 1942, is also invalid because it has been superseded by a Joint Resolution of Congress of June 22, 1942.[4] Here Congress, after describing the pledge of allegiance to the flag, provided as follows:

> "However, civilians will always show full respect to the flag when the pledge is given by merely standing at attention, men removing their headdress. Persons in uniform shall render the military salute."

The defendants moved to dismiss the action for various reasons, including the constitutionality of the West Virginia regulation and the fact the complaint goes counter to the decision of this Court in the Gobitis case.

The district court of three judges, declining to follow the Gobitis decision, held the compulsory flag salute unconstitutional in so far as it applies to children having conscientious scruples, and enjoined its enforcement as to them. 47 F. Supp. 251 (1942). The defendants have appealed.

The Committee's Position.

The Committee has no interest in this litigation save as its outcome will affect the integrity of the basic right to freedom of conscience. Consequently, this brief will not discuss the effect of the Joint Resolution of Congress. This omission does not indicate any belief on our part that this federal statute is immaterial,[5] but simply that our sole concern is with the proper scope of religious liberty.

The constitutional issues in this case are the same as those in the Gobitis case. Therefore, the Committee has filed this brief in the hope that the Court will now, upon a reconsideration of that case, decide to follow the opinion of the present Chief Justice.

---

[4] 56 Stat. 380; 36 U.S.C.A., 1942 Cum. Supp. § 172.

[5] In fact, the majority opinion gave as one reason for upholding the Pennsylvania local regulation in 1940: "It is to be noted that the Congress has not entered the field of legislation here under consideration." 310 U.S. at 600, n. 7. Congress has since entered the field by the Joint Resolution of 1942.

4

ARGUMENT.

The Committee believes that the constitutional prohibition against the deprivation of liberty without due process of law is violated by the enforcement of the compulsory flag salute against children who have sincere religious scruples against participating in this ceremony. The reasons for the invalidity of the regulation are set forth fully in the opinion of the present Chief Justice in the Gobitis case and in the brief which this Committee filed in that case, to which we respectfully beg the Court to refer. The two essential reasons for our position will be briefly stated in this brief.

I.

The flag salute in its application to the plaintiffs and their children should be treated by this Court as a religious ceremony.

Most of us may regard it as merely a beneficial training in patriotism, as a "gesture of respect for the symbol of our national life"; but it does have religious significance *for them*. They feel it to be an idolatrous worship abhorrent to their deep spiritual emotions, a deadly sin to be shunned under peril of damnation. Therefore *as to them* it must be judged as a restraint on religious liberty which can only be justified, if at all, by very strong contravening public good. This problem of justification will be discussed under our second argument, but our immediate point is that such justification is necessary. The court may have to prevent a man from following the pathway revealed to him by the inner light, but it must not tell him that the inner light does not shine. The right of private judgment as to the religious quality of one's own conduct should be held inviolate. For a court to deny that right would strike at the heart of religious freedom. No American judge should presume to tell any person that he is wrong in his opinion as to how he may best serve the God in whom he believes.

This conclusion results naturally from the traditional American attitude toward small religious groups, an attitude which

5

forms an integral part of our way of life. These small groups have been accorded all rights and privileges granted to the larger and more ancient religious bodies.

It is of course true, even under Bill of Rights, that particular religious views from time have had to yield to the paramount demands of public health, safety or morals. But that, as we have just said, is an entirely distinct problem. Courts are competent to judge when the public welfare is in fact jeopardized by a belief, but they are not competent to judge that the belief is not religious. Here analysis and logic must yield to simple faith. It should, we submit, be deemed inadmissible for a court to brush aside a *sincere* religious objection because the same scruple is not held by most of the people, or because in the court's own view the scruple is theologically unsound. Such an official determination would presuppose a unity between church and state which is foreign to our most basic institutions.

The issue as to whether the individual should be the sole judge of his own religious belief is a very old one. For centuries, various sects have honestly ascribed religious significance to acts and ceremonies that, to the vast majority, held no religious meaning whatever. The Jews in Pilate's time considered the carrying of busts of the Emperor Tiberius through the streets of Jerusalem to be a violation of the Biblical Commandment involved in the present case. The early Christian soldiers thought the wearing of laurel wreaths to be incompatible with Christianity. The Quakers in seventeenth-century England declined to uncover their heads in court. The record of history shows that the existence and seriousness of religious beliefs are not to be measured by the current opinion of the time. The truth is that the existence of religious scruples lies within the mind and heart of the individual man or woman, and nowhere else. Here a man is the only judge of himself. No outsider, not even legislature or court, can decide what pathway will lead his spirit to salvation or what road will take him to a moral or a physical hell. Therefore the compulsion of a child to participate in a ceremony which he considers idolatrous worship cannot be brushed aside as raising no issue of religious liberty. For that child religious liberty is just as much at stake in his expulsion from the only

6

school his parents can afford as it was at stake for the Scotch Covenanters who were harried for refusing to listen to the Anglican prayer-book or for the English Catholics when they were heavily fined for absence from the parish church.

II.

This impairment of religious liberty has no reasonable tendency to promote any public interest.

Since the compulsory flag salute thus impairs the religious liberty of these children to worship only in their own way and the liberty of these parents to bring up their children in their own faith, the regulation must be invalid *as to them* unless it be essential for the attainment of some public purpose which is so important as to outweigh even the right to religious freedom. We do not contend that religious liberty is unlimited, but only that limits must be justified by a plain and strong public need. No clear showing has been made here, we submit, of any public good which is served by a ceremony regarded by the unwilling participants as idolatrous.

In the first place, this legislation is of a sort new to America. It is an attempt to *compel* a particular expression as distinguished from *restraints* on certain kinds of expression. Judges have recognized the validity of prohibitions against various practices even though they were actuated by religious motives, such as bigamy and polygamy, human sacrifices, suttee, thuggery and the religious belief in assassination, promiscuous sexual intercourse, the possession of sacramental wine in excess of a statutory limit, burial customs dangerous to health, and spiritualistic fortune-telling.[6] There the individual was forbidden to do something which he believed holy. It is a much more serious interference with his religious liberty to order him to do something which he believes to be unholy like participation in a religious ceremony violative of his beliefs. There is no precedent prior to the flag salute legislation for requiring a person to perform a particular ceremony contrary to his religious beliefs. The present regulation is novel also in that the legislative power is not here exercised, as in the cases just listed, in furtherance of the safety, morals, physical health or economic welfare of the people. In the few situations where religion was held not to excuse the

---

[6] The authorities for these and other prohibitions are given in the Committee's *Gobitis* brief, p. 28.

failure to perform affirmative acts, those acts were important in themselves, not a ceremony, and they bore a close relation to the public health and safety like furnishing medical aid to sick children or military training.[7] But the object of the present law is not to obtain definitely useful services, but merely to produce a state of mind. Religious liberty is now to be limited for the novel purpose of presumably promoting loyalty and morale and national unity.

The vital question before the Court is whether there is any clear relation between these purposes and this ceremony when performed by children who believe it a deadly sin. The resplendence of national unity and loyalty should not blind the Court to the need for clear proof that these purposes will be furthered by the *coercion of these children*. The advocates of the union of Church and State have constantly argued that it would promote national unity for all citizens to join in a common religious ceremony. True enough if there were no dissenters to whom the ceremony is abhorrent. Since there are dissenters, we Americans learned long ago that nothing is gained by forcing them to join in acts which they think impious. Therefore, an extension of American legislative power in this direction should be viewed with suspicion, and, *in the absence of a showing of clear necessity*, should be condemned as a deprivation of individual liberty without due process of law.

In any search for the required proof, it is important to recognize that the compulsory flag salute by children who object to it on religious grounds is an entirely different thing from such a salute by children who accept it as a mere gesture of proper respect to the nation we love. Any arguments that the salute is useful training to children in general have no bearing on the problem of its value to the few children who abhor it as image-worship. No evidence has been offered to prove that the salute has any educational value to such objectors, and the probabilities are so strongly to the contrary that the gap cannot be filled by judicial notice. The contention that the morale and loyalty of the children participating willingly would suffer if

---

[7] See the authorities cited on page 29 of our *Gobitis* brief.

the objectors were excused from the ceremony also rests on no evidence in the case or common knowledge to serve as the basis of judicial notice; and it is squarely rebutted by the present Chief Justice:[8]

> ". . . I cannot say that the inconveniences which may attend some sensible adjustment of school discipline in order that the religious convictions of these children may be spared, presents a problem so momentous or pressing as to outweigh the freedom from compulsory violation of religious faith which has been thought worthy of constitutional protection."

The vital question whether there is any reasonable connection between the attainment of national unity and the compulsory flag salute *by these children* against their consciences should, we submit, be answered by this Court. And it is for this Court to decide whether this relationship, if it exist, is sufficiently close to outweigh the value of religious liberty. Judgments of this nature cannot be entrusted to legislatures or school boards in cases involving civil liberties under the Bill of Rights. Such has not been the practice of this Court. In *Hague* v. *Committee for Industrial Organization*, 307 U.S. 496 (1939), the Court did not accept the judgment of the government of Jersey City that there was a necessary relationship between closing the streets and parks to speakers and the promotion of public safety. Here there was much more of a possible relationship shown by experience than that between a hateful ceremony and national unity, but the Court examined the connection itself and held it too thin to offset the right of free assembly. In *Stromberg* v. *California*, 283 U.S. 359 (1931), the connection between punishing salutes of the red flag and public safety was much more obvious than that between unwillingly saluting the United States flag and national unity in the case at bar. Yet the Court did not accept the judgment of the California legislature as to the sufficiency of the connection. Indeed, the Court held that the relationship was too remote to constitute the clear and present danger of overt acts which is essential for the denial of freedom

---

[8] *Minersville School District v. Gobitis*, 310 U.S. at 607.

of speech. The same severe scrutiny of the alleged relationship between the compulsory flag salute and national unity seems indispensable, in the case at bar, unless this Court be ready to hold that religious liberty plays a less important part in our national life than liberty of speech.

This is not a contest between two powerful economic groups, where the side which suffers from a statute has a fair chance to obtain a revision of the law from another legislature after a fresh election through the use of normal democratic processes. In such contests this Court hesitates to substitute its judgment for that of the legislature. Here, however, the contest is hopelessly unequal as the Chief Justice points out:[9]

> "Here we have such a small minority entertaining in good faith a religious belief, which is such a departure from the usual course of human conduct, that most persons are disposed to regard it with little toleration or concern."

Such a small religious group is very unlikely to attain sufficient voting power to overthrow compulsory flag salute laws. It must obtain protection from the Bill of Rights, or nowhere. Surely the First Amendment was not written to put the religious liberty of small groups at the mercy of legislative majorities and school boards.

> "The Constitution expresses more than the conviction of the people that democratic processes must be preserved at all costs. It is also an expression of faith and a command that freedom of mind and spirit must be preserved, which government must obey, if it is to adhere to that justice and moderation without which no free government can exist."[10]

In *Hague* v. *Committee for Industrial Organization*, 307 U.S. 496 (1939), and in *Schneider* v. *New Jersey*, 308 U.S. 147 (1939), this Court held that, when the fundamental individual liberties are at stake, the government is *restricted in its choice of methods* and may even be required to adopt some relatively inefficient and inconvenient means when it wants to achieve a proper purpose.

---

[9] Minersville School District *v.* Gobitis, 310 U.S. at 606.
[10] Stone, J., in Minersville School District *v.* Gobitis, 310 U.S. at 606-7.

11

If this doctrine is applicable to freedom of speech, is it not applicable also to the equally basic guarantee of liberty of conscience?

The Committee submits that the present case falls squarely within the rule of the *Hague* and *Schneider* decisions, and that the petitioner school authorities are required by the Constitution to adopt some alternative method or methods of fostering patriotism in school children instead of insisting upon the imposition of the salute upon children who object to it on religious grounds. Various alternative methods of this end are available and will readily occur to the Court.

Therefore, we contend that no public interest has been established sufficient to justify the enforcement of the compulsory flag salute against these children. The only public interest alleged is the promotion of loyalty, morale, and national unity. Even if such vague concepts can ever validate a law which interferes with religious liberty, they should not do so unless such interference is shown to be clearly needed to attain these purposes. Since the constitutional protection of religious freedom requires the Court to pass upon the alleged relationship between the law and the public interest instead of accepting the judgment of the school authorities upon a constitutional issue, then we believe that the Court will find no proof of any sort that the enforced participation of these children in a ceremony which they regard as sinful idolatry will promote either their loyalty or the loyalty of their schoolmates.

III.

The subsequent effect of the Gobitis Case shows the soundness of the opinion of the present Chief Justice that the compulsory flag salute is unconstitutional as to these children.

Instead of further arguments, we shall devote the rest of this brief to material of an entirely different kind which has become available since that case was decided. This material will show the effect of the *Gobitis* case in three respects:

> 1. The opinion of the present Chief Justice has been overwhelmingly accepted by subsequent legal discussion as the sound presentation of the proper scope of religious liberty.
>
> 2. In so far as school authorities have been affected by the actual decision of the Court, the result has been harmful to religious liberty.
>
> 3. State courts, instead of being influenced by the actual decision, have tended to follow the reasoning of the present Chief Justice.

We venture to hope that this material will assist the Court in reaching the conclusion that the opinion of the present Chief Justice should have been adopted as the decision of the Court in the *Gobitis* case, and that the Court will now adopt that opinion as the basis of constitutional protection for religious liberty.

1. *Legal discussion of the Gobitis decision overwhelmingly supports the opinion of the present Chief Justice.*

Legal discussion of a contemporary constitutional decision, so far as it gets into print, must be mainly obtained from legal periodicals, the reports of bar associations, and similar sources. Treatises are unlikely to be sufficiently up-to-date. A careful examination of the material just described shows that the Gobitis case has been discussed in 22 different legal publications (sometimes more than once). Out of these 22, 18 approve the opinion of the present Chief Justice; only 2 agree with the decision of the Court; and 2 simply describe the case without taking sides. Of course law is not made by counting the noses of law reviews and a moderate majority would have little importance for the present case. But when 18 out of the 20 publications taking sides on the issue regard the opinion of the present Chief Justice as the sound exposition of religious liberty, this fact shows a definite trend of professional opinion which ought not to be ignored. To find a precedent for such overwhelmingly adverse professional criticism of a decision by the Court, we should have to go back to *Adkins* v. *Children's Hospital*, 261 U.S. 525 (1923), which held that Congress could not constitutionally establish a minimum wage for women and children.

It is true that, if we leave aside the articles by law professors and practitioners, the comments cited were written by young men and women studying in law schools; but they are none the less important for being the thoughts of youth. The writers are among the ablest students in their respective schools. They are the bar and bench of the near future, so that their views forecast professional opinion. All of them wrote in 1940 and 1941 with the knowledge that they might soon be required to risk their lives in the defense of the nation. Therefore, the virtually unanimous belief of these young men and women that religious liberty must not be sacrificed for a supposed effort to promote patriotism is a strong indication that the opinion of the present Chief Justice truly expresses the meaning of the Bill of Rights.

Space permits only the quotation of a few brief extracts from this contemporary legal discussion of the *Gobitis* case. There is much of value in the other citations which are listed below.

Professor Thomas Reed Powell of Harvard Law School has written a careful examination of the decision in his essay, "Conscience and the Constitution," in a book edited by W. T. Hutchinson, *Democracy and Unity* (University of Chicago Press, 1941), pp. 18–31. He says (pp. 29, 30):

> "This is not to suggest that conscientious scruples can stand against all compulsion to do positive acts. Quite the contrary. The question is one of degree. I should think that

it requires more justification to compel a man or child to commit what he regards as sin than to restrict him in the areas in which he can practice what he regards as a command of the Lord. The public need should be pretty clear if it is to override conscientious objections against performing positive acts. The public need for armed defense may well be regarded as the most pressing public need of all. The public need for coerced and insincere saluting of the flag by little children seems to me to be trivial, and the effort to coerce it seems to me likely to be self-defeating. . . . .

"The dissent exposes the deficiencies in this particular compulsion of the young and points to alternative and better ways of attaining the very ends so strongly emphasized in the opinion of the majority. Clearly a contrary decision would have been no threat of the danger of making the state too weak to maintain its own existence."

Professor Robert E. Cushman of Cornell University, "Constitutional Law in 1939–40," 35 Am. Pol. Sci. Rev. 250, 271 (1941).

"[The majority opinion] falls far short of proving that national unity or any other desirable result will come from compelling school children publicly to affirm unfelt loyalties. All of the eloquence by which the majority extol the ceremony of flag saluting as a free expression of patriotism turns sour when used to describe the brutal compulsion which requires a sensitive and conscientious child to stultify himself in public."

W. G. Fennell, "The 'Reconstructed Court' and Religious Freedom: The Gobitis Case in Retrospect," 19 N.Y. Univ. L.Q. Rev. 31, 47 (1941).

"To exercise care in seeing that no legislation is permitted to stand which threatens the processes whereby political changes may ordinarily be effected is necessary, but alone it is not enough. . . . It is in such situations where prejudice against minorities curtails the operation of ordinary political processes that the Supreme Court has a duty to scrutinize even more carefully legislation which violates the rights of religious or racial minorities. . . .

15

> "If the ... [Court] continues to adhere in cases involving religious liberty to the doctrine of the majority in the *Gobitis* case, the scope of the state police power will be immeasurably enhanced and religious liberty will be at the mercy of shifting political majorities. It is to the lasting credit of the new Chief Justice that he comprehended that the Constitution expresses more than the conviction that democratic processes must be preserved at all costs; it is also an expression of faith and a command *which government itself must obey* that freedom of mind and spirit must be preserved."

Father Joseph T. Tinnelly, C.M., in 15 St. John's L. Rev. 95, 97 (1940) (it will be remembered that Jehovah's witnesses are bitter opponents of the Catholic Church).

> "It is conceded that there may be times when the government may lawfully demand a public and external manifestation of the loyalty of its citizens. But it has no right, in the face of religious protests, to demand that that manifestation assume a particular, arbitrary form, when some other and religiously unobjectionable form would serve its purpose equally well. If national unity may be attained and freedom of conscience left uninfringed by the use of means other than the flag salute, those means should be used. [A footnote refers to the fact that religious objections to the customary swearing of witnesses are respected by the provision of the alternative method of affirmation.] ... Patriotism and loyalty were not born in this country with the enactment of the first flag salute statute and the educational system which cannot foster them without infringing liberty of conscience is on the verge of pedagogical bankruptcy.

> "To be sure, national unity, freedom and security are fostered by external marks of respect for the flag which symbolizes them. But they are, nevertheless, independent of these acts. To forget this fact is to risk falling into a dangerous formalism; it is to confuse the symbol with the thing symbolized; the shadow with the reality; flag waving with patriotism. The patriotism of the Gobitis children is not on trial. The lower courts found that there was no question of their substantial loyalty. And when we have the substance of loyalty we can well afford to overlook the children's refusal to externalize it by some accidental and

16

arbitrary form to which they objected on religious grounds. The greater danger lies in false professions of loyalty; the undetected enemy saluting the flag he plans to destroy. There seems to be no valid reason, then, for the denial to the Gobitis children of their freedom of conscience and the compulsory flag salute would appear to be an unjustified and unconstitutional use of the police power."

The opinion of the present Chief Justice is also approved by the following:

1 Bill of Rights Rev. 267 (1941).

H. G. Balter, "Freedom of Religion interpreted . . ." 15 Cal. St. Bar J. 161 (1940).

14 Univ. Cincinnati L. Rev. 444; *id.* 570, 571 (1940).

26 Cornell L.Q. 127 (1940).

4 Univ. Detroit L. J. 38 (1940).

Dean Ignatius M. Wilkinson of Fordham Law School, "Some Aspects of the Constitutional Guarantees of Civil Liberty," 11 Fordham L. Rev. 50 (1942).

29 Georgetown L. J. 112 (1940).

9 Internat. Juridical Assn. Bull. 1 (1940).

T. H. Skemp, "Freedom of Religious Worship," 25 Marquette L. Rev. 19 (1940).

39 Michigan L. Rev. 149 (1940).

6 Missouri L. Rev. 106 (1941).

18 N. Y. Univ. L. Q. Rev. 124 (1940).

Professor Charles E. Carpenter, Southern California Law School, in 14 Univ. So. Cal. L. Rev. 56 (1940).

14 Univ. So. Cal. L. Rev. 73 (1940).

15 Wash. L. Rev. 265 (1940).

J. R. Green, "Liberty under the Fourteenth Amendment," 27 Wash. Univ. L. Q. 497 (1942).

17

Only two law reviews have been found since the Gobitis case which favor constitutionality:

> 9 Jo. Bar Assn. of Kansas 276 (1941) [but compare the later Kansas decision stated *infra* p. 23].
>
> 14 Temple L. Q. 545 (1940).

The remaining discussions of the Gobitis case in legal periodicals take no position on either side:

> C. G. Galston, "Conscription of the Mind in Support of the Bill of Rights," 1 Bill of Rights Rev. 269 (1941).
>
> 3 Ga. Bar J. No. 2, p. 66 (Nov. 1940). The reversed decision by the Circuit Court of Appeals was approved in 2 *id*. No. 4, p. 74 (May, 1940).
>
> H. Wright, "Religious Liberty under the Constitution of the United States," 27 Va. L. Rev. 75 (1940).

To complete the picture of law review opinion, we may mention that several reviews which did not discuss the decision of the Court in the Gobitis case had already opposed the validity of the compulsory flag-salute in reviewing the case below or state cases.

> 20 Boston Univ. L. Rev. 356 (1940).
>
> 9 Brooklyn L. Rev. 205 (1940).
>
> 51 Harv. L. Rev. 1418 (1938).
>
> 23 Ia. L. Rev. 424 (1938).
>
> F. W. Grinnell, "Children, the Bill of Rights and the American Flag," 24 Mass. L.Q.No.2, p. 1 (April-June 1939), *id*. No. 3, p. 1 (July-Sept. 1939), *id*. No. 4, p. 18 (Oct.-Dec. 1939).
>
> 23 Minn. L. Rev. 247 (1939).
>
> 74 New York L. Rev. 4 (1940).
>
> 18 Ore. L. Rev. 122 (1939).
>
> 86 Univ. Pa. L. Rev. 431 (1938).
>
> 2 Univ. Pittsburgh L. Rev. 206 (1936).
>
> 12 Rocky Mt. L. Rev. 202 (1940).

18

By contrast only two law reviews upheld the compulsory flag-salute in these earlier discussions:

8 Geo. Wash. L. Rev. 1094 (1940).

Professor E. M. Million of University of Idaho Law School, "Validity of Compulsory Flag Salutes in Public Schools," 28 Ky. L.J. 306 (1940) (questioning wisdom of compulsion).

The following law reviews were non-committal:

6 Kans. City L. Rev. 217 (1938).

14 Notre Dame Lawy. 115 (1938).

2 Law Journal of the Student Bar Assn., Ohio State Univ., 151 (1936) (questioning wisdom of regulation).

2. *The continued enforcement of the flag salute against children with religious scruples, which the* Gobitis *decision permitted, has been harmful to religious liberty.*

The decision in the *Gobitis* case merely held that the children could be expelled from a public school for refusing to salute the flag. It did not say what was to happen to them afterwards. But the decision left the children and their parents in a dilemma. Unless they were wealthy enough to send them to a private school, what was to be done? If the children went to another public school, they would merely suffer another expulsion. If they stayed at home, the parents would be prosecuted and imprisoned. Furthermore, statutes could easily be construed to make the expelled children juvenile offenders for their disobedience of a valid school regulation. The line is very thin between wrongdoing which deserves expulsion from a public school and wrongdoing which deserves commitment to a reform school. The parents too became liable to prosecution in some states for not returning their children to the very public school from which they had been expelled. Attempts have even been made to remove children from the custody of their parents on the ground of unfitness to bring them up.[11]

---

[11] See Fennell, *op. cit. supra*, 19 N.Y.U.L.Q. Rev. at 42; Plaintiff's Bill of Complaint, Record pp. 8–10; "The *Gobitis* Case in Retrospect," 1 Bill of Rts. Rev. 267

Some of these harsh proceedings were checked by court decisions, as we shall show, often because of some technical loophole in the school-laws; but for every parent or child thus judicially rescued there were possibly many more who went to jail or reform school because the local statute offered no hopeful loophole or because the family was too poor to resort to the courts.

Although the decision of this Court did not go so far as to send children to reform school or their fathers to jail, nevertheless the *Gobitis* decision by sanctioning expulsion made it easy for school boards to take the first step in a process which would naturally end in imprisoning somebody unless the board was willing to let the law become a dead-letter. And nothing in the decision provides a safeguard against the incarceration of father and child. Professor Thomas Reed Powell describes the whole situation:[12]

> "For the inanity of thinking that the ancient Hebrews gave or had authority to give any command not to salute the American flag, I have no real respect. Yet for little children I have great sympathy, however misguided the teachings and compulsions of their simple-minded, unintelligent parents. For the folly of excluding them from the benefits of public education I have nothing but contempt, on the very basis of the hopes of making them loyal Americans and of promoting national unity and patriotism. To commit them to institutions for the wayward and make them scholars in the schools of vice is to be guilty of an outrage that would make my blood boil. The decision under review does not sanction that . . . I cannot believe that the Supreme Court will permit such degradation and disgrace, although it left the Gobitis children to such poor and meager instruction as impecunious parents can provide, and it refrained from caveats that would distinguish other penalties from that of expulsion from public schools."

(1941). The actual operation of the compulsory flag salute with its attendant criminal proceedings is fully reviewed by Professor E. M. Million of Idaho University College of Law, 28 Ky. L.J. 306 (1940), written before the Gobitis case.

[12] *Op. cit. supra* p. 13 of this brief, at p. 28.

The truth is that this chaotic situation is bound to continue so long as the *Gobitis* decision stands. The only lawful ways out of the dilemma created by the compulsory flag salute for a family of Jehovah's witnesses are (a) compliance with the salute regulation, which is for them a deadly sin; and (b) a private school for which these persons, largely working people, cannot pay. If the sect provides its own school, this means tearing the children from home for an education inferior to that in the public schools. All other ways out are illegal and lead straight to jail if the compulsory salute law is worth enforcing.

Since no one benefits from a continuance of this chaos, there seems to be little public good to justify the prolongation of interference with religious liberty.

3. *State courts, instead of being influenced by the actual decision in the* Gobitis *case, have tended to follow the reasoning of the present Chief Justice.*

The three years which have elapsed since the *Gobitis* case have shown an extraordinary preponderance of professional opinion, set forth under heading 1 of this brief, that the opinion of the present Chief Justice was sound; and there has also been a striking desire on the part of courts to follow that opinion. In addition to the decision by the three-judge district court in the case at bar, this tendency has been exhibited in state courts. Before the *Gobitis* case a large number of state courts of last resort had upheld the constitutionality of the compulsory flag salute, whereas since the publication of the opinion of the present Chief Justice not a single state decision in a court of last resort has been found which sustains the expulsion of a child from public schools for refusing on religious grounds to salute the flag. States which previously favored constitutionality have continued to do so, but no new state has been added to the list. The trend has been in the opposite direction. While school authorities have been active in enforcing the compulsory flag salute by expulsions and prosecutions of parents and children, yet judges, whenever they had the opportunity to review a case, have taken a much more lenient attitude toward the dissenting children and their parents. The state court cases fall into two groups. The first group has kept the enforcement of the compulsory flag salute within narrow limits, and the second group has prevented its enforcement altogether.

In the first group of state cases children have been expelled from school for refusing to salute the flag, but the validity of this expulsion had either been settled by a previous decision or was not before the court. Instead, the court had to consider the question whether the school authorities could follow up the expulsion by sending the child to a reform school as a delinquent juvenile or by prosecuting the father for failing to send his child to public school. The following cases quashed such prosecutions:

Commonwealth v. *Johnson,* 309 Mass. 476, 35 N.E. 2d 801 (1941).

Although the Massachusetts statutes had previously been construed to permit the expulsion of the child from school, such exclusion was held not to imply such wrongdoing that the child could be committed to a county training school as a habitual offender. This severe penalty should not be imposed in the absence of express statutory provisions therefor. The constitutional question was expressly left aside.

State v. *Lefebvre* (N.H.), 20 A. 2d 185 (1941).

Children expelled from school for refusal to salute the flag had been adjudged delinquent and been committed to the Industrial School for their minorities. A powerful opinion by Judge Page refused to let family life be broken up and discharged the children, expressly relying on the opinion of the present Chief Justice.

Matter of Jones, 175 Misc. 451, 24 N.Y.S. 2d 10 (1940), same point.

Re Reed, 262 App. Div. 814, 30 N.Y.S. 2d 702 (1941), same point.

Commonwealth v. *Nemchick,* Court of Quarter Sessions. Luzerne County, Pa. (Nov. 20, 1942), unreported.

In Pennsylvania, the very state where the *Gobitis* case arose, the conviction of a mother for failure to have her expelled children attend school was reversed. The decision rested partly on the fact that the school authorities did not give the required written notice three days before proceeding against her; but the court also held that the entire regulation prescribing the compulsory flag salute was invalidated by the Act of Congress of June 22, 1942, quoted in the Introduction in this brief.

Bolling v. *Superior Court for Clallam County*, Supreme Court of Washington (January 29, 1943), not yet reported.

Children of Jehovah's witnesses were expelled from school for refusal to salute the flag. The parents had no other means of educating them. The children were brought before the juvenile court as delinquent and declared to be wards of the court. They were taken away from their parents on a finding that the parents had neglected and refused to provide and permit proper training and education, and were placed in charge of their older sister. The Supreme Court of Washington issued a writ of prohibition to prevent the enforcement of this order, holding it to violate the Fourteenth Amendment, the Joint Resolution of Congress quoted *supra* page 3, and Amendment 4 to the Washington Constitution. The court, through Judge Beals, relied on the opinion of the former Chief Justice, which was quoted at length, and expressed entire agreement with the decision of the District Court in the case at bar. Although the validity of the expulsions was not before the court, the reasoning of the opinion is completely opposed to any enforcement of the compulsory flag salute against these children.

The material portion of the Constitution of the State of Washington, Amendment 4, reads: "Absolute freedom of conscience in all matters of religious sentiment, belief and worship, shall be guaranteed to every individual, and no one shall be molested or disturbed in person or property on account of religion; but the liberty of conscience hereby secured shall not be so construed as to excuse acts of licentiousness or justify practices inconsistent with the peace and safety of the state. . . ."

The preceding cases leave the children and their parents safely at home, although the children remain deprived of any education.[12a] The cases now to be considered reached the still

---

[12a] But see State *v.* Davis (Ariz.) 120 P. 2d 808 (1942) as to criminality of parents for instructing their children.

more desirable result of restoring the children to their normal status in a public school.

> *State* v. *Smith*, 155 Kans. 588, 127 P. 2d 518 (1942).

In reversing a criminal prosecution against the parents of expelled children, the Supreme Court of Kansas expressly invalidated the earliest of all the compulsory flag salute statutes, holding that it could not be constitutionally construed to support the expulsion of children from school if they refused on religious grounds to participate in the ceremony. Religious liberty was held to receive a wider protection from the Kansas Bill of Rights than under the national Bill of Rights as construed in the Gobitis case. The Kansas Bill of Rights, § 7, reads:

> "The right to worship God according to the dictates of conscience shall never be infringed; nor shall any person be compelled to attend or support any form of worship; nor shall any control or interference with the rights of conscience be permitted, nor any preference given by law to any religious establishment or mode of worship. No religious test or property qualification shall be required for any office of public trust, nor for any vote at any election, nor shall any person be incompetent to testify on account of religious belief."

In Minnesota a District Court judge held that the expulsion of children from school for refusing on religious grounds to salute the flag violated the First and Fourteenth Amendments and also paragraph 16 of the Minnesota Bill of Rights.

> *Brown* v. *Skustad*, District Court for the Eleventh Judicial District, St. Louis County, Minnesota (December 12, 1942).

We respectfully submit that liberty of religion under the First and Fourteenth Amendments should have the same breadth as under the more detailed constitutional provisions of Kansas, Minnesota, and Washington.

Thus the three years since the Gobitis case have supplied much evidence as to the actual operation of the compulsory flag

24

salute. The nature of most of the recent cases has obliged staet judges to focus their attention upon what the enforcement of the law does to these children and their parents, rather than upon what it is supposed to do to the nation. The state courts have had before them children, otherwise loyal and well behaved, who had been rendered stubborn and rebellious at a critical time in their lives when steady growth and freedom from unnecessary emotional strains is essential. Their education has been demoralized by the expulsions which this Court sanctioned; some get piecemeal instructions from their parents; some are sent away to a distant sectarian school; others are torn from their homes and committed for the rest of their adolescence to institutions for juvenile delinquents. The state judges have had to deal with fathers and even mothers who have also been torn from their homes and sent to jail for no other crime than teaching their simple faith to their own offspring. These ugly facts have made glowing abstractions about loyalty and national unity seem increasingly remote from the enforced salute. When men see how enforcement of the flag salute against a conscientious child disunites his school and his family, they doubt the reasonableness of its power to unite the nation.

CONCLUSION

The regulation forcing the children of these plaintiffs to engage in a ceremony which they believe to be sinful is an interference with religious liberty. We recognize that some interferences with religious liberty are constitutional, for it is not unlimited. The value of religious liberty must be weighed in the scales against the value of the conduct which the law requires. It is a problem of balancing. But this Court in view of the constitutional mandate must do this balancing itself. Religious liberty has been the cherished possession of small minorities, and would lose all its safeguards were it entrusted to the judgment of majorities in legislatures or administrative bodies.[13]

Everybody recognizes that national unity is a great ideal, but the whole question is whether national unity has anything to do with the case. What is to be weighed in the scales is the value of the conduct which the law requires. The law does not require national unity and it could not. National unity is a creation of the spirit, and the wind of the spirit "bloweth where it listeth." What the law does require is the salute of the flag by children who regard such saluting as a damnable sin. What must be weighed is the value of that ceremony as performed *by these children*—not by some other children who welcome it but by these children who detest it as forbidden by the Word of God. On that alone should the attention of the Court be concentrated. Everything then turns on the question whether there is any *reasonable* connection between the enforced participation of the children in a sinful ceremony and the promotion of national unity. The more one looks squarely at facts and probabilities, the better he can see that there never was any *reasonable* connection. The means are wholly unfit to attain the end which we all desire. As the present Chief Justice observes:[14]

> "And while such expressions of loyalty, when voluntarily given, may promote national unity, it is quite another matter to say that their compulsory expression by children

---

[13] See Stone, J., Minersville School District *v.* Gobitis, 310 U.S. at 604–605.
[14] Minersville School District *v.* Gobitis, 310 U.S. at 605.

in violation of their own and their parents' religious convictions can be regarded as playing so important a part in our national unity as to leave school boards free to exact it despite the constitutional guarantee of freedom of religion."

The nation which survived Valley Forge and the dark days of the Civil War without compulsory flag salutes will not go to rack and ruin because a few children fail to participate in this novel ceremony on account of their religious beliefs. We respectfully urge the Court to adopt the view of the present Chief Justice that their absence will not endanger the safety of the nation. Robert Frost, the poet, put this whole case in a nutshell when he recently said in reply to the observation that Mr. Justice Stone's opinion showed no such fears:

"Yes, he knew the flag was all right, any way."

Accordingly, the Committee submits that the judgment of the lower court should be affirmed.

Respectfully submitted,

THE COMMITTEE ON THE BILL OF RIGHTS, OF THE AMERICAN BAR ASSOCIATION

DOUGLAS ARANT, *Chairman*
(of the Alabama Bar)

JULIUS BIRGE
(of the Indiana Bar)

WILLIAM D. CAMPBELL
(of the California Bar)

ZECHARIAH CHAFEE, JR.
(of the Rhode Island Bar)

L. STANLEY FORD
(of the New Jersey Bar)

ABE FORTAS
(of the Connecticut Bar)

GEORGE I. HAIGHT
(of the Illinois Bar)

H. AUSTIN HAUXHURST
(of the Ohio Bar)

MONTE M. LEMANN
(of the Louisiana Bar)

ALVIN RICHARDS
(of the Oklahoma Bar)

EARL F. MORRIS
(of the Ohio Bar)

BURTON W. MUSSER
(of the Utah Bar)

BASIL O'CONNOR
(of the New York Bar)

IN THE
SUPREME COURT OF THE UNITED STATES
OCTOBER TERM, 1942

No. 591

THE WEST VIRGINIA STATE BOARD OF EDUCATION, composed of HONORABLE W. W. TRENT, President, MARY H. DAVISSON, THELMA B. LOUDIN, RAYMOND BREWSTER, LYDIA C. HERN, L. V. THOMPSON, and MRS. DOUGLAS W. BROWN, and all other boards, officials, teachers and persons subject to the jurisdiction and control of said STATE BOARD OF EDUCATION,
Defendants-Appellants,

vs.

WALTER BARNETTE, PAUL STULL, and LUCY McCLURE,
Plaintiffs-Appellees.

ON APPEAL FROM THE DISTRICT COURT OF THE UNITED STATES FOR THE SOUTHERN DISTRICT OF WEST VIRGINIA

BRIEF FOR AMERICAN CIVIL LIBERTIES UNION, *AMICUS CURIAE*

Preliminary Statement

The American Civil Liberties Union is a non-partisan, non-sectarian organization, national in scope, with members in the State of West Virginia. The purpose of the

American Civil Liberties Union is to defend the fundamental liberties guaranteed to all Americans, regardless of creed, class or condition, by the Bill of Rights. Because the American Civil Liberties Union firmly believes that "our democratic form of government functioning under the historic Bill of Rights has a high responsibility to accommodate itself to the religious views of minorities however unpopular and unorthodox those views may be" (cf. dissent of Justices Black, Douglas and Murphy in *Jones* v. *City of Opelika,* 316 U. S. 584 at 623 (1942)), this brief *amicus curiae* is filed. It is solely in the interests of religious tolerance and reasonable solutions that the undersigned—none of whom are members of Jehovah's Witnesses or subscribers to their view on flag-saluting—have subscribed their names to this brief in support of the unanimous decision of the District Court for the Southern District of West Virginia (sitting as a three-judge court) (47 F. Supp. 251) (R. 48-54)*. It is submitted that the opinion of Circuit Judge Parker correctly decided the case and should be upheld by this Court.

The Issue

The only issue before the Court below, and the only issue before this Court on appeal, is whether the regulation of the West Virginia Board of Education**, which requires all pupils in public schools to salute the flag in a specified manner and provides that failure to salute shall be dealt with as "insubordination", when applied to the appellees, who admittedly have religious scruples about

---

* References to the Record are indicated "R."

** The full text of this regulation, adopted Jan. 9, 1942, is set forth in Appendix A.

saluting the flag (see opinion below, R. 54, 47 F. Supp. 251, at 253), is a valid and constitutional regulation?

The Court below held "that the regulation of the Board requiring that school children salute the flag is void in so far as it applies to children having conscientious scruples against giving such salute and that, as to them, its enforcement should be enjoined" (47 F. Supp. 251, at 255).

Statement of the Case

The facts are well summarized in the first paragraph of the opinion of the Court below as follows (R. 49):

> "This is a suit by three persons belonging to the sect known as 'Jehovah's witnesses', who have children attending the public schools of West Virginia, against the Board of Education of that state. It is brought by plaintiffs in behalf of themselves and their children and all other persons in the State of West Virginia in like situation, and its purpose is to procure an injunction restraining the State Board of Education from enforcing against them a regulation of the Board requiring children in the public schools to salute the American flag. They allege that they and their children and other persons belonging to the sect of 'Jehovah's witnesses' believe that a flag salute of the kind required by the Board is a violation of the second commandment of the Decalogue, as contained in the 20th chapter of the book of Exodus; that because of this belief they cannot comply with the regulation of the Board; that, if they fail to comply, the children will be expelled from school, and thus be deprived of the benefits of the state's public school system; and that plaintiffs, in such event, will have to provide them education in private schools at great expense or be subjected to prosecution for crime for failing to send them to school, as required

by the compulsory school attendance law of the state. They contended, therefore, that the regulation amounts to a denial of religious liberty and is violative of rights which the first amendment to the federal Constitution protects against impairment by the federal government and which the 14th Amendment protects against impairment by the States."

The defendants-appellants moved to dismiss the bill on the ground that the regulation of the Board was a proper exercise of the statutory power vested in it and that under the doctrine of *Minersville School District* v. *Gobitis*, 310 U. S. 586, the flag salute, which the regulation requires, cannot be held a violation of the rights of the plaintiffs-appellees (R. 43-45). The parties agreed that it be submitted for final decree on the bill and motion to dismiss. The Court denied the motion and issued an injunctive order enjoining the Board from enforcing the regulation against children having conscientious scruples against giving such salute (R. 45-46).

The appellants are the acting Board of Education of the State of West Virginia and joined with them are all other boards, officials and teachers subject to its control. This Board has general supervision over all public schools in West Virginia and is given power to determine the State's educational policies (except those of the State University) and to "make rules for carrying into effect the laws and policies of the State relating to education". (*The West Virginia Code of 1937,* Sec. 1730, Chap. 18, Art. 2, Sec. 5.) The statutes further provide that minors must attend public schools, or obtain equivalent private instruction, until they reach the age of sixteen. (*Op. Cit.* 1941 Cumulative Supplement, Sec. 1847, Chap. 18, Art. 8, Sec. 1.)

The instruction to be given in public schools includes "instruction in the history of the United States, in civics, and in the constitutions of the United States and of the State of West Virginia, for the purpose of teaching, fostering and perpetuating the ideals, principles and spirit of Americanism." (*Op. Cit.* Sec. 1734, Chap. 18, Art. 2, Sec. 9.)

On January 9, 1942, The West Virginia State Board of Education adopted the regulation here in question. The full text of the regulation is set forth in Appendix A. It will be noted that the regulation requires all teachers and pupils to participate in the "commonly accepted salute to the Flag of the United States" as a "regular part of the program of activities in the public schools". The prescribed salute as stated in the regulation is as follows: "the right hand is placed upon the breast and the following pledge is repeated in unison: 'I pledge allegiance to the Flag of the United States of America and to the Republic for which it stands; One Nation, indivisible, and with liberty and justice for all.'"

It is not to be overlooked that the regulation provides for a penalty for failure to perform the salute (in the precise manner prescribed) as follows:

> "provided, however, that the refusal to salute the Flag be regarded as an act of insubordination and shall be dealt with accordingly."

The West Virginia Code (1941 Cumulative Supplement, Sec. 1851, Chap. 18, Art. 8, Sec. 5a) provides for dealing with insubordination of pupils as follows:

> "If a child be dismissed, suspended or expelled from school because of refusal of such child to meet the legal and lawful requirements of the school and the established regulations of the county and/or

state board of education, further admission of the child to school shall be refused until such requirements and regulations be complied with. Any such child shall be treated as being unlawfully absent from the school during the time he refuses to comply with such requirements and regulations, and any person having legal or actual control of such child shall be liable to prosecution under the provisions of this article for the absence of such child from school.''

By Sec. 1851 and Sec. 1847 of the Code (*Op. Cit.*) such persons would be guilty, if convicted, of a misdemeanor and subject to a fine not exceeding $50 and a jail term of not exceeding thirty days.

Furthermore the children may be proceeded against as delinquents under Chap. 49, Art. 1, Sec. 4 and Art. 5, Sec. 1 of *The West Virginia Code* (1941 Cumulative Supplement, Sec. 4904 (4) and 4904 (49)).

The views of Jehovah's Witnesses on flag-saluting are so well known to this Court that it is unnecessary to summarize them here at length. (Cf. Briefs filed in *Minersville School District* v. *Gobitis*, 310 U. S. 586 (1940); *Johnson* v. *Deerfield*, 306 U. S. 621 (1939); *Hering* v. *State Board*, 303 U. S. 624 (1938); *Leoles* v. *Landers*, 302 U. S. 65 (1937).) They are sufficiently summarized for this appeal in the excerpt from the opinion of the Court below quoted at page 3 above. A full exposition may be found in the sole Exhibit introduced in the proceedings in the Court below (R. 16-43), which is a pamphlet entitled ''God and the State''. It should be noted that Jehovah's Witnesses are taught, and in turn teach their children, that saluting the flag is idolatrous, that it violates the second commandment of the Decalogue (Exodus 20:3-5) (R. 49) and that if they salute the flag in violation of that commandment, the penalty is "death everlasting, from which there is no resurrection"; while if they refuse to salute, "the most severe punishment the State can inflict upon him is death, from which death God will resurrect his faithful servants who have been put to death by man because of faithfulness to God." (Exhibit A, R. 41.)

Summary of Argument

In support of the decision of the District Court, argument is submitted on the following points:

1. The decision of this Court in *Minersville School District* v. *Gobitis*, 310 U. S. 586, should be reversed.

2. Enforcement of the regulation of the State Board, in so far as persons holding a religious belief and doctrine against giving the flag salute are concerned, deprives such persons of religious liberty and violates the Fourteenth Amendment to the Constitution of the United States.

3. Such deprivation of religious liberty is without due process of law since the State Board's regulation is not a proper exercise of the State's police power.

4. Congress having entered the field of legislation by the enactment of Sec. 7 of the Act of June 22, 1942, and having expressed the national policy in the matter of saluting the Flag of the United States, the regulation of the State Board is invalid.

POINT I

The decision of this Court in *Minersville School District* v. *Gobitis* (310 U. S. 586) should be reversed.

Affirmance of the decision of the Court below requires that this Court reverse its decision in *Minersville School District* v. *Gobitis,* 310 U. S. 586. The facts in that case were in all essential respects the same as in this case save for the fact that a regulation of the Minersville School District of Pennsylvania, instead of a regulation of the West Virginia State Board of Education was in issue.

We urge, first, that the *Gobitis* case was wrongly decided. This assertion is based, not upon the opinion of the legal profession generally (although such opinion has been preponderantly unfavorable to the *Gobitis* decision); but upon the expressed opinion of four of the seven justices, now members of this Court, who participated in the *Gobitis* decision. (*Op. Cit.,* 310 U. S. 586, dissenting opinion; *Jones* v. *City of Opelika,* 316 U. S. 584, special dissenting opinion.)

Only one of the unfortunate effects of the *Gobitis* decision has been the efforts to use it to justify the conviction of children refusing to give the salute on the ground that they are delinquents, and to take such children from their homes and confine them to State Reformatories. To the credit of all the higher courts, which have considered the question, however, they have "shrunk from so barbaric a result". (Cf. *"The Gobitis Case in Retrospect"* (1941), 1 Bill of Rights Rev. 627.) As the Supreme Court of New Hampshire said in such a case (*State* v. *Lefebvre,* 20 A. (2d) 185, 187 (N. H. 1941):

> "If the order appealed from is executed, these three children and their parents will be visited with

the breaking up of the family, an institution of primary value in our social life. * * * it is impossible for us to attribute to the Legislature an intent to authorize the breaking up of family life for no other reason than because some of its members have conscientious religious scruples not shared by the majority of the community * * *.''

Other courts have reached the same decision as the New Hampshire Supreme Court in refusing to carry the implications of the *Gobitis* decision to such an extreme result. *Commonwealth* v. *Johnson,* 309 Mass. 476; *Kansas* v. *Smith,* 155 Kansas 588; *Bolling* v. *Superior Court,* Washington S. C. No. 28909, Filed Jan. 29, 1943, opinion as yet unpublished; *In re Reed,* 262 App. Div. (N. Y.) 858; *Commonwealth* v. *Nemchik* (unpublished) (Court of Quarter Sessions, Luzerne Co., Penna.).

The precise question at issue in these cases admittedly was not before this Court in the *Gobitis* case. Now, however, that this Court has an opportunity to reverse that unfortunate decision, the record of attempts to apply it so as to make criminals of school children whose only "crime" is, in obedience to conscience, to refuse to salute the flag, cannot be overlooked by this Court.

Chief Justice Stone's dissent in the *Gobitis* case has impressed us deeply and the following short paragraph from his opinion sets forth in moving and succinct fashion the doctrine which we hope this Court may now think it proper to adopt:

"The guaranties of civil liberty are but guaranties of freedom of the human mind and spirit and of reasonable freedom and opportunity to express them. They presuppose the right of the individual to hold such opinions as he will and to give them reasonable free expression, and his freedom, and that of the state as well, to teach and persuade others by the communication of ideas. The very essence of the liberty which they guarantee is the freedom of the individual from compulsion as to what he shall think and what he shall say, at least where the compulsion is to bear false witness to his religion. If these guaranties are to have any meaning they must, I think, be deemed to withhold from the state any authority to compel belief or the expression of it where that expression violates religious convictions, whatever may be the legislative view of the desirability of such compulsion."

Minersville School District, et al. v. *Gobitis*, 310 U. S. 586, 604.

We urge as a second ground for reversal the fact that Congress, since the *Gobitis* case was decided, has entered "the field of legislation here under discussion". (Cf. *Minersville School District* v. *Gobitis*, 310 U. S. 586, prevailing opinion at 600.) By Act of June 22, 1942 (Title 36 U. S. C. A. Supp. 1942, Sec. 172) Congress has prescribed the manner in which the flag of the United States shall be saluted. Since this is a Congressional enactment in a field of national cognizance, a statute or regulation of any State (especially if it conflicts with the Act of Congress) must be invalid.

Our Points II and III, which follow, are directed at sustaining the first ground and our Point IV, the second ground, for reversal of the *Gobitis* case, as stated above.

11

POINT II

Enforcement of the regulation of the State Board, in so far as persons holding a religious belief and doctrine against giving the flag salute are concerned, deprives such persons of religious liberty and violates the Fourteenth Amendment to the Constitution of the United States.

A. Liberty of religious belief and doctrine is protected by the Fourteenth Amendment against impairment by the States.

Since the decision of this Court in *Cantwell* v. *Connecticut*, 310 U. S. 296, there is no longer any doubt that religious liberty is protected from impairment by the States by the Fourteenth Amendment.

In that case (at p. 303) this Court said:

> "The fundamental concept of liberty embodied in that amendment (i.e. the Fourteenth Amendment) embraces the liberties guaranteed by the First Amendment. The First Amendment declares that Congress shall make no law respecting an establishment of religion or prohibiting the free exercise thereof. The Fourteen Amendment has rendered the legislatures of the states as incompetent as Congress to enact such laws."

B. The belief and doctrine of appellees is religious in character.

The fact that the vast majority of Americans do not see in the salute to the national Flag other than a "ceremony calculated to inspire in the pupils a proper love of country and reverence for its institutions" (opinion below) (R. 50-51) does not belie the fact that Jehovah's Witnesses are quite honest and sincere in their belief that saluting the flag is idolatrous. The inability of the majority to comprehend the religious significance of the flag salute to which these appellees are opposed should not lead the Court to attempt to decide when a belief is a religious one.

On this point we quote also the opinion of the Court below (R. 51):

> "Courts may decide whether the public welfare is jeopardized by acts done or omitted because of religious belief; but they have nothing to do with determining the reasonableness of the belief. That is necessarily a matter of individual conscience. There is hardly a group of religious people to be found in the world who do not hold to beliefs and regard practices as important which seem utterly foolish and lacking in reason to others equally wise and religious; and for the courts to attempt to distinguish between religious beliefs or practices on the ground that they are reasonable or unreasonable would be for them to embark upon a hopeless undertaking and one which would inevitably result in the end of religious liberty."

This Court has forcefully condemned as "censorship of religion" a State Statute which conferred on a public official the power to determine whether or not a cause was a religious one. (*Cantwell* v. *Connecticut*, 310 U. S. 296, 305.)

The Supreme Court of Washington in a recent case (*Bolling* v. *The Superior Court* (opinion as yet unpublished) No. 28909, Filed Jan. 29, 1943) gives an interesting historical example of the religious significance of a gesture:

"Many examples of the importance of a mere gesture may be found in history. In the time of the Roman empire it was customary for the people to burn a pinch of incense before a statue of the emperor. The early Christians, while recognizing the sovereignty of the emperor, refused to perform this ceremony, deeming it idolatrous. Pliny the Younger, a lawyer of distinction, acting as governor of a Roman province in Asia Minor, had occasion to write to his friend, the Emperor Trajan, describing his difficulties in ferreting out and punishing Christians, as such, residing within his jurisdiction. He refers to the fact that an order to offer incense before the statue of the emperor was one test applied to ascertain whether or not a particular individual was a Christian. A refusal to perform the rite was equivalent to an affirmation that the one refusing was a Christian, and subject to the severe penalties of the Roman law. A phrase, or the making of a gesture, which to most people may seem either right or possibly unimportant, may to others appear to be of great significance."

C. The State of West Virginia deprives the appellees of liberty guaranteed to them by the Fourteenth Amendment by requiring them to surrender it as a condition of attending public schools of that State.

The West Virginia State Board of Education has been constituted by the Legislature of that State to have control over that State's public school system. (*The West Virginia Code*, Sec. 1730, Ch. 18, Art. 2, Sec. 5.) Accordingly action of that Board is state action for the purposes of this case. (*Lovell* v. *City of Griffin*, 303 U. S. 444; *Missouri ex rel. Gaines* v. *Canada*, 305 U. S. 337.)

The provisions of the regulation of the State Board (App. A) are clear: a child must salute the flag, and if he refuses he is guilty of an act of insubordination; he may be expelled and proceeded against as a delinquent. (*The West Virginia Code*, 1941 Cumulative Supplement, Sec. 4904 (4) and 4949 (49).) Since every child is required to attend school until he is sixteen (*Op. Cit.*, Sec. 1847) the regulation of the State Board, as applied to children of these appellees, amounts to withholding from them the privileges of public school education unless they abjure their religious convictions. This, we submit, is to deprive them of their religious liberty. (*Terral* v. *Burke Construction Co.*, 257 U. S. 529; and cf. *Missouri ex rel. Gaines* v. *Canada*, 305 U. S. 337, and *Hamilton* v. *Regents*, 293 U. S. 245.)

The question then arises as to whether they are deprived of such liberty by due process of law.

POINT III

Such deprivation of religious liberty is without due process of law since the State Board's regulation is not a proper exercise of the State's police power.

Discussion of this point brings us to the main point of dispute in this case. Of the sincerity of the religious beliefs of these appellees no question has been raised. The State has threatened to deprive them of their religious liberty and to deprive them of other liberties and privileges. In the language of the opinion below, "*Can it be said * * * that the requirement that school children salute the flag has such a direct relation to the safety of the state, that the conscientious objections of plaintiffs must give way?*"

A. The Courts and not the State legislative authorities must decide when religious liberty must yield to the exercise of a State's police power.

With due respect it is nevertheless submitted that one of the most unfortunate aspects of the *Gobitis* decision was the expressed doctrine that the courts are not free to pass judgment upon the legislative opinion that "the country will be better served by conformity than by the observance of the religious liberty which the Constitution prescribed." To say that "the courtroom is not the arena for debating issues of educational policy" is to overlook entirely the religious liberty aspect of the present issue. The State Board by its regulation (App. A) is not trying *to educate* the children of the appellees in any true sense; it is admittedly trying *to compel* them to perform an act (which their religion forbids them to perform). If this Court holds that it will no longer scrutinize legislation to determine when constitutional rights must yield to the exercise of the police power, then it will be abdicating the most important duty which rests on it under the Constitution. The effect of any such doctrine will be to enhance beyond any previous conception the police power of the states and religious liberty will be at the mercy of shifting political majorities. "Constitutional rights are not subject to nullification by reference to a popularity poll." (Alexander, J., dissenting in *Cummings* v. *State* (Supreme Court of Mississippi, No. 35155, Jan. 25, 1943, opinion not yet published).) We cannot believe that this Court has intended to hold—or will hold—that religious liberty, or any liberty guaranteed by the Bill of Rights, is a "local question".

We approve the language of the opinion of Judge Parker in the Court below (R. 53):

16

"This bill of rights is not a mere guide for the exercise of legislative discretion. It is part of the fundamental law of the land, and is to be enforced as such by the courts. If legislation or regulations of boards conflict with it, they must give way; for the fundamental law is of superior obligation."

B. In a case involving minorities, the Courts should make an even more searching judicial inquiry to see that any abridgment of the liberties of such minorities is by due process of law.

The appellees in this case are members of a religious minority which has been subjected to persecutions unparalleled in this country since the days of the Mormons. The whole story of the prejudice against, and persecution of, Jehovah's Witnesses has been told many times elsewhere. (Cf. for example, the pamphlet of the American Civil Liberties Union, "Jehovah's Witnesses and the War", Jan. 1943, a copy of which is annexed to this brief.) It is even safe to assume that the regulation of the School Board (adopted in January, 1942) (App. A) which is involved in this case was conceived in the milieu of prejudice which has grown up against these people because of their misunderstood attitude on flag-saluting.

It is submitted that this is "a special condition, which tends seriously to curtail the operation of those political processes ordinarily to be relied upon to protect minorities", and calls "for a correspondingly more searching judicial inquiry". (*United States* v. *Carolene Products Co.*, 304 U. S. 144, 152-153.)

It is not enough that the "effective means of inducing political changes are left free from interference". (*Minersville School District* v. *Gobitis*, 310 U. S. 586, 600.)

In the case of minorities such as Jehovah's Witnesses the effectiveness of such means may be purely illusory. A persecuted minority may suffer long before it can alleviate its burdens by way of the ballot box. It looks, and has the right to look under our Constitutional system, to the courts, and particularly to this Court, for redress of grievances.

It may be significant that since the *Gobitis* case was decided in 1940 no legislature or school board, so far as we know, has repealed or modified a compulsory flag salute law or regulation. Indeed some additional states have adopted it—including West Virginia, whose regulation is at issue in this case. Pragmatically, this does not commend the doctrine that somehow legislative authorities will themselves abandon "foolish legislation" if "the effective means of inducing political changes are left free".

We maintain that compulsion has never in this country been the handmaiden to patriotism. Neither the Constitution nor the courts are powerless to exorcise the whiplash of tyranny over a religious minority from our national scene. In the words of Chief Justice Stone in his dissent in the *Gobitis* case:

> "The Constitution expresses more than the conviction of the people that democratic processes must be preserved at all costs. It is also an expression of faith and a command that freedom of mind and spirit must be preserved, which government must obey, if it is to adhere to that justice and moderation without which no free government can exist. For this reason it would seem that legislation which operates to repress the religious freedom of small minorities, which is admittedly within the scope of the protection of the Bill of Rights, must at least be subject to the same judicial scrutiny as legis-

lation which we have recently held to infringe the constitutional liberty of religious and racial minorities.''

Minersville School District, et al. v. *Gobitis,* 310 U. S. 586, 606, 607.

C. The test to be applied is whether the failure to salute the flag as required by the State Board's regulation presents such a "clear and present danger to the community" as to justify the State's exercise of its police power to the extent of overriding appellees' religious liberty.

Freedom of religion implies not only freedom of belief but also freedom to act upon belief, so long as such action does not endanger the safety of the State. (*Cantwell* v. *Connecticut,* 310 U. S. 296.) No one contends "that what a man may do or refrain from doing in the name of religious liberty is without limitations". (Opinion below (R. 52).) This Court has held that he may not refuse to bear arms (*Hamilton* v. *Regents,* 293 U. S. 245) and he may not engage in polygamy or other practices which endanger the public health, morals or safety of the community. (*Davis* v. *Beason,* 133 U. S. 333.)

In cases involving freedom of speech and the exercise of police power this Court has wisely announced and applied the "clear and present danger" rule. This means that freedom of speech is not to be abridged unless its exercise presents a clear and present danger to the community. (*Bridges* v. *California,* 314 U. S. 252; *Herndon* v. *Lowry,* 301 U. S. 242; Cf. *Reynolds* v. *United States,* 98 U. S. 145, 163.) There is every reason to apply this same rule to the exercise of religious freedom.

Can it be said that the religious freedom of the appellees must give way because there is a clear and present danger to the State if these school children do not salute the flag? If grown men can advocate doctrines tending to the overthrow of the government under the constitutional guaranty of freedom of speech (so long as their advocacy does not present a clear and present danger to society), it is absurd to say that the failure of school children to salute the flag presents any greater danger to public safety.

Indeed the policy implicit in the State Board's regulation—to compel the child to salute and to punish him as a delinquent if he does not—not only has no tendency to instruct the children of West Virginia in loyalty to the flag and Constitution of the United States, but on the contrary, instils hatred and bitterness in such children and their parents. As such the conduct of the State Board —not the children who fail to salute—is the more "clear and present danger" to society.

As succinctly stated by Judge Parker in the opinion below (R. 54):

> "The salute of the flag is an expression of the homage of the soul. To force it upon one who has conscientious scruples against giving it, is petty tyranny unworthy of the spirit of this Republic and forbidden, we think, by the fundamental law. This court will not countenance such tyranny but will use the power at its command to see that rights guarteed by the fundamental law are respected."

The fact that we have constitutional guaranties requires accommodation of the powers which government normally exercises, when no question of civil liberties is involved, to the constitutional demand that those liberties be protected against the action of government itself. (*Minersville School District* v. *Gobitis*, 310 U. S. 586, 603.) "Unnecessary clashes" between the proper demands of the State and the dictates of conscience should be avoided. (*United States* v. *McIntosh*, 283 U. S. 605.)

POINT IV

Congress having entered the field of legislation by the enactment of Sec. 7 of the Act of June 22, 1942 (Public Law 623, 77th Cong. Ch. 435, 2nd Sess., Tit. 36 U. S. C. A. Supp. 1942, Sec. 172), and having expressed the national policy in the matter of saluting the flag of the United States, the regulation of the State Board is invalid.

At the time that the *Gobitis* case was decided by this Court, Congress had not entered the field of legislation and the opinion of the majority in the *Gobitis* case took note of this fact. (310 U. S. 586, 600.) However, on June 22, 1942, Congress enacted the following as a part of a codification of the rules and customs regarding the use of and respect due the flag of the United States:

> "Sec. 7. That the pledge of allegiance to the flag, 'I pledge allegiance to the flag of the United States of America and to the Republic for which it stands, one Nation indivisible, with liberty and justice for all', be rendered by standing with the right hand over the heart; extending the right hand, palm upward, toward the flag at the words 'to the flag' and holding this position until the end, when the hand drops to the side. However, civilians will always show full respect to the flag when the pledge is given by merely standing at attention, men removing the headdress. Persons in uniform shall render the military salute."

Since it is the purpose of the salute to the flag to promote "national cohesion" and "national unity" (*Minersville School District* v. *Gobitis*, 310 U. S. 586, 596-7), the subject is of national cognizance and the Act of Congress renders the acts and regulations of State legislative authorities invalid, whether or not they conflict with the Act of Congress.

Two flags float above the State House of most states—on the left the flag of the state, on the right the flag of the United States. Each is the emblem of an independent political society organized directly by its citizens. If the government in Washington should assume to imprison West Virginia children for refusing to salute the emblem of that state, citizens of West Virginia would feel very properly that the representatives of New York and California were meddling in matters with which they had no concern. It is for the citizens of West Virginia to determine what observance the state demands of children, and to decide what laws will best support the honor of their flag.

Conversely, it is not for West Virginia to put the Stars and Stripes in the position where innocent children following the dictates of religious training might suffer physical injury or impairment of their intellectual development because the children do not yield it what West Virginia considers suitable respect. This is a matter that concerns Maine, and New York, and California. It concerns the unity of a hundred and thirty million people. Only the representatives of that hundred and thirty million can establish the ceremony for saluting the American flag and define and punish the offense of disloyalty to the common emblem of the United States.

We submit that the present case is governed, in principle, by *Hines* v. *Davidowitz,* 312 U. S. 52. There a Pennsylvania statute for the registration of aliens was held invalid because Congress had dealt with the same subject in a national act. There was nothing in the Federal Constitution to forbid Pennsylvania to register aliens, nor did the Pennsylvania statute conflict with the Act of Congress in the sense that it was not perfectly practicable for aliens to obey both at once. Nevertheless the Pennsylvania statute was declared invalid because the subject was one of national cognizance and because Congress had indicated by its enactment the policy which it had determined to pursue. We submit that the obligation of citizens towards the national emblem is even more clearly of national cognizance.

Nevertheless in this case the situation is not merely that Congress and the State Board are occupying the same field with perfectly consistent legislation. The fact is that the State Board's prescribed method of saluting the flag *conflicts* with that prescribed by Congress. *Congress says:* "* * * civilians will always show full respect to the flag when the pledge is given by merely standing at attention * * *". *The West Virginia State Board orders:* "* * * that the commonly accepted salute to the Flag of the United States—the right hand is placed upon the breast and the following pledge repeated * * * and that all teachers * * * and pupils * * * shall be required to participate in the salute * * *".

If Congress in a field of national cognizance says that proper respect for the flag may be shown merely by standing at attention, it is not proper for West Virginia or any other state or local authority to require more and to seek to compel a particular form of salute which Congress has not seen fit to adopt. (*Adams Express Co.* v. *Croninger,* 226 U. S. 491, 506; *Charleston & Western Carolina Railway Co.* v. *Varnville Furniture Co.,* 237 U. S. 597.)

Furthermore and of great importance is the fact that Congress did not deem it wise, or see fit, to impose any penalties for failure to salute the flag. Obviously West Virginia may not create an offense and prescribe a penalty as to a matter of national concern, as to which Congress has legislated, but for which it has prescribed no penalty.

In *Charleston & Western Carolina Railway Co. v. Varnville Furniture Co.*, 237 U. S. 597, at 604, Justice Holmes said:

> "When Congress has taken the particular subject matter in hand coincidence is as ineffective as opposition, and a state law is not to be declared a help because it attempts to go farther than Congress has seen fit to go. *Chicago, R. I. & Pacific Ry. v. Hardwick Elevator Co.*, 226 U. S. 426, 435, *Southern Railway v. Indiana Railroad Commission*, 236 U. S. 439, 446, 447. The legislation is not saved by calling it an exercise of the police power * * *."

Conclusion

The regulation of the State Board is unconstitutional, and it is invalid because it is in conflict with an Act of Congress legislating in a field of national cognizance. The decision in *Minersville School District v. Gobitis* (310 U. S. 586) should be reversed and the decision of the District Court should be affirmed.

Respectfully submitted,

WILLIAM G. FENNELL,
OSMOND K. FRAENKEL,
ARTHUR GARFIELD HAYS,
Of the New York Bar,

HOWARD B. LEE,
Of the West Virginia Bar,
Attorneys for the American Civil Liberties Union, Amicus Curiae.

WEST VIRGINIA STATE BOARD OF EDUCATION ET AL. *v.* BARNETTE ET AL.

APPEAL FROM THE DISTRICT COURT OF THE UNITED STATES FOR THE SOUTHERN DISTRICT OF WEST VIRGINIA.

No. 591. Argued March 11, 1943.—Decided June 14, 1943.

1. State action against which the Fourteenth Amendment protects includes action by a state board of education. P. 637.
2. The action of a State in making it compulsory for children in the public schools to salute the flag and pledge allegiance—by extending the right arm, palm upward, and declaring, "I pledge allegiance to the flag of the United States of America and to the Republic for which it stands; one Nation, indivisible, with liberty and justice for all"—violates the First and Fourteenth Amendments. P. 642.

So *held* as applied to children who were expelled for refusal to comply, and whose absence thereby became "unlawful," subjecting them and their parents or guardians to punishment.
3. That those who refused compliance did so on religious grounds does not control the decision of this question; and it is unnecessary to inquire into the sincerity of their views. P. 634.
4. Under the Federal Constitution, compulsion as here employed is not a permissible means of achieving "national unity." P. 640.

5. *Minersville School Dist.* v. *Gobitis,* 310 U. S. 586, overruled; *Hamilton* v. *Regents,* 293 U. S. 245, distinguished. Pp. 642, 632.

47 F. Supp. 251, affirmed.

APPEAL from a decree of a District Court of three judges enjoining the enforcement of a regulation of the West Virginia State Board of Education requiring children in the public schools to salute the American flag.

Mr. W. Holt Wooddell, Assistant Attorney General of West Virginia, with whom *Mr. Ira J. Partlow* was on the brief, for appellants.

Mr. Hayden C. Covington for appellees.

Briefs of *amici curiae* were filed on behalf of the Committee on the Bill of Rights, of the American Bar Association, consisting of *Messrs. Douglas Arant, Julius Birge, William D. Campbell, Zechariah Chafee, Jr., L. Stanley Ford, Abe Fortas, George I. Haight, H. Austin Hauxhurst, Monte M. Lemann, Alvin Richards, Earl F. Morris, Burton W. Musser,* and *Basil O'Connor;* and by *Messrs. Osmond K. Fraenkel, Arthur Garfield Hays,* and *Howard B. Lee,* on behalf of the American Civil Liberties Union,—urging affirmance; and by *Mr. Ralph B. Gregg,* on behalf of the American Legion, urging reversal.

MR. JUSTICE JACKSON delivered the opinion of the Court.

Following the decision by this Court on June 3, 1940, in *Minersville School District* v. *Gobitis,* 310 U. S. 586, the West Virginia legislature amended its statutes to require all schools therein to conduct courses of instruction in history, civics, and in the Constitutions of the United States and of the State "for the purpose of teaching, fostering and perpetuating the ideals, principles and spirit of Americanism, and increasing the knowledge of the organization and machinery of the government." Appellant Board of Education was directed, with advice of the State Superintendent of Schools, to "prescribe the courses of study covering these subjects" for public schools. The Act made it the duty of private, parochial and denominational schools to prescribe courses of study "similar to those required for the public schools." [1]

The Board of Education on January 9, 1942, adopted a resolution containing recitals taken largely from the Court's *Gobitis* opinion and ordering that the salute to the flag become "a regular part of the program of activities in the public schools," that all teachers and pupils "shall be required to participate in the salute honoring the Nation represented by the Flag; provided, however, that refusal to salute the Flag be regarded as an act of insubordination, and shall be dealt with accordingly." [2]

---

[1] § 1734, West Virginia Code (1941 Supp.):

"In all public, private, parochial and denominational schools located within this state there shall be given regular courses of instruction in history of the United States, in civics, and in the constitutions of the United States and of the State of West Virginia, for the purpose of teaching, fostering and perpetuating the ideals, principles and spirit of Americanism, and ncreasing the knowledge of the organization and machinery of the government of the United States and of the state of West Virginia. The state board of education shall, with the advice of the state superintendent of schools, prescribe the courses of study covering these subjects for the public elementary and grammar schools, public high schools and state normal schools. It shall be the duty of the officials or boards having authority over the respective private, parochial and denominational schools to prescribe courses of study for the schools under their control and supervision similar to those required for the public schools."

[2] The text is as follows:

"WHEREAS, The West Virginia State Board of Education holds in highest regard those rights and privileges guaranteed by the Bill of Rights in the Constitution of the United States of America and in the Constitution of West Virginia, specifically, the first amendment to the Constitution of the United States as restated in the fourteenth amend-

The resolution originally required the "commonly accepted salute to the Flag" which it defined. Objections to the salute as "being too much like Hitler's" were raised by the Parent and Teachers Association, the Boy and Girl

---

ment to the same document and in the guarantee of religious freedom in Article III of the Constitution of this State, and

"WHEREAS, The West Virginia State Board of Education honors the broad principle that one's convictions about the ultimate mystery of the universe and man's relation to it is placed beyond the reach of law; that the propagation of belief is protected whether in church or chapel, mosque or synagogue, tabernacle or meeting house; that the Constitutions of the United States and of the State of West Virginia assure generous immunity to the individual from imposition of penalty for offending, in the course of his own religious activities, the religious views of others, be they a minority or those who are dominant in the government, but

"WHEREAS, The West Virginia State Board of Education recognizes that the manifold character of man's relations may bring his conception of religious duty into conflict with the secular interests of his fellowman; that conscientious scruples have not in the course of the long struggle for religious toleration relieved the individual from obedience to the general law not aimed at the promotion or restriction of the religious beliefs; that the mere possession of convictions which contradict the relevant concerns of political society does not relieve the citizen from the discharge of political responsibility, and

"WHEREAS, The West Virginia State Board of Education holds that national unity is the basis of national security; that the flag of our Nation is the symbol of our National Unity transcending all internal differences, however large within the framework of the Constitution; that the Flag is the symbol of the Nation's power; that emblem of freedom in its truest, best sense; that it signifies government resting on the consent of the governed, liberty regulated by law, protection of the weak against the strong, security against the exercise of arbitrary power, and absolute safety for free institutions against foreign aggression, and

"WHEREAS, The West Virginia State Board of Education maintains that the public schools, established by the legislature of the State of West Virginia under the authority of the Constitution of the State of West Virginia and supported by taxes imposed by legally constituted measures, are dealing with the formative period in the development

Scouts, the Red Cross, and the Federation of Women's Clubs.[3] Some modification appears to have been made in deference to these objections, but no concession was made to Jehovah's Witnesses.[4] What is now required is the "stiff-arm" salute, the saluter to keep the right hand raised with palm turned up while the following is repeated: "I pledge allegiance to the Flag of the United States of

in citizenship that the Flag is an allowable portion of the program of schools thus publicly supported.

"Therefore, be it RESOLVED, That the West Virginia Board of Education does hereby recognize and order that the commonly accepted salute to the Flag of the United States—the right hand is placed upon the breast and the following pledge repeated in unison: 'I pledge allegiance to the Flag of the United States of America and to the Republic for which it stands; one Nation, indivisible, with liberty and justice for all'—now becomes a regular part of the program of activities in the public schools, supported in whole or in part by public funds, and that all teachers as defined by law in West Virginia and pupils in such schools shall be required to participate in the salute, honoring the Nation represented by the Flag; provided, however, that refusal to salute the Flag be regarded as an act of insubordination, and shall be dealt with accordingly."

[3] The National Headquarters of the United States Flag Association takes the position that the extension of the right arm in this salute to the flag is not the Nazi-Fascist salute, "although quite similar to it. In the Pledge to the Flag the right arm is extended and raised, palm UPWARD, whereas the Nazis extend the arm practically *straight to the front* (the finger tips being about even with the eyes), *palm* DOWNWARD, and the Fascists do the same except they raise the arm slightly higher." James A. Moss, The Flag of the United States: Its History and Symbolism (1914) 108.

[4] They have offered in lieu of participating in the flag salute ceremony "periodically and publicly" to give the following pledge:

"I have pledged my unqualified allegiance and devotion to Jehovah, the Almighty God, and to His Kingdom, for which Jesus commands all Christians to pray.

"I respect the flag of the United States and acknowledge it as a symbol of freedom and justice to all.

"I pledge allegiance and obedience to all the laws of the United States that are consistent with God's law, as set forth in the Bible."

America and to the Republic for which it stands; one Nation, indivisible, with liberty and justice for all."

Failure to conform is "insubordination" dealt with by expulsion. Readmission is denied by statute until compliance. Meanwhile the expelled child is "unlawfully absent"[5] and may be proceeded against as a delinquent.[6] His parents or guardians are liable to prosecution,[7] and if convicted are subject to fine not exceeding $50 and jail term not exceeding thirty days.[8]

Appellees, citizens of the United States and of West Virginia, brought suit in the United States District Court for themselves and others similarly situated asking its injunction to restrain enforcement of these laws and regulations against Jehovah's Witnesses. The Witnesses are an unincorporated body teaching that the obligation imposed by law of God is superior to that of laws enacted by temporal government. Their religious beliefs include a literal version of Exodus, Chapter 20, verses 4 and 5, which says: "Thou shalt not make unto thee any graven image, or any likeness of anything that is in heaven above, or that is in the earth beneath, or that is in the water under the earth; thou shalt not bow down thyself to them nor serve them." They consider that the flag is an "image" within this command. For this reason they refuse to salute it.

---

[5] § 1851 (1), West Virginia Code (1941 Supp.):

"If a child be dismissed, suspended, or expelled from school because of refusal of such child to meet the legal and lawful requirements of the school and the established regulations of the county and/or state board of education, further admission of the child to school shall be refused until such requirements and regulations be complied with. Any such child shall be treated as being unlawfully absent from school during the time he refuses to comply with such requirements and regulations, and any person having legal or actual control of such child shall be liable to prosecution under the provisions of this article for the absence of such child from school."

[6] § 4904 (4), West Virginia Code (1941 Supp.).

[7] See Note 5, *supra*.

[8] §§ 1847, 1851, West Virginia Code (1941 Supp.).

Children of this faith have been expelled from school and are threatened with exclusion for no other cause. Officials threaten to send them to reformatories maintained for criminally inclined juveniles. Parents of such children have been prosecuted and are threatened with prosecutions for causing delinquency.

The Board of Education moved to dismiss the complaint setting forth these facts and alleging that the law and regulations are an unconstitutional denial of religious freedom, and of freedom of speech, and are invalid under the "due process" and "equal protection" clauses of the Fourteenth Amendment to the Federal Constitution. The cause was submitted on the pleadings to a District Court of three judges. It restrained enforcement as to the plaintiffs and those of that class. The Board of Education brought the case here by direct appeal.[9]

This case calls upon us to reconsider a precedent decision, as the Court throughout its history often has been required to do.[10] Before turning to the *Gobitis* case, however, it is desirable to notice certain characteristics by which this controversy is distinguished.

The freedom asserted by these appellees does not bring them into collision with rights asserted by any other individual. It is such conflicts which most frequently require intervention of the State to determine where the rights of one end and those of another begin. But the refusal of these persons to participate in the ceremony does not interfere with or deny rights of others to do so. Nor is there any question in this case that their behavior is peaceable and orderly. The sole conflict is between authority and rights of the individual. The State asserts power to condition access to public education on making a prescribed sign and profession and at the same time to coerce

---

[9] § 266 of the Judicial Code, 28 U. S. C. § 380.

[10] See authorities cited in *Helvering* v. *Griffiths*, 318 U. S. 371, 401, note 52.

attendance by punishing both parent and child. The latter stand on a right of self-determination in matters that touch individual opinion and personal attitude.

As the present CHIEF JUSTICE said in dissent in the *Gobitis* case, the State may "require teaching by instruction and study of all in our history and in the structure and organization of our government, including the guaranties of civil liberty, which tend to inspire patriotism and love of country." 310 U. S. at 604. Here, however, we are dealing with a compulsion of students to declare a belief. They are not merely made acquainted with the flag salute so that they may be informed as to what it is or even what it means. The issue here is whether this slow and easily neglected [11] route to aroused loyalties constitutionally may be short-cut by substituting a compulsory salute and slogan.[12] This issue is not prejudiced by

---

[11] See the nation-wide survey of the study of American history conducted by the New York Times, the results of which are published in the issue of June 21, 1942, and are there summarized on p. 1, col. 1, as follows:

"82 per cent of the institutions of higher learning in the United States do not require the study of United States history for the undergraduate degree. Eighteen per cent of the colleges and universities require such history courses before a degree is awarded. It was found that many students complete their four years in college without taking any history courses dealing with this country.

"Seventy-two per cent of the colleges and universities do not require United States history for admission, while 28 per cent require it. As a result, the survey revealed, many students go through high school, college and then to the professional or graduate institution without having explored courses in the history of their country.

"Less than 10 per cent of the total undergraduate body was enrolled in United States history classes during the Spring semester just ended. Only 8 per cent of the freshman class took courses in United States history, although 30 per cent was enrolled in European or world history courses."

[12] The Resolution of the Board of Education did not adopt the flag salute because it was claimed to have educational value. It seems to have been concerned with promotion of national unity (see footnote

the Court's previous holding that where a State, without compelling attendance, extends college facilities to pupils who voluntarily enroll, it may prescribe military training as part of the course without offense to the Constitution. It was held that those who take advantage of its opportunities may not on ground of conscience refuse compliance with such conditions. *Hamilton* v. *Regents,* 293 U. S. 245. In the present case attendance is not optional. That case is also to be distinguished from the present one because, independently of college privileges or requirements, the State has power to raise militia and impose the duties of service therein upon its citizens.

There is no doubt that, in connection with the pledges, the flag salute is a form of utterance. Symbolism is a primitive but effective way of communicating ideas. The use of an emblem or flag to symbolize some system, idea, institution, or personality, is a short cut from mind to mind. Causes and nations, political parties, lodges and ecclesiastical groups seek to knit the loyalty of their followings to a flag or banner, a color or design. The State announces rank, function, and authority through crowns and maces, uniforms and black robes; the church speaks through the Cross, the Crucifix, the altar and shrine, and clerical raiment. Symbols of State often convey political ideas just as religious symbols come to convey theological ones. Associated with many of these symbols are appropriate gestures of acceptance or respect: a salute, a bowed or bared head, a bended knee. A person gets from a

---

2), which justification is considered later in this opinion. No information as to its educational aspect is called to our attention except Olander, Children's Knowledge of the Flag Salute, 35 Journal of Educational Research 300, 305, which sets forth a study of the ability of a large and representative number of children to remember and state the meaning of the flag salute which they recited each day in school. His conclusion was that it revealed "a rather pathetic picture of our attempts to teach children not only the words but the meaning of our Flag Salute."

symbol the meaning he puts into it, and what is one man's comfort and inspiration is another's jest and scorn.

Over a decade ago Chief Justice Hughes led this Court in holding that the display of a red flag as a symbol of opposition by peaceful and legal means to organized government was protected by the free speech guaranties of the Constitution. *Stromberg* v. *California,* 283 U. S. 359. Here it is the State that employs a flag as a symbol of adherence to government as presently organized. It requires the individual to communicate by word and sign his acceptance of the political ideas it thus bespeaks. Objection to this form of communication when coerced is an old one, well known to the framers of the Bill of Rights.[13]

It is also to be noted that the compulsory flag salute and pledge requires affirmation of a belief and an attitude of mind. It is not clear whether the regulation contemplates that pupils forego any contrary convictions of their own and become unwilling converts to the prescribed ceremony or whether it will be acceptable if they simulate assent by words without belief and by a gesture barren of meaning. It is now a commonplace that censorship or suppression of expression of opinion is tolerated by our Constitution only when the expression presents a clear and present danger of action of a kind the State is empowered to prevent and punish. It would seem that involuntary affirmation could be commanded only on even more immediate and urgent grounds than silence. But here the power of com-

---

[13] Early Christians were frequently persecuted for their refusal to participate in ceremonies before the statue of the emperor or other symbol of imperial authority. The story of William Tell's sentence to shoot an apple off his son's head for refusal to salute a bailiff's hat is an ancient one. 21 Encyclopedia Britannica (14th ed.) 911–912. The Quakers, William Penn included, suffered punishment rather than uncover their heads in deference to any civil authority. Braithwaite, The Beginnings of Quakerism (1912) 200, 229–230, 232–233, 447, 451; Fox, Quakers Courageous (1941) 113.

pulsion is invoked without any allegation that remaining passive during a flag salute ritual creates a clear and present danger that would justify an effort even to muffle expression. To sustain the compulsory flag salute we are required to say that a Bill of Rights which guards the individual's right to speak his own mind, left it open to public authorities to compel him to utter what is not in his mind.

Whether the First Amendment to the Constitution will permit officials to order observance of ritual of this nature does not depend upon whether as a voluntary exercise we would think it to be good, bad or merely innocuous. Any credo of nationalism is likely to include what some disapprove or to omit what others think essential, and to give off different overtones as it takes on different accents or interpretations.[14] If official power exists to coerce acceptance of any patriotic creed, what it shall contain cannot be decided by courts, but must be largely discretionary with the ordaining authority, whose power to prescribe would no doubt include power to amend. Hence validity of the asserted power to force an American citizen publicly to profess any statement of belief or to engage in any ceremony of assent to one, presents questions of power that must be considered independently of any idea we may have as to the utility of the ceremony in question.

Nor does the issue as we see it turn on one's possession of particular religious views or the sincerity with which they are held. While religion supplies appellees' motive for enduring the discomforts of making the issue in this case, many citizens who do not share these religious views

---

[14] For example: Use of "Republic," if rendered to distinguish our government from a "democracy," or the words "one Nation," if intended to distinguish it from a "federation," open up old and bitter controversies in our political history; "liberty and justice for all," if it must be accepted as descriptive of the present order rather than an ideal, might to some seem an overstatement.

hold such a compulsory rite to infringe constitutional liberty of the individual.[15] It is not necessary to inquire whether non-conformist beliefs will exempt from the duty to salute unless we first find power to make the salute a legal duty.

The *Gobitis* decision, however, *assumed,* as did the argument in that case and in this, that power exists in the State to impose the flag salute discipline upon school children in general. The Court only examined and rejected a claim based on religious beliefs of immunity from an unquestioned general rule.[16] The question which underlies the

---

[15] Cushman, Constitutional Law in 1939–40, 35 American Political Science Review 250, 271, observes: "All of the eloquence by which the majority extol the ceremony of flag saluting as a free expression of patriotism turns sour when used to describe the brutal compulsion which requires a sensitive and conscientious child to stultify himself in public." For further criticism of the opinion in the *Gobitis* case by persons who do not share the faith of the Witnesses see: Powell, Conscience and the Constitution, in Democracy and National Unity (University of Chicago Press, 1941) 1; Wilkinson, Some Aspects of the Constitutional Guarantees of Civil Liberty, 11 Fordham Law Review 50; Fennell, The "Reconstructed Court" and Religious Freedom: The Gobitis Case in Retrospect, 19 New York University Law Quarterly Review 31; Green, Liberty under the Fourteenth Amendment, 27 Washington University Law Quarterly 497; 9 International Juridical Association Bulletin 1; 39 Michigan Law Review 149; 15 St. John's Law Review 95.

[16] The opinion says "That the flag-salute is an allowable portion of a school program *for those who do not invoke conscientious scruples* is *surely not debatable.* But for us to insist that, *though the ceremony may be required, exceptional immunity must be given to dissidents,* is to maintain that there is no basis for a legislative judgment that such an exemption might introduce elements of difficulty into the school discipline, might cast doubts in the minds of the other children which would themselves weaken the effect of the exercise." (Italics ours.) 310 U. S. at 599–600. And elsewhere the question under consideration was stated, "When does the constitutional guarantee *compel exemption* from doing what society thinks necessary for the promotion of some great common end, or from a penalty for conduct which appears dangerous to the general good?" (Italics ours.) *Id.* at 593. And again, ". . .

flag salute controversy is whether such a ceremony so touching matters of opinion and political attitude may be imposed upon the individual by official authority under powers committed to any political organization under our Constitution. We examine rather than assume existence of this power and, against this broader definition of issues in this case, reëxamine specific grounds assigned for the *Gobitis* decision.

1. It was said that the flag-salute controversy confronted the Court with "the problem which Lincoln cast in memorable dilemma: 'Must a government of necessity be too *strong* for the liberties of its people, or too *weak* to maintain its own existence?' " and that the answer must be in favor of strength. *Minersville School District* v. *Gobitis, supra,* at 596.

We think these issues may be examined free of pressure or restraint growing out of such considerations.

It may be doubted whether Mr. Lincoln would have thought that the strength of government to maintain itself would be impressively vindicated by our confirming power of the State to expel a handful of children from school. Such oversimplification, so handy in political debate, often lacks the precision necessary to postulates of judicial reasoning. If validly applied to this problem, the utterance cited would resolve every issue of power in favor of those in authority and would require us to override every liberty thought to weaken or delay execution of their policies.

Government of limited power need not be anemic government. Assurance that rights are secure tends to diminish fear and jealousy of strong government, and by making us feel safe to live under it makes for its better support. Without promise of a limiting Bill of Rights it is

---

whether school children, like the Gobitis children, must be *excused from conduct required of all the other children* in the promotion of national cohesion. . . ." (Italics ours.) *Id.* at 595.

doubtful if our Constitution could have mustered enough strength to enable its ratification. To enforce those rights today is not to choose weak government over strong government. It is only to adhere as a means of strength to individual freedom of mind in preference to officially disciplined uniformity for which history indicates a disappointing and disastrous end.

The subject now before us exemplifies this principle. Free public education, if faithful to the ideal of secular instruction and political neutrality, will not be partisan or enemy of any class, creed, party, or faction. If it is to impose any ideological discipline, however, each party or denomination must seek to control, or failing that, to weaken the influence of the educational system. Observance of the limitations of the Constitution will not weaken government in the field appropriate for its exercise.

2. It was also considered in the *Gobitis* case that functions of educational officers in States, counties and school districts were such that to interfere with their authority "would in effect make us the school board for the country." *Id.* at 598.

The Fourteenth Amendment, as now applied to the States, protects the citizen against the State itself and all of its creatures—Boards of Education not excepted. These have, of course, important, delicate, and highly discretionary functions, but none that they may not perform within the limits of the Bill of Rights. That they are educating the young for citizenship is reason for scrupulous protection of Constitutional freedoms of the individual, if we are not to strangle the free mind at its source and teach youth to discount important principles of our government as mere platitudes.

Such Boards are numerous and their territorial jurisdiction often small. But small and local authority may feel less sense of responsibility to the Constitution, and agencies of publicity may be less vigilant in calling it to account. The action of Congress in making flag observance voluntary [17] and respecting the conscience of the objector in a matter so vital as raising the Army [18] contrasts sharply with these local regulations in matters relatively trivial to the welfare of the nation. There are village tyrants as well as village Hampdens, but none who acts under color of law is beyond reach of the Constitution.

3. The *Gobitis* opinion reasoned that this is a field "where courts possess no marked and certainly no controlling competence," that it is committed to the legislatures as well as the courts to guard cherished liberties and that it is constitutionally appropriate to "fight out the wise use of legislative authority in the forum of public opinion and before legislative assemblies rather than to transfer such a contest to the judicial arena," since all the "effective means of inducing political changes are left free." *Id.* at 597–598, 600.

The very purpose of a Bill of Rights was to withdraw certain subjects from the vicissitudes of political controversy, to place them beyond the reach of majorities and officials and to establish them as legal principles to be applied by the courts. One's right to life, liberty, and property, to free speech, a free press, freedom of worship and assembly, and other fundamental rights may not be submitted to vote; they depend on the outcome of no elections.

---

[17] Section 7 of House Joint Resolution 359, approved December 22, 1942, 56 Stat. 1074, 36 U. S. C. (1942 Supp.) § 172, prescribes no penalties for nonconformity but provides:

"That the pledge of allegiance to the flag, 'I pledge allegiance to the flag of the United States of America and to the Republic for which it stands, one Nation indivisible, with liberty and justice for all,' be rendered by standing with the right hand over the heart. However, civilians will always show full respect to the flag when the pledge is given by merely standing at attention, men removing the headdress . . ."

[18] § 5 (a) of the Selective Training and Service Act of 1940, 50 U. S. C. (App.) § 307 (g).

In weighing arguments of the parties it is important to distinguish between the due process clause of the Fourteenth Amendment as an instrument for transmitting the principles of the First Amendment and those cases in which it is applied for its own sake. The test of legislation which collides with the Fourteenth Amendment, because it also collides with the principles of the First, is much more definite than the test when only the Fourteenth is involved. Much of the vagueness of the due process clause disappears when the specific prohibitions of the First become its standard. The right of a State to regulate, for example, a public utility may well include, so far as the due process test is concerned, power to impose all of the restrictions which a legislature may have a "rational basis" for adopting. But freedoms of speech and of press, of assembly, and of worship may not be infringed on such slender grounds. They are susceptible of restriction only to prevent grave and immediate danger to interests which the State may lawfully protect. It is important to note that while it is the Fourteenth Amendment which bears directly upon the State it is the more specific limiting principles of the First Amendment that finally govern this case.

Nor does our duty to apply the Bill of Rights to assertions of official authority depend upon our possession of marked competence in the field where the invasion of rights occurs. True, the task of translating the majestic generalities of the Bill of Rights, conceived as part of the pattern of liberal government in the eighteenth century, into concrete restraints on officials dealing with the problems of the twentieth century, is one to disturb self-confidence. These principles grew in soil which also produced a philosophy that the individual was the center of society, that his liberty was attainable through mere absence of governmental restraints, and that government should be entrusted with few controls and only the mildest supervision over men's affairs. We must transplant these rights to a soil in which the *laissez-faire* concept or principle of non-interference has withered at least as to economic affairs, and social advancements are increasingly sought through closer integration of society and through expanded and strengthened governmental controls. These changed conditions often deprive precedents of reliability and cast us more than we would choose upon our own judgment. But we act in these matters not by authority of our competence but by force of our commissions. We cannot, because of modest estimates of our competence in such specialties as public education, withhold the judgment that history authenticates as the function of this Court when liberty is infringed.

4. Lastly, and this is the very heart of the *Gobitis* opinion, it reasons that "National unity is the basis of national security," that the authorities have "the right to select appropriate means for its attainment," and hence reaches the conclusion that such compulsory measures toward "national unity" are constitutional. *Id.* at 595. Upon the verity of this assumption depends our answer in this case.

National unity as an end which officials may foster by persuasion and example is not in question. The problem is whether under our Constitution compulsion as here employed is a permissible means for its achievement.

Struggles to coerce uniformity of sentiment in support of some end thought essential to their time and country have been waged by many good as well as by evil men. Nationalism is a relatively recent phenomenon but at other times and places the ends have been racial or territorial security, support of a dynasty or regime, and particular plans for saving souls. As first and moderate methods to attain unity have failed, those bent on its accomplishment must resort to an ever-increasing severity.

As governmental pressure toward unity becomes greater, so strife becomes more bitter as to whose unity it shall be. Probably no deeper division of our people could proceed from any provocation than from finding it necessary to choose what doctrine and whose program public educational officials shall compel youth to unite in embracing. Ultimate futility of such attempts to compel coherence is the lesson of every such effort from the Roman drive to stamp out Christianity as a disturber of its pagan unity, the Inquisition, as a means to religious and dynastic unity, the Siberian exiles as a means to Russian unity, down to the fast failing efforts of our present totalitarian enemies. Those who begin coercive elimination of dissent soon find themselves exterminating dissenters. Compulsory unification of opinion achieves only the unanimity of the graveyard.

It seems trite but necessary to say that the First Amendment to our Constitution was designed to avoid these ends by avoiding these beginnings. There is no mysticism in the American concept of the State or of the nature or origin of its authority. We set up government by consent of the governed, and the Bill of Rights denies those in power any legal opportunity to coerce that consent. Authority here is to be controlled by public opinion, not public opinion by authority.

The case is made difficult not because the principles of its decision are obscure but because the flag involved is our own. Nevertheless, we apply the limitations of the Constitution with no fear that freedom to be intellectually and spiritually diverse or even contrary will disintegrate the social organization. To believe that patriotism will not flourish if patriotic ceremonies are voluntary and spontaneous instead of a compulsory routine is to make an unflattering estimate of the appeal of our institutions to free minds. We can have intellectual individualism and the rich cultural diversities that we owe to exceptional minds only at the price of occasional eccentricity and abnormal attitudes. When they are so harmless to others or to the State as those we deal with here, the price is not too great. But freedom to differ is not limited to things that do not matter much. That would be a mere shadow of freedom. The test of its substance is the right to differ as to things that touch the heart of the existing order.

If there is any fixed star in our constitutional constellation, it is that no official, high or petty, can prescribe what shall be orthodox in politics, nationalism, religion, or other matters of opinion or force citizens to confess by word or act their faith therein. If there are any circumstances which permit an exception, they do not now occur to us.[19]

We think the action of the local authorities in compelling the flag salute and pledge transcends constitutional limitations on their power and invades the sphere of intellect and spirit which it is the purpose of the First Amendment to our Constitution to reserve from all official control.

The decision of this Court in *Minersville School District* v. *Gobitis* and the holdings of those few *per curiam* decisions which preceded and foreshadowed it are overruled, and the judgment enjoining enforcement of the West Virginia Regulation is

Affirmed.

MR. JUSTICE ROBERTS and MR. JUSTICE REED adhere to the views expressed by the Court in *Minersville School*

---

[19] The Nation may raise armies and compel citizens to give military service. *Selective Draft Law Cases*, 245 U. S. 366. It follows, of course, that those subject to military discipline are under many duties and may not claim many freedoms that we hold inviolable as to those in civilian life.

District v. *Gobitis,* 310 U. S. 586, and are of the opinion that the judgment below should be reversed.

MR. JUSTICE BLACK and MR. JUSTICE DOUGLAS, concurring:

We are substantially in agreement with the opinion just read, but since we originally joined with the Court in the *Gobitis* case, it is appropriate that we make a brief statement of reasons for our change of view.

Reluctance to make the Federal Constitution a rigid bar against state regulation of conduct thought inimical to the public welfare was the controlling influence which moved us to consent to the *Gobitis* decision. Long reflection convinced us that although the principle is sound, its application in the particular case was wrong. *Jones* v. *Opelika,* 316 U. S. 584, 623. We believe that the statute before us fails to accord full scope to the freedom of religion secured to the appellees by the First and Fourteenth Amendments.

The statute requires the appellees to participate in a ceremony aimed at inculcating respect for the flag and for this country. The Jehovah's Witnesses, without any desire to show disrespect for either the flag or the country, interpret the Bible as commanding, at the risk of God's displeasure, that they not go through the form of a pledge of allegiance to any flag. The devoutness of their belief is evidenced by their willingness to suffer persecution and punishment, rather than make the pledge.

No well-ordered society can leave to the individuals an absolute right to make final decisions, unassailable by the State, as to everything they will or will not do. The First Amendment does not go so far. Religious faiths, honestly held, do not free individuals from responsibility to conduct themselves obediently to laws which are either imperatively necessary to protect society as a whole from grave and pressingly imminent dangers or which, without any general prohibition, merely regulate time, place or manner of religious activity. Decision as to the constitutionality of particular laws which strike at the substance of religious tenets and practices must be made by this Court. The duty is a solemn one, and in meeting it we cannot say that a failure, because of religious scruples, to assume a particular physical position and to repeat the words of a patriotic formula creates a grave danger to the nation. Such a statutory exaction is a form of test oath, and the test oath has always been abhorrent in the United States.

Words uttered under coercion are proof of loyalty to nothing but self-interest. Love of country must spring from willing hearts and free minds, inspired by a fair administration of wise laws enacted by the people's elected representatives within the bounds of express constitutional prohibitions. These laws must, to be consistent with the First Amendment, permit the widest toleration of conflicting viewpoints consistent with a society of free men.

Neither our domestic tranquillity in peace nor our martial effort in war depend on compelling little children to participate in a ceremony which ends in nothing for them but a fear of spiritual condemnation. If, as we think, their fears are groundless, time and reason are the proper antidotes for their errors. The ceremonial, when enforced against conscientious objectors, more likely to defeat than to serve its high purpose, is a handy implement for disguised religious persecution. As such, it is inconsistent with our Constitution's plan and purpose.

MR. JUSTICE MURPHY, concurring:

I agree with the opinion of the Court and join in it.

The complaint challenges an order of the State Board of Education which requires teachers and pupils to participate in the prescribed salute to the flag. For refusal to conform with the requirement, the State law prescribes expulsion. The offender is required by law to be treated as unlawfully absent from school and the parent or guardian is made liable to prosecution and punishment for such absence. Thus not only is the privilege of public education conditioned on compliance with the requirement, but noncompliance is virtually made unlawful. In effect compliance is compulsory and not optional. It is the claim of appellees that the regulation is invalid as a restriction on religious freedom and freedom of speech, secured to them against State infringement by the First and Fourteenth Amendments to the Constitution of the United States.

A reluctance to interfere with considered state action, the fact that the end sought is a desirable one, the emotion aroused by the flag as a symbol for which we have fought and are now fighting again,—all of these are understandable. But there is before us the right of freedom to believe, freedom to worship one's Maker according to the dictates of one's conscience, a right which the Constitution specifically shelters. Reflection has convinced me that as a judge I have no loftier duty or responsibility than to uphold that spiritual freedom to its farthest reaches.

The right of freedom of thought and of religion as guaranteed by the Constitution against State action includes both the right to speak freely and the right to refrain from speaking at all, except insofar as essential operations of government may require it for the preservation of an orderly society,—as in the case of compulsion to give evidence in court. Without wishing to disparage the purposes and intentions of those who hope to inculcate sentiments of loyalty and patriotism by requiring a declaration of allegiance as a feature of public education, or unduly belittle the benefits that may accrue therefrom, I am impelled to conclude that such a requirement is not essential to the maintenance of effective government and orderly society. To many it is deeply distasteful to join in a public chorus of affirmation of private belief. By some, including the members of this sect, it is apparently regarded as incompatible with a primary religious obligation and therefore a restriction on religious freedom. Official compulsion to affirm what is contrary to one's religious beliefs is the antithesis of freedom of worship which, it is well to recall, was achieved in this country only after what Jefferson characterized as the "severest contests in which I have ever been engaged." [1]

I am unable to agree that the benefits that may accrue to society from the compulsory flag salute are sufficiently definite and tangible to justify the invasion of freedom and privacy that is entailed or to compensate for a restraint on the freedom of the individual to be vocal or silent according to his conscience or personal inclination. The trenchant words in the preamble to the Virginia Statute for Religious Freedom remain unanswerable: ". . . all attempts to influence [the mind] by temporal punishments, or burdens, or by civil incapacitations, tend only to beget habits of hypocrisy and meanness, . . ." Any spark of love for country which may be generated in a child or his associates by forcing him to make what is to him an empty gesture and recite words wrung from him contrary to his religious beliefs is overshadowed by the desirability of preserving freedom of conscience to the full. It is in that freedom and the example of persuasion, not in force and compulsion, that the real unity of America lies.

Mr. Justice Frankfurter, dissenting:

One who belongs to the most vilified and persecuted minority in history is not likely to be insensible to the freedoms guaranteed by our Constitution. Were my purely personal attitude relevant I should wholeheartedly associate myself with the general libertarian views in the Court's opinion, representing as they do the thought and

---

[1] See Jefferson, Autobiography, vol. 1, pp. 53–59.

action of a lifetime. But as judges we are neither Jew nor Gentile, neither Catholic nor agnostic. We owe equal attachment to the Constitution and are equally bound by our judicial obligations whether we derive our citizenship from the earliest or the latest immigrants to these shores. As a member of this Court I am not justified in writing my private notions of policy into the Constitution, no matter how deeply I may cherish them or how mischievous I may deem their disregard. The duty of a judge who must decide which of two claims before the Court shall prevail, that of a State to enact and enforce laws within its general competence or that of an individual to refuse obedience because of the demands of his conscience, is not that of the ordinary person. It can never be emphasized too much that one's own opinion about the wisdom or evil of a law should be excluded altogether when one is doing one's duty on the bench. The only opinion of our own even looking in that direction that is material is our opinion whether legislators could in reason have enacted such a law. In the light of all the circumstances, including the history of this question in this Court, it would require more daring than I possess to deny that reasonable legislators could have taken the action which is before us for review. Most unwillingly, therefore, I must differ from my brethren with regard to legislation like this. I cannot bring my mind to believe that the "liberty" secured by the Due Process Clause gives this Court authority to deny to the State of West Virginia the attainment of that which we all recognize as a legitimate legislative end, namely, the promotion of good citizenship, by employment of the means here chosen.

Not so long ago we were admonished that "the only check upon our own exercise of power is our own sense of self-restraint. For the removal of unwise laws from the statute books appeal lies not to the courts but to the ballot and to the processes of democratic government."

FRANKFURTER, J., dissenting. 319 U.S.

United States v. *Butler*, 297 U. S. 1, 79 (dissent). We have been told that generalities do not decide concrete cases. But the intensity with which a general principle is held may determine a particular issue, and whether we put first things first may decide a specific controversy.

The admonition that judicial self-restraint alone limits arbitrary exercise of our authority is relevant every time we are asked to nullify legislation. The Constitution does not give us greater veto power when dealing with one phase of "liberty" than with another, or when dealing with grade school regulations than with college regulations that offend conscience, as was the case in *Hamilton* v. *Regents*, 293 U. S. 245. In neither situation is our function comparable to that of a legislature or are we free to act as though we were a super-legislature. Judicial self-restraint is equally necessary whenever an exercise of political or legislative power is challenged. There is no warrant in the constitutional basis of this Court's authority for attributing different rôles to it depending upon the nature of the challenge to the legislation. Our power does not vary according to the particular provision of the Bill of Rights which is invoked. The right not to have property taken without just compensation has, so far as the scope of judicial power is concerned, the same constitutional dignity as the right to be protected against unreasonable searches and seizures, and the latter has no less claim than freedom of the press or freedom of speech or religious freedom. In no instance is this Court the primary protector of the particular liberty that is invoked. This Court has recognized, what hardly could be denied, that all the provisions of the first ten Amendments are "specific" prohibitions, *United States* v. *Carolene Products Co.*, 304 U. S. 144, 152, n. 4. But each specific Amendment, in so far as embraced within the Fourteenth Amendment, must be equally respected, and the function of this

FRANKFURTER, J., dissenting.

Court does not differ in passing on the constitutionality of legislation challenged under different Amendments.

When Mr. Justice Holmes, speaking for this Court, wrote that "it must be remembered that legislatures are ultimate guardians of the liberties and welfare of the people in quite as great a degree as the courts," *Missouri, K. & T. Ry. Co.* v. *May,* 194 U. S. 267, 270, he went to the very essence of our constitutional system and the democratic conception of our society. He did not mean that for only some phases of civil government this Court was not to supplant legislatures and sit in judgment upon the right or wrong of a challenged measure. He was stating the comprehensive judicial duty and rôle of this Court in our constitutional scheme whenever legislation is sought to be nullified on any ground, namely, that responsibility for legislation lies with legislatures, answerable as they are directly to the people, and this Court's only and very narrow function is to determine whether within the broad grant of authority vested in legislatures they have exercised a judgment for which reasonable justification can be offered.

The framers of the federal Constitution might have chosen to assign an active share in the process of legislation to this Court. They had before them the well-known example of New York's Council of Revision, which had been functioning since 1777. After stating that "laws inconsistent with the spirit of this constitution, or with the public good, may be hastily and unadvisedly passed," the state constitution made the judges of New York part of the legislative process by providing that "all bills which have passed the senate and assembly shall, before they become laws," be presented to a Council of which the judges constituted a majority, "for their revisal and consideration." Art. III, New York Constitution of 1777. Judges exercised this legislative function in New York for nearly fifty years. See Art. I, § 12, New York Constitution of 1821. But the framers of the Constitution denied such legislative powers to the federal judiciary. They chose instead to insulate the judiciary from the legislative function. They did not grant to this Court supervision over legislation.

The reason why from the beginning even the narrow judicial authority to nullify legislation has been viewed with a jealous eye is that it serves to prevent the full play of the democratic process. The fact that it may be an undemocratic aspect of our scheme of government does not call for its rejection or its disuse. But it is the best of reasons, as this Court has frequently recognized, for the greatest caution in its use.

The precise scope of the question before us defines the limits of the constitutional power that is in issue. The State of West Virginia requires all pupils to share in the salute to the flag as part of school training in citizenship. The present action is one to enjoin the enforcement of this requirement by those in school attendance. We have not before us any attempt by the State to punish disobedient children or visit penal consequences on their parents. All that is in question is the right of the State to compel participation in this exercise by those who choose to attend the public schools.

We are not reviewing merely the action of a local school board. The flag salute requirement in this case comes before us with the full authority of the State of West Virginia. We are in fact passing judgment on "the power of the State as a whole." *Rippey* v. *Texas*, 193 U. S. 504, 509; *Skiriotes* v. *Florida*, 313 U. S. 69, 79. Practically we are passing upon the political power of each of the forty-eight states. Moreover, since the First Amendment has been read into the Fourteenth, our problem is precisely the same as it would be if we had before us an Act of Congress for the District of Columbia. To suggest that we are here concerned with the heedless action of some village tyrants is to distort the augustness of the constitutional issue and the reach of the consequences of our decision.

Under our constitutional system the legislature is charged solely with civil concerns of society. If the avowed or intrinsic legislative purpose is either to promote or to discourage some religious community or creed, it is clearly within the constitutional restrictions imposed on legislatures and cannot stand. But it by no means follows that legislative power is wanting whenever a general non-discriminatory civil regulation in fact touches conscientious scruples or religious beliefs of an individual or a group. Regard for such scruples or beliefs undoubtedly presents one of the most reasonable claims for the exertion of legislative accommodation. It is, of course, beyond our power to rewrite the State's requirement, by providing exemptions for those who do not wish to participate in the flag salute or by making some other accommodations to meet their scruples. That wisdom might suggest the making of such accommodations and that school administration would not find it too difficult to make them and yet maintain the ceremony for those not refusing to conform, is outside our province to suggest. Tact, respect, and generosity toward variant views will always commend themselves to those charged with the duties of legislation so as to achieve a maximum of good will and to require a minimum of unwilling submission to a general law. But the real question is, who is to make such accommodations, the courts or the legislature?

This is no dry, technical matter. It cuts deep into one's conception of the democratic process—it concerns no less the practical differences between the means for making these accommodations that are open to courts and to legislatures. A court can only strike down. It can only say "This or that law is void." It cannot modify or qualify, it cannot make exceptions to a general requirement. And it strikes down not merely for a day. At least the finding of unconstitutionality ought not to have ephemeral significance unless the Constitution is to be reduced to the fugitive importance of mere legislation. When we are dealing with the Constitution of the United States, and more particularly with the great safeguards of the Bill of Rights, we are dealing with principles of liberty and justice "so rooted in the traditions and conscience of our people as to be ranked as fundamental"—something without which "a fair and enlightened system of justice would be impossible." *Palko* v. *Connecticut,* 302 U. S. 319, 325; *Hurtado* v. *California,* 110 U. S. 516, 530, 531. If the function of this Court is to be essentially no different from that of a legislature, if the considerations governing constitutional construction are to be substantially those that underlie legislation, then indeed judges should not have life tenure and they should be made directly responsible to the electorate. There have been many but unsuccessful proposals in the last sixty years to amend the Constitution to that end. See Sen. Doc. No. 91, 75th Cong., 1st Sess., pp. 248–51.

Conscientious scruples, all would admit, cannot stand against every legislative compulsion to do positive acts in conflict with such scruples. We have been told that such compulsions override religious scruples only as to major concerns of the state. But the determination of what is major and what is minor itself raises questions of policy. For the way in which men equally guided by reason appraise importance goes to the very heart of policy. Judges should be very diffident in setting their judgment against that of a state in determining what is and what is not a major concern, what means are appropriate to proper ends, and what is the total social cost in striking the balance of imponderables.

What one can say with assurance is that the history out of which grew constitutional provisions for religious equality and the writings of the great exponents of religious freedom—Jefferson, Madison, John Adams, Benjamin Franklin—are totally wanting in justification for a claim by dissidents of exceptional immunity from civic measures of general applicability, measures not in fact disguised assaults upon such dissident views. The great leaders of the American Revolution were determined to remove political support from every religious establishment. They put on an equality the different religious sects—Episcopalians, Presbyterians, Catholics, Baptists, Methodists, Quakers, Huguenots—which, as dissenters, had been under the heel of the various orthodoxies that prevailed in different colonies. So far as the state was concerned, there was to be neither orthodoxy nor heterodoxy. And so Jefferson and those who followed him wrote guaranties of religious freedom into our constitutions. Religious minorities as well as religious majorities were to be equal in the eyes of the political state. But Jefferson and the others also knew that minorities may disrupt society. It never would have occurred to them to write into the Constitution the subordination of the general civil authority of the state to sectarian scruples.

The constitutional protection of religious freedom terminated disabilities, it did not create new privileges. It gave religious equality, not civil immunity. Its essence is freedom from conformity to religious dogma, not freedom from conformity to law because of religious dogma. Religious loyalties may be exercised without hindrance from the state, not the state may not exercise that which except by leave of religious loyalties is within the domain of temporal power. Otherwise each individual could set up his own censor against obedience to laws conscientiously deemed for the public good by those whose business it is to make laws.

The prohibition against any religious establishment by the government placed denominations on an equal footing—it assured freedom from support by the government to any mode of worship and the freedom of individuals to support any mode of worship. Any person may therefore believe or disbelieve what he pleases. He may practice what he will in his own house of worship or publicly within the limits of public order. But the lawmaking authority is not circumscribed by the variety of religious beliefs, otherwise the constitutional guaranty would be not a protection of the free exercise of religion but a denial of the exercise of legislation.

The essence of the religious freedom guaranteed by our Constitution is therefore this: no religion shall either receive the state's support or incur its hostility. Religion is outside the sphere of political government. This does not mean that all matters on which religious organizations or beliefs may pronounce are outside the sphere of government. Were this so, instead of the separation of church and state, there would be the subordination of the state on any matter deemed within the sovereignty of the religious conscience. Much that is the concern of temporal authority affects the spiritual interests of men. But it is not enough to strike down a non-discriminatory law that it may hurt or offend some dissident view. It would be too easy to cite numerous prohibitions and injunctions to which laws run counter if the variant interpretations of the Bible were made the tests of obedience to law. The validity of secular laws cannot be measured by their conformity to religious doctrines. It is only in a theocratic state that ecclesiastical doctrines measure legal right or wrong.

An act compelling profession of allegiance to a religion, no matter how subtly or tenuously promoted, is bad. But an act promoting good citizenship and national allegiance is within the domain of governmental authority and is therefore to be judged by the same considerations of power and of constitutionality as those involved in the many claims of immunity from civil obedience because of religious scruples.

That claims are pressed on behalf of sincere religious convictions does not of itself establish their constitutional validity. Nor does waving the banner of religious freedom relieve us from examining into the power we are asked to deny the states. Otherwise the doctrine of separation of church and state, so cardinal in the history of this nation and for the liberty of our people, would mean not the disestablishment of a state church but the establishment of all churches and of all religious groups.

The subjection of dissidents to the general requirement of saluting the flag, as a measure conducive to the training of children in good citizenship, is very far from being the first instance of exacting obedience to general laws that have offended deep religious scruples. Compulsory vaccination, see *Jacobson* v. *Massachusetts*, 197 U. S. 11, food inspection regulations, see *Shapiro* v. *Lyle*, 30 F. 2d 971, the obligation to bear arms, see *Hamilton* v. *Regents*, 293 U. S. 245, 267, testimonial duties, see *Stansbury* v. *Marks*, 2 Dall. 213, compulsory medical treatment, see *People* v. *Vogelgesang*, 221 N. Y. 290, 116 N. E. 977—these are but illustrations of conduct that has often been compelled in the enforcement of legislation of general applicability even though the religious consciences of particular individuals rebelled at the exaction.

Law is concerned with external behavior and not with the inner life of man. It rests in large measure upon compulsion. Socrates lives in history partly because he gave his life for the conviction that duty of obedience to secular law does not presuppose consent to its enactment or belief in its virtue. The consent upon which free government rests is the consent that comes from sharing in the process of making and unmaking laws. The state is not shut out from a domain because the individual conscience may deny the state's claim. The individual conscience may profess what faith it chooses. It may affirm and promote that faith—in the language of the Constitution, it may "exercise" it freely—but it cannot thereby restrict community action through political organs in matters of community concern, so long as the action is not asserted in a discriminatory way either openly or by stealth. One may have the right to practice one's religion and at the same time owe the duty of formal obedience to laws that run counter to one's beliefs. Compelling belief implies denial of opportunity to combat it and to assert dissident views. Such compulsion is one thing. Quite another matter is submission to conformity of action while denying its wisdom or virtue and with ample opportunity for seeking its change or abrogation.

In *Hamilton* v. *Regents*, 293 U. S. 245, this Court unanimously held that one attending a state-maintained university cannot refuse attendance on courses that offend his religious scruples. That decision is not overruled today, but is distinguished on the ground that attendance at the institution for higher education was voluntary and therefore a student could not refuse compliance with its conditions and yet take advantage of its opportunities. But West Virginia does not compel the attendance at its public schools of the children here concerned. West Virginia does not so compel, for it cannot. This Court denied the right of a state to require its children to attend public schools. *Pierce* v. *Society of Sisters*, 268 U. S. 510. As to its public schools, West Virginia imposes conditions which it deems necessary in the development of future citizens precisely as California deemed necessary the requirements that offended the student's conscience in the *Hamilton* case. The need for higher education and the duty of the state to provide it as part of a public educational system, are part of the democratic faith of most of our states. The right to secure such education in institutions not maintained by public funds is unquestioned.

FRANKFURTER, J., dissenting.

But the practical opportunities for obtaining what is becoming in increasing measure the conventional equipment of American youth may be no less burdensome than that which parents are increasingly called upon to bear in sending their children to parochial schools because the education provided by public schools, though supported by their taxes, does not satisfy their ethical and educational necessities. I find it impossible, so far as constitutional power is concerned, to differentiate what was sanctioned in the *Hamilton* case from what is nullified in this case. And for me it still remains to be explained why the grounds of Mr. Justice Cardozo's opinion in *Hamilton v. Regents, supra,* are not sufficient to sustain the flag salute requirement. Such a requirement, like the requirement in the *Hamilton* case, "is not an interference by the state with the free exercise of religion when the liberties of the constitution are read in the light of a century and a half of history during days of peace and war." 293 U. S. 245, 266. The religious worshiper, "if his liberties were to be thus extended, might refuse to contribute taxes . . . in furtherance of any other end condemned by his conscience as irreligious or immoral. The right of private judgment has never yet been so exalted above the powers and the compulsion of the agencies of government." *Id.,* at 268.

Parents have the privilege of choosing which schools they wish their children to attend. And the question here is whether the state may make certain requirements that seem to it desirable or important for the proper education of those future citizens who go to schools maintained by the states, or whether the pupils in those schools may be relieved from those requirements if they run counter to the consciences of their parents. Not only have parents the right to send children to schools of their own choosing but the state has no right to bring such schools "under a strict governmental control" or give "affirmative direction concerning the intimate and essential details of such schools, entrust their control to public officers, and deny both owners and patrons reasonable choice and discretion in respect of teachers, curriculum, and textbooks." *Farrington* v. *Tokushige,* 273 U. S. 284, 298. Why should not the state likewise have constitutional power to make reasonable provisions for the proper instruction of children in schools maintained by it?

When dealing with religious scruples we are dealing with an almost numberless variety of doctrines and beliefs entertained with equal sincerity by the particular groups for which they satisfy man's needs in his relation to the mysteries of the universe. There are in the United States more than 250 distinctive established religious denominations. In the State of Pennsylvania there are 120 of these, and in West Virginia as many as 65. But if religious scruples afford immunity from civic obedience to laws, they may be invoked by the religious beliefs of any individual even though he holds no membership in any sect or organized denomination. Certainly this Court cannot be called upon to determine what claims of conscience should be recognized and what should be rejected as satisfying the "religion" which the Constitution protects. That would indeed resurrect the very discriminatory treatment of religion which the Constitution sought forever to forbid. And so, when confronted with the task of considering the claims of immunity from obedience to a law dealing with civil affairs because of religious scruples, we cannot conceive religion more narrowly than in the terms in which Judge Augustus N. Hand recently characterized it:

"It is unnecessary to attempt a definition of religion; the content of the term is found in the history of the human race and is incapable of compression into a few words. Religious belief arises from a sense of the inadequacy of reason as a means of relating the individual to his fellowmen and to his universe. . . . [It] may justly be regarded as a response of the individual to an inward mentor, call it conscience or God, that is for many persons at the present time the equivalent of what has always been thought a religious impulse." *United States* v. *Kauten,* 133 F. 2d 703, 708.

Consider the controversial issue of compulsory Bible-reading in public schools. The educational policies of the states are in great conflict over this, and the state courts are divided in their decisions on the issue whether the requirement of Bible-reading offends constitutional provisions dealing with religious freedom. The requirement of Bible-reading has been justified by various state courts as an appropriate means of inculcating ethical precepts and familiarizing pupils with the most lasting expression of great English literature. Is this Court to overthrow such variant state educational policies by denying states the right to entertain such convictions in regard to their school systems, because of a belief that the King James version is in fact a sectarian text to which parents of the Catholic and Jewish faiths and of some Protestant persuasions may rightly object to having their children exposed? On the other hand the religious consciences of some parents may rebel at the absence of any Bible-reading in the schools. See *Washington ex rel. Clithero* v. *Showalter,* 284 U. S. 573. Or is this Court to enter the old controversy between science and religion by unduly defining the limits within which a state may experiment with its school curricula? The religious consciences of some parents may be offended by subjecting their children to the Biblical account of creation, while another state may offend parents by prohibiting a teaching of biology that contradicts such Biblical account. Compare *Scopes* v. *State,* 154 Tenn. 105, 289 S. W. 363. What of conscientious objections to what is devoutly felt by parents to be the poisoning of impressionable minds of children by chauvinistic teaching of history? This is very far from a fanciful suggestion for in the belief of many thoughtful people nationalism is the seed-bed of war.

There are other issues in the offing which admonish us of the difficulties and complexities that confront states in the duty of administering their local school systems. All citizens are taxed for the support of public schools although this Court has denied the right of a state to compel all children to go to such schools and has recognized the right of parents to send children to privately maintained schools. Parents who are dissatisfied with the public schools thus carry a double educational burden. Children who go to public school enjoy in many states derivative advantages such as free textbooks, free lunch, and free transportation in going to and from school. What of the claims for equality of treatment of those parents who, because of religious scruples, cannot send their children to public schools? What of the claim that if the right to send children to privately maintained schools is partly an exercise of religious conviction, to render effective this right it should be accompanied by equality of treatment by the state in supplying free textbooks, free lunch, and free transportation to children who go to private schools? What of the claim that such grants are offensive to the cardinal constitutional doctrine of separation of church and state?

These questions assume increasing importance in view of the steady growth of parochial schools both in number and in population. I am not borrowing trouble by adumbrating these issues nor am I parading horrible examples of the consequences of today's decision. I am aware that we must decide the case before us and not some other case. But that does not mean that a case is dissociated from the past and unrelated to the future. We must decide this

FRANKFURTER, J., dissenting.

case with due regard for what went before and no less regard for what may come after. Is it really a fair construction of such a fundamental concept as the right freely to exercise one's religion that a state cannot choose to require all children who attend public school to make the same gesture of allegiance to the symbol of our national life because it may offend the conscience of some children, but that it may compel all children to attend public school to listen to the King James version although it may offend the consciences of their parents? And what of the larger issue of claiming immunity from obedience to a general civil regulation that has a reasonable relation to a public purpose within the general competence of the state? See *Pierce* v. *Society of Sisters,* 268 U. S. 510, 535. Another member of the sect now before us insisted that in forbidding her two little girls, aged nine and twelve, to distribute pamphlets Oregon infringed her and their freedom of religion in that the children were engaged in "preaching the gospel of God's Kingdom." A procedural technicality led to the dismissal of the case, but the problem remains. *McSparran* v. *Portland,* 318 U. S. 768.

These questions are not lightly stirred. They touch the most delicate issues and their solution challenges the best wisdom of political and religious statesmen. But it presents awful possibilities to try to encase the solution of these problems within the rigid prohibitions of unconstitutionality.

We are told that a flag salute is a doubtful substitute for adequate understanding of our institutions. The states that require such a school exercise do not have to justify it as the only means for promoting good citizenship in children, but merely as one of diverse means for accomplishing a worthy end. We may deem it a foolish measure, but the point is that this Court is not the organ of government to resolve doubts as to whether it will fulfill its purpose. Only if there be no doubt that any reasonable mind could entertain can we deny to the states the right to resolve doubts their way and not ours.

That which to the majority may seem essential for the welfare of the state may offend the consciences of a minority. But, so long as no inroads are made upon the actual exercise of religion by the minority, to deny the political power of the majority to enact laws concerned with civil matters, simply because they may offend the consciences of a minority, really means that the consciences of a minority are more sacred and more enshrined in the Constitution than the consciences of a majority.

We are told that symbolism is a dramatic but primitive way of communicating ideas. Symbolism is inescapable. Even the most sophisticated live by symbols. But it is not for this Court to make psychological judgments as to the effectiveness of a particular symbol in inculcating concededly indispensable feelings, particularly if the state happens to see fit to utilize the symbol that represents our heritage and our hopes. And surely only flippancy could be responsible for the suggestion that constitutional validity of a requirement to salute our flag implies equal validity of a requirement to salute a dictator. The significance of a symbol lies in what it represents. To reject the swastika does not imply rejection of the Cross. And so it bears repetition to say that it mocks reason and denies our whole history to find in the allowance of a requirement to salute our flag on fitting occasions the seeds of sanction for obeisance to a leader. To deny the power to employ educational symbols is to say that the state's educational system may not stimulate the imagination because this may lead to unwise stimulation.

The right of West Virginia to utilize the flag salute as part of its educational process is denied because, so it is argued, it cannot be justified as a means of meeting a "clear and present danger" to national unity. In passing it deserves to be noted that the four cases which unanimously sustained the power of states to utilize such an educational measure arose and were all decided before the present World War. But to measure the state's power to make such regulations as are here resisted by the imminence of national danger is wholly to misconceive the origin and purpose of the concept of "clear and present danger." To apply such a test is for the Court to assume, however unwittingly, a legislative responsibility that does not belong to it. To talk about "clear and present danger" as the touchstone of allowable educational policy by the states whenever school curricula may impinge upon the boundaries of individual conscience, is to take a felicitous phrase out of the context of the particular situation where it arose and for which it was adapted. Mr. Justice Holmes used the phrase "clear and present danger" in a case involving mere speech as a means by which alone to accomplish sedition in time of war. By that phrase he meant merely to indicate that, in view of the protection given to utterance by the First Amendment, in order that mere utterance may not be proscribed, "the words used are used in such circumstances and are of such a nature as to create a clear and present danger that they will bring about the substantive evils that Congress has a right to prevent." *Schenck v. United States,* 249 U. S. 47, 52. The "substantive evils" about which he was speaking were inducement of insubordination in the military and naval forces of the United States and obstruction of enlistment while the country was at war. He was not enunciating a formal rule that there can be no restriction upon speech and, still less, no compulsion where conscience balks, unless imminent danger would thereby be wrought "to our institutions or our government."

The flag salute exercise has no kinship whatever to the oath tests so odious in history. For the oath test was one of the instruments for suppressing heretical beliefs.

Saluting the flag suppresses no belief nor curbs it. Children and their parents may believe what they please, avow their belief and practice it. It is not even remotely suggested that the requirement for saluting the flag involves the slightest restriction against the fullest opportunity on the part both of the children and of their parents to disavow as publicly as they choose to do so the meaning that others attach to the gesture of salute. All channels of affirmative free expression are open to both children and parents. Had we before us any act of the state putting the slightest curbs upon such free expression, I should not lag behind any member of this Court in striking down such an invasion of the right to freedom of thought and freedom of speech protected by the Constitution.

I am fortified in my view of this case by the history of the flag salute controversy in this Court. Five times has the precise question now before us been adjudicated. Four times the Court unanimously found that the requirement of such a school exercise was not beyond the powers of the states. Indeed in the first three cases to come before the Court the constitutional claim now sustained was deemed so clearly unmeritorious that this Court dismissed the appeals for want of a substantial federal question. *Leoles* v. *Landers,* 302 U. S. 656; *Hering* v. *State Board of Education,* 303 U. S. 624; *Gabrielli* v. *Knickerbocker,* 306 U. S. 621. In the fourth case the judgment of the district court upholding the state law was summarily affirmed on the authority of the earlier cases. *Johnson* v. *Deerfield,* 306 U. S. 621. The fifth case, *Minersville District* v. *Gobitis,* 310 U. S. 586, was brought here because the decision of the Circuit Court of Appeals for the Third Circuit ran counter to our rulings. They were reaffirmed after full consideration, with one Justice dissenting.

What may be even more significant than this uniform recognition of state authority is the fact that every Justice—thirteen in all—who has hitherto participated in judging this matter has at one or more times found no constitutional infirmity in what is now condemned. Only the two Justices sitting for the first time on this matter have not heretofore found this legislation inoffensive to the "liberty" guaranteed by the Constitution. And among the Justices who sustained this measure were outstanding judicial leaders in the zealous enforcement of constitutional safeguards of civil liberties—men like Chief Justice Hughes, Mr. Justice Brandeis, and Mr. Justice Cardozo, to mention only those no longer on the Court.

One's conception of the Constitution cannot be severed from one's conception of a judge's function in applying it. The Court has no reason for existence if it merely reflects the pressures of the day. Our system is built on the faith that men set apart for this special function, freed from the influences of immediacy and from the deflections of worldly ambition, will become able to take a view of longer range than the period of responsibility entrusted to Congress and legislatures. We are dealing with matters as to which legislators and voters have conflicting views. Are we as judges to impose our strong convictions on where wisdom lies? That which three years ago had seemed to five successive Courts to lie within permissible areas of legislation is now outlawed by the deciding shift of opinion of two Justices. What reason is there to believe that they or their successors may not have another view a few years hence? Is that which was deemed to be of so fundamental a nature as to be written into the Constitution to endure for all times to be the sport of shifting winds of doctrine? Of course, judicial opinions, even as to questions of constitutionality, are not immutable. As has been true in the past, the Court will from time to time reverse its position. But I believe that never before these Jehovah's Witnesses cases (except for minor deviations subsequently retraced) has this Court overruled decisions so as to restrict the powers of democratic government. Always heretofore, it has withdrawn narrow views of legislative authority so as to authorize what formerly it had denied.

In view of this history it must be plain that what thirteen Justices found to be within the constitutional authority of a state, legislators can not be deemed unreasonable in enacting. Therefore, in denying to the states what heretofore has received such impressive judicial sanction, some other tests of unconstitutionality must surely be guiding the Court than the absence of a rational justification for the legislation. But I know of no other test which this Court is authorized to apply in nullifying legislation.

In the past this Court has from time to time set its views of policy against that embodied in legislation by finding laws in conflict with what was called the "spirit of the Constitution." Such undefined destructive power was not conferred on this Court by the Constitution. Before a duly enacted law can be judicially nullified, it must be forbidden by some explicit restriction upon political authority in the Constitution. Equally inadmissible is the claim to strike down legislation because to us as individuals it seems opposed to the "plan and purpose" of the Constitution. That is too tempting a basis for finding in one's personal views the purposes of the Founders.

The uncontrollable power wielded by this Court brings it very close to the most sensitive areas of public affairs. As appeal from legislation to adjudication becomes more frequent, and its consequences more far-reaching, judicial self-restraint becomes more and not less important, lest we unwarrantably enter social and political domains wholly outside our concern. I think I appreciate fully the objections to the law before us. But to deny that it presents a question upon which men might reasonably differ appears to me to be intolerance. And since men may so reasonably differ, I deem it beyond my constitutional power to assert my view of the wisdom of this law against the view of the State of West Virginia.

Jefferson's opposition to judicial review has not been accepted by history, but it still serves as an admonition against confusion between judicial and political functions. As a rule of judicial self-restraint, it is still as valid as Lincoln's admonition. For those who pass laws not only are under duty to pass laws. They are also under duty to observe the Constitution. And even though legislation relates to civil liberties, our duty of deference to those who have the responsibility for making the laws is no less relevant or less exacting. And this is so especially when we consider the accidental contingencies by which one man may determine constitutionality and thereby confine the political power of the Congress of the United States and the legislatures of forty-eight states. As to attitude of judicial humility which these considerations enjoin is not an abdication of the judicial function. It is a due observance of its limits. Moreover, it is to be borne in mind that in a question like this we are not passing on the proper distribution of political power as between the states and the central government. We are not discharging the basic function of this Court as the mediator of powers within the federal system. To strike down a law like this is to deny a power to all government.

The whole Court is conscious that this case reaches ultimate questions of judicial power and its relation to our scheme of government. It is appropriate, therefore, to recall an utterance as wise as any that I know in analyzing what is really involved when the theory of this Court's function is put to the test of practice. The analysis is that of James Bradley Thayer:

". . . there has developed a vast and growing increase of judicial interference with legislation. This is a very different state of things from what our fathers contemplated, a century and more ago, in framing the new system. Seldom, indeed, as they imagined, under our system, would this great, novel, tremendous power of the courts be exerted,—would this sacred ark of the covenant be taken from within the veil. Marshall himself expressed truly one aspect of the matter, when he said in one of the later years of his life: 'No questions can be brought before a judicial tribunal of greater delicacy than those which involve the constitutionality of legislative acts. If they become indispensably necessary to the case, the court must meet and decide them; but if the case may be determined on other grounds, a just respect for the legislature requires that the obligation of its laws should not be unnecessarily and wantonly assailed.' And again, a little earlier than this, he laid down the one true rule of duty for the courts. When he went to Philadelphia at the end of September, in 1831, on that painful errand of which I have spoken, in answering a cordial tribute from the bar of that city he remarked that if he might be permitted to claim for himself and his associates any part of the kind things they had said, it would be this, that they had 'never sought to enlarge the judicial power beyond its proper bounds, nor feared to carry it to the fullest extent that duty required.'

"That is the safe twofold rule; nor is the first part of it any whit less important than the second; nay, more; today it is the part which most requires to be emphasized. For just here comes in a consideration of very great weight. Great and, indeed, inestimable as are the advantages in a popular government of this conservative influence,—the power of the judiciary to disregard unconstitutional legislation,—it should be remembered that the exercise of it, even when unavoidable, is always attended with a serious evil, namely, that the correction of legislative mistakes comes from the outside, and the people thus lose the political experience, and the moral education and stimulus that come from fighting the question out in the ordinary way, and correcting their own errors. If the decision in Munn *v.* Illinois and the 'Granger Cases,' twenty-five years ago, and in the 'Legal Tender Cases,' nearly thirty years

624   FRANKFURTER, J., dissenting.

ago, had been different; and the legislation there in question, thought by many to be unconstitutional and by many more to be ill-advised, had been set aside, we should have been saved some trouble and some harm. But I venture to think that the good which came to the country and its people from the vigorous thinking that had to be done in the political debates that followed, from the infiltration through every part of the population of sound ideas and sentiments, from the rousing into activity of opposite elements, the enlargement of ideas, the strengthening of moral fibre, and the growth of political experience that came out of it all,—that all this far more than outweighed any evil which ever flowed from the refusal of the court to interfere with the work of the legislature.

"The tendency of a common and easy resort to this great function, now lamentably too common, is to dwarf the political capacity of the people, and to deaden its sense of moral responsibility. It is no light thing to do that.

"What can be done? It is the courts that can do most to cure the evil; and the opportunity is a very great one. Let them resolutely adhere to first principles. Let them consider how narrow is the function which the constitutions have conferred on them—the office merely of deciding litigated cases; how large, therefore, is the duty intrusted to others, and above all to the legislature. It is that body which is charged, primarily, with the duty of judging of the constitutionality of its work. The constitutions generally give them no authority to call upon a court for advice; they must decide for themselves, and the courts may never be able to say a word. Such a body, charged, in every State, with almost all the legislative power of the people, is entitled to the most entire and real respect; is entitled, as among all rationally permissible opinions as to what the constitution allows, to its own choice. Courts, as has often been said, are not to think of the legislators, but of the legislature—the great, continuous body itself, abstracted from all the transitory individuals who may happen to hold its power. It is this majestic representative of the people whose action is in question, a coördinate department of the government, charged with the greatest functions, and invested, in contemplation of law, with whatsoever wisdom, virtue, and knowledge the exercise of such functions requires.

"To set aside the acts of such a body, representing in its own field, which is the very highest of all, the ultimate sovereign, should be a solemn, unusual, and painful act. Something is wrong when it can ever be other than that. And if it be true that the holders of legislative power are careless or evil, yet the constitutional duty of the court remains untouched; it cannot rightly attempt to protect the people, by undertaking a function not its own. On the other hand, by adhering rigidly to its own duty, the court will help, as nothing else can, to fix the spot where responsibility lies, and to bring down on that precise locality the thunderbolt of popular condemnation. The judiciary, today, in dealing with the acts of their coördinate legislators, owe to the country no greater or clearer duty than that of keeping their hands off these acts wherever it is possible to do it. For that course—the true course of judicial duty always—will powerfully help to bring the people and their representatives to a sense of their own responsibility. There will still remain to the judiciary an ample field for the determinations of this remarkable jurisdiction, of which our American law has so much reason to be proud; a jurisdiction which has had some of its chief illustrations and its greatest triumphs, as in Marshall's time, so in ours, while the courts were refusing to exercise it." J. B. Thayer, John Marshall, (1901) 104–10.

Of course patriotism can not be enforced by the flag salute. But neither can the liberal spirit be enforced by judicial invalidation of illiberal legislation. Our constant preoccupation with the constitutionality of legislation rather than with its wisdom tends to preoccupation of the American mind with a false value. The tendency of focussing attention on constitutionality is to make constitutionality synonymous with wisdom, to regard a law as all right if it is constitutional. Such an attitude is a great enemy of liberalism. Particularly in legislation affecting freedom of thought and freedom of speech much which should offend a free-spirited society is constitutional. Reliance for the most precious interests of civilization, therefore, must be found outside of their vindication in courts of law. Only a persistent positive translation of the faith of a free society into the convictions and habits and actions of a community is the ultimate reliance against unabated temptations to fetter the human spirit.

The Flag-Salute Case

THE GOBITIS CHILDREN can now go back to public school in Minersville, Pennsylvania, without having to salute the American flag. The eight-to-one Supreme Court decision which three years ago sanctioned their exclusion is now reversed by a vote of six to three in West Virginia State Board of Education v. Barnette. Mr. Justice Frankfurter dissents in a nineteen-page opinion in which the dominant and sustained note is that of the duty of judicial deference to the judgment of the legislature. This note would have come with more power had not its sponsor voted to condemn on constitutional grounds an ordinance forbidding picketing on the sidewalk and an injunction issued by a chancellor against such picketing. It would seem that Mr. Justice Frankfurter must see a significant constitutional difference between forbidding picketing and requiring the flag salute as a condition of attending public schools or else he must design his latest pronouncement as a recantation or qualification of his earlier overriding of legislative judgment.

Justices Roberts and Reed do not join in Mr. Justice Frankfurter's opinion, possibly because of some expressions of a personal nature, but they dissent from the decision with the simple announcement that they adhere to the views expressed by the Court in the Gobitis Case. The Gobitis opinion was written by Mr. Justice Frankfurter, and the reasons which he there gave for sustaining the school-imposed flag salute are dealt with in detail in Mr. Justice Jackson's opinion for the Court in the Barnette Case. The frame of the Barnette opinion is largely that of a dissent from the Gobitis opinion.

In the interim between the two cases, Justices Black, Douglas and Murphy had announced that they had become convinced that they erred in their earlier vote to sustain the flag-salute order, and they now write independently of their change of view, putting somewhat more emphasis on the religious aspect of the problem than does Mr. Justice Jackson. This triple defection would not have been enough by itself to overturn the earlier case. The reversal came with the aid of Justices Jackson and Rutledge, who for the first time participated in the Supreme Court's consideration of the issue.

The fact that thirteen other members of the Supreme Court in prior cases have at one time or another treated the flag-salute requirement as constitutional is invoked by Mr. Justice Frankfurter in support of his dissent. This invocation he follows by saying that "The Court has no reason for existence if it merely reflects the pressures of the day." Whatever implication or innuendo there may be in this is not wholly negatived by the succeeding statement that "Our system is built on the faith that men set apart for this special function, freed from the influences of immediacy and from the deflections of worldly ambition, will become able to take a view of longer range than the period of responsibility entrusted to Congress and legislatures."

It seldom furthers enlightenment on the substantive issue to impugn, in however veiled and backhanded fashion, the motives or the capacities of those with whom one disagrees. Reversals of judicial judgment are not a complete novelty or always without merit, as the dissenting opinion recognizes when it says: "But I believe that never before has this Court changed its views so as to restrict the powers of democratic government. Always heretofore, it has withdrawn narrow views of legislative authority so as to authorize what formerly it had denied."

This is far from true as a matter of fact. Not only is there the record of the Taft Court in the field of taxation, but there is the later expansion of judicial censorship both of legislative censorship and of state criminal procedures. Nevertheless one may cherish the ideal that judicial recantation should always be in favor of sustaining legislation, however much it may have been dishonored in the breach. Its dishonoring in the pres-

-ent instance is brought to bear on the most fundamental of issues by the paragraph which follows:

In view of this history it must be plain that what thirteen Justices found to be within the constitutional authority of a state, legislators cannot be deemed unreasonable in enacting. Therefore, in denying to the states what heretofore has received such impressive judicial sanction, some other tests of unconstitutionality must surely be guiding the Court than the absence of a rational justification for the legislation. But I know of no other test which this Court is authorized to apply in nullifying legislation.

This invites analysis. The *ad hominem* invocation of "impressive legal sanction" seems to assume that the thirteen Justices stamped their personal commendation on the legislation by not invalidating it, an inference which Mr. Justice Frankfurter denies for himself in his insistence that the judicial function is limited to determining whether there is a rational justification for the state action. On such an issue, judges as well as others may differ, and judges as well as others may revise their initial judgment. They may even give weight to adverse professional and editorial response to their earlier acquiescence, without warranting any suspicion of seeking favor with the multitude for any reason whatsoever, selfish or otherwise.

It therefore does not follow that the reversal of judicial judgment on the flag-salute issue is the product of any other test of constitutionality than that which Mr. Justice Frankfurter invokes. His is the view of judicial review that in a season not long past was widely acclaimed by dissenting Justices and by those who favored the ameliorating social legislation of the time. It has been the profession reiterated in Supreme Court opinions, often when it seemed to be least translated into practice. Yet always the criteria of constitutional adjudication have involved the weighing of competing considerations and often the rejection of the policy preferred by legislatures. Judicial tolerance, if carried to the extreme of the postulates in its favor, would mean the denial of constitutionally secured civil liberties. Somewhere the line has to be drawn, as Mr. Justice Frankfurter has recognized in cases where he has condemned or joined in condemnation. He would draw it here if he believed the law before him to be akin to the suppression of freedom of utterance.

The crux of his particularistic difference with the majority appears in the following paragraph:

The flag-salute exercise has no kinship whatever to the oath tests so odious in history. For the oath test was one of the instruments for suppressing heretical beliefs. Saluting the flag suppresses no belief nor curbs it. Children and their parents may believe what they please, avow their belief and practise it. It is not even remotely suggested that the requirement for saluting the flag involves the slightest restriction against the fullest opportunity on the part both of the children and of their parents to disavow as publicly as they choose to do so the meaning that others attach to the gesture of salute. All channels of affirmative free expression are open to both children and parents. Had we before us any act of the state putting the slightest curbs upon such free expression, I should not lag behind any member of this Court in striking down such an invasion of the right to freedom of thought and freedom of speech protected by the Constitution.

This misses the point of the conscientious objection to the flag salute. The children cannot by any affirmative statement cure the infirmity of the flag salute for them. To disavow in words what it means to others is largely beside the point, even if this includes avowal of what it means to them. Their belief is that they must refrain from the flag salute in obedience to an injunction against idolatry, and such is their conforming practice. They can hardly cherish freedom to avow their belief if in practice they are coerced to traduce it. Freedom to practise their belief is denied if the flag salute is compulsory. Only if they are wholly free to refrain without consequent disabilities have they a full measure of freedom to practise their belief. If on the basis of a rational ideal of liberty, distinctions are to be drawn between what Mr. Justice Frankfurter would condemn and what he would condone, it is hard to reject the judgment of Mr. Justice Jackson that "It would seem that involuntary affirmation could be commanded only on more immediate and urgent grounds than silence."

While the paragraph last quoted speaks of the requirement to salute the flag, perhaps it should be read in the light of the earlier dissenting insistence that "All that is in question is the right of the State to compel participation in this exercise by those who choose to attend the public schools." To any reliance on a special public power over public schools, the majority opinion answers that "Free public education, if faithful to the ideal of secular instruction and political neutrality, will not be partisan or enemy of any class, creed, party or faction." To this the dissent replies by posing various other academic rituals that may give rise to objections based on religious or political grounds which, it suggests, the Court certainly cannot be called upon to evaluate in order to choose between constitutional rejection or sanction.

The official disputants disagree, too, upon the distinction between requiring students in state universities to participate in military training, which the Court sanctions, and requiring school children to participate in the flag ceremony. Mr. Justice Jackson is technically in error in saying that "In the present case attendance is not optional." It is settled that students need not go to public schools if they go to suitable other schools. The opportunity, however, is not always available. We shall now never know whether the Court would have condemned compulsion in private schools had it continued to sustain it in public schools. Mr. Justice Frankfurter, without drawing explicit conclusions therefrom, quotes some general statements from an earlier Supreme Court opinion, pointing to limitations on state power over private schools, and he might condemn the ceremonial requirement in private schools notwithstanding the duty of judicial deference to legislative judgment, and notwithstanding justifications which he has advanced for that judgment. However this all might have been, attendance at a state university is certainly voluntary, and for the requirement of military training there Mr. Justice Jackson invokes the additional justification of the "power of the State to raise militia and impose the duties of service therein upon its citizens."

This gives enough of the argumentation to show that the constitutional and judicial issue is not so simple as some zealots might lead one to infer. Those who would have a court condemn everything that they detest must recognize that they invoke a standard of judicial conduct that they have roundly condemned when practised against what they desire. They may narrow their contention by noting with Mr. Justice Jackson that "The freedom asserted by these respondents does not bring them into collision with rights asserted by any other individual." They may, in view of the explicitness of the First Amendment now incorporated into the Fourteenth, put civil liberties on a more exalted plane than all others. They will then object most pointedly to Mr. Justice Frankfurter's seeming refusal to do so when he denies any difference of degree in the duty of judicial deference to legislative judgment "depending upon the nature of the challenge to the legislation."

In a purely formal sense it may be quite accurate to say that "The Constitution does not give us greater veto power when dealing with one phase of 'liberty' than with another"; but it denies the whole history of judicial review to imply that there is no hierarchy of individual and social interests which is of constitutional concern. As the greater public exigency in time of war may warrant unusually drastic interference with both liberty and property, so are there particular freedoms so deeply cherished and so part and parcel of the professions and the strivings of the hard ascent from barbarism that their curtailment demands justification by a higher and more immediate public need than is required for invasions of interests of lesser moment.

Such valuing and comparing has been of the essence of judicial application of constitutional constraints. It is the underlying canon of the majority's attribution of high constitutional concern for freedom to refrain from expression as well as for freedom of utterance and of worship. Mr. Justice Frankfurter's feeling for a judicial duty of equal deference to legislative judgments whatever the interests and the ideals at stake points strongly in the direction of legislative absolutism.

There is undoubtedly much truth in his concluding thought that "It is self-delusive to believe that the liberal spirit can be enforced by judicial invalidation of illiberal legislation." Perhaps it would have been as well if we had never looked to courts as guardians of a spiritual sanctuary. Mr. Justice Frankfurter's plea for well-nigh complete judicial abdication comes from him with the greater force when applied to restraints which he as an individual has most zealously striven to lift or to prevent. Doubtless he will be misunderstood by those who do not make or do not regard the distinction between the judicial and the personal attitude on which he insists. To some of this misunderstanding he may contribute by details of his argumentation subordinate to his main theme. For he cannot refrain from differentiations and evaluations while insisting that they are beyond his province. His philosophy of judicial restraint does not extend to restraint of debating zeal which carries him farther than he needs to go and perhaps farther than he really means to go.

To spasmodic excess of zeal rather than to anything more fundamental must doubtless be attributed such occasional examples of intricate blundering in analysis and reasoning as have been noted. Argumentative ineptitudes may be merely superfluous frail props for a conclusion thoroughly well bottomed on other grounds. They are not necessarily the propelling forces leading to the conclusion. They need not drag the judgment with them in their own collapse. Yet if sufficiently numerous and serious, they may rob the position taken of the support of esoteric or technical considerations and leave the question one on which wise laymen may claim as much intellectual authority as members of the bar or bench.

The opinion of the Court in the Barnette Case might have been stronger had it not been so preponderantly devoted to answering the arguments which Mr. Justice Frankfurter made earlier for the Court in sustaining the flag-salute requirement in the Gobitis Case. This destructive polemic was not a difficult task, and it was done with entire adequacy by Mr. Justice Jackson. One of the important points in his opinion for the Court is that the liberty here given constitutional sanction is not confined to cases where the objections to compulsion to participate in ceremonials are based on religious grounds. The freedom of silence and the freedom of abstention extend to those who have other than religious objections to compulsion of public avowals. Subject to certain exceptions, notably in military service, the opinion concludes that "If there is any fixed star in our constitutional constellation, it is that no official, high or petty, can prescribe what shall be orthodox in politics, nationalism, religion or other matters of opinion or force citizens to confess by word or act their faith therein."

THOMAS REED POWELL

Freedom of Thought and Religious Liberty Under the Constitution

Louis B. Boudin

I

JEHOVAH'S WITNESSES AND THE COURTS.

Jehovah's Witnesses have been frequently before the Courts in recent years. But aside from the Flag Salute Cases,[1] they never came in voluntarily, but were brought in as criminals by the police. None of their cases involved a Federal statute, and only two involved a State statute. All of the other cases involved City or School Board ordinances. In the only case which involved a State statute, aside from the second Flag Salute case, that of *Cantwell v. Connecticut*,[2] the statute involved was not declared unconstitutional, even though the decision was in their favor. In that case Jehovah's Witnesses were charged with violating a statute which provided that "no person shall solicit money, services, subscriptions or any valuable thing for any alleged religious, charitable or philanthropic cause, from other than a member of the organization for whose benefit such person is soliciting * * * unless such cause shall have been approved by the secretary of the public welfare council." And the decision of the U. S. Supreme Court was to the effect that "the statute, *as construed and applied to the appellants*, deprives them of their liberty without due process of law in contravention of the Fourteenth Amendment."[3]

It should be added, however, that the form of the decision notwithstanding, this decision actually did declare the statute in question unconstitutional insofar as it involved the unlicensed solicitation of funds for religious purposes. But, on the other hand, the case was not a genuine case of "judicial review",—*i.e.*, a case of the nullification by the courts of the deliberate action of a legislature representing a majority of the people,—even insofar as the State of Connecticut was concerned, for the simple reason that the Connecticut legislation which enacted the statute probably never even dreamed that it was curtailing religious liberty, and did not have in mind the actual constitutional problem presented to the Supreme Court. This brings into relief one phase of the civil liberties cases which Prof. Commager, in his book[4] discussed in my last article,[5] completely overlooks when he assimilates them to the problem of judicial review of economic legislation. A study of the history of the cases dealing with the latter subject will reveal the fact that every piece of social economic legislation which the courts have nullified, or the nullification of which by the courts has been sought, was adopted after long agitation and, usually, careful deliberation by the legislature —usually after the legislation was long overdue as far as public opinion was concerned. On the other hand, the civil liberties cases are usually the outgrowth of temporary excitement, either general or local; and are frequently the result of action which is the reverse of deliberate. Even if the cases arise under a statute designed to accomplish a purpose like the one involved in the judgment sought to be annulled by an appeal to the Constitution, the actual situation has but seldom been encompassed by the legislature which adopted the statute. The case of *Gitlow v. New York*[6] is an instance in point.

---

1. *Minersville School District v. Gobitis*, 310 U. S. 586 (1940); *West Virginia Board of Education v. Barnette*, 319 U. S. 624 (1943).
2. 310 U. S. 296 (1940).
3. 310 U. S. 296 at p. 303. Italics here and throughout are the author's.

4. *Majority Rule and Minority Rights:* A study in Jeffersonian Democracy and Judicial Review. New York. (Oxford University Press, pp. 92, $1.50.)
5. Boudin, Majority Rule and Constitutional Limitations, IV Lawyers Guild Review, No. ?, p. 1.
6. 268 U. S. 652 (1925) aff'g 234 N. Y. 132. In that case the defendant, a Communist, was convicted under a New York statute known as the Criminal Anarchy Law. That statute was passed in 1902, following the shooting of President McKinley at Buffalo in the Fall of 1901 by an avowed anarchist—this outrage having been preceded by a long series of similar outrages perpetrated by anarchists throughout the world. At the time of its adoption Communism in its present form was unknown; and by the time Gitlow came to trial anarchism had become practically extinct. But because of the hysteria caused by World War I and its aftermath, this statute, which had apparently never been used against any anarchist during the entire intervening period of some twenty years, was dug up and applied against a group of people who were utterly dissimilar in their views upon Government than those against whom the statute had been aimed.

In many cases the legislature did not even have in mind the *kind* of situation presented by the case in which the appeal to constitutional guarantees is made. So, in the *Cantwell* case, the legislature was clearly concerned with the prevention of frauds and impostures in the name of religion and charity. The chances are that it was passed at the solicitation of religious and charitable institutions; and the legislators who voted for the statute would probably have been shocked to learn that it had abridged the freedom of religion. What actually happened in this case was, that a "pestiferous" minority group got on the nerves of the powers that be—who may or may not represent a majority of the locality in question—and an old statute, passed for an entirely different purpose, was used to squelch them.

It would serve no purpose to discuss here the reason why Jehovah's Witnesses were disliked, although the *Cantwell* case furnishes some clues. They were an extremely fanatical group, whose methods were likely to provoke not only those whose religious views they considered it their duty to attack, while appealing to the freedom of religion guaranteed by the Constitution, but also those who generally believed in religious freedom as well as in religious toleration.[6a] This is evidenced by the kind of offenses charged against them as reflected by such of their cases as have reached the Supreme Court. This requires some further consideration of the methods of "worship" as practiced by Jehovah's Witnesses. The facts involved in the *Cantwell* case were thus stated by Mr. Justice Roberts in his opinion:

> "The facts which were held to support the conviction of Jesse Cantwell on the fifth count were that he stopped two men in the street, asked and received permission to play a phonograph record, and played the record 'Enemies,' which attacked the religion and church of the two men, who were Catholics."[7]

Other Jehovah's Witnesses cases show that they made a specialty of attacking the Catholic religion and that their "worship" consisted, among other things, in circulating books and pamphlets attacking that religion. Their methods of circulation were to offer to "give away" a book or a pamphlet to anyone who was willing to "donate" to the cause a certain small sum of money, but often gave them away without pay when the recipient could not afford to pay. The persons who did the selling or giving away were "ordained" as ministers, and the distribution of the literature was claimed to be their method of "worshipping God." It was the fact that they were giving away the books while asking for "donations", that brought them within the toils of the law in Connecticut, since that was considered "solicitation of funds" within the terms of the statute. In other places where there were no statutes against solicitation, and there were statutes requiring licenses for selling merchandise by peddlers, they were deemed by the local authorities to be *sellers of merchandise,* and they were brought within the purview of the law on that score. Such was the situation in the famous case of *Jones* v. *Opelika*[8] and other cases which will be discussed further below. It is primarily for such situations that constitutional guarantees are intended; although they may be needed, and be properly invoked, where the hysteria is more widespread and results in local statutes or ordinances intended to cover the particular situation.

In the *Cantwell* case the Constitutional guarantee of Freedom of Religion was properly invoked, and its observance trenched nowhere upon the legitimate purpose of the statute involved—the protection of the community against frauds. In delivering the opinion of the Supreme Court on the basic Constitutional question involved, Mr. Justice Roberts said:

> "It will be noted, however, that the Act requires an application to the secretary of the public welfare council of the State; that he is empowered to determine whether the cause is a religious one, and that the issue of a certificate depends upon his affirmative action. If he finds that the cause is

---

6a. And this was increased by the spirit of intolerance which has certainly been growing apace of late in this country, and of which the fanaticism of Jehovah's Witnesses is itself a manifestation. A history of the struggle for religious freedom is replete with evidence that the intolerance of established churches and the fanaticism of dissident sects rise and fall together.

7. 310 U. S. 296 at pp. 302-3.

8. 316 U. S. 584 (1942).

not that of religion, to solicit for it becomes a crime. He is not to issue a certificate as a matter of course. His decision to issue or refuse it involves appraisal of facts, *the exercise of judgment, and the formation of an opinion.* He is authorized to withhold his approval if he determines that the cause is not a religious one. Such a censorship of religion as the means of determining its right to survive is a denial of liberty protected by the First Amendment and included in the liberty which is within the protection of the Fourteenth."[9]

II

THE MUTATIONS OF A CONSTITUTIONAL ISSUE.

Cantwell v. Connecticut was decided by a unanimous Court; and so was the earlier case of *Lovell v. Griffin*[10]—the first Jehovah's Witnesses case taken up by the Supreme Court and decided in their favor. But from then on the Court was to divide sharply, and sometimes bitterly. In order that we may fully appreciate the present division in the Supreme Court, and properly appraise the position which the various justices have taken as these case came up, it is necessary to go a step back even of *Lovell v. Griffin*. Shortly before *Lovell v. Griffin* was argued in the Supreme Court,—on October 11, 1937, to be exact,—the Supreme Court dismissed the appeal in the case of *Coleman v. Griffin*,[11] on the ground that it did not present a Federal question. Coleman had been charged with the same offense as Alma Lovell, in whose case the Supreme Court did grant *certiorari*, and made the first important decision in this series of cases. The difference in the Supreme Court's attitude towards these two cases was due to the fact that in the *Coleman* case the only issue that was raised was Freedom of Religion, while in the *Lovell* case counsel had pleaded that the ordnance for the violation of which she had been arrested was violative of both Freedom of Religion and Freedom of the Press.[12]

The Supreme Court apparently thought when the *Coleman* case was presented to it on an appeal that the fact that Jehovah's Witnesses believed that they were performing a religious rite when distributing the circulars in question, did not raise a Federal question, because the requirement of a license for the distribution of circulars advertising a religious tract was not a curtailment of the freedom of religion. But it did consider it a curtailment of the freedom of the press; and therefore granted *certiorari* in the *Lovell* case, and then reversed the state court. In holding the ordinance unconstitutional the Supreme Court said:

> "We think that the ordinance is invalid on its face. Whatever the motive which induced its adoption, *its character is such that it strikes at the very foundation of the freedom of the press by subjecting it to license and censorship.* The struggle for the freedom of the press was primarily directed against the power of the licensor. It was against that power that John Milton directed his assault by his 'Appeal for the Liberty of Unlicensed Printing'. And the liberty of the press became initially a right to publish *'without a license* what formerly could be published only with one.' While this freedom from previous restraint upon publication cannot be regarded as exhausting the guarantee of liberty, the prevention of that restraint was a leading purpose in the adoption of the constitutional provision. * * *[13]

The decision, therefore, turned not upon any special freedom of religious literature which

---

9. 310 U. S. 296 at p. 305.
10. 303 U. S. 444 (1938).
11. 302 U. S. 636.

12. The ordinance and the act constituting the violation are stated thus by Mr. Chief Justice Hughes in the *Lovell* case:
"The ordinance in question is as follows:
"'Section 1. That the practice of distributing, either by hand or otherwise, circulars, handbooks, advertising, or literature of any kind, whether said articles are being delivered free, or whether same are being sold, within the limits of the City of Griffin, without first obtaining written permission from the City Manager, of the City of Griffin, such practice shall be deemed a nuisance, and punishable as an offense against the City of Griffin. * * *'
"The violation, which is not denied, consisted of the distribution without the required permission, of a pamphlet and magazine in the nature of religious tracts, setting forth the gospel of the 'Kingdom of Jehovah.' Appellant did not apply for a permit, as she regarded herself as 'sent by Jehovah to do His work', and that such an application 'would have been an act of disobedience to His commandment'." (303 U. S. 444 at pp. 447-8.)
13. Id. at pp. 451-2.

protected it against restraints upon circulation, but the freedom of all literature from such restraint. In other words, freedom of religion was treated as part of freedom of thought and freedom of expression.

The *Lovell* case was decided on March 28, 1938. On November 22, 1939, the Supreme Court decided a group of four cases generally cited as *Schneider v. Irvington*,[14] dealing with municipal ordinances in various parts of the country prohibiting or curbing the distribution of circulars. Only one of the defendants was a Jehovah's Witness. Of the others, one was charged with distributing circulars in connection with a strike; another with distributing circulars calling a meeting of Friends of the Lincoln Brigade; and still another had distributed circulars for a protest meeting in connection with the administration of State Unemployment Insurance. But the Supreme Court saw no difference between the case of Jehovah's Witnesses and the other defendants, and treated them all as cases involving the single issue of Freedom of Speech. Mr. Justice Roberts, who spoke for the Court, commenced his opinion with the following statement:

> "Four cases are here, *each of which* presents the question of whether regulations embodied in a municipal ordinance abridge the freedom of speech and the press secured against State invasion by the Fourteenth Amendment of the Constitution."[15]

And in his dissenting opinion in the first Flag Salute case, Mr. Justice (now Mr. Chief Justice) Stone still treats the question in the same way.

> "The guaranties",—says he—"*of civil liberty are but guaranties of freedom of the human mind and spirit and of reasonable freedom and opportunity to express them.*"[16]

Such was the situation up to June 8, 1942, when the Supreme Court divided five to four in *Jones v. Opelika*.[17] The decision which goes under that title embraced a group of three cases which had arisen in Alabama, Arizona, and Arkansas, all involving Jehovah's Witnesses, who had been convicted for the distribution, without a license, of their literature, which the state courts held to be "sales", and, therefore, subject to licensing and the payment of license fees. The question actually presented for decision was a very narrow one, whether the distribution of their literature by the Witnesses constituted "sales", that is, business transactions, or religious activities in the nature of "worship", as claimed by the Witnesses, or at least fund-raising for religious purposes assimilable to religious activities. But the three opinions delivered in the case went into elaborate discussions of the whole problem of Religious Freedom, and injected two new issues: the issues of immunity from taxation of "fund-raising" for the protected activities, and the issue of the position of Freedom of Religion as compared with the other freedoms protected by the First and Fourteenth Amendments. The majority of the Court, in an opinion delivered by Mr. Justice Reed, held that the protection which the Constitution extends to the three freedoms mentioned in the First Amendment, was intended to be, and is, a protection against prohibition, interference or abridgment, but does not confer any special privilege which would exempt their votaries from the ordinary duties of citizenship or the burdens of contributing to the support of Government. Agreeing that the activities of the Witnesses were "sales", as held by the state courts, and that the taxes involved were general and non-discriminatory, the Court, therefore, affirmed the convictions. Mr. Chief Justice Stone, in an opinion concurred in by Justices Black, Douglas, and Murphy, disagreed with the state courts and the majority of the Supreme Court that the activities of the Witnesses were "sales"; but he went a step further, asserting that the First Amendment was not intended merely to *protect* these freedoms from invasion, but to give them a *preferred position* with respect to taxation. He did not discuss the extent of the exemption advocated by him, nor the exact nature of the preference claimed. His language was as follows:

---

14. *Schneider v. Irvington; Young v. California; Snyder v. City of Milwaukee; Nichols v. Massachusetts,* 308 U. S. 147 (1939).
15. Id. at pp. 153-4.
16. 310 U. S. 586 at p. 604.
17. *Jones v. City of Opelika; Bowden v. City of Fort Smith; Jobin v. Arizona,* 316 U. S. 584 (1942).

"The First Amendment is not confined to safeguarding freedom of speech and freedom of religion against discriminatory attempts to wipe them out. On the contrary, the Constitution, by virtue of the First and the Fourteenth Amendments, has put those freedoms in a *preferred position.* Their commands are not restricted to cases where the protected privilege is sought out for attack. They extend at least to every form of taxation which, because it is a condition of the exercise of the privilege, is capable of being used to control or suppress it."[18]

But for the "at least", the rule laid down in the last sentence, which I believe to be a correct one, does not imply any preference at all, for without it the *protection* would be of little value. It is the insertion of the "at least" in the rule, and the position of *preference* claimed as a principle, that raises one of the serious issues which have disturbed the peace and harmony of the Court, which had theretofore existed with respect to these cases, and may well disturb all those who are interested in the harmonious working of our constitutional system. In this connection attention must be called to the fact that in the *Schneider* case, Mr. Justice Roberts, speaking for the Court—unanimous but for Mr. Justice McReynolds, who is no longer of the Court—referred to previous decisions of the Court in which the freedoms in question were referred to as "fundamental" rights and liberties, and then said:

"The phrase is not an empty one and was not lightly used. * * *
"*In every case, therefore,* * * * *the Courts should be astute to examine the effect of the challenged legislation.* Mere legislative preferences or beliefs respecting matters of public convenience may well support regulation directed at other personal activities, but be insufficient to justify such as diminishes the exercise of rights so vital to the maintenance of democratic institutions."[19]

The minority of the Court would, therefore, have been well within the rule previously laid down by the whole Court if they claimed that the judgments involved in the *Opelika* case should be reversed because the States had not met the burden imposed upon them by the Constitution. The fact that the Chief Justice did not take that position, but asserted a special preferred position for the protected freedoms, in the nature of a special privilege with respect to taxation, makes that opinion a departure from his own previous position, as well as that of the Court, and challenges attention and thought.

An even greater departure, and a greater challenge, is presented by the second issue— that of an alleged *preferred position* of the Freedom of Religion among the freedoms protected by the Constitution. This new issue was injected by Mr. Justice Murphy, in an opinion concurred in by Justices Black and Douglas, as well as the Chief Justice.[19a] In this opinion Mr. Justice Murphy goes over briefly the question of Freedom of Speech and Freedom of the Press, discussed at great length in the Chief Justice's opinion, and then proceeds as follows:

"Under the foregoing discussion of freedom of speech and freedom of the press any person would be exempt from taxation upon the act of distributing information or opinion of any kind, whether political, scientific or religious in character, when done solely in an effort to spread knowledge and ideas, with no thought of commercial gain. But there is another and perhaps *more precious* reason why these ordinances cannot constitutionally apply to petitioners. Important as free speech and a free press are to a free government and a free citizenry, *there is a right even more dear to many individuals—the right to worship their Maker* according to their needs and the dictates of their souls *and to carry their message or their gospel to every living creature.*"[20]

[19a] While the Chief Justice and Mr. Justice Black concurred in Mr. Justice Murphy's separate dissenting opinion which claims this preferential position for freedom of religion, it seems to me that there is a difference of emphasis at least between the position of the Chief Justice and Mr. Justice Black on the one hand and that of Justices Murphy and Douglas on the other. The very fact that the Chief Justice thought it necessary to write a separate opinion in which the specially preferred position claimed in Mr. Justice Murphy's dissenting opinion for freedom of religion is omitted, would indicate that he is not quite ready to follow Mr. Justice Murphy to the end of the road. And a comparison of Mr. Justice Black's opinion for the Court in the case of *Martin v. City of Struthers*, decided with the second *Opelika* case, with the concurring opinion of Mr. Justice Murphy in that case, would indicate a similar reservation on the part of Mr. Justice Black.

18. Id. at 608.
19. 308 U. S. 147 at p. 161.
20. 316 U. S. 586 at pp. 620-1.

This makes an invidious distinction between the Freedom of Religion on the one hand and the Freedom of Speech and Freedom of the Press on the other, in so far as they are used for secular concerns, such as the propagation of political or economic views.

III

FREEDOM OF RELIGION AND FREEDOM
FROM TAXATION

What is the position of religion under the Constitution?

The First Amendment, as far as material here, reads as follows:

"Congress shall make no law respecting an establishment of religion, or prohibiting the free exercise thereof; or abridging the freedom of speech, or of the press * * *."

From a mere reading of this Amendment one is apt to conclude that the protection intended to be given to Freedom of Religion is a much narrower one than that which was intended to be given to Freedom of Speech and Freedom of the Press: Aside from prohibiting the *establishment* of a particular religion, the only protection extended to religion is that against the *prohibition* of its *free exercise* while freedom of speech and freedom of the press are protected against *abridgment*, a much wider term than *prohibition of exercise*. I believe, however, that such reading of the First Amendment would be a mistaken one, although the framers of the Amendment were undoubtedly very careful in their choice of language. *Prohibition* is a narrower term than *abridgment*, and was meant to be. But it was also meant to cover the subject, and it is adequate for that purpose. The *exercise* of religion moves within a narrow orbit and has a well defined meaning which can be completely protected by providing against its *prohibition*. On the other hand, Freedom of Speech and Freedom of the Press have many facets, and the word "prohibition", if used, would not give all of the protection that was intended. But aside from the *exercise of religion*,—which is equivalent to "worship", there are other things that are of importance. Such are the right of proselytizing,—of using the spoken as well as the written word in an effort to spread one's religious beliefs in order to make converts to the same. That also needs protection. But that protection is given by the wider protection extended to Freedom of Speech and Freedom of the Press.

It was, therefore, a correct construction of the Constitution when the Supreme Court, in the *Lovell* case, brought the activities of Jehovah's Witnesses within the protection not of Freedom of Religion but of Freedom of Speech and Freedom of the Press. Clearly, calling the sale of books and pamphlets the "worship of God" is using the Lord's name in vain; even though it may be perfectly proper to say that it is doing religious work in a broad sense,—that is to say, in the sense of *propagating* one's religious beliefs. The State Court, in the *Opelika* case, was therefore, perfectly correct when it refused to admit evidence of the fact that the defendant in the case had been "ordained" as a minister of religion; a minister is ordained for the purpose of performing religious rites,—which the selling or giving away of pamphlets is not, and no ordination is necessary for the purpose of propagating religious ideas, since the free propagating of ideas is everyone's right.

"In the Beginning was the Word." But before the "Word" was the Thought; and all the three freedoms covered by the First Amendment are meant to protect the basic freedom, Freedom of Thought, as was correctly stated by the Chief Justice in the passage quoted above from his dissenting opinion in the First Flag Salute Case.

There can, therefore, be no preferential position for any one of these freedoms as against the other, for it is the same Freedom of Thought that is involved whether we think of religion, science, politics, or economics. And it is the same right to freely express our thoughts that is used whether we preach the Gospel, teach the science of Evolution, or advocate political or social or economic change. The suppression of the free expression of any of these ideas would be equally fatal to democracy and progress. But so would be *a privilege* given to the expression of one kind of thought as compared with another. It is that position of privilege claimed for political thought that Mr. Justice Stone protested against in his dissenting opinion in the first Flag Salute case; and now the majority of the Court must be warned against putting religion in the privileged position which has been denied to politics. So far the decisions of the Supreme Court, both before and since the second *Opelika* case,[21] are reassuring, at least outside the sphere of taxation. So, in the case of *Cox* v. *New Hampshire*,[22] decided before either of the *Opelika* cases, the Supreme Court held that a religious parade is not any different from any other kind of parade; and, therefore, comes within a municipal ordinance which prescribes reasonable regulations for the organization of street parades. In the case of *Prince* v. *Commonwealth of Massachusetts*,[23] decided since the second *Opelika* case, the Supreme Court held that the claim of a Jehovah's Witness that her little girl was "worshipping God" when she was selling Jehovah's Witnesses pamphlets, was no protection against prosecution under a state statute which prohibited children of that age from selling newspapers or other printed matter on the streets. Therefore, so far as the present Court is concerned, at least, there is no danger that Child Labor Laws and similar social legislation may be broken down because of a claim that they interfere with the "free exercise of religion". But there is no telling to what a breaking down of the equality between the various freedoms protected by the First Amendment may lead, once invidious distinctions between them are established. And while this danger may be remote, the question of taxation is of present importance and deserves careful consideration.

21. *Jones* v. *Opelika*, 319 U. S. 103 (1943), reversing and vacating, after reargument, the prior judgments (316 U. S. 584).
22. 312 U. S. 569 (March, 1941).
23. 88 L. Ed. 403, decided January 31, 1944.

To get the full bearing of the decision of the Court in the *Opelika* cases on the problem of taxation of fund-raising activities, or activities which result in income which is used for the activities protected by the First and Fourteenth Amendments, we must, first of all, look at the municipal ordinances under which the three cases grouped in the *Opelika* decision arose; for they were not alike, even though neither the majority nor the minority of the Supreme Court differentiated between them. The ordinance involved in the *Opelika* case proper, specifically mentioned book agents and taxed them as such. The other two ordinances contained no reference to book agents, being of a general tenor, taxing all sales. The opinion delivered for the majority of the Court in the first *Opelika* case overlooked this difference, treating all as if they had no reference to book agents as such. Pointing to the supposedly general and non-discriminatory character of the ordinances, which taxed all business alike, and apparently without undue hardship to any business, the Court came to the conclusion that the business of selling pamphlets for a religious purpose is no different from selling them for purely commercial reasons, and, therefore, subject to the payment of the tax. The minority of the Court, claiming a preferred position in the nature of a privilege for the constitutionally-protected activities, contended that where the sale is not purely commercial, but is made for the purpose of raising funds for a constitutionally-protected activity, it is exempt from general taxation. Both the Chief Justice and Mr. Justice Murphy, in their opinions, conceded that there were limits to the exemption, although neither would draw a line of demarcation. It is the establishment of this broad principle of exemption without indicating any definite limiting principle, which became the law in the second *Opelika* case, that disturbed the present minority of the Court and led to their vehement opposition to the decision in that case,—repeated since with even greater vehemence in *Follett* v. *McCormick*.[24] In giving his reasons for the exemption claimed by him apparently for all the constitutionally-protected

24. 88 L. Ed. 588, decided March 27, 1944.

activities, the Chief Justice said, in his dissenting opinion in the first *Opelika* case:

> "No one could doubt that taxation which may be freely laid upon activities not within the protection of the Bill of Rights could—when applied to the dissemination of ideas, be made the ready instrument for destruction of that right. Few would deny that a license tax laid specifically on the privilege of disseminating ideas would infringe the right of free speech. For one reason among others, if the State may tax the privilege it may fix the rate of tax and, through the tax, control or suppress the activity which it taxes."[25]

To which Justices Roberts, Frankfurter, and Jackson, in a dissenting opinion in the *Follett* case, retort by saying:

> "If exactions on the business or occupation of selling cannot be enforced against Jehovah's Witnesses they can no more be enforced against publishers or vendors of books, whether dealing with religion or other matters of information. The decision now rendered must mean that the guarantee of freedom of the press creates an immunity equal to that here upheld as to teaching or preaching religious doctrine. Thus the decision precludes nonoppressive, nondiscriminatory licensing or occupation taxes on publishers, and on news vendors as well, since, without the latter the dissemination of news would be impossible. This court disavowed any such doctrine with respect to freedom of the press in *Grosjean* v. *American Press Co.*, and it is unthinkable that those who publish and distribute for profit newspapers and periodicals should suggest that they are in a class apart, untouchable by taxation upon their enterprises for the support of the government which makes their activities possible."[26]

It may now seem "unthinkable" that the publishers should put forward such extravagant claims. But the records of the Supreme Court show that much less founded and much more extravagant claims were put forward by them when they attacked the constitutionality of the National Labor Relations Act; and another record now on its way to the Supreme Court shows no less unfounded and quite as extravagant claims with respect to alleged abridgment of the freedom of the press if anti-trust laws should be enforced against them.

Nor is the history of the Supreme Court itself on the subject of exemption from taxation very reassuring,—in view of the history of the exemption from taxation of "state instrumentalities". In 1819 the Court, speaking through Chief Justice Marshall in the famous case of *McCulloch* v. *Maryland*,[27] held that a State could not tax the *operations* of Federal Governmental instrumentalities,—a self-evident proposition. Nearly a quarter of a century later the Court, in *Dobbins* v. *Erie*,[28] relying upon the self-evident proposition announced by Marshall in the *McCulloch* case, decided that a State could not, as part of a general system of taxation which applied to all property and "offices", exact a tax from one of the citizens who held a Federal office, when it involved the taxing of the office *eo nomine*,—making the considerable jump from *operations* of the Federal Governmental instrumentalities to the income of Federal officials. Then, in *Collector* v. *Day*,[29] decided in 1871, the Court, with *Dobbins* v. *Erie* as a jumping-off place, decided that state officials were exempt from a general income tax laid by the Federal Government. This involved a double jump— each jump involving an enormous distance on a different constitutional plane: In the first place, the decision in *Dobbins* v. *Erie* was based specifically on the circumstance that the tax attempted to be collected by the State was laid *eo nomine* on a Federal office, while the tax involved in *Collector* v. *Day* was a general income tax which taxed all income, no matter from what source, and the state officials were not asked where their income came from, nor was the law concerned with it. But an even greater jump was involved in the introduction of a so-called equality or reciprocity rule which placed state matters with respect to Federal taxation on the same plane as Federal

---

25. 316 U. S. 586 at p. 608.
26. 88 L. Ed. 588 at p. 592.
27. 4 Wheat. 316.
28. 16 Pet. 435 (1842).
29. 11 Wall. 113.

matters with respect to state taxation. Nor was that the end of the story: *Collector v. Day,* in its turn, led to a series of further steps on the road of exemption, until we reached a point at which the exemptions involved were much more extravagant than the publishers' claims which the learned Justices now think would be "unthinkable".

The matter finally became a serious menace to the finances of the United States Government. So much so that demands came from all sides for a constitutional amendment to meet the threatened danger. And on February 8, 1933, Mr. Cordell Hull, then a Senator from Tennessee, arose in the United States Senate and actually offered a constitutional amendment in order to do away with an exemption which would have seemed "unthinkable" not only to Marshall when he delivered the opinion in *McCulloch v. Maryland* but even to Mr. Justice Wayne when he spoke for the Supreme Court in *Dobbins v. Erie,* and probably even to the Court which decided *Collector v. Day.* It is true that the Supreme Court finally discovered that no constitutional amendment was necessary, and that the job could be done by the simple process of overruling the series of cases commencing with *Collector v. Day.* But that involved a revolution in thinking on the part of our profession and great courage on the part of the members of the Supreme Court,—both aided by an economic crisis which Mr. Justice Brandeis characterized as "more serious than war." We must, therefore, be vigilantly on the watch against departures from correct principle, as nothing is "unthinkable" in this field except at the time when the first step in the wrong direction is still under discussion.

Nor is this all. There is still another aspect of the case which requires very serious consideration. In his dissenting opinion in the second *Opelika* case,[30] Mr. Justice Reed, speaking for the entire minority of four members of the Court,[31] pointed out that the exemption claimed, and allowed by the Court in that case, was actually a subsidy. And in the *Follett* case, his three associates who still persisted in the dissent,[31a] speaking of the *preferred* exemption claimed on behalf of Freedom of Religion, said:

"In effect, the decision grants not free exercise of religion, in the sense that such exercise shall not be hindered or limited, but, on the other hand, requires that the exercise of religion be *subsidized.* Trinity Church, owning great property in New York City, devotes the income to religious ends. Must it, therefore, be exempt from paying its fair share of the cost of government's protection of its property?"[32]

This requires some further consideration of the position of Freedom of Religion among the three freedoms involved in this discussion. I have said before that Freedom of Religion is not in a *subordinate* position among those three freedoms. But that is only true with respect to real freedom, *i.e.,* with respect to *freedom from interference or abridgment.* That is decidedly *not* the case when it comes to the question of subsidies. There is no constitutional prohibition against the subsidizing by Government of the spread of *secular knowledge.* In fact, the Federal Government has been granted specific power to do so.[33] But there is in the Constitution, what I believe to be, a definite prohibition against subsidizing religion, as an examination of the constitutional text, and the history of the development of Freedom of Religion clearly demonstrate. The Constitution, as already pointed out, has two provisions with respect to religion: one guarantees the free exercise of religion, while the other prohibits the

---

30. 319 U. S. 103 at p. 117.
31. Justices Frankfurter, Jackson and Roberts joined in Reed's dissent.

31a. Mr. Justice Reed did not join in the dissent in the *Follett* case. Not, however, because he had changed his views on the constitutional question involved, but because he accepted the decision in the second *Opelika* case as "the law of the land", and did not see any substantial difference between the *Opelika* case and the *Follett* case. His three associates in the dissent in the *Opelika* case, however, saw in the *Follett* case a *further step* in the wrong direction. As to the position of Mr. Justice Reed in accepting a wrong constitutional decision as "the law of the land", see discussion of the problem of *stare decisis* in constitutional law in, Boudin, *Government by Judiciary.* Also, Boudin, the Problem of *Stare Decisis in Our Constitutional Theory,* 8 NYU Law Quarterly Review, 589-639.
32. 88 L. Ed. at p. 592. Religious and charitable organizations have been no more backward in putting forward extravagant and "unthinkable" claims with respect to exemption from taxation than the publishers. Notwithstanding the very liberal exemptions granted by state constitutions and state laws, these organizations have never failed to grasp for more. One of the latest examples of the grasping nature of these organizations with respect to exemptions, showing even more extravagant claims,—if that were possible,—than those which the three learned Justices thought "unthinkable", is shown by the case of *S.L.R.B. v. Trustees of Columbia University,* now pending in the courts of New York.
33. U. S. Constit. Art. I, sec. 8.

establishment of an official religion. The two provisions are different in character, and were prompted by different considerations. The freedom that we have discussed until now, and the only one discussed by the Supreme Court in the cases referred to, is the guarantee of the free exercise of religion. But the prohibitory provision must also be considered if we are to cover the entire ground and come to a correct conclusion with respect to the question as to what the guarantee of free exercise of religion actually means. We now turn to that subject.

Congress is forbidden by the First Amendment to pass any law establishing a religion. That, clearly, is not the same as the guarantee of "free exercise" of religion, which follows the prohibition against the establishment of any religion. An established church may co-exist with Freedom of Religion, just a monarchy may co-exist with democracy. England has both a Monarchy and an Established Church, but no one would claim that England is not a democratic country or that its inhabitants do not enjoy religious freedom. But our Founding Fathers wanted to abolish both monarchy and religious establishment; and so they guaranteed to each State a republican form of government in the original Constitution, and provided against an Established Church, at least as far as the Federal Government is concerned, by the First Amendment. And the provision *against* the religious Establishment was considered at the time as important as the guarantee *of* the "free exercise" of religion. But the guarantee against a religious Establishment, in a country which enjoys absolute freedom of religion means nothing else than *the freedom from being taxed for the support of religion.* That the feeling against being taxed by the state for the support of religion was strong among the proponents of our Bill of Rights, is attested by the history of the times.[33a]

In other words, the Freedom of Religion is in a class by itself, to the extent that the *enlargement* of one man's freedom in that respect is considered *a diminution of another man's religious freedom;* and a privilege or exemption extended to one man's religion is a discrimination against and a burdening of all others. It must be borne in mind in this connection, that Freedom of Religion includes freedom *from* religion,—*i.e.,* religious freedom involves the right *not to have any religion* and *not to be burdened* in any way because others *do* have religion. The underlying thought of our constitutional theory on this subject is that religion is completely divorced from the state; and the exercise thereof, as well as the *means* of its support, must be the result of voluntary action and voluntary contributions. Any attempt to read into the First Amendment a *privilege* in favor of any religious institution, enterprise or activity, by way of exemption from general taxation, is, therefore, clearly contrary to the spirit of that Amendment, and an infringement of the freedom which it was designed to establish.

There is one other matter which must be considered in this connection,—a matter which concerns not only Freedom of Religion, which was paramount in the minds of Justices Murphy and Douglas, but all of the three freedoms which the decision in the second *Opelika* case was intended to uphold and promote. In all of the opinions written on behalf of the present majority of the Supreme Court in these cases emphasis is laid upon the fact that freedom from taxation is particularly important to poor and struggling sects; and the Chief Justice in his dissenting opinion in the first *Opelika* case, said:

> "When applied as it is here to activities involving the exercise of religious freedom its vice is emphasized in that it is levied and paid in advance of the activities taxed, and applied at rates well calculated to suppress these activities save only as others may volunteer to pay the tax. *It requires a sizeable out-of-pocket expense by someone who may never succeed in raising a penny in this exercise of the privilege which is taxed.*"[34]

33a. We find in the "Statute of Religious Freedom", adopted by Virginia in 1785, the following provision:
"Be it enacted by the General Assembly, That no man shall be compelled to frequent *or support* any religious worship, place, or ministry whatsoever, nor shall he be enforced, restrained, molested, or *burthened* in his body or goods, nor shall otherwise suffer on account of his religious opinions or beliefs; but that all men shall be free to profess, and by argument to maintain, their opinion in matters of religion, and that the same shall in no wise diminish, *enlarge,* or affect their civil capacities".

34. 316 U. S. 586 at 609.

Although this was said in connection with Freedom of Religion, it applies to all of the three freedoms we have been discussing,—protection is particularly needed by poor and struggling organizations or groups, whether in the field of religion, economics, or politics. And since there is no constitutional impediment as far as the latter two classes are concerned, with respect to subsidies by the state, one would be inclined to fall in with the argument of the Chief Justice that they should be extended the privilege of exemption from general taxation. But this argument overlooks the fact that a privilege of exemption from taxation *is itself frequently a privilege in favor of the rich rather than the poor*. Even where the privilege is based on theoretical equality, the equality is apt to be a snare and a delusion, because of the unequal distribution of property among religious, educational, and similar establishments. There is some dispute as to whether or not the Jehovah's Witnesses are actually a poor and struggling sect. But assuming that they are a poor and struggling sect, the privilege of exemption from taxation, if it were to be extended to property, would certainly benefit Trinity Church and similar rich congregations, more than Jehovah's Witnesses. The same is true, of course, in the field of knowledge. And I am inclined to believe that an extension of the exemption from general taxation, such as is contended for in the opinions of the majority of the Court and is claimed in the *Columbia University Case* referred to above, would lead to the very institutionalization of thought which the First Amendment was designed to prevent.

Does that mean that our freedoms are fated to be wrecked either on Scylla or Charybdis? Must we choose between the alternatives of the right of the States to regulate, and possibly extinguish, our freedoms by taxing them, —or exempt them entirely from taxation and run the risk of the evils just referred to? I believe that we are not confronted with any such alternative if we bear in mind the distinction between general taxation and special taxation,—a distinction frequently drawn by the Supreme Court in connection with the problem of Federal relations. I believe that the true constitutional rule is that the freedoms protected by the First Amendment cannot be taxed *as such,—eo nomine*, as *Dobbins v. Erie* has it,—but that they are not exempt from *general* taxation. I would therefore differentiate between the three ordinances involved in the three cases covered by the first *Opelika* decision. The City of Opelika ordinance was, in my opinion, clearly unconstitutional,—and not only as applied to Jehovah's Witnesses,—because it laid a tax on book agents by name, thus putting a tax on the dissemination of argument and knowledge, both secular and religious. On the other hand, the ordinances of the two other cities I would hold constitutional against all comers, since they taxed trading, irrespective of the wares traded in. I believe that this distinction furnishes complete protection to the freedoms involved, without running the risks pointed out in the opinions written by the various members of the present minority of the Supreme Court in these cases.

IV

The Flag Salute Cases and the Problem of Conformity.

We now come to the flag salute cases,—the cases which have evoked the most bitter controversy on the Supreme Bench, and have led Professor Commager to issue his curious clarion call to the liberals discussed in my last article.[35] It is unfortunate that this question came to the Supreme Court on the initiative of Jehovah's Witnesses, as that has led to a confusion of the real issues involved,—a confusion emanating, in the first instance, from the Bar, but threatening to engulf the Court. Being Jehovah's Witnesses cases, it was only natural that the problem of religious freedom should be the one stressed by counsel for the parties directly concerned. But it seems that the large array of counsel who argued on behalf of various organizations interested in civil liberties generally, followed the lead of counsel for the parties directly involved, —due largely, we take it, because they found it

---
35. Note 5, *supra*.

difficult to argue on behalf of "free speech" in a case which did not involve any speech. Mr. Justice Frankfurter, speaking for the Court in the first Flag Salute case, therefore, began his opinion with the following statement:

> "A grave responsibility confronts this Court whenever, in course of litigation, it must reconcile the conflicting claims of liberty and authority. *But when the liberty invoked is liberty of conscience, and the authority is authority to safeguard the nation's fellowship, judicial conscience is put to its severest test. Of such a nature is the present controversy.*"[36]

And a little further on in his opinion he said:

> "We must decide whether the requirement of participation in such a ceremony, exacted from a child who refuses upon sincere *religious grounds,* infringes without due process of law the liberty guaranteed by the Fourteenth Amendment."[37]

Mr. Justice Frankfurter then proceeded to develop his argument for the constitutionality of the flag salute legislation by discussing in two aspects: the nature of the constitutional guarantee of religious freedom, and the extent of the powers of the state to require conformity of conduct. Mr. Justice Frankfurter's point of departure on the first branch of his argument, is, that in dealing with religious freedom as guaranteed by the United States Constitution, we are dealing with a "historic concept"; and that historically that guarantee was not intended, nor even held, to exclude "legislation of general scope not directed against doctrinal loyalties of particular sects." Since it must be conceded that the legislation in question was general in scope, and was not directed against the "doctrinal loyalties" of Jehovah's Witnesses, that really disposed of the case which Mr. Justice Frankfurter said the Court was called upon to decide. Since, however, the general question of civil liberties and due process had been adumbrated, Mr. Justice Frankfurter proceeded to make an elaborate argument proving the authority of the state to prescribe conduct which it deems necessary for its protection or for the advancement of the general welfare of the people. This branch of the argument, while apparently merely subsidiary to the main argument on the nature of the constitutional guarantee of religious freedom, is important not only because it affects the question of civil liberties generally, but because it goes far to explain Mr. Justice Frankfurter's attitude toward many other problems which seems to have puzzled many of his friends and admirers.

It must be borne in mind in this connection that Mr. Justice Frankfurter belongs to the generation which looked upon the States as "laboratories of social experimentation" and was battling for the Lord against judicial interference with such experimentation. In the storm and stress of these times we are apt to forget that great historic struggle and its importance in the history of the development of our constitutional law; and to lose sight of the fact that the history of the development of our constitutional law demonstrates that it is unsafe to sacrifice general positions in order to achieve specific gains. It is this which accounts for what may seem to some too great a sensitivity to "State Rights" at a time when the nation provides a much greater "laboratory" for social experimentation, and a much more effective one. It seems to me, however, that the difficulty is largely of our own making. We are not confronted here with the problem of National versus State power. If we bear in mind the fact that the Constitution is *not* an economic document, and *does* contain specific guarantees of personal freedom[38] it will be found that both the Nation and the States can be used as "laboratories of social experimentation", both laboratories working at full blast at the same time.[39]

Unfortunately, the circumstances under which these cases came before the Supreme Court, and particularly the manner in which the second Flag Salute case came before that Court, created such confusion as to the real issues in-

---

36. 310 U. S. 586 at p. 591.
37. Id. at 592-3.
38. See IV Lawyers Guild Review No. 2 at pages 2-4.
39. Except, of course, that the state "laboratories" may not work upon the same object or in the same field with the national "laboratory", insofar as the national laboratory has preempted the field by actually working therein in a manner which would make the working of the state laboratories an interference with the national laboratory, or where the field by its very nature belongs in the national domain.

volved, that even so perspicacious a jurist as Mr. Justice Frankfurter was led astray as to the real question before the Court, and missed a distinction which he should have been the first to recognize, in view of his great contribution to the clarification of thought in this field.

I have already referred to the fact that the argument at bar in the first Flag Salute case stressed largely the question of religious freedom. To this should be added that on four previous occasions the Supreme Court refused to grant *certiorari* in similar cases on the ground that freedom of religion—which was the only point raised—was not trenched upon by the flag salute ordinances complained of. And the only member of the Court who dissented in the first Flag Salute case, Mr. Justice (now Mr. Chief Justice) Stone, stressed the religious aspect of the case,—even though he used some language which was applicable to civil liberties generally. And it was the religious aspect of the subject which apparently led to the recantation on the part of three of the members of the Court who had joined in the decision of the majority in the first Flag Salute case. It will be recalled that when *Jones v. Opelika* was first before the Supreme Court, Justices Black, Douglas and Murphy made a dramatic announcement of their change of position on the flag salute issue in a statement which began as follows:

> "The opinion of the Court sanctions a device which, in our opinion, suppresses or tends to suppress *the free exercise of a religion practiced by a minority group. This is but another step in the direction which Minersville School District v. Gobitis took against the same religious minority and is a logical extension of the principles upon which that decision rested.* Since we joined in the opinion in the *Gobitis Case*, we think this is an appropriate occasion to state that *we now believe that it was also wrongly decided.*"[40]

It was this dramatic announcement that has led to the reversal of its position by the Supreme Court on the flag salute issue, and to one of the most remarkable dissenting opinions in the history of the Supreme Court.

No one can read Mr. Justice Frankfurter's dissenting opinion in the second Flag Salute case without being deeply stirred by the emotion with which it is charged,—an emotion evoked by the importance of the issues before the Court as Mr. Justice Frankfurter conceived them. And notwithstanding the depth of emotion which pervades it, Mr. Justice Frankfurter's opinion is closely reasoned,— on the assumption from which it proceeds, namely, that the question before the Court was whether the Jehovah's Witnesses' children are entitled to an exemption from performing an act *which other children may be compelled to perform.* In a long opening paragraph, Mr. Justice Frankfurter states the basic issue involved,—*the proper function of the courts under our constitutional system,*— in the spirit of Justices Holmes, Brandeis, and Cardozo:

> "As a member of this Court I am not justified in writing my private notions of policy into the Constitution, no matter how deeply I may cherish them or how mischievous I may deem their disregard. The duty of a judge who must decide which of two claims before the Court shall prevail, that of a State to enact and *enforce laws within its general competence* or that of an individual to refuse obedience because of the demands of his conscience, is not that of the ordinary person. It can never be emphasized too much that one's own opinion about the wisdom or evil of a law should be excluded altogether when one is doing one's duty on the bench. The only opinion of our own even looking in that direction that is material is our opinion *whether legislators could in reason have enacted such a law.* In the light of all the circumstances, including the history of this question in this Court, it would require more daring than I possess to deny that reasonable legislators could have taken the action which is before us for review. Most unwillingly, therefore, I must differ from my brethren with regard to legislation like this. I cannot bring my mind to believe that the "liberty" secured by the Due Process Clause gives this Court authority to deny to the State of West Virginia the attainment of that which we all recognize as a legitimate legislative end, namely, *the promotion of*

---

40. 316 U. S. 584 at pp. 623-4.

good citizenship, by employment of the means here chosen."[41]

Having thus delimited the province of Judicial Review in our constitutional system, he proceeds to state the immediate constitutional problem before the Court, as he conceives it, *namely, whether the constitutional guarantee of religious freedom means equality of all religions or special privileges in favor of religion:*

> "What one can say with assurance is that the history out of which grew constitutional provisions for religious equality and the writings of the great exponents of religious freedom—Jefferson, Madison, John Adams, Benjamin Franklin —are totally wanting in justification for a claim by dissidents of exceptional immunity from civic measures of general applicability, measures not in fact disguised assaults upon such dissident views. The great leaders of the American Revolution were determined to remove political support from every religious establishment. They put on an equality the different religious sects— Episcopalians, Presbyterians, Catholics, Baptists, Methodists, Quakers, Huguenots —which, as dissenters, had been under the heel of the various orthodoxies that prevailed in different colonies. So far as the state was concerned, there was to be neither orthodoxy nor heterodoxy. And so Jefferson and those who followed him wrote guarantees of religious freedom into our constitutions. Religious minorities as well as religious majorities were to be equal in the eyes of the political state. But Jefferson and the others also knew that minorities may disrupt society. It never would have occurred to them to write into the Constitution the subordination of the general civil authority of the state to sectarian scruples.
>
> "The constitutional protection of religious freedom terminated disabilities, *it did not create new privileges.* * * *
>
> "The validity of secular laws cannot be measured by their conformity to religious doctrines. *It is only in a theocratic state that ecclesiastical doctrines measure legal right or wrong."*[42]

On the issue thus stated, on the assumptions thus made, Mr. Justice Frankfurter's position is unassailable. The real difficulty with this position is that the assumptions are unwarranted,—the real question before the Court being not whether Jehovah's Witnesses' children are entitled to exemptions from the provisions of a law which others are bound to obey, but whether the law in question is such that *anybody* need obey it. It is difficult to say what Mr. Justice Frankfurter's position would be had the situation not been complicated by the justified fear of equality before the law being turned into special privilege. Let us hope that that fear will soon be removed,—clearing the way for a recognition of a clear distinction between the function of the courts in cases involving economic problems, which are properly within the competence of the legislative organs of our Governments, State and National, and the specific freedoms guaranteed by the Constitution, which are expressly withdrawn from their competence.

This distinction was really made, although not expressly stated, in *Schneider* v. *Irvington,* when the Court said, speaking through Mr. Justice Roberts:

> "This Court has characterized the freedom of speech and that of the press as fundamentally personal rights and liberties. The phrase is not an empty one and was not lightly used. * * *
>
> "In every case, therefore, where legislative abridgment of the rights is asserted, the Courts should be *astute* to examine the effect of the challenged legislation. Mere legislative preferences or beliefs respecting matters of public convenience may well support regulations directed at other personal activities, but be insufficient to justify such as diminishes the exercise of rights so vital to the maintenance of democratic institutions."[43]

Mr. Justice Frankfurter joined in the decision in that case, and presumably in the opinion delivered by Mr. Justice Roberts. And he also joined in the decision of the Supreme Court in *Thornhill* v. *Alabama,*[44] in which the Court again expressed the same thought,—this time speaking through Mr. Justice Murphy, who said:

---

41. 319 U. S. 624 at pp. 646-7.
42. Id. at pp. 652-4.

43. 308 U. S. 147 at p. 161.
44. 310 U. S. 88 (1940).

"Mere legislative preference for one rather than another means for combatting substantive evils, therefore, may well prove an inadequate foundation on which to rest regulations which are aimed at or in their operation diminish the effective exercise of rights so necessary to the maintenance of democratic institutions. It is imperative that, when the effective exercise of these rights is claimed to be abridged, the Courts should 'weigh the circumstances', and 'appraise the substantiality of the reasons advanced' in support of the challenged regulations".[45]

The distinction is now made explicit in Mr. Justice Jackson's opinion in the second Flag Salute case:

"The Gobitis opinion reasoned that that is a field 'where Courts possess no marked and certainly no controlling competence', that it is committed to the legislatures as well as the courts to guard cherished liberties and that it is constitutionally appropriate to 'fight out the wise use of legislative authority in the forum of public opinion and before legislative assemblies rather than to transfer the contest to the judicial arena' ". * * *

"The very purpose of a Bill of Rights was to *withdraw* certain subjects from the vicissitudes of political controversy, to place them beyond the reach of majorities and officials and to establish them as legal principles to be applied by the courts. One's right to life, liberty, and property, to free speech, a free press, freedom of worship and assembly, and other fundamental rights may not be submitted to vote; they depend on the outcome of no elections.

"In weighing arguments of the parties it is important to distinguish between the due process clause of the Fourteenth Amendment as an instrument for transmitting the principles of the First Amendment and those cases in which it is applied for its own sake. The test of legislation which collides with the Fourteenth Amendment, because it also collides with the principles of the First, *is much more definite* than the test when only the Fourteenth is involved. Much of the vagueness of the due process clause disappears when the *specific prohibitions* of the First become its standard. The right of a state to regulate, for exam-

ple, a public utility may well include, so far as the due process test is concerned, power to impose all of the restrictions which a legislature may have a 'rational basis' for adopting. But freedoms of speech and of press, of assembly, and of worship may not be infringed on such slender grounds. They are susceptible of restriction only to prevent grave and immediate danger to interests which the state may lawfully protect".[46]

This is the first time, as far as I know, that the Supreme Court has explicitly recognized the distinction between cases dealing with economic problems *which are properly the subject of legislation,* and the freedoms of the First Amendment, now protected by the Fourteenth Amendment from state interference, which are *withdrawn* from the sphere of legislation. This recognition is of such tremendous importance in the development of our constitutional law as to overshadow the particular question involved in the flag salute cases.[46a]

Turning now, however, to the specific problem involved in the flag salute question, we must be thankful to Mr. Justice Jackson for clarifying the situation with respect to the nature of the freedom involved. I think Mr. Justice Frankfurter was right in that portion of his opinion in the *Gobitis* case which dealt with the question of "religious worship". But it is "freedom of conscience" that is involved in the requirement to salute the flag, rather than "freedom of worship." And "freedom of conscience" is merely another name for Freedom of Thought, from which all the other freedoms flow. This, too, is made plain by Mr. Justice

---

45. Id. at pp. 95-6.

46. 319 U. S. 624 at pp. 638-9.

46a. It, incidentally, gives a complete answer to Professor Commager's plea that we sacrifice our civil liberties lest we may offend against an imaginary abstract principle of majority rule, supposed to have been believed in by Thomas Jefferson. As pointed out in the first of these articles, Jefferson deliberately intended to place the Bill of Rights under the protection of the courts. So long as the courts used the power granted to them in this respect for the illegitimate purpose of interfering with economic legislation, it may have been arguable that we give up this protection—which in the past has been of little practical value—in the hope that we would stay the hands of the courts from interfering with economic experimentation. Now, however, that the Supreme Court has recognized the distinction between economic legislation and the freedoms guaranteed by the Constitution, there certainly is no reason why we should sacrifice a single iota of the freedoms guaranteed by the United States Constitution.

Jackson, speaking for the Court in the second Flag Salute case:

> "Nor does the issue as we see it turn on one's possession of particular religious views or the sincerity with which they are held. While religion supplies appellees' enduring motive for enduring the discomforts of making the issue in this case, many citizens who do not share these religious views hold such a compulsory rite to infringe constitutional liberty of the individual. It is not necessary to inquire whether non-conformist beliefs will exempt from the duty to salute unless we first find power to make the salute a legal duty."[47]

The Court never reached the question whether the religious motives which impelled Jehovah's Witnesses to violate the statute, put them in a separate category. The only question, therefore, is: *What are the limits of the power of the State to require conformity?*

And the answer to this question is two-fold:

First: *The State has no authority whatsoever in the domain of thought. Freedom of thought is absolute.*

Second: In the domain of *conduct* the State has a right to protect itself against imminent *serious* danger.

This is, of course, the doctrine which was formulated by Mr. Justice Holmes during the First World War and is now the official doctrine of the Supreme Court. The difficulty arises from a failure to correlate the problem of freedom of thought. This relation, as given by the majority of the Supreme Court may be stated thus: Democracy, the foundation of *our* State and the guarantee of its safety, presupposes absolute freedom of thought, and is only possible where the formulation of thought is left absolutely free. To permit the State to require the expression of assent to a given mode of thought is destructive of that freedom of thought which lies at the basis of its safety as a democratic state. It is not solicitude for the individual who harbors non-conformist thoughts that led to the insertion of these guarantees into our Constitution, but the conviction that free institutions can only result from free thoughts freely expressed. The habit of free expression of one's thoughts is vital to free society. The requirement of conformity,—breeding the *habit* of conformity,—is its mortal enemy.

Saluting the flag, like genuflection and similar bodily gestures, is an expression of thought; and it is this that lies behind the requirement, whether by law or custom. Whenever required, whether by the state or by a group, it is intended to show conformity to the thought which the state or the group considers important. It is this that lay behind the various requirements for the salute which have been exacted from time to time by various agencies, state and other, which sought to impose their will upon others. The Hitler salute is only the last of a long series of such tyrannical requirements. And it is a safe guess that at least some of the members of the Supreme Court were influenced in their decision by the horrible example of this latest manifestation of human tyranny.

People have, of course, saluted heroes and symbols of heroism, freedom, and the struggle for freedom. But those have always come freely from free people. They cease to have any meaning—nay, turn into their opposite—when they come as the result of imposed conformity.

Our heritage of freedom is largely the result of the struggle of the English people over the centuries to preserve and enlarge their liberties. In this struggle the "non-conformist conscience," religious as well as secular, has played a decisive role. The decision of the Supreme Court in the second Flag Salute case is in line with that glorious tradition; and is particularly to be welcomed at a time when the temptation is great to overlook the nature of the means we employ in an effort to achieve a good result. The unity of the nation is a desirable immediate end. But it is only a means to an ultimate end,—a united *free* nation. But that is not achieved by an *imposed* national unity. Religious freedom as well as secular freedom was achieved in the fight *against* the slogan: "One God, one King, one Country!"

---

47. Id. at pp. 634-5.

Justice Frankfurter's Opinions in the Flag Salute Cases: Blending Logic and Psychologic in Constitutional Decisionmaking*

Richard Danzig**

Although their roles have been established in mature form for more than 180 years, there has been remarkably little insight into how the Justices of the Supreme Court of the United States arrive at their decisions in constitutional cases, and scarcely more agreement about how they ought to arrive at those decisions. Most informed observers no longer believe that the legal universe operates according to enduring, classical, and objectively determinable rules. No longer do we believe that a Supreme Court Justice has "only . . . to lay the article of the Constitution which is invoked beside the statute which is challenged and to decide whether the latter squares with the former."[1] But although the old theory of objective rules has been largely displaced, the newer, "more realistic" theory has put little in its stead.

Legal realists and their political science cousins, judicial behavioralists, tell us that a judge's values and perceptions shape his decisions.[2] This assertion rests first on the observation that the corpus of legal rules is in most respects too ambiguous and contradictory to compel the application in any given fact situation of a single rule

---

* Work on this essay was supported by the Harvard Society of Fellows and The Rockefeller Foundation. I thank both organizations for their generosity. I am also grateful to friends and colleagues at my law firm, Latham, Watkins and Hills, and at Chicago, Georgetown, Harvard, Iowa, Stanford, and Yale Law Schools, where, at various times, drafts of this essay were presented or reviewed. I would like particularly to note the special thoughtfulness of Jay Casper, Paul Freund, Fred Konefsky, Tom Krattenmaker, Sandy Levinson and Jan Vetter in making this a better product than it otherwise would be.

** B.A. 1965, Reed College; B. Phil. 1967, D. Phil. 1968, Oxford University; J.D. 1971, Yale University; Partner, Latham, Watkins and Hills (Washington, D.C.).

1. United States v. Butler, 297 U.S. 1, 62 (1936).
2. *See, e.g.*, Danelski, *Values as Variables in Judicial Decision-Making: Notes Toward a Theory*, 19 VAND. L. REV. 721, 728 (1966).

that would yield an inevitable and straightforward result.[3] This assertion is further supported by the recognition that rules cannot be applied to facts until after fact situations are characterized as falling under one or another rule—a characterization that will depend on the judge's values and perceptions. These two propositions are buttressed by studies that demonstrate that the Justices' opinions form patterns that seem more consistent with realist-behavioralist hypotheses than with the Justices' avowed constitutional theories.[4]

But "[f]or the most part, discussion has ceased at this point."[5] Though biographers describe their impressions that a Justice's background or beliefs affected a particular decision, and though casual comments to this effect abound in the corridors of courts[6] and universities, scholars have not given us a study that demonstrates precisely

---

3. Perhaps the most famous statement of this observation is that of Justice Holmes: "General propositions do not decide concrete cases." Lochner v. New York, 198 U.S. 45, 76 (1905) (Holmes, J., dissenting). On contradictions in legal rules and therefore the freedom of judges and advocates, see K. LLEWELLYN, THE COMMON LAW TRADITION: DECIDING APPEALS app. C (1960); Llewellyn, *Remarks on the Theory of Appellate Decision and the Rules or Canons About How Statutes Are to be Construed*, 3 VAND. L. REV. 395 (1950).

4. *See, e.g.,* G. SCHUBERT, THE JUDICIAL MIND (1965). A useful survey of such studies may be found in W. MURPHY & C. PRITCHETT, COURTS, JUDGES AND POLITICS (2d ed. 1974), especially in the appendix, *Modes of Research and Analysis, id.* at 693-700. Among criticisms of this type of analysis, Spaeth & Peterson, *The Analysis and Interpretation of Dimensionality: The Case of Civil Liberties and Decisionmaking,* 15 MIDWEST J. POL. SCI. 415 (1971), is particularly worthwhile.

5. R. WASSERSTROM, THE JUDICIAL DECISION 20 (1961).

6. See, for example, Justice Jackson's admission of predispositions in judging cases:
You try to approach each case without predictions, or pre-judgments, but sometimes that's difficult. One shouldn't, of course, make up his mind until he's heard the argument on both sides, but sometimes in his own experience he's been up against the problem or is familiar with it in some way, and he's very apt to have an impression from the mere statement of the question as to which way he feels about it . . . . My own weakness as a judge, I feel, is that I'm perhaps too quick to make up my mind which way I'll go. Perhaps I don't give enough consideration to it. I pretty quickly make up my mind as to which side of any question I want to be on.
R. JACKSON, ORAL HISTORY MEMOIR, pt. VIII, at 20-21 (Phillips ed. 1952) (on file at the Oral History Project Office, Columbia University) [hereinafter cited as JACKSON ORAL HISTORY MEMOIR].

Justice Douglas made similar comments on the issue of judges' predispositions being translated into decisions:
A judge's reaction to vague statutory language is bound to be like his reaction to the generalities of constitutional clauses. The language that he construes gathers meaning and overtones, significance and relevancy in terms of his own life and experience, his personal set of values, his training and education, and the genes of the blood stream of his ancestors. It would be as futile to argue that judges are not human as it would to prove that politics and legislatures can be divorced."
Douglas, *The Dissenting Opinion,* 8 LAW. GUILD REV. 467, 468 (1948). *See generally* B. CARDOZO, THE NATURE OF THE JUDICIAL PROCESS (1921); Hutcheson, *The Judgment Intuitive: The Function of the "Hunch" in Judicial Decision,* 14 CORNELL L.Q. 274 (1929).

how a specific judge's personal values and perceptions entered into the legal calculus in a particular act of judging.[7] Instead, the realist critic has typically contented himself with demonstrating simply that a judge was predisposed to choose A rather than B, and that he in fact chose A. This "proof" of a parallelism between private preference and public decision, however, is like the work of a detective who can place his suspect at the scene of a crime and delineate his motives but cannot describe how the deed was done. A convincing demonstration of psychological motivation in judging should trace how and at which points a judge's personal, subjective considerations supplemented or subordinated his impersonal, objective judgments.

By committing himself to the task of showing a judge's way as well as his will, the realist would establish a discipline that I think is necessary. A showing that a man or woman brought to the bench a psychological syndrome, an ethnic prejudice, or an ideological inclination proves only that the judge was human. To separate true insight into judging from gossip about judges, realists ought, I believe, to insist on a demonstration of the particular respects in which private predispositions infiltrate legal analysis. Demonstrations of this kind are needed also if we are to understand the art of judging and the place of judges in our constitutional system. For only by offering a detailed description of the ways of judging can we effectively prescribe what those ways should be.

In this essay, I attempt an analysis of the merger of the personal and the impersonal in constitutional decisionmaking by reviewing a judicial performance that has recently attracted intense commentary from so-called psychohistorians: Justice Frankfurter's opinions in the flag salute cases.[8] In June of 1940, the Supreme Court of the United

---

7. The best study of how personal values and perceptions are brought into the legal calculus still renders analyses with much less particularity than I think is necessary. *See* J. HOWARD, MR. JUSTICE MURPHY (1968); *see also* Ulmer, *Bricolage and Assorted Thoughts on Working in the Papers of Supreme Court Justices*, 35 J. POL. 286 (1973). Other biographical efforts are weak when compared with Howard's. *See, e.g.*, L. BAKER, FELIX FRANKFURTER (1969); G. DUNNE, HUGO BLACK AND THE JUDICIAL REVOLUTION (1977); F. HARPER, JUSTICE RUTLEDGE AND THE BRIGHT CONSTELLATION (1965); H. HIRSCH, THE ENIGMA OF FELIX FRANKFURTER (1981); A. MASON, HARLAN FISKE STONE: PILLAR OF THE LAW (1956). The commendable M. PARRISH, FELIX FRANKFURTER AND HIS TIMES: THE REFORM YEARS (1982) does not attempt to cover Frankfurter's activities as a Justice. For a dated, but useful general summary of the biographical literature on Supreme Court Justices, see Howard, *Judicial Biography and the Behavioral Persuasion*, 65 AM. POL. SCI. REV. 704 (1971).

8. *See* H. HIRSCH, *supra* note 7. Professor Hirsch's book has provoked several reviews. *See, e.g.*, Dorsen, Book Review, 95 HARV. L. REV. 367 (1981); Stone, Book Review, 95 HARV. L. REV. 346 (1981). I do not believe the book meets the criteria I have set for a useful realist analysis of judging. Professor Hirsch argues that Justice Frankfurter was a "textbook case of

States held, by a vote of eight to one in *Minersville School District v. Gobitis*,[9] that expelling Jehovah's Witnesses children from public schools for refusing to salute the flag was constitutionally tolerable. Felix Frankfurter wrote the majority opinion. Three years later, in June of 1943, the Court held, by a vote of six to three in *West Virginia Board of Education v. Barnette*,[10] that such expulsions and the concomitant compelled flag salutes were constitutionally repugnant and thus must cease. Felix Frankfurter wrote a fierce dissent. By examining these opinions, I aim to show how Justice Frankfurter integrated personal and psychological propositions with legal and logical ones and how the circumstances of these important constitutional cases encouraged, indeed demanded, this integration. Neither a doctrinal nor a psychological analysis alone properly tells the story: The two must be combined to understand constitutional decisionmaking. After demonstrating this integration in the context of Justice Frankfurter's performance in the flag salute cases, I conclude with some suggestions regarding what I think this one study implies about how constitutional decisionmaking ought to proceed.

I. THE DOCTRINAL CONTEXT OF JUSTICE FRANKFURTER'S FLAG SALUTE OPINIONS

An odd thing happened during litigation in the first flag salute case. As the case made its way up the judicial ladder, the Gobitas family name was spelled less and less often as Gobitas and more and more often as Gobitis.[11] By the time the matter was decided by the Supreme Court of the United States, the petitioner and his children were carefully and invariably referred to by the latter, mistaken, spelling. Insignificant in itself, this event may be viewed as symbolizing the reduction of human reality to legal reality in the course of

---

a neurotic personality," H. HIRSCH, *supra* note 7, at 5, whose "behavior places him within the narcissistic category." *Id.* at 203. There is reason to dispute these characterizations, *see* Stone, *supra*, at 352-53, but even if they were to be accepted I do not believe that Professor Hirsch compellingly connects them (or similar assertions) to Justice Frankfurter's jurisprudence. Perhaps this is simply a statement about the kind of book Professor Hirsch chose to write: THE ENIGMA OF FELIX FRANKFURTER is devoted more to analyzing the development of Justice Frankfurter's personality and to asserting the effects of that personality on his relations with his colleagues than to assessing the connection between Justice Frankfurter's personality and his jurisprudence.

9. 310 U.S. 586 (1940).
10. 319 U.S. 624 (1943).
11. D. MANWARING, RENDER UNTO CAESAR 278 n.3 (1962); *see also* Record at 6, *Gobitis* (name is sometimes spelled Gobitas and sometimes Gobitis).

In this essay, I will use the now conventional spelling of Gobitis.

litigation, especially Supreme Court litigation. Disputes arise in human terms, but before the bar, in the Justices' chambers, and in the opinions delivered from the bench, issues are abstracted and their factual premises abbreviated and caricatured. That Gobitis never existed by that name was and is of small moment because from the time the litigation began he ceased to be important as a man and became instead only the starting point for a legal argument. As such, he was inevitably left further and further behind as the "matter" advanced through the courts.

Justice Frankfurter's opinion for the majority in *Gobitis* illustrates this tendency towards legal abstraction. Near the beginning of his opinion, the Justice sketched the facts of the case in the barest detail: "Lillian Gobitis, aged twelve, and her brother William, aged ten" were from a family of Jehovah's Witnesses, "for whom the Bible as the Word of God [was] the supreme authority. The children had been brought up conscientiously to believe that [saluting] the flag was forbidden by command of Scripture."[12] They refused to salute and consequently were expelled from the Minersville, Pennsylvania, public schools. Having been described in a few sentences, the Gobitis children departed the opinion. After sparking the dispute, they became irrelevant to the discourse by which it was resolved. Instead, Justice Frankfurter posed "[t]he problem" as a legal abstraction: "Our present task, then, as so often the case with courts, is to reconcile two rights . . . ."[13]

Though expressed in one phrase as a predicate to the legal analysis rather than as a part of it, the transition from a factual discussion of schoolchildren in Minersville to a legal discussion of rights was immensely important. For the movement from the realm of events to the realm of ideas required a doctrinal characterization—the placement of a dispute originally innocent of constitutional labels into a preexisting framework of legal thought. That such a characterization is necessary prior to judicial decision is uncontroversial. The *particular* characterization of an issue is, however, hotly debatable, for it affects the entire legal analysis and thus the end result of the matter.

---

12. *Gobitis*, 310 U.S. at 591-92.
13. *Gobitis*, 310 U.S. at 594.

Justice Jackson's majority opinion in *Barnette* is yet starker in its abstraction. There the case was presented in the form of a petition for an injunction restraining the enforcement of a state flag salute ordinance. Without any specific incident precipitating the matter, all discussion between the litigants and judges proceeded entirely on a constitutional plane. *See Barnette*, 319 U.S. at 633-36; *see also* J. NOONAN, JR., PERSONS AND MASKS OF THE LAW (1976) (discussion of the effects of abstraction on legal discussion generally).

One may therefore ask at the outset what doctrinal alternatives might Justice Frankfurter have used to characterize the situation in *Gobitis,* and why did he select the one he did?

A. *The Advocates' Doctrinal Characterization of the Factual Issues in* Gobitis

The plaintiff's lawyers accomplished the first doctrinal characterization of the *Gobitis* case. They reconceived the factual dispute in Minersville in legal outline and reworked it—highlighting, slighting, or ignoring facts and authorities—to suit their legal conception. They translated the dispute from the medium of everyday life into the medium of litigation.

Gobitis' lawyers saw this case as a conflict between the individual's right of free exercise of religion and the secular authority's power to coerce conduct. Their picture of the litigation was in large measure a consequence of the angle from which they viewed the case. This case—like little litigation before it, but like much litigation after it—was intended to further the interests of a movement.[14] The Gobitis family refused to salute the flag on the instructions of a leader of the Jehovah's Witnesses, "Judge" Rutherford, and Rutherford and the lawyers he employed (all of whom were Jehovah's Witnesses) made the resulting expulsions (as they made expulsions throughout the country) the occasion for litigation in the federal courts. The Gobitis family's individual circumstances were apparently no more significant to the advocates in fact than they were to Justice Frankfurter in theory.

Three years later, the successor flag salute case, *West Virginia Board of Education v. Barnette,* would be argued and decided on a free speech theory.[15] But in 1940, Rutherford and his colleagues entirely over-

---

14. *See generally* Hakman, *The Supreme Court's Political Environment: The Processing of Noncommercial Litigation,* in FRONTIERS OF JUDICIAL RESEARCH 199 (J. Grossman & J. Tanenhaus eds. 1969) (comprehensive study of "litigation lobbying" in 1175 noncommercial Supreme Court cases between 1928 and 1966, discussing the representation of group interests, including those of religious groups, before the Supreme Court).

15. [T]he compulsory flag salute and pledge requires [sic] affirmation of a belief and an attitude of mind . . . . To sustain the compulsory flag salute we are required to say that a Bill of Rights which guards the individual's right to speak his own mind, left it open to public authorities to compel him to utter what is not in his mind.

. . . .

. . . Compulsory unification of opinion achieves only the unanimity of the graveyard.

It seems trite but necessary to say that the First Amendment to our Constitu-

looked this line of argument. To them, *Gobitis* was a suit about the clash between their religion and secular authority. They made this perspective salient not only by concentrating on it exclusively but also by advancing their legal arguments in a starkly religious manner. The Witnesses' advocates ran roughshod over the mores of Supreme Court discourse in much the same way that the children refused to conform to the secular mores of the school. The first words of argument a Justice would have seen in the brief for Gobitis were:

> The vital question in the instant case is this: Shall the creature man be free to exercise his conscientious belief in God and his obedience to the law of Almighty God, the Creator, or shall the creature man be compelled to obey the law or rule of the State, which law of the State, as the creature conscientiously believes, is in direct conflict with the law of Almighty God?[16]

In the twenty-five pages of argument that followed, the fifteen judicial opinions cited were swamped by references to sixty-one biblical passages, which were sometimes labeled "divine precedents." And of the cases cited, seven were at one time or another invoked for no more particularized a proposition than that "[t]his is a Christian nation."[17] In sum, the Justices were presented with an argument that was more religious than secular. Further, insofar as that argument was based upon the Constitution, it was expressed solely in terms of the importance of free exercise of religion. The Witnesses did not mention freedom of speech, and any tendencies to see a secular as well as a religious defense for their conduct were buried beneath an avalanche of religious verbiage.

In giving the case its ultimate constitutional coloration, the Justices painted over this sketch drawn by the advocates. The Justices slighted the free speech aspects of the compelled flag salute when they considered it in 1940. And it was perfectly in keeping with the arguments that he read and heard[18] for Justice Frankfurter to write

---

tion was designed to avoid these ends by avoiding these beginnings . . . . We set up government by consent of the governed, and the Bill of Rights denies those in power any legal opportunity to coerce that consent.

Barnette, 319 U.S. at 633-634, 641.

16. Respondent's Brief at 9, *Gobitis*, 310 U.S. 586, *reprinted in* 310 U.S. at 589.
17. Respondent's Brief at 23, *Gobitis*.
18. The Supreme Court did not keep transcripts of oral arguments in 1940, and contemporary press summaries of the argument are rather uninformative. Judge Rutherford's oral argument was, however, preserved "by the courtesy of a press reporter" who provided what appears to be a transcript to a Jehovah's Witnesses magazine, which reprinted Rutherford's speech. *See* CONSOLATION, May 29, 1940, at 19. In this report, the argument tracks the style of the brief. *See id.* at 23, 24.

A handwritten note that was apparently passed to Justice Murphy by Justice Frank-in *Gobitis* that "[t]he manifold character of man's relations may bring his conception of religious duty into conflict with the secular interest of his fellow-men . . . . Our present task . . . is to reconcile [these] two rights in order to prevent either from destroying the other."[19]

B. *Justice Frankfurter's Doctrinal Characterization of the Factual Issues in* Gobitis

Even more striking than the influence of the advocates on the Justices' perceptions of the rights in question was the disjunction between the advocates' argument and the opinion that was handed down. The *Gobitis* opinion ended with the "present task" of reconciling religious freedom and secular power entirely ignored. Instead, the Court confronted and resolved another, quite different, problem. If the Witnesses saw the dispute in the context of their concern with establishing a boundary between the domains of God and Caesar, Justice Frankfurter found in it an occasion for charting an unmapped part of the boundary between the domains of courts and legislatures. These two views of the dispute had a certain logical connection and, I hope to show, a definite psychological relationship, but the shift in focus from the authority of the Supreme Being to the authority of the Supreme Court placed the case in a context that had not been considered or addressed by the litigants.

Justice Frankfurter effected the shift by asserting that issues of institutional power preempted issues of individual right:

> The case before us must be viewed as though the legislature of Pennsylvania had itself formally directed the flag-salute for the children of Minersville . . . . The precise issue, then, for us to decide is whether the legislatures of the various states and the authorities in a thousand counties and school districts of this country are barred [from enacting such laws] . . . . To stigmatize legislative judgment . . . would amount to no less than the pronouncement of pedagogical and psychological dogma in a field where courts possess no marked and certainly no controlling competence . . . . [T]he end is legitimate. And the effective means for its attainment are still so uncertain and so unauthenticated by science as to preclude us from putting the widely prevalent belief in flag-saluting

---

furter during the *Gobitis* argument reinforces the predominance of the religious issue. "Is it at all probable," Justice Frankfurter wrote, "that the framers of the Bill of Rights would have thought that a requirement to salute the flag violates the protection of the free exercise of religion?" Note from Felix Frankfurter to Frank Murphy (April 25, 1946), Murphy Papers, Box 60, File 690 (available at University of Michigan Law Library).

19. *Gobitis,* 310 U.S. at 593-94.

beyond the pale of legislative power.[20]

Following this reasoning, Justice Frankfurter concluded that the Jehovah's Witnesses' proper course was "[t]o fight out the wise use of legislative authority in the forum of public opinion and before legislative assemblies rather than to transfer such a contest to the judicial arena . . . ."[21]

This shift in the focus of discussion exemplifies a common phenomenon: the reworking of a case between argument and opinion so that in its final disposition a matter reflects less the concerns of the litigants than the agenda of the Justices. Lawyers who are aware of the Court's concerns may be able to lessen the gap between argument and opinion by tailoring their arguments to the Court's agenda. Eventually, as the Jehovah's Witnesses' lawyers appeared and reappeared in the Supreme Court, they developed a history of interchange with the Court and gained some sensitivity to the Justices' concerns.[22] But insofar as their *Gobitis* brief is representative, one can say with some confidence that they had not yet developed such sensitivity when Rutherford argued before the Court in the spring of 1940. For though Rutherford showed no appreciation of it, *Gobitis* was an early incident in the Justices' post-New Deal struggle

---

20. *Id.* at 597-98.

21. *Id.* at 600. The transformation of issues is even more manifest in a private letter written by Justice Frankfurter to Justice Stone just after Justice Stone indicated that he might dissent from Justice Frankfurter's majority opinion. In this letter, Justice Frankfurter gives a nod to the conflict of secular and religious imperatives that so mattered to the litigants, but he does not pretend either to order or to reconcile these "rights." "Here we have the clash of rights, not the clash of wrongs. For resolving such a clash we have no calculus." Instead,

> There is for me, and I know also for you, a great makeweight for dealing with this problem, namely that we are not the primary resolvers of the clash. We are not exercising an independent judgment; we are sitting in judgment upon the judgment of the legislature . . . . [M]y intention—and I hope my execution did not lag too far behind—was to use this opinion as a vehicle for preaching the true democratic faith of not relying on the Court , . . . [W]e ought to let the legislative judgment stand and put the responsibility for its exercise where it belongs.

Letter from Felix Frankfurter to Harlan Fiske Stone (May 27, 1940), Stone Papers, Box 65, File 690 (available at the Library of Congress). Copies of this letter are also extant. *See, e.g.,* Frankfurter Papers, Box 105, File 2197, (available at the Library of Congress); Frankfurter Papers, Box 10, File 26 and Box 171, File 19 (available at Harvard Law School); Murphy Papers, Box 60, File 690 (available at University of Michigan Law Library).

22. The assimilation of the Witnesses' lawyers is crudely quantifiable in terms already used. In the 1939 *Gobitis* brief, 61 biblical references overshadowed 15 judicial citations. *See* text accompanying note 17 *supra*. In a key 1941 brief, 54 biblical citations were buttressed by 86 case citations. Brief for the Appellant, Jobin v. Arizona, 316 U.S. 584 (1942). By the time of *Barnette* in 1943, though the table of statutes cited still began with "Almighty God, Law of," the normal quota of biblical citations (in this instance 71) was outstripped by 133 case citations. Brief for the Appellee, *Barnette*, 319 U.S. 624.

to define the Court's role in national life. To understand the primacy of that concern and the immediate cause of its crystallization in *Gobitis*, we need to look backwards a bit.

1. *The Court's post-New Deal retreat:* Erie *and* Carolene Products.

In 1937, in the wake of Roosevelt's court-packing plan,[23] the Justices had begun a full-scale retreat from the activist administration of substantive federal law and substantive due process that had characterized the preceding decades.[24] On April 28, 1938, the Court completed the renunciation of this activism by handing down *Erie Railroad Co. v. Tompkins*[25] and *United States v. Carolene Products.*[26] Though not commonly noticed, the temporal coincidence of these two famous opinions reflected their conceptual kinship. Both opinions raised basic questions about the Supreme Court's function by renouncing traditional Court powers. In *Erie,* the Court seized on an apparent clash between state and federal common law as an occasion for announcing—to the complete surprise of the litigants[27]—that henceforth there would be no federal common law diversity cases; instead, federal courts would defer to the common law opinions of state judges. And in *Carolene Products,* the Court, in the course of re-

---

23. *See generally* L. BAKER, BACK TO BACK—THE DUEL BETWEEN FDR AND THE SUPREME COURT (1967); A. COPE & F. KRINSKY, FRANKLIN D. ROOSEVELT AND THE SUPREME COURT (rev. ed. 1969).

24. *Compare* West Coast Hotel Co. v. Parrish, 300 U.S. 379 (1937) (holding minimum wage laws constitutional) *and* NLRB v. Jones & Laughlin Steel Corp., 301 U.S. 1 (1937) (sustaining the constitutionality of the National Labor Relations Act) *and* Helvering v. Davis, 301 U.S. 619 (1937) (rebuffing a challenge to the Federal Social Security Act) *with* Schechter Poultry Corp. v. United States, 295 U.S. 495 (1935) (invalidating the National Industrial Recovery Act of 1933) *and* Carter v. Carter Coal Co., 298 U.S. 238 (1936) (striking down aspects of the Bituminous Coal Conservation Act of 1935).

25. 304 U.S. 64 (1938).

26. 304 U.S. 144 (1938).

27. *See Erie,* 304 U.S. at 82 (Butler, J., concurring) ("No constitutional question was suggested or argued below or here.").

> I cannot help but feel a special sympathy with losing counsel in that case:
> Down went Tompkins, thirty [actually thirty-three] thousand blown to the winds, a lifetime on relief to face. Down went the thousands that [the firm representing Tompkins] had spent on the case. [The money was spent among other things on hiding Tompkins so that the railroad could not pressure him into settling.] And down went [Aaron] Danzig [who wrote the brief for Tompkins]. It was a blow from which I could not arise. For two years I had waited for the future to come to me. It was time for me to make my own future. I asked my father if he thought it possible that I could get a job selling coffee. He thought I could . . . ."

A. Danzig, For This Is My Portion 288 (undated) (unpublished manuscript) (in the possession of both Danzigs, senior and junior). *See generally* Younger, *What Happened in Erie,* 56 TEX. L. REV. 1011 (1978) (recounting the personal side of the case).

jecting a constitutional challenge to the Federal Filled Milk Act, summarized the new modesty of recent opinions and reemphasized what had developed into a rule of decision: Henceforth federal legislation would generally be upheld if there was a "rational basis" for the legislative judgment.[28]

Taken together, these two opinions left the Supreme Court almost without function in what had previously been an important part of its docket. If *Erie* mandated deference to state common law decisions and if the *Carolene Products* rationality test meant that the Court would hold constitutionally infirm only those laws that no one could reasonably have enacted, then the Court's role would be significant only in policing federal-state relationships, interpreting and elaborating federal statutes, and developing areas of law that, like patent and admiralty law, the Constitution proscribed to the states.

At the same time that *Carolene Products* employed the self-effacing rationality test, however, it opened the door, in one of the most famous footnotes in Supreme Court history,[29] to a new institutional role for the Court. As originally drafted in Justice Stone's chambers,[30] footnote four of that opinion introduced, in two paragraphs, two important qualifications. In the footnote that was ultimately published, these paragraphs took the following form:

> It is unnecessary to consider now whether legislation which restricts those political processes which can ordinarily be expected to bring about repeal of undesirable legislation, is to be subjected to more exacting judicial scrutiny under the general prohibitions of the Fourteenth Amendment than are most other types of legislation . . . .
>
> Nor need we enquire whether similar considerations enter into the review of statutes directed at particular religions, or national or racial minorities: whether prejudice against discrete and insular minorities may be a special condition, which tends seriously to curtail the operation of those political processes ordinarily to be relied upon to protect minorities, and which may call for a correspondingly more searching judicial inquiry.[31]

When they were circulated for approval, Chief Justice Hughes suggested some uncertainty about these paragraphs. To assuage his concern that the original paragraphs might be too limiting, an addi-

---

28. *Carolene Products*, 304 U.S. at 152.
29. *Id.* at 152 n.4.
30. *See* A. MASON, *supra* note 7, at 513-14 (describing the drafting process). Justice Stone's original circulation may be found in the Stone Papers, Box 63, File 640 (available at the Library of Congress).
31. *Carolene Products*, 304 U.S. at 152 n.4 (citations omitted).

tional paragraph was drafted, noting that "[t]here may be narrower scope for operation of the presumption of constitutionality when legislation appears on its face to be within a specific prohibition of the Constitution, such as those of the first ten amendments, which are deemed equally specific when held to be embraced within the Fourteenth."[32] This new paragraph became the first paragraph in the footnote; Justice Stone's "political processes" point became the second; and his concern over "discrete and insular minorities" became the third.

2. Gobitis: *the first dispute over the* Carolene Products *footnote.*

Overshadowed by *Erie,* the *Carolene Products* footnote, holding the germ of a full-blown jurisprudence, lay dormant for some time after it was handed down. In the 1939 October Term, however, the issues raised by the Jehovah's Witnesses in the *Gobitis* case made immediate much of what had been deferred in the *Carolene Products* footnote, and the footnote in turn gave structure and significance to the opinions rendered in that case. Though *Carolene Products* was not mentioned by the parties and was cited only once in the opinions of the Justices, it was in the context of the ideas presented in the footnote—rather than in regard to the flag salute *per se*—that *Gobitis* had special meaning for Justices Stone and Frankfurter. It was for this reason that both Justice Frankfurter's majority opinion and Justice Stone's lone dissent turned on the manner in which the Court was to decide the case rather than on the substantive issues presented by the advocates.

Cast in the language of *Carolene Products,* the issues in *Gobitis* were these: Was the Court to review the requirement of a flag salute according to the standard applied in the text of *Carolene Products* or according to that hinted at in the footnote? If the footnote controlled, was it endorsed in its entirety? What standard or standards followed from it? Were the flag salute statutes to be assessed under paragraph one, as an allegedly clear violation of the first amendment, applied through the fourteenth? Or was this a paragraph three case because the salute requirement derogated the interests of a discrete and insu-

---

32. *Id.* For a history of the drafting of the footnote, see A. MASON, *supra* note 7, at 513–15; *see also* Letter from Charles Evans Hughes to Harlan Fiske Stone (April 18, 1938), Stone Papers, Box 63, File 640 (available at the Library of Congress); Letter from Harlan Fiske Stone to Charles Evans Hughes (April 19, 1938), Stone Papers, *supra*; Lusky, *Footnote Redux: A Carolene Products Reminiscence,* 82 COLUM. L. REV. 1093 (1982) (reviewing the history of the footnote and reproducing the correspondence between the Chief Justice and Justice Stone).

lar minority? Did it matter under which heading analysis proceeded?

Though it mentioned *Carolene Products* only once,[33] Justice Stone's dissent was clearly cast along the lines of the footnote's first and third paragraphs. It stated that the salute requirement "operates to repress the religious freedom of small minorities, which is admittedly within the scope of the protection of the Bill of Rights . . . ."[34] To press his paragraph one attack, Justice Stone placed special emphasis on the "specificity of [the constitutional command] where freedom of speech and of religion are concerned . . . ."[35] Stressing his paragraph three concern about minorities, Justice Stone wrote:

> Here we have . . . a small minority entertaining in good faith a religious belief, which is such a departure from the usual course of human conduct, that most persons are disposed to regard it with little toleration or concern. In such circumstances careful scrutiny of legislative efforts to secure conformity of belief and opinion by a compulsory affirmation of the desired belief, is especially needful if civil rights are to receive any protection. Tested by this standard, I am not prepared to say that the right of this small and helpless minority . . . is to be overborne by the interest of the state in maintaining discipline in the schools.[36]

Justice Frankfurter, in contrast, offered a view that emasculated paragraph one and implicitly excised the concerns of paragraph three from those to which he was willing to afford special protection. In his view, the Court's mandate to apply more than a rationality test to challenged legislation extended only to instances when the democratic process that might effect a legislative correction was itself impaired. For Justice Frankfurter, the only acceptable part of the *Carolene Products* footnote was paragraph two.[37]

He did not say so explicitly, but the implication was clear. In the midst of considering *Gobitis,* he wrote a personal letter about the footnote to Justice Stone in which he attempted to collapse the whole footnote into its second paragraph:

> I am aware of the important distinction which you so skillfully adumbrated in your footnote four (particularly the second paragraph of it) in the Carolene Products Co. case. I agree with that distinction; I regard it as basic. I have taken over that distinction in its central aspect, however inadequately, in the present opinion by in-

---

33. *Gobitis,* 310 U.S. at 606 (Stone, J., dissenting).
34. *Id.* at 607 (Stone, J., dissenting).
35. *Id.* at 602 (Stone, J., dissenting).
36. *Id.* at 606 (Stone, J., dissenting).
37. *See* Lusky, *supra* note 32, at 1103.

sisting on the importance of keeping open all those channels of free expression by which undesirable legislation may be removed, and keeping unobstructed all forms of protest against what are deemed invasions of conscience, however much the invasion may be justified on the score of the deepest interests of national wellbeing.[38]

Justice Frankfurter's *Gobitis* opinion also reflected this approach:

> Except where the transgression of constitutional liberty is too plain for argument, personal freedom is best maintained—so long as the remedial channels of the democratic process remain open and unobstructed—when it is ingrained in a people's habits and not enforced against popular policy by the coercion of adjudicated law.[39]

Despite the stress in Justice Stone's *Gobitis* dissent on the discrete and insular minority concerns of the third paragraph of the *Carolene Products* footnote, Justice Frankfurter's majority opinion said nothing about the minority status of the Jehovah's Witnesses. Indeed, Justice Frankfurter's conclusion that the Witnesses should "fight out the wise use of legislative authority in the forum of public opinion and before legislative assemblies rather than . . . transfer such a contest to the judicial arena" because "all the effective means of inducing political changes [were] left free from interference"[40] implied either that the Witnesses were not a discrete and insular minority (and if they were not, what group was?) or that such status was without significance in constitutional litigation.

As to Justice Stone's paragraph one argument that compulsory flag salutes transgressed "on their face" guarantees of freedom of religion and to a lesser extent speech, Justice Frankfurter responded simply by saying that these claims were not "too plain for argument."[41] The right of free exercise had not previously been taken to warrant exclusion from general legislation. And even if the salute requirement implicated the right of free speech (referred to, but not stressed, by Justice Stone), the question remained whether the legislative preference for this method of effecting national cohesion outweighed that right.[42]

These different doctrinal approaches to *Gobitis* led Justices Stone and Frankfurter to apply quite different standards in assessing the constitutionality of the flag salute requirement and hence to reach different conclusions about its validity. But it is suggestive of the

---

38. Letter from Felix Frankfurter to Harlan Fiske Stone, *supra* note 21.
39. *Gobitis*, 310 U.S. at 599 (footnote omitted).
40. *Id.* at 600.
41. *Id.* at 599.
42. *Id.* at 595.

unsettled nature of the debate that each Justice was either ambivalent or ambiguous as to the standard he was applying. In places, Justice Stone's words suggested the absolutist position later made famous by Justice Black.[43] In other places, he wrote as though the legislature needed to show only that it had pursued a legitimate end by what later came to be called the "least drastic means."[44] But he always applied more than a simple rationality test. Justice Frankfurter's discussion of the standard he was applying was also blurred, but on the whole he appeared to use in *Gobitis* the same rationality test that had been endorsed in the text of *Carolene Products* in the context of legislation affecting economic interests.[45]

In his letter to Justice Stone, Justice Frankfurter clearly identified his use of the rationality test:

---

43. *See, e.g.*, *id.* at 604 (Stone, J., dissenting) ("If these guarantees are to have any meaning they must, I think, be deemed to withhold from the state any authority to compel belief or the expression of it where that expression violates religious convictions, whatever may be the legislative view of the desirability of such compulsion."); *id.* at 605 (Stone, J., dissenting) ("I cannot conceive that in prescribing, as limitations upon the powers of government, the freedom of the mind and spirit secured by the explicit guarantees of freedom of speech and religion, [the framers] intended or rightly could have left any latitude for a legislative judgment that the compulsory expression of belief which violates religious convictions would better serve the public interest than their protection.").

44. Justice Stone contended that in previous cases the Court had "pointed out" that

> where the performance of governmental functions is brought into conflict with specific constitutional restrictions, there must, when that is possible, be reasonable accommodation between them so as to preserve the essentials of both and that it is the function of courts to determine whether such accommodation is reasonably possible. In the cases just mentioned the Court was of [the] opinion that there were ways enough to secure the legitimate state end without infringing the asserted immunity . . . .

Id. at 603 (Stone, J., dissenting). Coming to the case at hand, Justice Stone argued that

> there are other ways to teach loyalty and patriotism . . . than by compelling the pupil to affirm that which he does not believe . . . . I cannot say that government here is deprived of any interest or function which it is entitled to maintain at the expense of the protection of civil liberties by requiring it to resort to the alternatives . . . .

Id. at 603-04.

Justice Stone's wavering between absolutist and accommodationist positions was paralleled in other areas of his post-1937 jurisprudence. Thus, Professor Gunther notes that in South Carolina Highway Dep't v. Barnwell Bros., 303 U.S. 177 (1938), Justice Stone "suggest[ed] a virtually complete withdrawal from review of state regulations challenged under the commerce clause," while in Southern Pac. Co. v. Arizona, 325 U.S. 761 (1945), he "made [it] clear that a more intense 'balancing' mode of review was appropriate in implementing the dormant commerce clause barrier." G. GUNTHER, CASES AND MATERIALS ON CONSTITUTIONAL LAW 541 n.3 (10th ed. 1980).

45. *See e.g., Gobitis*, 310 U.S. at 598 ("Surely . . . the [legislature's] end is legitimate. And the effective means for its attainment are still so uncertain and so unauthenticated by science as to preclude us from putting the widely prevalent belief in flag-saluting beyond the pale of legislative power.").

I want to avoid the mistake comparable to that made by those whom we criticized when dealing with the control of property . . . . I cannot rid myself of the notion that it is not fantastic, although I think foolish and perhaps worse, for school authorities to believe—as the record in this case explicitly shows the school authorities to have believed—that to allow exemption to some of the children goes far toward disrupting the whole patriotic exercise. And since certainly we must admit the general right of the school authorities to have such flag-saluting exercises, it seems to me that we do not trench on an undebatable territory of libertarian immunity to permit the school authorities a judgment as to the effect of this exemption in the particular setting of our time and circumstances.[46]

Three years later, this view reappeared in Justice Frankfurter's dissent in *Barnette*:

[I]t would require more daring than I possess to deny that reasonable legislators could have taken the action which is before us for review. . . . Only if there be no doubt that any reasonable mind could entertain can we deny to the states the right to resolve doubts their way and not ours.[47]

Justice Frankfurter had adopted a legal view of the flag salute cases that powerfully disposed him against the claims of the Jehovah's Witnesses. His doctrinal characterization of these cases as presenting the issue of the extent of the Court's power and his further determination that they did not deserve special scrutiny under the *Carolene Products* footnote—a characterization that differed from the majority in *Barnette*—remained constant.

This observation is the beginning of my analysis, however, not its conclusion. In the next part, I attempt to show that Justice Frankfurter's doctrinal characterization grew from his personal values and philosophies about society and minorities, and that these values and philosophies in turn reflected his psychological makeup.

II. The Psychological Context of Justice Frankfurter's Flag Salute Opinions

In one of his first law review articles, Felix Frankfurter wrote about the special characteristics of constitutional law:

Called upon late in life to teach constitutional law, a great teacher of property law, after a brief trial, gave it up in despair on the ground that constitutional law "was not law at all, but politics." . . . Undoubtedly, such a field of law by the very nature of the

---

46. Letter from Felix Frankfurter to Harlan Fiske Stone, *supra* note 21.
47. *Barnette*, 319 U.S. at 647, 661-62 (Frankfurter, J., dissenting).

issues sought to be settled, by reason of the interests sought to be enforced, leaves wider scope and calls for the exercise of a broader experience than the familiar domains of the common law. . . . [T]he necessary flexibility makes the personality of the justices so much more important in their decisions on constitutional law than in questions of property or corporation law.[48]

The fact that Justice Frankfurter perceived the flag salute cases in the context of *Carolene Products* advances our understanding of his approach in those cases only a little. For Justice Stone's dissent in *Gobitis* (and Justice Jackson's opinion for the Court in *Barnette*) make it clear that perceiving the flag salute cases in that context did not mandate the specific conclusion reached by Justice Frankfurter. Why did Justice Frankfurter rigidly overlook, and thus override, concerns about discrete and insular minorities? Why did he insist that a mere rationality test should be applied to a requirement that was challenged on free exercise grounds? The Constitution, after all, did not offer any indication of what standard of review should be applied to government acts that arguably contravened its amendments. Why, while rejecting the first and third paragraphs of the footnote, did he endorse the second paragraph's political process concerns? To answer these questions, we must reconstruct the values and perceptions that determined Felix Frankfurter's choice of doctrine in these particular cases. As Justice Frankfurter wrote in *Barnette*: "This is no dry, technical matter. It cuts deep into one's conception of the democratic process . . . ."[49]

A. *Justice Frankfurter's Aversion to the Paragraph Three "Discrete and Insular Minorities" Argument*

Near the beginning of *Felix Frankfurter Reminisces*, Justice Frankfurter related an anecdote that touched on problems similar to those raised by *Gobitis*. I reproduce it at length because its recounting of one nonjudicial incident reveals much about the man who rebuffed the Jehovah's Witnesses' arguments.

Despite Felix Frankfurter's exceptional record at Harvard Law School, as his graduation approached he apparently became concerned about his employment prospects. An acquaintance encouraged him by remarking "that a good office needs a good man just as much as a good man needs a good office."[50]

---

48. Frankfurter, *The Constitutional Opinions of Justice Holmes*, 29 HARV. L. REV. 683, 683 (1916).
49. *Barnette*, 319 U.S. at 651 (Frankfurter, J., dissenting).
50. H. PHILLIPS, FELIX FRANKFURTER REMINISCES 36 (1960). This book is drawn

That was a revelation from heaven. That put the thing in proper perspective, that I wasn't a mendicant, that I had something they wanted as much as they something I wanted. There was one office, Hornblower, Byrne, Miller & Potter, that was one of the best offices at the time. Lots of Harvard people were in there. I'd heard that they had never taken a Jew and wouldn't take a Jew. I decided that that was the office I wanted to get into not for any reason of truculence, but I was very early infused with, had inculcated in me, a very profoundly wise attitude toward the whole fact that I was a Jew, the essence of which is that you should be a biped and walk on the two legs that man has. To me as a philosophy of action, as an attitude, it's as simple as saying you should neither be truculent nor subservient, you should just be a biped. You should take that ultimate fact that you were born of these parents instead of some other parents as much for granted as the fact that you've got green-brown eyes instead of blue eyes.

An uncle of mine said to me when I was a boy, "You'll encounter a great deal of anti-Semitism in your life, but don't go around sniffing anti-Semitism."

Some of the lads at the Harvard Law School occasionally—a Jewish lad who failed and then thought there might be reasons for that—were soon made to realize that I was not a Jewish professor at the Harvard Law School, but I was a Harvard Law School professor who happened to be a Jew. In fact, I know that I exacted higher standards from Jews than from other people, and perhaps that was on the whole a good thing for Jews who have any capacity.

But this is partly a result of the way you're made. I have evidently a great deal of vivacity and buoyancy. I don't have much hate in my composition, and I'm a great believer in reason. I have a romantic view about reason. You've got nothing else except that poor reed of reason to lean on in order to get away as far as possible from the jungle and earth from whence we all come and a good deal of which we have in us. So I thought that a rule like that, not to take a Jew into a law office, was just born of ignorance, stupidity and ignorance. I thought it would be interesting just to go there and have them realize that this was just an artifact of theirs, that a Jew was something different. That's where I wanted to go.

Well, I was so highly recommended, particularly to the junior partner who was hiring the people, that I went in there to get a job.

---

from transcripts of tape recorded interviews conducted (mainly, but apparently not exclusively, by the editor) with Justice Frankfurter between 1953 and 1957. The published volume tracks the available transcribed text with only minor corrections and the frequent deletion of the interviewer's questions. *Cf.* Columbia Oral History Project, Felix Frankfurter Reminisces (microfiche available from Columbia University). *See also* B. Goldstein, The Tape and Book Media of Communication as Precious Helpmeets (private printing, Saint Xavier College, Chicago, Illinois, April 1, 1965) (available at the Library of Congress and at the Library of the Supreme Court of the United States).

> This fellow, who was a distinguished younger product of the Harvard Law School, evidently took a kind of shine to me. He was a bachelor, and he sort of thought he'd be my patron. He talked to me, as he said, like a warm friend. He said that now that I had started life, as it were that life was beginning, "this is a good time to change your name. Frankfurter—you know, there's nothing the matter with it, but it's odd, fun-making."
>
> That's the way to begin life. Up to this time I hadn't lived, and since I was going to begin living, he suggested, "Give yourself an appropriate name."
>
> I said, "Thank you very much," but I thought I'd better get along with what circumstances had given me, and he thought that was very foolish. Anyhow I began at Hornblower, Byrne, Miller & Potter for $1000 a year.[51]

The fact that Justice Frankfurter recited this account on several occasions in the half-century after its occurrence, the contemporary importance of the experience it relates, and the account's description of the experience as reinforcing a preexisting "philosophy of action" that "was very early infused . . . inculcated in me," all suggest that this anecdote is psychologically significant. The raw facts of the experience, like the raw facts of the *Gobitis* case, could have been interpreted in a number of ways. The experience could add to a despair over the pervasiveness of anti-Semitism or buttress a conviction that anti-Semitism could be readily overcome; it could be seen as emphasizing the importance of connections or underscoring the ultimate power of merit. It is probably impossible to discern how Felix Frankfurter's upbringing, education, and exposure to the then-prevalent philosophies of pragmatism and progressivism shaped his interpretation of this event. But the resulting interpretation and the world view that underlay it are relatively clear.

1. *Justice Frankfurter's perceptions of reason and assimilation and their relationship to democracy.*

Reason, the "poor reed" that alone could get us "away as far as possible from the jungle and the earth," held a central position in Felix Frankfurter's thought.[52] He believed that people and positions

---

51. H. PHILLIPS, *supra* note 50, at 36-39.
52. There are several strands in Justice Frankfurter's background that may have contributed to the intensity of his view. The Jewish culture of the time emphasized "scholarship . . . as the pathway . . . to God." I. HOWE, WORLD OF OUR FATHERS 8 (1976). Within this tradition, "[s]tudy was a technique for sublimating feeling into thought, for transposing dreams into syllogisms . . . ." *Id.* at 13 (quoting Abraham Heschel).

Justice Frankfurter's secular education encouraged his focus on reason and his compartmentalization of emotion, both as a matter of practice and as an ideal. *See* notes 60, 61 *infra*;

were not normally irreconcilable[53]—that the power of persuasion by rational argument was very great.[54] Almost no faction should be written off as uneducable, no end as unachievable by persuasion.[55] The key was to effect the proper education, in political as well as in university life.[56] From these premises, Felix Frankfurter generated a "buoyant" view of American life and an energizing prescription for participating in it.[57]

---

see also Letter from Felix Frankfurter to Robert Jackson (Feb. 23, 1944), Frankfurter Papers, (available at the Library of Congress) ("You see, my dear Bob, one drawback of a professor is that he does believe in reason and profoundly believes that the mode by which results are reached is as important—maybe even more important—in the evolution of society as the result itself.").

53. Of course [William Jennings Bryan's] influence waned. He had a certain naiveté, and a very parochial outlook, no sense of the forces he was fighting . . . . He made a terrible break when he came East. He said "I'm now entering the enemy's country." You don't tell an audience whom you want to woo that you regard them as your enemies, and therefore, by implication you're their enemy.

H. PHILLIPS, *supra* note 50, at 6. *See also* Letter from Felix Frankfurter to Morris Cohen (Oct. 3, 1916), *reprinted in* L. ROSENFIELD, PORTRAIT OF A PHILOSOPHER: MORRIS R. COHEN IN LIFE AND LETTERS at 247-48 (1962) (noting first that "the Republican or the Democratic Party means nothing to you or me. We have to work out an association with either, or neither, on purely rational grounds," then explaining that for Chief Justice Hughes there was an "emotional association" with the Republican Party through his family history, but then arguing that whatever his party allegiance, [Chief Justice] Hughes was "subject to the impact of the facts").

54. In his reminiscences, Justice Frankfurter described a four-hour argument with Alice Longworth in which he began by accusing her of showing "biases and prejudices" and she by addressing him in an "icy voice." At the end of the argument, he reported:

[S]he turned from me to [her husband] and said, "Nick, I've always told you that this was a good man" . . . . [T]hat made a great impression on me; the impression was great in the sense of indicating that if you have time enough to probe these problems and the mind you're dealing with isn't really imprisoned, has any sense of pursuing reason and a desire to know, is open to consideration of relevant facts, unless you yourself are unreasonable you can get somewhere. In short, as my wife says, I'm a romantic believer in reason.

H. PHILLIPS, *supra* note 50, at 138-39.

55. *Cf., e.g.,* Letter from Felix Frankfurter to Henry Stimson (Feb. 1, 1919), Frankfurter Papers, Box 103, Folder 2147 (available at the Library of Congress) ("We ought to be able to work out industrial democracy as we have worked out political democracy—without revolution. Undoubtedly it is a slow process of education—education in the widest sense, the education that comes particularly through the participation of the masses.").

56. *See* Letter from Felix Frankfurter to Franklin D. Roosevelt (Nov. 8, 1928), *reprinted in* M. FREEDMAN, ROOSEVELT AND FRANKFURTER: THEIR CORRESPONDENCE, 1928-1945, at 39 (1967) ("[Y]ou have, as Smith has, the conception of government which seems to me indispensable to the vitality of a democratic government, namely, the realization that the processes of government are essentially educational processes.").

57. His view called for "[d]isinterested enthusiasm, freedom from imprisoning dogmatism, capacity for fresh insight, unflagging industry, [and] ardor for difficulties." Frankfurter, *The Young Men Go to Washington,* 13 FORTUNE 61 (1936), *reprinted in* A. MACLEISH & E. PRITCHARD, JR., LAW AND POLITICS: OCCASIONAL PAPERS OF FELIX FRANKFURTER 1913-1938, at 246-47 (1939); *see also* H. PHILLIPS, *supra* note 50, at 242-43; Howe, *Felix Frank-*

Reason was intimately linked to a second value: assimilation.[58] Reason—his own skill at it and others' receptivity to it—had powered Felix Frankfurter to something he craved: acceptance and then importance in American society.[59] His experience—the immensely gratifying progression of a twelve-year-old, non-English-speaking immigrant through a school system that rewarded his intellectual merit, to a profession he viewed as celebrating reason,[60] through a series of governmental posts in which his brains and his zest brought him influence, back as a professor to that Pantheon of hard-headed rationality, the Harvard Law School,[61] and ultimately to a position on the Supreme Court, a position he saw as charged with the duty of dispassionate reasoning[62]—reached its apogee when Frankfurter found

---

furter, 78 HARV. L. REV. 1526, 1526 (1965) (describing Justice Frankfurter: "Did he not, perhaps, innocently misjudge the character of his fellowmen and assume that his intensities were matched in most other human beings? . . . If you take a restraining hand from the impulses of most of us we will not set many fires or agitate many rebellions. . . . The mind and spirit of Felix Frankfurter, however, were charged with . . . an effervescent ardor . . . ."); F. Frankfurter, Diary Entry (May 5, 1943), Frankfurter Papers, Box 2 (available at the Library of Congress), *reprinted in* J. LASH, FROM THE DIARIES OF FELIX FRANKFURTER 235 (1975) (describing a visit in which two of Justice Frankfurter's protégés appeared depressed about current affairs, noting that "I rather talked Dutch to them and indicated that defeatism and pessimism are luxuries we cannot afford, that they seem to forget that reforms are not to be won over night, and that the goals of a decent society constitute a process which must be constantly fought for, and that they must not get weary of welldoing.").

58. Put differently, these values were congruent. "[C]ongruency . . . refers to the harmony between a specific value and other values held by a judge." Danelski, *supra* note 2, at 728.

59. *Cf.* M. HIMMELFARB, THE JEWS OF MODERNITY 23, 49 (1973) ("reason was the modern Jew's ally; from this it was only a small step to a reverence for Reason . . . . In the name of universal reason and ideals, all would be active and equal citizens alike, and Jews would come in from the cold. Actually, to be universally rational and idealistic you may have to abolish all distinctions between Christian and Jew . . . maybe there should no longer be Christian and Jew at all, only men who are citizens.").

60. "I do take law very seriously, deeply seriously," he once explained, "because fragile as reason is and limited as law is as the expression of the institutionalized medium of reason, that's all we have standing between us and the tyranny of mere will and the cruelty of unbridled, undisciplined feeling." L. BAKER, *supra* note 7, at 16 (quoting TIME, Sept. 7, 1962, at 15); *see also* Dennis v. United States, 341 U.S. 494, 525 (1951) (Frankfurter, J., concurring); Frankfurter, *John Marshall and the Judicial Function*, 69 HARV. L. REV. 217, 235 (1955); Letter from Felix Frankfurter to Henry Stimson (Mar. 22, 1921), Frankfurter Papers, Box 103, Folder 2150 (available at the Library of Congress) ("[L]aw is . . . deeper than passing popular passion.").

61. "[F]eeling was feeling and thinking was thinking. . . . It is the tradition of [the Harvard Law] School to foster intellectual discipline. May it never relax its insistence." Address by Felix Frankfurter, Dean James Barr Ames and the Harvard Law School, Law School-Graduate School Alumni Day (June 13, 1956), *reprinted in* P. KURLAND, OF LAW AND LIFE & OTHER THINGS THAT MATTER 32-33 (1965).

62. *See* Public Utils. Comm'n v. Pollak, 343 U.S. 451, 466-67 (1952) (Frankfurter, J., recusing himself); *see also* Hutchinson, *Felix Frankfurter and the Business of the Supreme Court, O.T.*

himself writing *Gobitis,* his first major constitutional opinion for a Supreme Court majority that agreed with his thinking.[63] Felix Frankfurter's advancement and assimilation depended at every step on his whole-hearted and hard-headed commitment to rationality. He used "that poor reed of reason to lean on in order to get away . . . from whence we all come."[64]

It was also important that Justice Frankfurter had used "that poor reed of reason . . . to get away as far as possible from the jungle and earth, *a good deal of which we have in us.*"[65] Experiences of assimilation and advancement further intertwined with the idea of rationality in Justice Frankfurter's mind because of the fact that his gains were achieved in the face of tendencies in others and temptations in himself to regard his prospects as limited by his status as a Jew and an immigrant. Felix Frankfurter refused to hide his background.[66] He believed that assimilation could be made compatible with a distinctive ethnic and religious identity by insisting on the irrelevance of "race or religion or the accidents of antecedents"[67] in the realms to

---

1946-O.T. 1961, 1980 SUP. CT. REV. 143, 164-203 (chronicling fifteen years of effort by Justice Frankfurter to expand time for discussion in the Supreme Court on the theory that rational discussion would lead to sounder decisionmaking); Letter from Felix Frankfurter to Harold Burton (Dec. 27, 1946), Burton Papers, Box 336 (available at the Library of Congress) ("Your concurrence . . . is but another proof of the conscientious disinterestedness of your mind—your readiness to have it take you wherever it guides, regardless of your previous inclination. That, if I may say so, is the judicial function at its best."); *cf.* F. Frankfurter, Diary Entry (Oct. 20, 1946), *reprinted in* J. LASH, *supra* note 57, at 276 ("Schlesinger said that there is a school of thought, particularly centered in Yale, which believes . . . it is a question of whether your side or the other side is going to use the Supreme Court for its purposes. I told him that such an attitude was of course just as wicked as it was dishonest.").

63. Justice Frankfurter had previously written a unanimous opinion in a commerce clause case of little significance. *See* Hale v. Bimco Trading, Inc., 306 U.S. 375 (1939).

64. H. PHILLIPS, *supra* note 50, at 37.

65. *Id.* (emphasis added).

66. In retelling the quoted anecdote, *see* text accompanying note 51 *supra*, in other circumstances, Justice Frankfurter added that "I have no doubt that my mother's advice, 'hold yourself dear,' made me reject the idea. 'My name,' I told my friend, 'is part of me and I ought to respect it as part of my self-respect.'" P. KURLAND, *supra* note 61, at 39. Justice Frankfurter spoke of his mother's admonition as having "saved me from making a deplorable decision on [this] crucial matter immediately after I came out of law school." *Id.*

The suggestion that he change his name may have been especially salient to Justice Frankfurter because one of his brothers did, reportedly, change his name to Frankfort. Interview with Esther Austern, Secretary to Felix Frankfurter at Harvard and, from 1939-1940, at the Supreme Court of the United States (Apr. 24, 1976).

67. *See* M. FREEDMAN, *supra* note 56, at 589 (attributing phrase to speech honoring Oliver Wendell Holmes that was drafted by Felix Frankfurter and delivered by Franklin D. Roosevelt).

which he sought admission.[68] Such assertions grew from the idea of rationality. Rationality depended on adopting a "disinterested" position. Merit had to be established and assessed without regard to idiosyncrasies of background or belief.[69] This norm of rationality enabled Felix Frankfurter to demand that he be viewed as detached from his background even while he maintained his personal integrity by refusing to deny that background.[70] It was rather as if he erected, to employ a phrase used in another context, "a wall of separation"[71] between his public, secular, professional functioning and his private, religious, personal being.[72]

---

68. In this, the assimilation he endorsed and achieved was different from that advocated by Jews who thought Americanization could only be achieved by abandoning Jewishness.

69. Justice Frankfurter believed that merit must be determined without preconceptions of the one whose person or argument was being considered:
   I remember saying to a dear friend of mine, "Don't talk to me about this report as the report of the president of Harvard University! You must go from the report to Mr. Lowell, not from Mr. Lowell to the report. You must deal with this report as though it was an anonymous report written on parchment, on papyrus, which was discovered way back in some catacomb, and some archaeologist who was able to decipher it said, 'This is a report on the conviction of two men. I can't figure out their names—something like Sacco and Vanzetti. This is two thousand-odd years ago, and I'm happy to report that buried with it is the six thousand pages of minutes, so that we can check what was said in this report about these two men against the permanent and controlling facts—the stenographic minutes.'
   You are not thus led to the plausibility of this report by the author of the report. . . ."
H. PHILLIPS, *supra* note 50, at 204.

70. In retelling the story of his refusal to change his name, *see* text accompanying note 51 *supra*, Justice Frankfurter coupled it with an anecdote about his insistence on rational discourse divorced from personal references and cited both anecdotes as "instances" of his adherence to his mother's admonition to "hold yourself dear." For him, the preservation of the personal and its divorce from the professional were two sides of the same coin. For the story of his rejection of a name change, see note 66 *supra*. He told the connected anecdote as follows:
   A few years after [Justice Frankfurter's report to the President on the Mooney case], the fairness of the investigation conducted by me was violently attacked by a nationally known lawyer who then held the distinguished office of Solicitor General of the United States. He was not content to deal with the facts of my report; he made a rather vituperative attack on my character. Considering the source, his article could hardly be left unnoticed. But the natural temptation to strike back and deal with the personal attack was suppressed by the still voice that whispered to me "hold yourself dear." In this situation it meant "don't get down to the other fellow's level," so I confined myself in my reply to an austere statement of facts.
P. KURLAND, *supra* note 61, at 40.

71. Illinois *ex rel.* McCollum v. Board of Educ., 333 U.S. 203, 247 (1948) (wall between church and state).

72. Felix Frankfurter's reaction was hardly idiosyncratic. *See, e.g.,* Auerbach, *Dual Loyalty (Again)*, MOMENT, April 1976, at 53-54 (1976), speaking of American Jews generally: "It was easy enough to be Jewish *and* American if Jewishness was religious rather than nationalistic in content. Confine Jewish identity to religious affiliation and the problem of dual

In the recited anecdote, one sees these points—and even a little more. The tale is one of acceptance in the face of ethnic prejudice. The teller refuses "to begin life" anew. Instead, he retains his name and the integrity of his private identity. But he gets the job. The triumph results from a reliance on rationality. The hero, "a great believer in reason . . . a romantic . . . about reason," enjoys a "revelation" about the power of merit. Inspired, he presents himself not as a "mendicant," not as a Jew, but as a "biped" of proven achievement. In a place where good men (intellectually able men) are needed, he is certifiably a good man, neither more nor less. (Later, he would "make" others realize that "I was not a Jewish professor at the Harvard Law School, but I was a Harvard Law School professor who happened to be a Jew.")

The manner in which the teller recounts his actions reinforces the emphasis on rationality. Where emotion appears ("[t]hat's where I wanted to go") it is described as though born of rational reflection ("it would be *interesting* just to go there").[73] Moreover, just as in his retelling, Frankfurter speaks as though careful thought were the father of worthy emotions, so he depicts his counter-players as thoughtless when their emotions seem unworthy. Prejudice is not an inbred, irremediable, emotional phenomenon; it is an "artifact." Prejudice can be overcome with evidence because it is "just born of ignorance, stupidity and ignorance."

Only one comment hints that Jewishness is relevant to the secular world—that the speaker, who is "neither truculent nor subservient," is in any way affected in his public conduct by his private person. "In fact," he tells us, "I know that I exacted higher standards from Jews than from other people, and perhaps that was on the whole a good thing for Jews who have any capacity."

Felix Frankfurter's notions of rationality and assimilation were basic to his conception of democracy—a conception that had little to do with majoritarian rule. His conception of democracy centered on

---

identity would disappear . . . . Nomenclature is revealing: we speak of Irish Americans or Mexican Americans, but not of Jewish Americans; but rather of American Jews."

73. *Cf.* H. PHILLIPS, *supra* note 50, at 233 ("There were only two temptations I had not to turn the nomination [to the Supreme Judicial Court of Massachusetts] down. There were only two things that seemed to appeal to that part of my nature which is whimsical, why I should like to have accepted. [One of them was that] [i]n those days the seven members of the Supreme Judicial Court of Massachusetts went in lock step every day from where the court was sitting on Ashburton Place, right near the State House, to lunch at the Union Club in formal dress and top hat. I thought that would be an *interesting* thing—to go in lock step in top hat to the Union Club for lunch.") (emphasis added).

a vision of a meritocratic society that endorsed notions of assimilation and rationality similar to his own.[74] His description of Harvard Law School reflects this vision:

> You very quickly got into the atmosphere. There was a dominating atmosphere, first, of professionalism, and what I think is an indispensable quality of true professionalism, the democratic spirit. What mattered was excellence in your profession to which your father or your face was equally irrelevant. And so rich man, poor man, were just irrelevant titles to the equation of human relations. The thing that mattered was what you did professionally.... And so I say, as I've said often in talking to the young, the *Harvard Law Review* in particular and the Harvard Law School in general are to me the most complete practices in democracy that I have ever known anything about.[75]

Justice Frankfurter's reminiscence of his first year as a student at Harvard Law School also reflects his admiration for—indeed, dedication to—the ideals of rationality and absorption and his perception of their connection with his meritocratic conception of democracy. Here the recollection is more personal, and characteristic religious metaphors are reinforced by references to himself as a small man[76] seeking acceptance in a land of giants:

---

74. *See* Frankfurter, *Amherst Commencement Address*, 13 AMHERST ALUMNI COUNCIL NEWS 133 (1940), Frankfurter Papers, Box 198, File 3868 (available at the Library of Congress) ("Democratic society is merely a hypocritical pretense unless in daily life, in college, in shop, in the marketplace, in the halls of legislatures, in Courts, wherever men may gather together, the process of reasoning, the process of exchange of mind, prevails."); F. Frankfurter, Democracy and False Shibboleths, Commencement Address at Radcliffe College (June 8, 1941), *reprinted in* RADCLIFFE Q. (Aug. 1941) ("In the long course of human experience [democracy] has proven itself the only form of social arrangement which adequately respects, and by so doing helps to unfold, the richness of human diversity.... Democracy furnishes the political framework within which alone reason can thrive most imaginatively on the widest scale—least hampered by the accidents of personal antecedents and most regardful of the intrinsic qualities of man."); F. Frankfurter, The Permanence of Jefferson, Address on the Occasion of the Bicentennial of Thomas Jefferson's Birth (April 13, 1943) Frankfurter Papers, Box 198, File 3686, at 10 (available at the Library of Congress).

Higham, *Ethnic Pluralism in Modern American Thought*, in SEND THESE TO ME: JEWS AND OTHER IMMIGRANTS IN URBAN AMERICA 208 (J. Higham ed. 1975) shows the contemporary context in which Frankfurter's views fit, but comments insightfully that the "pluralist thesis from the outset was encapsulated in white ethnocentrism.... Could anyone have designed a pluralism that would have suited blacks as well as Jews, the minorities that were left behind as well as those that were thriving?"); *see also* J. AUERBACH, UNEQUAL JUSTICE: LAWYERS AND SOCIAL CHANGE IN MODERN AMERICA 29 (1976) (calling Justice Frankfurter "the conspicuous exception, not the prototypical product of a democratic meritocracy" and criticizing his views accordingly).

75. H. PHILLIPS, *supra* note 50, at 26-27.

76. "[H]e was less than five feet, five inches." J. LASH, *supra* note 57, at 3; *see also* L. BAKER, *supra* note 7, at 214 ("In appearance, [Justice] Frankfurter did not quite live up to his own idea of what a Supreme Court Justice ought to look like: 'Supreme Court Justices should

> I had never seen Cambridge or Boston before . . . . [T]here was a fellow who seemed small in stature ahead of us. My new friend . . . whispered to me in an awed breath, "That's the editor of the *Harvard Law Review.*"
>
> If he had said, "That's the Archangel Gabriel," he couldn't have been more awed. "My God," I said to myself, "the head of the *Harvard Law Review.* He must be a giant."
>
> The first day I went to my classrooms I had one of the most intense frights of my life. I looked about me. Everybody was taller. I wasn't as tall as I am now. That is a joke. I was a little fellow. I was much thinner. There were a lot of big fellows, tall fellows, robust fellows, self-confident creatures around . . . .
>
> . . . I said, "My God, this is a place for giants, not for a minnow like me." I wanted to leave and go back to Mama probably—you know, psychoanalytically—to return to the womb. I said, "This is too fast a crowd for me."
>
> In no time I reveled in the place. . . .
>
> . . . I buckled down and ended up by being the first in the class, which I continued to be for the three years that I was there, but which I did not know about at the time. I knew I had a high mark because I was made one of the editors of the *Law Review.*
>
> I have a quasi-religious feeling about the Harvard Law School. I regard it as the most democratic institution I know anything about. By "democratic" I mean regard for the intrinsic and for nothing else.[77]

I believe that these anecdotes (and others to which I shall refer) are to Felix Frankfurter's judicial writings as the underplots in Shakespeare's plays are to the main themes. In an everyday context, comparatively naked values are revealed to us that are later shown to operate in more elaborate clothing at more exalted levels.

2. *The manifestation of these perceptions in the flag salute cases.*

Justice Frankfurter's values and perspectives were complex, self-contradictory, and indubitably more extensive than suggested by this narrowly focused summary. But once sensitized to the central ideas I have noted, we find them reflected in the architecture and the detail of Justice Frankfurter's flag salute opinions—opinions that he used, as he expressed it to Justice Stone, as "a vehicle for preaching the true democratic faith."[78] Consider first the famous words with which Frankfurter began his dissent in *Barnette*:

---

be tall and broad and have a little bit of bay window,' he once said. At fifty-six years of age, [Justice] Frankfurter was short and rather slight, with an appearance of tenseness and physical energy.").

77. H. PHILLIPS, *supra* note 50, at 17–19.
78. Letter from Felix Frankfurter to Harlan Fiske Stone, *supra* note 21.

One who belongs to the most vilified and persecuted minority in history is not likely to be insensible to the freedoms guaranteed by our Constitution. Were my purely personal attitude relevant I should wholeheartedly associate myself with the general libertarian views in the Court's opinion, representing as they do the thought and action of a lifetime. But as judges we are neither Jew nor Gentile, neither Catholic nor agnostic. We owe equal attachment to the Constitution and are equally bound by our judicial obligations whether we derive our citizenship from the earliest or the latest immigrants to these shores.[79]

These four sentences of overture—so starkly personal and superficially irrelevant to the issue at hand—sounded the twin themes that dominated Justice Frankfurter's view of the issues raised by the flag salute cases and made it clear that they were intertwined. The opening note suggests the writer's isolation, his position as "one who belongs to the most vilified and persecuted minority in history." Yet the third sentence asserts his assimilation: "But as judges we are neither Jew nor Gentile, neither Catholic nor agnostic." And the fourth reinforces the point. Assimilation is achieved through the suppression of the personal. "Were . . . personal attitude[s] relevant," personal background might distinguish judges and validate or undermine their claims to authority. But personal attitudes are not relevant. Instead, they are walled off from the judicial function. A judge can and must function with dispassionate attachment to the Constitution and to his judicial obligation.[80]

The allegedly impersonal prologue foreshadowed the substance of

---

79. *Barnette,* 319 U.S. at 646-47 (Frankfurter, J., dissenting).
80. Justice Frankfurter's diary entry for the day on which *Barnette* came down underscores this state of mind:

> Before we went on the bench, F[rank] M[urphy] said he would like to say to me "as a friend" and "for your benefit" that it would be a mistake for me to keep in the opening sentences of my Flag Salute opinion. I asked him why. He told me he thought them "too personal" and that they would be "catapulting a personal issue into the arena. I said I could understand that a reference to the fact that I am a Jew would be deemed to be personal if I drew on that fact as a reason for enforcing some minority rights and invoking the protection of the Constitution to declare legislation unconstitutional. But I do not see what is "personal" about referring to the fact that although a Jew, and therefore naturally eager for the protection of minorities, on the Court it is not my business to yield to such considerations, etc. In any event, the sentences will stay in because they are not the products of a moment's or an hour's or a day's or a week's thought—I had thought about the matter for months and I deem it necessary to say and put into print in the U.S. Reports what I conceive to be basic to the function of this Court and the duty of the Justices of this Court.

F. Frankfurter, Diary Entry (June 14, 1943), Frankfurter Papers, Box 2, File 7 (available at the Library of Congress), *reprinted in* J. LASH, *supra* note 57, at 254; *see also* F. Frankfurter, Diary Entry (June 13, 1943), Frankfurter Papers, Box 2, File 7 (available at the Library of

the assertedly impersonal opinion. Felix Frankfurter set the same course for the Jehovah's Witnesses that he had charted for himself. The opinion told them that as citizens we are "neither Jew nor Gentile" and that we are all equally constrained by an "attachment to the Constitution" and by obligations that demand a subordination (though *not* an abandonment) of personal preference and belief. Justice Frankfurter underscored the parallel between his own situation and that of the litigants by intertwining references to their claims of unbounded freedom to act in accord with their consciences with references to restraints he imposed on his own actions as a judge, despite qualms of conscience. This intertwining appeared in Justice Frankfurter's *Gobitis* opinion in a particularly evident use of the word "conscience" in both contexts: "A grave responsibility confronts this Court. . . . [W]hen the liberty invoked is liberty of conscience, and the authority is authority to safeguard the nation's fellowship, judicial conscience is put to its severest test."[81]

This parallel between the testing of the litigants' consciences and the testing of Justice Frankfurter's judicial conscience was deepened by a fact that was unmentioned in the opinions. As a personal matter, Justice Frankfurter's conscience pulled in the same direction as did the litigants':

> [N]othing has weighed so much on my conscience, since I have come on this Court, as has this case. . . . [C]onstitutional power is on one side and my private notions of liberty and tolerance and good sense are on the other. After all, the vulgar intrusion of law in the domain of conscience is for me a very sensitive area. For various reasons—I suppose the most dominant one is the old colored man's explanation that Moses was just raised that way—a good part of my mature life has thrown whatever weight it has against foolish and harsh manifestations of coercion . . . .[82]

The demands on these Jehovah's Witnesses and this Jew were the same. For both, "law" preempted "conscience" in the domain of the secular. Though "raised that way," "Moses" was obliged to put aside "private notions" in order to participate in "the nation's fellowship."

The parallelism between these reflections on duty results, I believe, from the fact that both grew from the underlying philosophy I have sketched. For himself and for others, Felix Frankfurter built an

---

Congress), *reprinted in* J. LASH, *supra* note 57, at 253-34 (recounting a similar exchange with Justice Roberts).

81. *Gobitis*, 310 U.S. at 591.
82. Letter from Felix Frankfurter to Harlan Fiske Stone, *supra* note 21.

impersonal standard of duty from an intensely personal conviction. No less than those activist judges he criticized,[83] he constitutionalized his own world view.

Nor could it be otherwise. Like most important constitutional cases, the flag salute controversies called at every turn for judgments about the world that could not be resolved simply by referring to the constitutional document or to the doctrine it had spawned.[84] Paragraph three of the *Carolene Products* footnote advanced a proposition that, as the law clerk who drafted it later remarked, made "no reference to the words or the intentions of the Constitutors." It spoke, "rather, of the dynamics of government."[85] It could not be wrestled with other than in political and thus personal terms. For Felix Frankfurter, it rang false. He was not a Jewish judge, any more than he was a Jewish professor at the Harvard Law School:

> I remember how shocked I was when entre nous in my early days down here [Henry] Stimson said that [President] Taft had asked him to ask me for some suggestions of Jewish lawyers because he wanted to appoint a Jew as a district judge. I told Stimson to count me out on such business. And so far as I take any personal satisfaction in being here, at least I feel entitled to feel that whatever wise or unwise considerations brought me here, my appointment at that time was despite and not because I was a Jew.[86]

The Jehovah's Witnesses could not be anything but citizens. Headway in the world had come to Felix Frankfurter "despite and not

---

83. *See, e.g.*, H. PHILLIPS, *supra* note 50, at 293 ("[Justices] McReynolds, Butler, Sutherland and Van Devanter . . . are a perfect illustration of that against which de Toqueville warned us, not to confuse the familiar with the necessary."); Memorandum from Felix Frankfurter to Franklin D. Roosevelt (untitled, attached to a letter of Feb. 18, 1937), *reprinted in* M. FREEDMAN, *supra* note 56, at 387 ("Nor is it admissible that we should yield our constitutional destiny to the personal judgment of a few men, however sincere . . . . Judges who cannot rise above their private views are not free judges.").

84. *See* note 48 *supra* and accompanying text; *see also* JACKSON ORAL HISTORY MEMOIR, *supra* note 6, pt. VII, at 23, *repeated in part in* Jackson, *Full Faith and Credit—The Lawyer's Clause of the Constitution*, 45 COLUM. L. REV. 1, 1 (1945) ("Once there was a vacancy on the New York Court of Appeals and my name, along with many others, appeared as a possible appointee, or nominee, for that position. I called on Judge Cardozo in his apartments in Washington that afternoon. He mentioned what he'd read. He said, 'Jackson, if you have a chance to go on the New York Court of Appeals, go on the New York Court of Appeals. That's a lawyer's court. Those are the kinds of problems you'll enjoy. Over on this court there are two kinds of questions—statutory construction, which no one can make interesting, and politics.'

"Of course he didn't mean politics in the sense of party politics, but in the sense of public policy. There's a great deal of truth in his observation . . . .").

85. L. LUSKY, BY WHAT RIGHT?: A COMMENTARY ON THE SUPREME COURT'S POWER TO REVISE THE CONSTITUTION 109 (1975).

86. Letter from Felix Frankfurter to Learned Hand (Dec. 4, 1939), Frankfurter Papers, Box 64, File 1232 (available at the Library of Congress).

because" he was a Jew. From Jews, he in turn "exacted higher standards than from other people and perhaps that was on the whole a good thing for Jews who had any capacity." Were the Jehovah's Witnesses to be kept from the need to participate in the political process because they were "a discrete and insular minority"? It would be surprising if such a step were thought desirable by Felix Frankfurter.[87]

Nor was such a step necessary. Stanley Reed saw his colleague clearly at the time:

> The . . . protest against both the Brandeis and the Frankfurter appointments was merely a manifestation of anti-Semitism, I thought, active anti-Semitism . . . . I don't think that [Justice Frankfurter] felt that any particular abuse was heaped upon him at this time. No, I don't think the name calling bothered him—not in the slightest. He was perfectly sure of himself. Of course, I knew him fairly well when he first came on the Court . . . . But in all the years I've known him, I'm [sic] never heard him criticize any of the people for their critizing of him. I don't think he had any feeling of the anti-Semitism. I've heard him frequently say that he never felt any disadvantages from the fact that he was of the Jewish faith. I really don't know whether he's a "practicing Jew" or not; but I know that he's never felt any bitterness about it, or certainly never expressed it, and I've heard him say frequently that he never experienced any disadvantages from it, which I can well believe, as I don't know anyone who is more acceptable to more people than Justice

---

87. A half-jocular exchange in handwritten notes passed between Justices Murphy and Frankfurter in Conference a week before *Barnette* was handed down renders another clue to Justice Frankfurter's adamant belief that Jews and other minorities should not be treated with favoritism:

> [Frankfurter to Murphy] Are you writing the Indian cases on the assumption that rights depend on 'ancestry'? If so—I cannot give my imprimatur to such racial discrimination!
>
> [Murphy to Frankfurter] I would protect rights on the basis of ancestry—but I would never deny them. [Frankfurter to Murphy] That's not good enough for me. *I don't want any of my fellow-citizens to be treated as objects of favor, i.e., as inferiors!*

Murphy Papers, Box 63, File 870 (available at University of Michigan Law Library) (emphasis added). Justice Frankfurter's diary entry for June 5, 1943, puts these notes in context. They were passed while the Conference discussed Hirabayashi v. United States, 320 U.S. 81 (1943) (upholding a war-related curfew on Japanese living on the West Coast). Justice Frankfurter reports that after Justice Murphy expressed concern about *Hirabayashi,* "I good humoredly chided him about his Indian opinions—their being based on the fact of ancestry, namely, on the fact that Indians are Indians." Frankfurter Papers, Box 3, File 7, (available at the Library of Congress), *reprinted in* J. LASH, *supra* note 57, at 252. The "Indian cases" involved claims (to which Murphy was sympathetic) of Indian exemption from federal taxation. *See* Board of County Comm'ns v. Seber, 318 U.S. 705 (1943); Creek Nation v. United States, 318 U.S. 629 (1943); Choctaw Nation of Indians v. United States, 318 U.S. 423 (1943).

Frankfurter.[88]

Felix Frankfurter interpreted his experience as demonstrating that prejudice fell away over the long term when minorities confronted it—that rational persuasion was a reliable vehicle for assimilation. In the flag salute cases, he seems to have unselfconsciously conceived the Jehovah's Witnesses and the world in which they functioned—persons and arenas he did not know—in the image of his own experience. For Justice Frankfurter, the political processes created the appropriate forum for resolving these cases. From *Gobitis*, his first major constitutional opinion, through *Baker v. Carr*, his last, this view remained a central tenet of Felix Frankfurter's "democratic faith."[89] Thus, his inclination to restrain legislative action was slight: "Tact, respect, and generosity toward variant views will always commend themselves to those charged with the duties of legislation so as to achieve a maximum of good will and to require a minimum of unwilling submission to a general law."[90] His propensity to protect an insular minority was low:

> Where all the effective means of inducing political changes are left free from interference, education in the abandonment of foolish legislation is itself a training in liberty. To fight out the wise use of legislative authority in the forum of public opinion and before legislative assemblies rather than to transfer such a contest to the judicial arena, serves to vindicate . . . self-confidence. . . .[91]

B. *Justice Frankfurter's Dismissal of the Paragraph One "Bill of Rights" Argument*

Though central to his disposition of the flag salute cases, Justice Frankfurter's aversion to granting special constitutional consideration to discrete and insular minorites does not fully explain his position in the flag salute cases. There were two lines of argument based on paragraph one of the *Carolene Products* footnote that Justice Frankfurter had to nullify or circumvent in order to reach his result. In his *Gobitis* dissent, Justice Stone contended that the expulsions posed a paragraph one as well as a paragraph three case because "on their

---

88. S. Reed, Oral History Memoir 256-57 (1960) (unpublished manuscript, Columbia University Oral History Project).
89. *See* Levinson, *The Democratic Faith of Felix Frankfurter*, 25 STAN. L. REV. 430, 430 (1973) (arguing that Frankfurter "accept[ed] absolutely the major premise underlying his theory of judicial restraint— namely, the United States is in fact an open polity, and there is therefore no need for an alert and active Court to further the development of greater openness").
90. *Barnette*, 319 U.S. at 651 (Frankfurter, J., dissenting).
91. *Gobitis*, 310 U.S. at 600.

face" they impeded the free exercise of religion. Similarly, the Witnesses, without mentioning *Carolene Products,* had rested their case on the first amendment's free exercise guarantee. A second type of attack climaxed three years later when Justice Jackson and a majority of the Court held in *Barnette* that compulsory salutes were repugnant to the right of free speech. Why did these free exercise and free speech arguments, which obviously convinced other members of the Court, have no effect on Justice Frankfurter's analysis? Because he conceived and recited the issues in the flag salute cases in a manner that undercut these points.

In his dissent in *Barnette,* Justice Frankfurter described the "precise" issue he saw in these cases:

> [T]he question here is whether the state may make certain requirements that seem to it desirable or important for the proper education of those future citizens who go to schools maintained by the states, or whether the pupils in those schools may be relieved from those requirements if they run counter to the consciences of *their parents.*[92]

"[T]he question" thus phrased, however, was not the question raised by the litigants or considered in the other opinions in these cases. The question they addressed involved instead a conflict between the consciences of the *children* and the demands of the state. Yet Justice Frankfurter's phrasing was not accidental. He described the *Gobitis* case even more explicitly as an instance of conflict between the control exercised by parents, who desired to mold their children in their own image, and the state, which intended to induct them into "the nation's fellowship":

> [The legislature] had made no exemption for children *whose parents* were possessed of conscientious scruples like those of the Gobitis family. . . .
>
> . . . .
>
> What the school authorities are really asserting is the right to awaken in the child's mind considerations as to the significance of the flag contrary to those implanted by the parent. In such an attempt the state is normally at a disadvantage in competing with the parent's authority, so long—and this is the vital aspect of religious toleration—as parents are unmolested in their right to counteract by their own persuasiveness the wisdom and rightness of those loyalties which the state's educational system is seeking to promote.[93]

In contrast, Justice Stone in *Gobitis* and Justice Jackson in *Barnette* apparently operated with a very different vision of the dispute. Jus-

---

92. 319 U.S. at 657 (Frankfurter, J., dissenting) (emphasis added).
93. *Gobitis,* 310 U.S. at 597, 599 (emphasis added).

tice Stone viewed the compelled flag salute as violating *the children's right of free exercise of religion*,[94] and Justice Jackson viewed it as violating their right of free speech.[95] But both Justices perceived the compulsion to be acting directly upon the children as individuals.

Differing statements of facts in the majority and dissenting opinions of Justices Frankfurter and Stone in *Gobitis* signalled these differing perceptions in a subtle yet vivid fashion. Justice Frankfurter began his opinion by stating that "Lillian Gobitis, aged twelve, and her brother William, aged ten, were expelled from the public schools of Minersville, Pennsylvania . . . ."[96] Justice Stone, in contrast, began by saying that "[t]wo youths, now fifteen and sixteen years of age, are by the judgment of this Court held liable to expulsion . . . ."[97] Thus, without either being inaccurate, the two Justices ascribed differing ages to the children. Justice Frankfurter emphasized their youth by reciting their ages at the time of their expulsion, while Justice Stone stressed their maturity by reciting their ages at the time he was writing.[98]

This contrast in perception arose because each Justice viewed the thin record he was handed in the context of his own experience. The three pages of transcript that recorded the trial testimony from the

---

94. For by this law the state seeks to coerce *these children* to express a sentiment, which as *they* interpret it, *they* do not entertain, and which denies *their* deepest religious convictions . . . . [I]t is said that . . . [the state] may coerce *the pupil* to make affirmation contrary to his belief and in violation of his religious faith . . . .

. . . .

. . . I am not prepared to say that the right of this small and helpless minority, including children having a strong religious conviction, whether they understand its nature or not, to refrain from an expression obnoxious to their religion, is to be overborne by the interest of the state . . . .

Id. at 601-02, 606 (Stone, J., dissenting) (emphasis added).

95. Here . . . we are dealing with a compulsion of *students* to declare a belief.

. . . .

. . . [T]he compulsory flag salute and pledge requires affirmation of a belief and an attitude of mind. It is not clear whether the regulation contemplates that *pupils* forego any contrary convictions of *their* own and become unwilling converts to the prescribed ceremony or whether it will be acceptable if they simulate assent by words without belief and by a gesture barren of meaning . . . . To sustain the compulsory flag salute we are required to say that a Bill of Rights which guards the individual's right to speak his own mind, left it open to public authorities to compel him to utter what is not in his mind.

Barnette, 319 U.S. at 631, 633-34 (emphasis added).

96. *Gobitis*, 310 U.S. at 591.

97. *Id.* at 601 (Stone, J., dissenting).

98. It is also noteworthy that Justice Stone placed responsibility for expulsion on the court, while Justice Frankfurter used language consonant with his message that responsibility lay elsewhere.

two children could convey no sense of the subtleties of their relations with their parents and the school authorities, or of the genuineness and the sources of their beliefs. In imagining the children, just as in spelling their father's name, all the Justices had to work with was a caricature. But while they could accept a caricature in spelling a name, they could not accept a caricature in deciding the substantive issues presented. To do their work, the Justices had to envision the circumstances that had generated this dispute[99] and would generate others like it in the future.

Other advocates or a different litigation process might have aided or enriched this act of imagination. As it was, Justices Frankfurter and Stone were forced to use their own experiences to construct a vision of the external world with which they were dealing. We can do little more than speculate about how this was accomplished. But I suggest that Justice Frankfurter, himself childless, appears to have envisioned the Jehovah's Witnesses children in his own image. From an adult perspective that was basically agnostic,[100] he saw his own Jewishness as an "accident of antecedence" rather than an act of faith: "the whole fact that I was a Jew" was traceable to "that ultimate fact that I was born of these parents instead of some other parents." Jewishness was to be taken "as much for granted as the fact that you've got green-brown eyes instead of blue eyes." In this light, Justice Frankfurter's attribution of the children's belief to their parents rather than to individual faith is not surprising. They were Jehovah's Witnesses simply by the accident of their birth, not because of any affirmative choice of their own. It followed that, in the free speech context, if the children fell silent during the salute they were

---

99. *Cf.* J. FRANK, IF MEN WERE ANGELS 74-75 (1930) ("For court purposes, the real conduct of the parties to the lawsuit does not count. All that counts is the judge's or the jury's guess as to that conduct."). Judge Frank directed his comments primarily towards the trial judge; he wanted to show that "what happens in the trial court is of transcendant importance." *Id.* at 80. My argument suggests that his observation about the idiosyncratic origins of factual suppositions could be applied to the Supreme Court as well as to trial courts. Indeed, one remark reported by Judge Frank supports this application (though he ignores its implications):

"In my experience in the conference room of the Supreme Court of the United States, which consists of nine judges," said Mr. Justice Miller, "I have been surprised to find how readily those judges came to an agreement upon questions of law, and how often they disagree in regard to questions of facts."

Id. at 78.

100. *See* H. PHILLIPS, *supra* note 50, at 291 (references by Justice Frankfurter to himself as a "believing unbeliever" and as a "reverent agnostic"); *see also* L. BAKER, *supra* note 7, at 18 (citing a letter from Justice Frankfurter to a clergyman in which the Justice refers to "Your God and My Equivalent").

symbolically affirming not their own views, but rather their parents' authority.

Justice Frankfurter's vision of the children as objects rather than actors in a tug-of-war greatly affected his perception of the flag salute cases. For by assuming away the children's individual rights, the central question became one of whose authority—parents' or boards' of education—prevailed in the schoolhouse. Thus forged, the issue involved a broader struggle between schools as welders of national unity and families as breeders of idiosyncracy. Whatever the genuineness of his deprecation of the flag salute requirement,[101] on this point there is little doubt about where Felix Frankfurter stood. His reminiscences clearly reveal his position: "[T]he greatest debt I owe my parents," he said, "is that they left me alone almost completely."[102] In contrast,

---

101. *See* note 82 *supra* and accompanying text; *see also Can the Supreme Court Guarantee Toleration?*, NEW REPUBLIC, June 17, 1925, at 85. In this unsigned editorial, Felix Frankfurter criticized Meyer v. Nebraska, 262 U.S. 390 (1923) and Pierce v. Society of Sisters, 268 U.S. 510 (1925), in which the Court struck down laws prohibiting teaching German and banning private schooling as a substitute for public education. Although he viewed such an exercise of judicial power as undesirable, he feared that the Court had left "much room for mischief" by conceding that the state might require "that certain studies plainly essential to good citizenship must be taught": "Here is ample room for the patrioteers [the state] to roll in their Trojan horses. And here is ample warning to the liberal forces that the real battles of liberalism are not won in the Supreme Court." *Id.* at 87.

102. H. PHILLIPS, *supra* note 50, at 9.

The contrast between Justice Frankfurter's extended reminiscences on his education at P.S. 25, the City College of New York, and Harvard Law School and his almost complete omission of any mention of his family underscores his allegiance to public schools rather than to families. *Felix Frankfurter Reminisces* says almost nothing of Justice Frankfurter's siblings or of his parents' personalities, occupations, relationships to him, or even names. Only an uncle, "the librarian-in-chief of the great library of the University of Vienna" is mentioned in any descriptive way. *Id.* at 5.

Justice Frankfurter's suppression of knowledge of his family was also evident in some unusual conduct. Late in her life (perhaps as early as the 1920's, but certainly by the 1930's), Justice Frankfurter's mother reportedly came to Cambridge and lived near her son until her death. Interview with Esther Austern, Secretary to Felix Frankfurter (April 24, 1976). So insulated were the lives of mother and son, however, that this fact was unknown to, and greatly surprised, many who knew Felix Frankfurter at the time. Interview with Professor Paul Freund, Harvard Law School (May 28, 1976).

This distancing from family may have been common for those with backgrounds similar to Justice Frankfurter's. One New York City historian found that settlement house workers on the lower East Side at the turn of the century were struck by the "gulf the teachers were creating between the foreign born parents and their native born children." I. HOWE, *supra* note 52, at 275.

> [T]he young could rarely avoid feelings of embarrassment. One's mother spoke English, if she spoke it at all, with a grating accent; one's father shuffled about in slippers and suspenders when company came, hardly as gallant in manner or as nicely groomed as he ought to be; and both mother and father knew little about

> I never heard a word of English spoken and never had spoken an English word when we arrived here in August 1894—not one word!
>
> School opened very shortly after I came here....
>
> ... We had a teacher, a middle-aged Irish woman, named Miss Hogan. I suppose she was one of my greatest benefactors in life because she was a lady of the old school. She believed in corporal punishment—I was going to say capital punishment. She evidently saw this ardent kid who by that time had picked up some English—I'm not a linguist and haven't got a good ear for languages—but she told the boys that if anybody was caught speaking German with me, she would punish him. She would give gentle uppercuts to the boys. It was wonderful for me that speaking English was enforced upon my environment in school, all thanks to Miss Hogan.[103]

Justice Frankfurter recalled this experience sixty years after it occurred. It is hard to believe that it did not affect opinion when he first asked himself in *Gobitis* whether the state's declared intent ("to awaken in the child's mind considerations . . . contrary to those implanted by the parent") was entitled to deference. Indeed, after the fact Justice Frankfurter told a friend that while the Court was discussing *Gobitis* he had made a "moving statement at conference on the role of the public school in instilling love of country in our pluralist society."[104]

> those wonders of the classroom—Shakespeare, the Monroe Doctrine, quadratic equations—towards which, God knows, they were nevertheless sufficiently respectful. The sense of embarrassment derived from a half-acknowledged shame before the perceived failings of one's parents, and both embarrassment and shame mounted insofar as one began to acquire the tastes of the world.

Id. at 262.

103. H. PHILLIPS, *supra* note 50, at 4–5. Again, this attitude may not have been peculiar to Felix Frankfurter:

> The bulk of memoirs dealing with East Side childhood contain warm, sometimes remarkably tender descriptions of the years in school. . . . Still, one wonders, were there no petty tyrants, no mean-spirited bigots teaching school in the immigrant Jewish neighborhoods? Very few, if one goes by the pupils' remembrances.
>
> Perhaps, in gratification at having escaped from the hardships of their youth, the writers of such memoirs indulged in a certain romanticizing of their days at school. . . . It appeared first as the familiar Jewish respect for institutions of learning, with the sheer architectural impressiveness of the newer school buildings helping occasionally to induce a bit of awe; and it emerged a bit later as a kind of idealistic calculation, with the school commonly taken to be a sure path to advancement.

I. HOWE, *supra* note 52, at 272–73.

104. Freund, *Charles Evans Hughes as Chief Justice,* 81 HARV. L. REV. 4, 41 (1967). Professor Freund's article does not cite a source for this statement, but I understand from him that he learned this from a conversation with Justice Frankfurter. Interview with Professor Paul Freund, Harvard Law School (May 23, 1976).

Justice Frankfurter's continued adherence to the free exercise issue after a majority of the Court had migrated to a free speech theory in *Barnette*[105] is perhaps the strongest evidence that his own experiences had a profound effect on his view of the flag salute cases. Justice Jackson's transition from *Gobitis'* free exercise rationale to a free speech theory was important. For once the Jehovah's Witnesses' conduct was linked to a free speech claim, the majority could follow an accepted formulaic approach that avoided both the passivity of Justice Frankfurter's minimum rationality standard and the uncabined activism implied by Justice Stone's *Carolene Products* ideas. By using a free speech theory, Justice Jackson was able to speak for the majority in terms of the "clear and present danger" test.[106] Thus characterized, the question in *Barnette* became whether or not the state could show that it would suffer a clear and present danger if it were unable to coerce school children into making the required affirmation. Not surprisingly, the majority concluded that no such clear and present danger could be shown. Given this phrasing of the question, the result was easy.

To judge by his opinion in *Barnette,* Justice Frankfurter hardly recognized the recasting of the issues in the free speech format. In twenty-five pages of dissent, he devoted fifteen paragraphs to slaying the dragon of free exercise and only two paragraphs to attacking the majority's resolution of the free speech issue. This failure to recognize that the debate had changed indicates that the religious issue resonated so strongly for Frankfurter that it dominated and therefore skewed his view of both the facts and the principles at issue. As with many cases of mistake or illogic by those who invest themselves in being careful and logical, the error in issue perception betrays the presence of a deep concern. The tone of the dissent in *Barnette,* its highly personal beginning, its length, and the intensity with which Justice Frankfurter worked on it and talked about it all suggest that it is best viewed as a *cri de coeur.*[107] Justice Frankfurter was not confronting the issues posed by the opinion to which he was supposedly responding. Instead, he was addressing issues inside himself.

---

105. *See* Thornhill v. Alabama, 310 U.S. 88, 105 (1940) (reciting "clear and present danger" test); Herndon v. Lowry, 301 U.S. 242, 256 (1937) (same). *See generally* Mendelson, *Clear and Present Danger—From Schenck to Dennis,* 52 COLUM. L. REV. 313 (1952) (reviewing development and implications of clear and present danger test for free speech claims).

106. *See Barnette,* 319 U.S. at 639 ("grave and immediate danger").

107. This phrase was invoked to describe this opinion in P. KURLAND, MR. JUSTICE FRANKFURTER AND THE CONSTITUTION 5 (1971).

III. THE SOCIOPOLITICAL CONTEXT OF JUSTICE FRANKFURTER'S FLAG SALUTE OPINIONS AND THE JUSTICE'S CONSEQUENT EMPHASIS ON THE PARAGRAPH TWO LEGISLATIVE PROCESS CONCERNS

If what I have said thus far is persuasive, it should be clear that doctrinal developments and personal history intertwined to pose the flag salute cases in certain ways and to make certain answers especially attractive to Felix Frankfurter. The Justice's angle of approach to the issues before him was—and had to be—a product of the times and the experiences that shaped his intellectual heritage. But to effect a complete understanding of Justice Frankfurter's thought one must add a third factor: the larger societal milieu in which the flag salute issues were considered and resolved.

I[108] and others[109] have written about these points elsewhere so I will not belabor them here. For our present purposes, the extrajudicial phenomena themselves—Hitler's increasing military success in Europe and Justice Frankfurter's correspondingly intense efforts to induce President Roosevelt to mobilize America for war[110]—are not as interesting as how Justice Frankfurter's concern about them manifested itself in his judicial work.[111] My observation, discussed elsewhere,[112] is that these external considerations shaped two critical doctrinal choices.

First, these considerations affected Justice Frankfurter's choice in *Gobitis* not to follow the precedent of *Schneider v. State.*[113] In that case, decided earlier that very term, Justice Roberts had written a majority opinion, which Justice Frankfurter had joined, that held that although four cities had acted rationally in prohibiting leafletting because it tended to lead to littering, their actions were nevertheless constitutionally intolerable, because "the purpose [of keeping] the

---

108. *See* Danzig, *How Questions Begot Answers in Felix Frankfurter's First Flag Salute Opinion,* 1977 SUP. CT. REV. 257, 261-71.

109. *See, e.g.,* R. MCCLOSKEY, THE MODERN SUPREME COURT 25 (1972) ("The first Flag Salute case had been decided in 1940 at a time when the prospect of war and the call for a new patriotism were obscuring the judicial vision even more than they did later.")

110. *See* Danzig, *supra* note 108, at 266-71; *see also* B. MURPHY, THE BRANDEIS/FRANKFURTER CONNECTION 186-200 (1982).

111. *See, e.g.,* Frank, Book Review, 32 J. LEGAL ED. 432, 442 (1982) ("What in retrospect appears to be Justice Frankfurter's most important opinion in terms of his own intellectual development, the first flag salute case, was referred to around the Supreme Court when I was there a year or so later as 'Felix's Fall-of-France' Opinion.").

112. *See* Danzig, *supra* note 108, at 261-66.

113. 308 U.S. 147 (1939).

streets clean" was "insufficient to justify" the adverse first amendment consequences.[114] Here were the seeds of the notion of preferred freedoms and of the thought that even in achieving legitimate ends by rational means the state, in undercutting those freedoms, needed at least to use the "least drastic means."

In his *Gobitis* opinion, Justice Frankfurter distinguished this potentially disquieting precedent by stating:

> We are dealing with an interest inferior to none in the hierarchy of legal values. National unity is the basis of national security. To deny the legislature the right to select appropriate means for its attainment presents a totally different order of problem from that of the propriety of subordinating the possible ugliness of littered streets to the free expression of opinion through distribution of handbills. Compare Schneider v. State, 308 U.S. 147.[115]

In deprecating one state purpose while deferring to another, this paragraph relies not on law or logic but on political philosophy.[116] The opinion papers over the personal choice inherent in the judgment by a technique I have dubbed "inflation" and described as follows:

> "National security" indeed might so commonly be thought to rank higher than the public interest in avoiding littering, that any judge at all alive to the world would think *Gobitis* a different case from *Schneider*. But such an analysis compared incommensurate concerns. "National security" was not self-evidently at stake in *Gobitis*. One might as well say that "public health" was at issue in *Schneider* and argue, as Frankfurter once argued in defense of a statute, "Health is the foundation of the state."
>
> On their face, the government actions questioned in *Gobitis* and *Schneider* prescribed flag saluting and proscribed littering. If Judges and other observers saw larger issues at play it was through individual acts of inflation. The facts presented by these controversies were like flaccid balloons waiting to be pumped up by those who interested themselves in the matter. The size the cases would reach when full blown, the heights of abstraction to which they would be lifted, would be determined by the heat of the principles with which they were injected and by the energy and intensity with which Justices pumped them.

---

114. *Id.* at 162.
115. *Gobitis*, 310 U.S. at 595.
116. Justice Frankfurter made this point himself when objecting to Justice Jackson's opinion for the majority in *Barnette*:
> We have been told that [secular] compulsions override religious scruples only as to major concerns of the state. But the determination of what is major and what is minor itself raises questions of policy. For the way in which men equally guided by reason appraise importance goes to the very heart of policy.

319 U.S. at 652 (Frankfurter, J., dissenting).

What Felix Frankfurter was doing in comparing *Schneider* and *Gobitis* was to take the former case in its uninflated, flaccidly factual state, and compare it with a fully inflated *Gobitis*. There is no reason to believe that the comparison was duplicitous. Rather, it seems simply that for Frankfurter, the state interest in *Schneider* consistently appeared limp— nothing in his thought or experience gave it buoyancy. In contrast, he invested the flag-salute controversy with issues of such great intensity that for him it always loomed full blown.[117]

Thus, the issues of national unity and national security, brought sharply into focus for Felix Frankfurter by events in Europe, dominated his view of the *Gobitis* case and supported his treating it differently from *Schneider*.

External political considerations also prompted a second instance of inflation, which was even more fundamental to Justice Frankfurter's presentation and treatment of the issues in *Gobitis*. The flag salute requirement was established in Minersville as a matter of custom. When challenged, it was rationalized by reference to nothing more substantial than a Pennsylvania State Board of Education regulation authorizing instruction in "civics, including loyalty." In *Cantwell v. Connecticut*,[118] yet another opinion by Justice Roberts—this one announced for a unanimous court in the very month in which the *Gobitis* opinion was being written—the court had overturned a conviction for "breach of peace" of a Jehovah's Witness who had played a virulently anti-Catholic phonograph record on a street corner:

> Conviction . . . was not pursuant to a statute evincing a legislative judgment that discussion of religious affairs, because of its tendency to provoke disorder, should be regulated. . . . Such a declaration of the State's policy would weigh heavily in any challenge of the law as infringing constitutional limitations. Here, however, the judgment is based on a common law concept of the most general and undefined nature.[119]

Felix Frankfurter was not moved by the possibilities of applying

---

117. Danzig, *supra* note 108, at 265–66 (footnotes omitted).
118. 310 U.S. 296 (1940).
119. *Id.* at 290, 307–08. Much more recently the argument for such an approach has been put forcefully by Professor Charles Black. Considering the case of judicial review of police conduct, he has said:

> It would, I think, be hard to state a sound political reason for the judicial branch's doing anything but walking into such a case with no presumption of constitutionality whatever, with no apparatus of self-denial. If the courts do not do that, then [the defendant] never gets a responsible and competent judgment on the constitutionality of what has been done to him, never gets a judgment from anybody except his formal adversaries in the criminal process. That cannot be right.

this precedent to the facts of *Gobitis*. Instead, he circumvented the question by a remarkable intellectual sleight-of-hand. Justice Frankfurter posed the issue in *Gobitis* by saying:

> The case before us must be viewed as though the legislature of Pennsylvania had itself formally directed the flag-salute for the children of Minersville; had made no exemption for children whose parents were possessed of conscientious scruples like those of the Gobitis family; and had indicated its belief in the desirable ends to be secured by having its public school children share a common experience . . . . The precise issue, then, for us to decide is whether the legislatures of the various states and the authorities in a thousand counties and school districts of this country are barred from determining the appropriateness of various means to evoke that unifying sentiment without which there can ultimately be no liberties, civil or religious.[120]

This too, I think is an act of inflation. My observation[121] is that as with the transition from the children's conduct to the assertion that aspects of the nation's security were at stake in this case, it required a substantial inflation for Justice Frankfurter to draw from a town school board meeting in Schuylkill County, Pennsylvania, an assertion that "the case before us must be viewed as though the legislature of Pennsylvania had itself formally directed the flag salute."[122] Yet even more imagination was required to replace the Minersville school board by "the legislatures of the various states and the authorities in a thousand counties and school districts."[123] Ultimately, Justice Frankfurter argued in *Gobitis* that the court should not strike down the salute requirement because to do so would be to "exercise censorship over the conviction of legislatures that a particular program or exercise will best promote in the minds of children who attend the common schools an attachment to the institutions of their

---

C. BLACK, STRUCTURE AND RELATIONSHIP IN CONSTITUTIONAL LAW 78 (1969).

For a strong endorsement of this approach, see Sandalow, *Racial Preferences in Higher Education: Political Responsibility and the Judicial Role*, 42 U. CHI. L. REV. 653, 695-701 (1975). Sandalow also criticizes *Gobitis*. *Id.* at 701 n.143.

The Justices have occasionally explicitly embraced the *Cantwell* approach. *See, e.g.*, Garner v. Louisiana, 368 U.S. 157, 196-207 (1961) (Harlan, J., concurring); Edwards v. South Carolina, 372 U.S. 229, 236-37 (1963). Though *Cantwell* is not often cited, one commentator has observed that in administering a vagueness test to shield first amendment freedoms, the Court has "consistently regarded" the "probability of [the] deprivation [of these freedoms] as a function of what kind of tribunal is empowered to make the potentially deprivative value judgment." Note, *The Void-for-Vagueness Doctrine in the Supreme Court*, 109 U. PA. L. REV. 67, 94 (1960).

120. 310 U.S. at 597.
121. This point is also made in similar language in Danzig, *supra* note 108, at 262.
122. 310 U.S. at 597.
123. *Id.*

country."[124] In the final analysis, deference was thus accorded not to the real acts of real men but to a mental image about a legislative "conviction" that never existed—a phantasm of Mr. Justice Frankfurter.

What accounts for this phantasm? Partly it can be described in terms of doctrine. Justice Frankfurter had leeway to assert that the acts of a subsidiary body had to be viewed as though they were the acts of the legislature because the question, like the questions emerging from the *Carolene Products* footnote, was a relatively new one. *Cantwell v. Connecticut* suggested one line of approach, but there was precedent in regard to economic claims that suggested the contrary.[125] Roosevelt's Justices must have been particularly sensitive to the idea that legislatures should be able to delegate decisions to agencies. Moreover, the new "modesty" which underlay *Erie Railroad Co. v. Tompkins*[126] ran counter to the idea that federal courts might pierce the veil of state relationships so as to pass on such delicate intrastate questions as whether a school board had the authority to do as it did. Finally, in choosing not to litigate in the state courts and in failing to raise the issue in the Supreme Court of the United States, the Witnesses arguably had waived the question of the board's authority.

But doctrine did not determine the issue—it merely left it open. As I have argued previously, the logic (as distinguished from the historical compulsion) behind the recently asserted policies of judicial deference, and thus restraint, "had to be premised at least in part on notions about legislatures: their representativeness, their responsiveness, and their capacity for making constitutional judgments. Were the same notions equally relevant to the decision of the Minersville

---

124. *Id.* at 599.
125. In Pacific States Box & Basket Co. v. White, 296 U.S. 176 (1935), Mr. Justice Brandeis, for a unanimous Court, upheld an order of Oregon's Department of Agriculture. There it was

> urged that this rebuttable presumption of the existence of a state of facts sufficient to justify the exertion of the police power attaches only to acts of legislature; and that where the regulation is the act of an administrative body, no such presumption exists, so that the burden of proving the justifying facts is upon him who seeks to sustain the validity of the regulation.

Id. at 185. To this, Mr. Justice Brandeis replied:

> The question of law may, of course, always be raised whether the legislature had power to delegate the authority exercised. But where the regulation is within the scope of authority delegated, the presumption of the existence of facts justifying its specific exercise attaches alike to statutes, to municipal ordinances, and to orders of administrative bodies.

Id. at 186 (footnotes omitted).
126. 304 U.S. 64 (1938).

School Board?"[127]

The material for addressing this question could have come in some significant measure from the advocates. The record in *Gobitis* contained references that, if pieced together, would have shown that the Gobitis children were victims of an *ex post facto* law. It contained hints indicating that the regulation that resulted in the children's expulsion was hastily passed to justify retaliation for their defiance. Beyond this were facts the legal record had screened out. Nothing in the record revealed that Minersville was a one-street town, of whose 8686 citizens some 80 percent were Catholic,[128] and that the Witnesses' proselytization, led in the region by the Gobitis father, himself converted from Catholicism,[129] was virulently anti-Catholic.

Without this information—or even with it—Mr. Justice Frankfurter and his colleagues had to rely very substantially on their own world view and experience. Felix Frankfurter, a child of the city, had, for all intents and purposes, no experience of a small town. Moreover, as has already been shown, his ambitions and accomplishments in other arenas led him to assume that assimilation and accommodation were generally achievable. He articulated this view in *Barnette* when he said that "[t]act, respect, and generosity toward variant views will always commend themselves to those charged with the duties of legislation."[130]

---

127. Danzig, *supra* note 108, at 263.
128. D. MANWARING, *supra* note 11, at 81.
129. *See* L. STEVENS, SALUTE!: THE CASE OF THE BIBLE VS. THE FLAG 22 (1973) ("He had recently gained an extra measure of public notice when he, who had been reared in the Catholic faith, became a Jehovah's Witness. Gobitis, in fact, was now overseer (leader) in a wide area of Pennsylvania around Minersville.") On reactions to the Witnesses' proselytizing, *see id.* at 26, 28. The Gobitis family was generally accepted in Minersville and experienced no hostility other than an implacable rejection of their religious views. *See* D. MANWARING, *supra* note 11, at 83; L. STEVENS, *supra*, at 36-39.
130. *Barnette*, 319 U.S. at 651 (1943) (Frankfurter, J., dissenting). Contrast Justice Jackson's comment in *Barnette*:

> The action of Congress in making flag observance voluntary and respecting the conscience of the objector in a matter so vital as raising the Army contrast sharply with these local regulations in matters relatively trivial to the welfare of the nation. There are village tyrants as well village Hampdens . . . .

Id. at 638 (footnotes omitted).

> It is interesting to compare the experiences that underlay the two Justices' contrasting views. Justice Jackson was raised in and practiced in small towns and cities.
> Standing and reputation came to him rapidly in that great school of trial advocates, the general, country and small-town practice . . . . It was during this period that Robert Jackson developed a social philosophy emphasizing the rights of the individual, of the under privileged, of small business, and opposing monopoly and oppression in all their forms.

Alderman, *In Memory of Robert Houghwait Jackson,* in PROCEEDINGS OF THE BAR AND OFFICERS

It was natural for Justice Frankfurter to imagine that Minersville was a miniature of the world he perceived—and that if it were not a miniature of that world the larger polity would modify it. In Justice Frankfurter's personal judgment it was therefore immaterial whether the rule in question originated in the Minersville School Board or in the Pennsylvania Legislature.

Doctrinal and personal considerations were reinforced by the political milieu. To do his job, a Justice has to imagine what is to come in future cases as well as to imagine what has occurred in the case before him. For Justice Frankfurter, who perceived a nation on the verge of war, there was a natural tendency to see a small case about a small town as a forerunner of larger cases about larger issues. Thus politics, personality, and precedent combined to shape opinion.

IV. Conclusion

In this study of the Flag Salute cases we have seen how Justice Frankfurter's development of doctrine (*Carolene Products*) and treatment of precedent (*Schneider v. State* and *Cantwell v. Connecticut*) were shaped by his perceptions of fact (the independence of children versus their subservience to their parents) and value (the role of the state as against that of parents in shaping children's beliefs). In turn, we have seen how these judgments of fact and value apparently derived from the Justice's own experience and from social circumstances at the time he considered his opinion. Thus, I hope the process by which subjective experience intertwines with objective reasoning in constitutional decision-making becomes more visible and admits of a better understanding.

This study of one Justice grappling with one issue can hardly pre-

---

OF THE SUPREME COURT OF THE UNITED STATES 1955, at 10-11 (1955) (private print). *See* Jackson, *The Country-Seat Lawyer*, 36 A.B.A. J. 497 (1950); Jackson, *Tribute to Country Lawyers: A Review*, 30 A.B.A. J. 136 (1944); *cf.* W. DOUGLAS, THE COURT YEARS 1939-1975, at 45-46 (1980):

> [Justice] Stone, who came off a New Hampshire farm and always pronounced Iowa as I-oh-way, never knew how the other half lived, nor had he any speaking acquaintance with the offbeat nonconformists of his time. But during World War I he had an experience that was to influence him throughout his life. He was made a member of the three-man board of inquiry named by the Secretary of War on June 1, 1918, to review the claims of those who had refused military service on the grounds of conscientious objection. The board traveled to the various containments, and the contacts, interviews, and cross-examinations of the objectors deeply affected Stone. He talked to me a lot about this experience and wrote an account of it . . . . I think it was this experience which made Stone particularly sensitive to the claims of the Jehovah's Witnesses in the flag-salute case.

tend to demonstrate universal truths about judging. This is particularly so because time, circumstance, subject matter, and the manner of the Witnesses' advocacy made the flag salute cases especially evocative of personal philosophy. Yet after observing how Felix Frankfurter's perceptions of the dispute before him were shaped by doctrinal, personal, and political factors, it seems to me likely that a similar shaping occurs in other major constitutional cases. As a possible contribution to policy debates and research that have long preceded this study and will long outlive it, I offer a half-dozen concluding observations, three of them descriptive and three prescriptive.

First, I believe that the act of imagining a case is a prerequisite to judging it. The circumstances in a case do not unfold before a judge's eyes; the pivotal issues are not self-evident; their resolution is not predetermined. A judge is asked to use the information he is given to conceive what has happened and what is likely to happen as a result of his judgment. To decide *Gobitis,* Justices Stone and Frankfurter (and their colleagues whom I have not discussed) had to imagine children in schools and their relations with their peers, their parents and their teachers. They had to imagine how a regulation came into being and how it might be repealed. They also had to imagine what the implications of their decision might be for minority groups, for freedom of religion, for the development of children, and for the country's ability to create a unified population that might have to mobilize for war. I anticipate that similar acts of imagination are required and accomplished in other major constitutional litigation.

Second, I believe that this study reinforces the hypothesis that, particularly in the Supreme Court of the United States, these acts of imagination are often personal. In envisioning what has happened, a Supreme Court Justice does not see witnesses, nor does he (at least typically) read through extended transcripts. Each advocate now normally has only a half-hour for oral argument and about the same amount of a Justice's reading time to convey what he thinks is important. In all but the rarest of cases, little of that time is devoted to building a richly textured description of the facts and circumstances at issue. Though the Jehovah's Witnesses were poor advocates in the early 1940's, I would hypothesize that other advocates at other times leave Justices largely on their own in imagining the cases before them. In such situations, the Justices naturally fall back on their own experience. Moreover, in looking beyond the case before him, each

Justice reflects the values and priorities he has developed over a lifetime, most especially those made salient by the circumstances at the time of decision. I do not believe that Felix Frankfurter acted idiosyncratically when he responded to one set of issues in *Gobitis* but not to a logically analogous set of issues in *Schneider* or in *Cantwell,* or when he acted as though paragraph two of *Carolene Products* resonated powerfully for him, while he rejected paragraph three. By what calculus is a Justice to reason about such matters if not from his own experience and his own values?

Third, however, there are institutional factors that if used skillfully can enable a Justice to enrich, to moderate, and in fact to transcend his personal understanding.[131] There is the constitutional requirement that the Justices pass judgment only on an actual "case or controversy." Thus, each case presents an occasion for a Justice to expand his experience, and a series of cases—like those involving the Jehovah's Witnesses, or segregated facilities, or searches and seizures—may educate a Justice so that his perceptions in the end are not the same as in the beginning. There is the power of recorded precedent, for the wise judge expands his own view of a case by reading about similar preceding cases and by seeing how they are resolved. There is the effect, on the Supreme Court, of each Justice dealing with the other eight. The need for a majority should limit if not cancel the significance of what is idiosyncratic to one Justice. There is a well-established commitment to ideals of rationality, continuity and consistency in judgment. Thus, a Supreme Court Justice is not free in Case X to take the position that this case alone might cause him to adopt. He must consider what he is likely to want to say in cases Y and Z that may arise in the future, and he is constrained by what he has already said in an alphabet of cases A through W earlier in his career.[132]

---

131. Writing about common law appellate litigation, Llewellyn called considerations of this type "steadying factors." K. LLEWELLYN, *supra* note 3, at 19.

132. These institutional factors may have been somewhat weaker in the flag salute cases than they are in other Supreme Court adjudications. *Gobitis* gave Felix Frankfurter unusual running room because it was his first major constitutional opinion, one of the first Jehovah's Witnesses cases, and one of the first cases to revolve around the emerging but not yet fullblown constitutional theories advanced in the *Carolene Products* footnote and in *Cantwell v. Connecticut.* Even here, however, the prior cases made themselves felt. Justice Stone's perceptions of *Gobitis* were influenced by what he had said in the *Carolene Products* footnote. Justice Frankfurter was strongly influenced by the ideas inherent in the opinions (including the text of *Carolene Products*) that rejected the notion of close judicial oversight of New Deal legislation. Eventually, Felix Frankfurter's personal convictions about the propriety of a salute were overruled by the views of a majority that saw things differently. That majority, in turn, profited

If the three descriptive hypotheses just advanced are borne out, I suggest an equivalent number of prescriptive implications. First, if Supreme Court judging of at least major constitutional issues is in substantial measure personal, we ought to give more weight to personal experience and personal philosophy in considering appointments to that bench. The case for creating diversity on the Court is strongest if we appreciate that these background factors are critical to the most important decisions.

Second, if personal factors are pervasive and important we ought to spend more effort both on identifying them and then—most significantly—in attempting to describe their proper roles. It has been suggested that there are three broad positions on one spectrum of constitutional commentary: an objectivist view, which sees decisionmaking as predominantly a logical, disinterested process; at the opposite pole a "nihilist" view which sees judging as inherently personal and discretionary; and an intermediate position that contends that decisionmaking involves a constrained subjectivity.[133] By this third view, constitutional judgments are like interpretations of texts in general: They demand a personal input but the text and professional mores of interpretation shape and constrain what may be said.

If this middle view is to prevail, it behooves those of us who take this position to develop a jurisprudence that guides the integration of the subjective and the objective. The descriptive work that I have attempted here may facilitate the development of this jurisprudence, but at best it clears the brush and surveys the terrain, rather than blueprints what might attractively be built. Should we, for example, encourage Justices to be more self-conscious and open about their predispositions, their relevant experiences and their values? Would such openness improve the evaluation of Supreme Court opinions, argument before the Justices, or discussion among the Justices? Along a similar line, I suspect there is much to be said against the modern tendency to cloister Justices and thus to leave them heavily dependent on ever-more-remote personal experiences. Justices who observe the workings of Congress and the executive branch, who see prisons, police, schools and bureaucracies at first hand, are more likely to decide cases involving these institutions wisely.

On the other hand, it may be that the mere fact that personal experience and philosophy intrude into opinions is no reason to facil-

---

from the development of doctrine and the enrichment of understanding that derived from looking at other cases in other contexts.

133. Fiss, *Objectivity and Interpretation*, 34 STAN. L. REV. 739 (1982).

itate that intrusion. Perhaps the present conventions desirably minimize personal factors, or at least mask them so as to maximize public support for what the Court does. I do not pretend to certainty on this point, but my intuition is that the present balance suppresses too much. I would urge more debate on these points, as well as more analysis—focused as I have focused it here—on what apparently has influenced the thought process of Justices in decisions now generally favored or disfavored.

Third, and last, the relationship between experience and personal outlook on the one hand and the development of doctrine and precedent on the other suggests for me a standard of good judging. If judging involves more than a logical manipulation of case law, then opinions cannot be criticised by logic alone. In this light it is tempting to say that Supreme Court opinions are more like works of art than like scientific proofs, and that the skill with which a Justice reconciles his experience and values with the demands of doctrine and precedent is the primary determinant—almost an aesthetic determinant—of our respect for his work. However, I believe that while this position captures an element of truth about the "art of judging," it too, is insufficient.

In the last analysis, I believe, a Supreme Court opinion faces a test beyond whether it is logically and aesthetically acceptable. This test is external[134] and practical: Our evaluation of a major opinion is powerfully—though not exclusively—moulded by our views of its impact on our national life. There was nothing wrong, I think, with the logic of the Court that repeatedly rejected Franklin Roosevelt's New Deal legislation. Nor do I detect any decisive error of logic in Felix Frankfurter's flag salute opinions. The fault in these judgments lies in their inconsistency with the development of the nation. The experience of life—not the logic of the law—proved these opinions ill-conceived,[135] as it has shown others (*Brown v. Board of Education* is

---

134. *Id.* at 748.
135. The psychological impact of the Supreme Court opinion in *Gobitis*, and the Justices' reactions to what had been wrought, are recorded more clearly than usual. The most comprehensive chronicler of the Flag Salute controversies summarized his detailed description of many incidents when he later wrote:

> [P]ersecution probably was more widespread and vigorous because of the Supreme Court's apparent indorsement. . . . [I]t must be emphasized that the public and private persecution of Jehovah's Witnesses did not *begin* in June 1940. . . . Still, the outburst[s] that followed [the *Gobitis* opinion] . . . were worse and much more numerous.

D. MANWARING, *supra* note 11, at 163-64.

Ten days after *Gobitis* was handed down, "Bob Jackson told [a Cabinet meeting] about

the best modern example) to be well-conceived. If judgments are to be measured in fact against so practical a standard, ought they not to be criticised and discussed in just such terms?

---

the hysteria that is sweeping the country against aliens and fifth columnists. He is particularly bitter about the decision recently handed down by the Supreme Court in the Jehovah's Witness cases." H. ICKES, 3 THE SECRET DIARY OF HAROLD ICKES 111 (1954). Over the next month it became increasingly evident that the credo advanced in *Gobitis* was not causing the Witnesses to become more assimilated, but less so. It is against this backdrop that one should read a remark of Justice Douglas recorded in Felix Frankfurter's diary: "[I]n the fall after we had decided the Flag Salute case . . . Douglas said, 'Hugo will now not go with you in the Flag Salute case.' I said, 'Why, has he reread the Constitution during the Summer?' Douglas replied, 'No, but he has read the papers.'" F. Frankfurter, Diary Entry (Mar. 12, 1943), *reprinted in* J. LASH, *supra* note 57, at 209.

THE FLAG SALUTE CASES AND THE FIRST AMENDMENT

STEPHEN W. GARD*

I.	INTRODUCTION	419
II.	JUSTICE JACKSON'S ABSOLUTISM VERSUS JUSTICE FRANKFURTER'S BALANCING	421
III.	TWO DIFFERING CONCEPTIONS OF THE JUDICIAL FUNCTION	430
IV.	*Barnett* AND THE BURGER COURT	435
V.	CONCLUSION	452

I. INTRODUCTION

IN *MINERSVILLE SCHOOL DISTRICT V. GOBITIS*[1] JUSTICE FRANKFURTER, speaking for a majority of the Court, held that public school students could be compelled constitutionally to participate in a daily pledge of allegiance and flag salute ceremony despite the children's sincere conscientious belief, as members of Jehovah's Witnesses, that such participation was explicitly forbidden by the Bible and would subject them to eternal damnation.[2] Justice Stone was the sole dissenter, arguing passionately that the compelled participation infringed upon the children's constitutionally protected rights to religious freedom.[3] Despite the overwhelming majority that Justice Frankfurter was able to garner in *Gobitis*, the opinion was short lived. A mere two years later, Justices Black, Douglas and Murphy, who had joined in Justice Frankfurter's majority opinion, took the extraordinary step of announcing in a dissenting opinion in another, unrelated Jehovah's Witnesses case: "Since we joined in

---

* Associate Professor of Law, Cleveland-Marshall College of Law, Cleveland State University. B.A., DePauw University; J.D., Indiana University, Indianapolis Law School; LL.M., University of Chicago.

[1] 310 U.S. 586 (1940).

[2] The belief of the Jehovah's Witnesses is based on a literal understanding of 20 *Exodus* 3-5:
    3. Thou shalt have no other gods before me.
    4. Thou shalt not make unto thee any graven image, or any likeness of anything that is in heaven above, or that is in the earth beneath, or that is in the water under the earth;
    5. Thou shalt not bow down thyself to them, nor serve them . . . .

[3] 310 U.S. at 601.

the opinion in the *Gobitis* case, we think this is an appropriate occasion to state that we now believe that it also was wrongly decided."[4] The following year *Gobitis* was reversed, in one of the most celebrated overrulings in American constitutional history, by *West Virginia State Board of Education v. Barnette.*[5]

In *Barnette* the majority opinion, written by Justice Jackson, held that the coerced flag ceremony contravened the freedom of speech guarantee of the first amendment.[6] Justices Black, Douglas and Murphy added concurring statements that the compelled pledge and salute also violated the constitutionally protected religious freedom of the children.[7] In stark contrast to Justice Frankfurter's leadership of the court in *Gobitis*, no other Justice joined his dissenting opinion in *Barnette.*[8]

The flag salute cases have been a source of endless fascination for legal and historical scholars.[9] Most of this large body of scholarship has focused on the apparent oddity of Justice Frankfurter's view that there was no constitutional infirmity in the "petty tyranny"[10] of a governmental requirement that school children engage in a hypocritical affirmation of belief.[11] Unfortunately, the doctrinal importance of the opinions of Justices Jackson and Frankfurter in the flag salute cases as contrasting statements on the interpretation of the freedom of speech guarantee of the first amendment[12]

---

[4] Jones v. Opelika, 316 U.S. 584, 623-24 (1942) (Black, Douglas and Murphy, JJ., dissenting). The dissenters' comments are even more striking in light of the pointed effort made by the *Jones* majority to distinguish *Gobitis* as inapplicable to that case. *Id.* at 598.

[5] 319 U.S. 624 (1943).

[6] *Id.* at 625.

[7] *Id.* at 643 (Black and Douglas, JJ., concurring); *id.* at 644 (Murphy, J., concurring).

[8] *See id.* at 646 (Frankfurter, J., dissenting). Justices Reed and Roberts also dissented but refused to concur in Justice Frankfurter's opinion. *Id.* at 642-43 (dissenting notation).

[9] *See, e.g.,* H. HIRSCH, THE ENIGMA OF FELIX FRANKFURTER (1981); D. MANWARING, RENDER UNTO CAESAR (1962); L. STEVENS, SALUTE! THE CASE OF THE BIBLE VS. THE FLAG (1973); H. THOMAS, FELIX FRANKFURTER—SCHOLAR ON THE BENCH 45-68 (1960); Danzig, *How Questions Begot Answers in Felix Frankfurter's First Flag Salute Opinion,* 1977 SUP. CT. REV. 257.

[10] Barnette v. West Virginia State Bd. of Educ., 47 F. Supp. 251, 255 (S.D.W.Va. 1942), *aff'd,* 319 U.S. 624 (1943).

[11] Thus, the suggestions have been made that Justice Frankfurter's view was attributable to the impact of "Frankfurter's own assimilation as an immigrant Jew into American Life," Danzig, *supra* note 9, at 274; his "conception of the role of the public schools as secular, nationalizing agencies," A. BICKEL, THE SUPREME COURT AND THE IDEA OF PROGRESS 33 (1978) and H. THOMAS, *supra* note 9; or his intense and contemporaneous involvement, as an advisor to President Roosevelt, in the preparation of the nation for military intervention into World War II, H. THOMAS, *supra* note 9, and Danzig, *supra* note 9, at 266-71.

[12] U.S. CONST. amend. I: "Congress shall make no law . . . abridging the freedom of speech . . . ."

and the function of the judiciary in preserving our most precious civil liberty has been almost wholly ignored.

There are several reasons why an examination of the cases from this perspective is especially important. First, the major casebooks almost uniformly treat *Barnette* and *Gobitis* as freedom of religion cases and ignore Justice Jackson's significant contribution to free speech theory.[13] Second, the flag salute controversy has been revived recently in several cases where the individual's motive for refusal to participate was not religiously based.[14] Third, a proper appreciation of *Barnette* as an important free speech precedent is necessary to a proper understanding of the constitutionality of analogous governmental regulations, such as the requirement that individuals, litigants and spectators alike, stand in a courtroom at specified times as a gesture of respect.[15] Finally, the United States Supreme Court has rediscovered *Barnette*, after years of desuetude, as a major doctrinal freedom of expression precedent.[16]

II. Justice Jackson's Absolutism Versus Justice Frankfurter's Balancing

The issue of whether "balancing" or "absolutism" is the appropriate mode of interpreting the constitutional guarantee of freedom of expression has always been of central importance in first amendment jurisprudence.[17] Unfortunately, the issue was obscured by the misleading

---

[13] *See, e.g.,* E. BARRETT, CONSTITUTIONAL LAW: CASES AND MATERIALS 1476 (5th ed. 1977); P. FREUND, A. SUTHERLAND, M. HOWE & E. BROWN, CONSTITUTIONAL LAW: CASES AND OTHER PROBLEMS 1345 (4th ed. 1977); P. KAUPER, CONSTITUTIONAL LAW: CASES AND MATERIALS 1247 (4th ed. 1972); W. LOCKHART, Y. KAMISAR & J. CHOPER, CONSTITUTIONAL LAW: CASES—COMMENTS—QUESTIONS 1265 (4th ed. 1975). The apparent exception, which perhaps proves the rule, is G. GUNTHER, CASES AND MATERIALS ON CONSTITUTIONAL LAW 1045 (9th ed. 1975).

[14] *See, e.g.,* Goetz v. Ansell, 477 F.2d 636 (2d Cir. 1973); Russo v. Central School Dist., 469 F.2d 623 (2nd Cir.), *cert. denied,* 411 U.S. 932 (1972); Banks v. Board of Public Educ., 314 F. Supp. 285 (S.D. Fla. 1970), *aff'd mem.,* 450 F.2d 1103 (5th Cir. 1971); Hanover v. Northrup, 325 F. Supp. 170 (D. Conn. 1970); Frain v. Baron, 307 F. Supp. 27 (E.D.N.Y. 1969).

[15] Findings of contempt of court for refusal to stand in a gesture of respect have been almost uniformly upheld. *See, e.g.,* United States v. Abascal, 509 F.2d 752 (9th Cir.), *cert. denied,* 422 U.S. 1027 (1975); *In re* Chase, 468 F.2d 128 (7th Cir. 1972); Comstock v. United States, 419 F.2d 1128 (9th Cir. 1969); United States *ex rel.* Robson v. Malone, 412 F.2d 848 (7th Cir. 1969). *Contra* United States v. Snider, 502 F.2d 645 (4th Cir. 1974).

[16] *See, e.g.,* Board of Educ., Island Trees Union Free School Dist. v. Pico, 457 U.S. ___, 102 S. Ct. 2799 (1982); Abood v. Detroit Bd. of Educ., 431 U.S. 209 (1977); Wooley v. Maynard, 430 U.S. 705 (1977); Elrod v. Burns, 427 U.S. 347 (1976).

[17] *See, e.g.,* Frantz, *The First Amendment in the Balance,* 71 YALE L.J. 1424 (1962); Mendelson, *On the Meaning of the First Amendment: Absolutes in the Balance,* 50 CALIF. L. REV. 821 (1962); Frantz, *Is the First Amendment Law?—A Reply to Professor Mendelson,* 51 CALIF. L. REV. 729 (1963); Mendelson, *The First Amendment and the Judicial Process: A Reply to Mr. Frantz,* 17 VAND. L. REV. 479 (1964).

and unproductive debate which occurred almost two decades ago between Justice Harlan, representing the balancers, and Justice Black, representing the absolutists.[18] This debate suffered not only because the absolutist position became hopelessly confused with Justice Black's reliance on a literal reading of the text of the first amendment,[19] but also because Justice Harlan "substitute[d] caricature for refutation"[20] by representing Justice Black's position as urging that the first amendment be treated as absolute in scope.[21] When the debate was waged in these terms it was a "fruitless one."[22] Two decades earlier, however, the debate was waged between Justice Jackson and Justice Frankfurter on terms which illuminated rather than obscured the real jurisprudential issue: whether the first amendment should be interpreted as positive law with some judicially discoverable essential meaning which it is the duty of the courts to enforce fully, or whether the constitutionally guaranteed freedom of expression should be treated by the courts as an interest which should be balanced pragmatically against other important, governmental interests.[23]

In *West Virginia State Board of Education v. Barnette*, Justice Jackson's majority opinion provided a lucid exposition of the absolutist view that the first amendment embodies an essential meaning to which it is the duty of the judiciary to afford absolute constitutional protection. Justice Jackson approached the case from the perspective of the governmental interests asserted in support of the flag salute requirement rather than from a focus on the nature of the conduct of the particular Jehovah's Witnesses children. The children's "possession of particular religious beliefs" merely "supplie[d] appellees' motive for enduring the discomforts of making the issue in this case,"[24] and was irrelevant to the process of

---

See also J. NOWAK, R. ROTUNDA & J. YOUNG, HANDBOOK ON CONSTITUTIONAL LAW 718-22 (1978); L. TRIBE, AMERICAN CONSTITUTIONAL LAW 582-84 (1978).

[18] See Konigsberg v. State Bar, 366 U.S. 36 (1961); *id.* at 56 (Black, J., dissenting); Barenblatt v. United States, 360 U.S. 109 (1959); *id.* at 134 (Black, J., dissenting).

[19] See, e.g., Konigsberg v. State Bar, 366 U.S. at 61 (Black, J., dissenting); Barenblatt v. United States, 360 U.S. at 140-41 (Black, J., dissenting); Cahn, *Justice Black and First Amendment "Absolutes": A Public Interview*, 37 N.Y.U. L. REV. 549, 552-54 (1962).

[20] Meiklejohn, *The First Amendment is an Absolute*, 1961 SUP. CT. REV. 245, 248.

[21] See Konigsberg v. State Bar, 366 U.S. at 49. Justice Black always placed clear limits on his absolutism. *See id.* at 64 (Black, J., dissenting); Barenblatt v. United States, 360 U.S. at 141-42 (Black, J., dissenting); Giboney v. Empire Storage & Ice Co., 336 U.S. 490 (1949). *See also* Tinker v. Des Moines Indep. Community School Dist., 393 U.S. 503, 515 (1969) (Black, J., dissenting); Adderley v. Florida, 385 U.S. 39 (1966); Brown v. Louisiana, 383 U.S. 131, 151 (1966) (Black, J., dissenting).

[22] Kalven, *Upon Rereading Mr. Justice Black on the First Amendment*, 14 U.C.L.A. L. REV. 428, 444 (1967).

[23] See West Virginia State Bd. of Educ. v. Barnette, 319 U.S. 624 (1943).

[24] *Id.* at 634.

constitutional decision-making. The crucial question was "whether such a ceremony so touching matters of opinion and political attitude may be imposed upon the individual by official authority under powers committed to any political organization under our Constitution."[25] Thus, for the *Barnette* majority the issue was not whether the children should be allowed an exemption from a required ceremony, but whether governmental officials had the legitimate authority to compel such participation in the first instance.[26] In order to answer this question it was necessary to identify the interest the government was attempting to protect or pursue by the means of the compulsory flag salute ceremony. Justice Jackson first emphasized that the government's interest in preventing disruption of the educational environment was not implicated in *Barnette*: "[T]he refusal of these persons to participate in the ceremony does not interfere with or deny rights of others to do so. Nor is there any question in these cases that their behavior is peaceable and orderly. The sole conflict is between authority and rights of the individual."[27]

Nor was the government's compulsion of the flag salute ceremony grounded upon any official claim that the ritual had educational value.[28] The sole governmental interest asserted in support of the officially mandated ceremony was the "promotion of national unity" or patriotism.[29] The question presented for judicial resolution in *Barnette*, reasoned Justice Jackson, was thus simply "whether under our Constitution compulsion as here employed is a permissible means for [the] achievement"[30] of national unity or patriotism.

Justice Jackson, by stating the issue as the constitutional permissibility of the asserted governmental power to enforce patriotism by the means of compelling an affirmation of belief rather than whether some individuals were entitled to an exemption from a presumptively proper exercise of governmental authority, avoided judicial consideration of the wisdom of the state's policy:

> Whether the First Amendment to the Constitution will permit officials to order observance of ritual of this nature does not depend upon whether as a voluntary exercise we would think it to be good, bad or merely innocuous. . . . [V]alidity of the asserted

---

[25] *Id.* at 636.

[26] *Id.* at 634-36.

[27] *Id.* at 630.

[28] *Id.* at 631 n.12.

[29] *Id.* at 626-28, 628 n.2, 631, 631 n.12, 640.

[30] *Id.* at 640. The *Barnette* majority stated that "[n]ational unity as an end which officials may foster by persuasion and example is not in question." *Id.* Clearly, the government, which spends millions attempting to convince its citizens of its goodness and virtue and persuade them of the wisdom of its policies and personnel, has a legitimate interest in such activities. *See, e.g.*, Linmark Assocs., Inc. v. Willingboro, 431 U.S. 85, 97 (1977); Wooley v. Maynard, 430 U.S. 705, 717 (1977); T. EMERSON, THE SYSTEM OF FREEDOM OF EXPRESSION 697-716 (1970).

power to force an American citizen publicly to profess any statement of belief or to engage in any ceremony of assent to one presents questions of power that must be considered independently of any idea we may have as to the utility of the ceremony in question.[31]

The majority opinion, rather than evaluating the wisdom of the governmental policy, focused on the freedom of speech clause of the first amendment and found that it contained a core of absolute protection which the government could not infringe constitutionally regardless of any perceived wisdom in so doing. No paraphrase can capture the eloquence of Justice Jackson's statement of principle: "If there is any fixed star in our constitutional constellation, it is that no official, high or petty, can prescribe what shall be orthodox in politics, nationalism, religion, or other matters of opinion or force citizens to confess by word or act their faith therein."[32]

This, *Barnette* holds, is the essential meaning of the first amendment which must be accorded absolute judicial protection: it is not the legitimate business of government in this nation to prescribe the "right" opinion for its citizens. False doctrine is absolutely protected by the first amendment and no governmental official is constitutionally empowered to penalize an individual for expressing a message the government disagrees with or for refusing to express or affirm an idea which the government endorses. This "freedom to differ is not limited to things that do not matter much. That would be a mere shadow of freedom. The test of its substance is the right to differ as to things that touch the heart of the existing order."[33] This is not the entire scope of the first amendment and no doubt the first amendment substantively limits governmental action beyond that which the government attempts to justify on the grounds of an official desire to penalize false doctrine.[34] But the *Barnette* majority clearly explicated the heart of the first amendment's command and had no need to consider the periphery.

Justice Jackson supported this judicial interpretation of the freedom of speech clause of the first amendment on both utilitarian and philosophical grounds. His first, pragmatic rationale was that the suppression of dissent inevitably leads to the suppression of dissenters and this, in return, leads to the disregard of all liberty: "Those who begin coercive elimination of dissent soon find themselves exterminating dissenters. Compulsory unification of opinion achieves only the unanimity of the graveyard."[35]

The progress of the flag salute controversy is itself evidence that Justice Jackson's argument was not fanciful. For the *Gobitis* majority the prac-

---

[31] 319 U.S. at 634.
[32] *Id.* at 642.
[33] *Id.*
[34] *Id.* at 633-34.
[35] *Id.* at 641.

tical consequence of an individual's refusal to participate in the flag salute ceremony was merely the expense of a private education.[36] In fact, however, as a result of official efforts to enforce the requirement, parents had been subjected to the threat of imprisonment, and children were subjected to the threat of being made wards of the state and of being removed from the custody of their parents.[37]

The *Barnette* majority was not content, however, to rest its opinion on utilitarian grounds. The majority ultimately based its interpretation of the freedom of speech clause on the very nature of our democratic form of government:

> There is no mysticism in the American concept of the State or of the nature or origin of its authority. We set up government by consent of the governed, and the Bill of Rights denies those in power any legal opportunity to coerce that consent. Authority here is to be controlled by public opinion, not public opinion by authority.[38]

Justice Jackson did not balance or "categorize" competing interests in *Barnette* and somehow decide that the government's interest in compelling an affirmation of belief in a "correct" point of view was out-weighed by an interest in being free of such coercion.[39] Instead, the *Barnette* majority enunciated an absolute first amendment principle traceable to the role of freedom of expression in a self-governing democracy.

There was nothing unique in Justice Jackson's recognition of the fundamental principle that, in a democracy, the government is absolutely barred from prescribing or proscribing any individual activity on the grounds of official agreement or disagreement with the ideological message the activity is believed by the government to express. A long line of impressive precedent supported this interpretation of the freedom of expression guarantee of the first amendment.[40] Indeed, this was the Supreme Court's explicit rationale, in *Stromberg v. California*,[41] for holding that

---

[36] Minersville School Dist. v. Gobitis, 310 U.S. 586, 592 (1940).

[37] *Barnette*, 319 U.S. at 629. *See also* Bolling v. Superior Court, 133 P.2d 803 (Wash. 1943) (reversing court order declaring children wards of the court and ordering their removal from parents' home); *In re* Latrecchia, 128 N.J.L. 472, 26 A.2d 881 (1942) (reversing criminal conviction).

[38] 319 U.S. at 641.

[39] Such is the mode of first amendment analysis offered by some modern first amendment theorists. *See, e.g.*, L. TRIBE, *supra* note 17, at 580-84; Ely, *Flag Desecration: A Case Study in the Roles of Categorization and Balancing in First Amendment Analysis*, 88 HARV. L. REV. 1482 (1975); Nimmer, *The Right to Speak from Times to Time: First Amendment Theory Applied to Libel and Misapplied to Privacy*, 56 CALIF. L. REV. 935 (1968).

[40] *See, e.g.*, Herndon v. Lowry, 301 U.S. 242 (1937); DeJonge v. Oregon, 299 U.S. 353 (1937); United States v. Schwimmer, 279 U.S. 644, 654-55 (1929) (Holmes, J., dissenting). *Cf.* Masses Publishing Co. v. Patten, 244 F. 535 (S.D.N.Y. 1917).

[41] 283 U.S. 359 (1931).

a state could not constitutionally penalize the display of a red flag as a symbol of opposition to organized government. The difference between *Barnette* and *Stromberg*, as Justice Jackson observed, was an emotional, not an analytical one: in *Barnette* "the flag involved [was] our own."[42]

The focus of the *Barnette* majority on the nature of the applicable governmental regulation rather than the character of the activity of the Jehovah's Witnesses children gave its opinion an analytical beauty and clarity which represents the finest tradition of first amendment jurisprudence.[43] The *Barnette* majority was thus able to avoid consideration of the wisdom of the state's policy,[44] consideration of the impossible issue of whether the children's refusal to participate in the ceremony constituted expression or action,[45] and consideration of whether the children's activity should be characterized as political or religious expression.[46] The reality, fully recognized by Justice Jackson, is that whenever the government seeks to compel or prohibit any activity because of the state's agreement or disagreement with the message that activity is officially believed to express, the government's conduct gives that activity both an expressive character and a political significance.[47] This is true regardless of whether the individual subjected to the governmental regulation is aware of the fact.[48] By reasoning from the perspective of the character

---

[42] 319 U.S. at 641.

[43] For more recent examples of this mode of first amendment analysis, see Police Dept. of Chicago v. Mosley, 408 U.S. 92 (1972); Cohen v. California, 403 U.S. 15 (1971); Street v. New York, 394 U.S. 576 (1969); New York Times v. Sullivan, 376 U.S. 254 (1964).

[44] 319 U.S. at 634.

[45] Thus, while Justice Jackson found that the state-mandated ceremony was expressive in character, he did not find it necessary to inquire whether the refusal to participate in such a ceremony was expressive. *Id.* at 632-34.

It is today recognized that no sound first amendment doctrine can be founded on a purported analytical distinction between expression and action. *See, e.g.*, L. TRIBE, *supra* note 17, at 598-601; Ely, *supra* note 39, at 1493-96; Kalven, *The Concept of the Public Forum; Cox v. Louisiana*, 1965 SUP. CT. REV. 1, 23.

[46] 319 U.S. at 634-35. Attempts have been made to ground first amendment theory on a supposed distinction between "political" speech and other categories of speech. *See, e.g.*, A. MEIKLEJOHN, FREE SPEECH AND ITS RELATION TO SELF-GOVERNMENT (1948); BeVier, *The First Amendment and Political Speech: An Inquiry into the Substance and Limits of Principle*, 30 STAN. L. REV. 299 (1978); Bork, *Neutral Principles and Some First Amendment Problems*, 47 IND. L.J. 1 (1971). The intellectual inadequacy of such attempts is explained in H. KALVEN, THE NEGRO AND THE FIRST AMENDMENT 46-50 (1965); Kalven, *The Metaphysics of the Law of Obscenity*, 1960 SUP. CT. REV. 1, 10-13.

[47] 319 U.S. at 631, 640-41.

[48] Thus, for example, in Linmark Assocs., Inc. v. Willingboro, 431 U.S. 85 (1977), the individuals merely wished to express a willingness to engage in a simple commercial transaction by placing "For Sale" signs on the front lawns of homes offered for sale, but the government attempted to prohibit such activity because it perceived the signs as expressing the message that the community was a racially

of the governmental regulation, the *Barnette* majority was able to announce an absolute first amendment principle: in a democracy the government has no lawful authority to compel the expression of a "correct" opinion or to prohibit the expression of an "erroneous" opinion.[49]

Justice Frankfurter's balancing approach in the flag salute controversy was different in every respect from the *Barnette* majority's reliance on absolute legal principles derived from the essential meaning of the first amendment. Indeed, Justice Frankfurter explicitly denied the very existence of absolute legal principles.[50] On the basis of this premise Justice Frankfurter necessarily perceived the court's role in the flag salute controversy as the pragmatic reconciliation of two competing interests.[51] Justice Frankfurter fortified his reliance upon a balancing approach by analogy[52] to the secular regulation rule which was then used by the court in freedom of religion cases.[53] Under the secular regulation rule, "[c]onscientious scruples [do not relieve] the individual from obedience to a general law not aimed at the promotion or restriction of religious beliefs."[54] Contrary to Justice Frankfurter's initial premise, the secular regulation rule did, by implication, recognize an absolute legal principle which even Justice Frankfurter was willing to honor: "If the avowed or intrinsic legislative purpose is either to promote or to discourage some religious community or creed, it is clearly within the constitutional restrictions imposed on legislatures and cannot stand."[55] The proper analogy from the freedom of religion clause to the freedom of speech clause would seem obvious; the former is designed to prohibit governmentally imposed

---

unstable, undesirable place to live. *Id.* at 96-97. *See also* Wooley v. Maynard, 430 U.S. 705 (1977); Virginia State Bd. of Pharmacy v. Virginia Citizens Consumer Council, Inc., 425 U.S. 748 (1976); Greer v. Spock, 424 U.S. 828 (1976).

Unfortunately, the Supreme Court has not always been true to Justice Jackson's insight. *See, e.g.,* Wooley v. Maynard, 430 U.S. 705, 713 n.10 (1977); Spence v. Washington, 418 U.S. 405, 410-11 (1974).

[49] 319 U.S. at 642. *See also* Thomas v. Collins, 323 U.S. 516, 545 (1945) (Jackson, J., concurring).

[50] Minersville School Dist. v. Gobitis, 310 U.S. 586, 594 ("[n]o single principle can answer all of life's complexities."). *See also* Dennis v. United States, 341 U.S. 494, 524 (1951) (Frankfurter, J., concurring).

[51] *Gobitis,* 310 U.S. at 594 ("Our present task, then, . . . is to reconcile two rights in order to prevent either from destroying the other.").

[52] *Id.* at 595 ("Nor does the freedom of speech assured by Due Process move in a more absolute circle of immunity than that enjoyed by religious freedom.").

[53] *See, e.g.,* Hamilton v. Regents, 293 U.S. 245 (1934); Davis v. Beason, 133 U.S. 333 (1890); Reynolds v. United States, 98 U.S. 145 (1878). The secular regulation doctrine has been since repudiated by the Supreme Court. *See, e.g.,* Wisconsin v. Yoder, 406 U.S. 205 (1972); Sherbert v. Verner, 374 U.S. 398 (1963). Eventually even Justice Frankfurter was to reject the secular regulation rule. *See* McGowan v. Maryland, 366 U.S. 420, 462 (1961) (Frankfurter, J., concurring).

[54] 310 U.S. at 594.

[55] *Barnette,* 319 U.S. at 651 (Frankfurter, J., dissenting); *Gobitis,* 310 U.S. at 593.

religious orthodoxy and the latter clause prohibits governmentally imposed political orthodoxy. Indeed, a respectable body of Supreme Court precedent has reached precisely this conclusion.[56] Justice Frankfurter, however, not only ignored these cases but also failed to recognize the analogy: "An act compelling profession of allegiance to a religion, no matter how subtly or tenuously promoted, is bad. But an act promoting good citizenship and national allegiance is within the domain of governmental authority . . . ."[57]

Justice Frankfurter also attempted to justify his balancing methodology by the citation of *Schneider v. State*,[58] a then recent free speech case in which the Supreme Court had utilized a similar mode of reasoning in order to invalidate state anti-littering statutes which prohibited the distribution of handbills. Unfortunately, *Schneider* was simply not apposite to the type of governmental regulation at issue in the flag salute cases. The statutes in *Schneider* were time, place and manner regulations which prohibited all handbilling without reference to the ideological message the handbills contained.[59] The flag salute requirement was fundamentally different because it was explicitly justified by reference to the ideological message the expression of which the government was attempting to coerce. In the past, when the Court had been confronted with similar content regulations, it had never used a balancing test.[60]

Even assuming that reliance on *Schneider v. State* supported rather than refuted the propriety of applying a balancing test in the flag salute cases, the issue remains whether Justice Frankfurter applied that test in a defensible manner. Here again we find Justice Frankfurter's mode of analysis seriously deficient. Justice Frankfurter not only assumed the crucial question of the very legitimacy of the governmentally compelled flag salute ceremony,[61] but he inflated its importance beyond recognition. Thus, in Justice Frankfurter's hands, the governmental purpose of instilling patriotism and national unity was equated with the government's interest in protecting the "national security" and labelled as "an interest inferior to none in the hierarchy of legal values."[62]

After inflating the governmental interest in compelling participation in a flag salute ceremony into an interest in preserving the security of

---

[56] *See supra* notes 40-41 and accompanying text.

[57] 319 U.S. at 654 (Frankfurter, J., dissenting).

[58] 308 U.S. 147 (1939).

[59] *Id.* at 154-58.

[60] *See, e.g.*, Hague v. C.I.O., 307 U.S. 496 (1939); Lovell v. Griffin, 303 U.S. 444 (1938); DeJonge v. Oregon, 299 U.S. 353 (1937). *See also* Kalven, *supra* note 45, at 23-25.

[61] *See Gobitis*, 310 U.S. at 598 ("Surely, however, the end is legitimate.").

[62] *Id.* at 595. For further discussion of Frankfurter's inflation and deflation of the characterization of governmental interests as a judicial technique, *see* Danzig, *supra* note 9, at 259-66.

the nation in time of war Justice Frankfurter then relied on this characterization of the importance of the governmental interest to justify a refusal to scrutinize judicially the appropriateness or efficacy of the means chosen by the government to achieve its purpose: "The wisdom of training children in patriotic impulses by those compulsions which necessarily pervade so much of the educational process is not for our independent judgment. Even were we convinced of the folly of such a measure, such belief would be no proof of its unconstitutionality."[63]

By the sleight of hand of inflating the governmental interest and then relying on that inflation to justify a refusal to scrutinize the means chosen by the government to achieve its purpose Justice Frankfurter wholly avoided the question, considered by Justice Jackson, of whether "the strength of the government to maintain itself would be impressively vindicated by . . . confirming power of the State to expel a handful of children from school."[64] Regardless of the importance of the state's ultimate interest, certainly it must be recognized that the means chosen to achieve that purpose may be so inefficient as to render the infringement on constitutionally protected liberties gratuitous: "[S]urely at some point, not too remote, the unwisdom of the state's policy undermines the legitimate interest of the state. Or to put this another way, the legitimate interest of a state in foolish legislation is difficult to isolate."[65]

Perhaps less apparent, but equally true, it is also possible that the means chosen by the state to achieve its goal might be positively counterproductive and destructive of the purposes sought to be attained by the state. This was precisely the situation regarding the compulsory flag salute ceremony in the eloquent concurring opinion of Judge Lehman of the New York Court of Appeals: "The flag is dishonored by a salute by a child in reluctant and terrified obedience to a command of secular authority which clashes with the dictates of conscience. The flag 'cherished by all our hearts' should not be soiled by the tears of a little child."[66]

When we shift our focus from the government's interest to the first amendment side of Justice Frankfurter's balance, his performance in the flag salute cases becomes no more impressive. Against the government's interest, Justice Frankfurter merely weighed the free speech interest of the Jehovah's Witnesses children instead of society's interest in freedom of expression.[67] The objection to such a skewed weighting of the competing interests is well known.[68] Justice Frankfurter, however, proceeded

---

[63] *Id.* at 598. *See also id.* at 595, *distinguishing* Schneider v. State, 308 U.S. 147 (1939).

[64] *Barnette*, 319 U.S. at 636.

[65] H. KALVEN, *supra* note 46, at 89.

[66] People *ex rel.* Fish v. Sandstrom, 279 N.Y. 523, 539, 18 N.E.2d 840, 847 (1939).

[67] *See Gobitis*, 310 U.S. at 594, 599-600; *Barnette*, 319 U.S. at 653, 655.

[68] *See* Barenblatt v. United States, 360 U.S. 109, 144-45 (1959) (Black, J., dissenting).

to diminish the free speech side of the scale even further by characterizing the Jehovah's Witnesses children as "dissidents"[69] whose religious beliefs were "obnoxious to the cherished beliefs of others."[70] When the government's interests in preserving national security, without regard to the efficacy of the means chosen to achieve this end, were weighed against the claim that "exceptional immunity . . . be given to dissidents,"[71] Justice Frankfurter's conclusion was foregone. All that remained was the gratuitous additional argument that the free speech claim of the Jehovah's Witnesses was further diminished because "the effective means of inducing political changes [were] left free from interference."[72] This argument, however, is nothing more than the old invocation of the right-privilege distinction[73] which had been rebutted in a similar context in *Schneider v. State*: "one is not to have the exercise of his liberty of expression in appropriate places abridged on the plea that it may be exercised in some other place."[74]

The contrast between the opinions of Justices Frankfurter and Jackson in the flag salute cases could not be more vivid. On the one hand, Justice Jackson resolved the compulsory flag salute issue by invoking an absolute principle traceable to the freedom of expression clause of the first amendment. Justice Frankfurter, on the other hand, never directly addressed the merits of the legal principle invoked by Justice Jackson, but dismissed it with the general observation that there could be no absolute legal principles. Instead of relying on principle to resolve the flag salute controversy, Justice Frankfurter judicially duplicated the pragmatic balancing of interests which had been undertaken by a coordinate branch of the state government upon the enactment of the flag salute requirement. Justice Frankfurter upheld the exertion of governmental power to coerce participation in a patriotic ceremony by assuming the legitimacy and importance of the state's interest, ignoring the efficacy of the means chosen to achieve that interest and devaluing the dignity of the freedom of expression claim championed by the Jehovah's Witnesses children.

III. Two Differing Conceptions of the Judicial Function

Justices Frankfurter and Jackson invoked two entirely different con-

---

[69] See *Gobitis*, 310 U.S. at 599-600; *Barnette*, 319 U.S. at 653, 655 (Frankfurter, J., dissenting).

[70] See *Gobitis*, 310 U.S. at 594.

[71] *Id.* at 599-600.

[72] *Id.* at 600.

[73] *Cf.* Van Alstyne, *The Demise of the Right-Privilege Distinction in Constitutional Law*, 81 Harv. L. Rev. 1439 (1968).

[74] 308 U.S. 147, 163 (1939). For modern invocations of this principle, *see* Virginia State Bd. of Pharmacy v. Virginia Citizens Consumer Council, Inc., 425 U.S. 748, 757 n.15 (1976); Southeastern Promotions, Ltd. v. Conrad, 420 U.S. 546, 556 (1975); Spence v. Washington, 418 U.S. 405, 411 n.4 (1974).

ceptions of the proper interpretation of the freedom of speech clause of the first amendment. In addition, both attempted to justify their flag salute opinions by reference to two entirely different conceptions of the appropriate judicial function in reviewing the constitutionality of governmental regulations.

Justice Frankfurter initiated the larger debate on the proper mode of utilization of the power of judicial review. He argued strenuously that his result in *Gobitis* upholding the compulsory flag salute ceremony was dictated by the necessity of observing appropriate limitations on the Court's power to determine the constitutionality of governmental regulations.[75] Arguably, his advocacy of judicial self-restraint did not influence his substantive decision on the freedom of expression issue; rather it was his mode of interpreting the first amendment which necessitated his philosophy of judicial self-restraint.

Justice Frankfurter emphasized three interrelated themes in support of his conception of the judicial function. First, in Justice Frankfurter's view, there is only one test of the constitutionality of governmental regulations regardless of which provision of the Bill of Rights is invoked in opposition to the claim of legitimate authority: "There is no warrant in the constitutional basis of this Court's authority for attributing different roles to it depending upon the nature of the challenge to the legislation. . . . [T]he function of this Court does not differ in passing on the constitutionality of legislation challenged under different Amendments."[76]

Second, the one universal test which Justice Frankfurter believed appropriate to test judicially the constitutionality of governmental regulations was the "rational basis" test:

> We may deem it a foolish measure, but the point is that this Court is not the organ of government to resolve doubts as to whether it will fulfill its purpose. Only if there be no doubt that any reasonable mind could entertain can we deny to the states the right to resolve doubts their way and not ours.[77]

Finally, the third underlying premise for Justice Frankfurter's philosophy of judicial self-restraint was his view that the institution of judicial review is fundamentally undemocratic:

> The reason why from the beginning even the narrow judicial authority to nullify legislation has been viewed with a jealous eye is that it serves to prevent the full play of the democratic pro-

---

[75] *Gobitis*, 310 U.S. at 598-600; *Barnette*, 319 U.S. at 646-71 (Frankfurter, J., dissenting).

[76] *Barnette*, 319 U.S. at 648-49 (Frankfurter, J., dissenting).

[77] *Id.* at 661-62. *See also id.* at 666: "[S]ome other tests of constitutionality must surely be guiding the Court than the absence of a rational justification for the legislation. But I know of no other test which this Court is authorized to apply in nullifying legislation."

cess. The fact that it may be an undemocratic aspect of our scheme of government does not call for its rejection or its disuse. But it is the best of reasons, as this Court has frequently recognized, for the greatest caution in its use.[78]

Justice Frankfurter clearly explained the interdependence of the three rationales for judicial self-restraint: "If the function of this Court is to be essentially no different from that of a legislature, if the considerations governing constitutional construction are to be substantially those that underlie legislation, then indeed judges should not have life tenure and they should be made directly responsible to the electorate."[79] Thus, for Justice Frankfurter the anti-majoritarianism of the Court's argument for judicial review was philosophically dependent on the appropriateness of the rational basis test of the constitutionality of governmental regulations. In addition to this philosophic argument, Justice Frankfurter suggested a pragmatic justification for judicial self-restraint which related to his concern for democratic self-government. In Justice Frankfurter's view, judicial self-restraint would result in the legislature taking its responsibilities more seriously and, consequently, lead to the "abandonment of foolish legislation."[80] Of course, such a normative proposition is incapable of empirical verification. But if the aftermath of the *Gobitis* opinion is any indication of the wisdom of Justice Frankfurter's argument, the verdict is unequivocal. After the *Gobitis* decision was announced there was a manifold increase in the number of state and local governments instituting or enforcing compulsory flag salute requirements[81] and a wave of anti-Jehovah's Witness persecution and violence swept across the country.[82]

Before considering the validity of Justice Frankfurter's underlying premise for judicial self-restraint and concern for democratic decisionmaking, that the proper judicial function is no different from the legislative function, the wisdom of the rational basis test he utilized to determine the constitutionality of governmental regulations should be addressed. What is most striking about this "test" is that it is not a test at all, but merely an admonition to judicial self-restraint. Thus, while Justice Frankfurter would caution that the wisdom of a governmental regulation is no criterion for its constitutionality,[83] the rational basis test is essentially a measure of legislative wisdom. Only if a statute is so unwise that no "legislators could in reason have enacted such a law" is the Court entitled to hold the statute unconstitutional.[84] The reason why the wisdom

---

[78] *Id.* at 650.
[79] *Id.* at 652.
[80] *Gobitis*, 310 U.S. at 600.
[81] *See* D. MANWARING, *supra* note 9, at 187.
[82] *See id.* at 163-86; L. STEVENS, *supra* note 9, at 106-16.
[83] *Barnette*, 319 U.S. at 647, 661, 670.
[84] *Id.* at 647.

of a statute will assure its constitutionality but the foolishness of a statute will not guarantee its unconstitutionality is simply Justice Frankfurter's belief in judicial self-restraint. In this light it is not surprising that the rational basis test is virtually always satisfied.[85] Not only does this test negatively define the freedom of speech guaranteed by the first amendment as that speech which no reasonable person could conceive of a reason to suppress,[86] but in the hands of Justice Frankfurter this test operated like a rachet to contract progressively the scope of constitutionally protected liberty. Thus, in Justice Frankfurter's view the fact that the Court previously had upheld the compulsory flag salute ceremony foreclosed the issue of whether reasonable minds could differ on its constitutionality.[87]

Justice Frankfurter's underlying premise for judicial self-restraint, that the only test of the constitutionality of governmental regulations is whether the regulation could have been enacted by a rational legislature, is itself subject to serious challenge. In passing on the constitutionality of the compulsory flag salute ceremony, Justice Frankfurter inquired only as to whether a reasonable legislator could believe that such a coerced ritual would further the governmental purpose of encouraging patriotism and national unity.[88] Justice Frankfurter did not attempt to determine judicially what the freedom of speech clause of the first amendment might say about the permissibility of such a ceremony. The irony of Justice Frankfurter's test of constitutionality is that in its application the Bill of Rights is irrelevant. Here, Justice Frankfurter's position that there are no absolutes, that the freedom of speech clause has no essential core meaning can be contrasted profitably with his opinion in *Illinois ex rel. McCollum v. Board of Education.*[89] The issue in *McCollum* was whether the "released time" program for religious instruction for public school premises violated the first amendment's proscription of the establishment of religion. Justice Frankfurter's position was that the program was unconstitutional, not because a reasonable mind could not entertain it, but because "the basic Constitutional principle of absolute separation was violated."[90] The absoluteness of Justice Frankfurter's interpretation of the establishment of religion clause was clear: "Separation means separation, not something less. . . . It is the Court's duty to enforce this principle in its full integrity."[91] Ultimately, the difference between his judicial

---

[85] *See* C. BLACK, THE PEOPLE AND THE COURT: JUDICIAL REVIEW IN A DEMOCRACY 205-10 (1960); M. SHAPIRO, FREEDOM OF SPEECH: *The Supreme Court and Judicial Review* 16 (1966).

[86] *See* Frantz, *The First Amendment in the Balance*, 71 YALE L.J. 1424, 1441-44 (1962).

[87] *See Barnette*, 319 U.S. at 664-65.

[88] See *id.* at 652, 661-62; *Gobitis*, 310 U.S. at 598-600.

[89] 333 U.S. 203, 212 (1948) (Frankfurter, J., concurring).

[90] *Id.* at 231.

[91] *Id.*

self-restraint in the flag salute cases and his refusal to defer to the legislative judgment in *McCollum* was simply that Justice Frankfurter believed that the establishment clause had a meaning, while he was unable to discover any core meaning in the freedom of speech clause. It is almost as if Justice Frankfurter declared the free speech clause of the first amendment void for vagueness.[92]

Justice Jackson's view of the judicial function was also dependent upon his interpretation of the first amendment. Since, in his view, the essential meaning of the first amendment was the prohibition of the use of governmental power in an attempt to coerce political orthodoxy, it was clear that the compelled flag salute ceremony struck at the very heart of constitutionally protected liberty.[93] While the courts should grant deference to legislative and executive policy judgments when governmental action touches the periphery of constitutional concerns,[94] no such deference is appropriate when governmental action contravenes the essential meaning of the first amendment: "The very purpose of a Bill of Rights was to withdraw certain subjects from the vicissitudes of political controversy, to place them beyond the reach of majorities and officials and to establish them as legal principles to be applied by the courts."[95]

Justice Jackson held that the Court's authority, indeed its duty, to interpret and enforce the freedom of speech clause of the first amendment is derived from the positive law status of that constitutional provision. Thus, Justice Jackson's majority opinion in *Barnette* foreshadowed the persuasive views of such eminent legal scholars as Professors Black and Wechsler and placed the judicial protection of the first amendment on the firmest possible foundation.[96]

Justice Jackson did not pretend that the Court's responsibility to ascertain the often murky purposes of the Bill of Rights was an easy one,[97] nor can it be doubted that the Court will occasionally err in the exercise of its duties. The Supreme Court is not unique in its capacity to err and the Constitution contains its own correctives for judicial missteps. Perhaps the most important point, however, is that in its exercise of the historically accepted power of judicial review the Court is not to act as a super-legislature or as a national school board, reweighing the wisdom of governmental policies. In Justice Jackson's words:

---

[92] *Cf.*, Mendelson, *The First Amendment and the Judicial Process: A Reply to Mr. Frantz*, 17 VAND. L. REV. 479 (1964); Mendelson, *On the Meaning of the First Amendment: Absolutes in the Balance*, 50 CALIF. L. REV. 821 (1962).

[93] *Barnette*, 319 U.S. at 642.

[94] *See, e.g.*, Cox v. New Hampshire, 312 U.S. 569 (1941); Cantwell v. Connecticut, 310 U.S. 296 (1940); Schneider v. State, 308 U.S. 147 (1939).

[95] *Barnette*, 319 U.S. at 638.

[96] *See* C. BLACK, *supra* note 85, Wechsler, *Toward Neutral Principles of Constitutional Law*, 73 HARV. L. REV. 1 (1959).

[97] *See* Thomas v. Collins, 323 U.S. 516, 545 (1945) (Jackson, J., concurring).

Nor does our duty to apply the Bill of Rights to assertions of official authority depend upon our possession of marked competence in the field where the invasion of rights occurs. . . . [W]e act in these matters not by authority of our competence but by force of our commissions. We cannot, because of modest estimates of our competence in such specialties as public education, withhold the judgment that history authenticates as the function of this Court when liberty is infringed.[98]

The function of the Supreme Court is to act as the expositor and guardian of the fundamental principles embodied in the Constitution. One of those principles, contained in the freedom of speech clause of the first amendment, is that the government is constitutionally proscribed from compelling the affirmation of a "correct" idea or from penalizing the expression of an "erroneous" idea. In a democracy there is no place for governmentally coerced political orthodoxy.

IV. *Barnette* AND THE BURGER COURT

A reconsideration of the implications of the Flag Salute cases is a particularly worthy enterprise at the present time because they bring together three themes of unparalleled contemporary interest. First, *West Virginia State Board of Education v. Barnette* and *Minersville School District v. Gobitis* provide an important perspective on the perennially controversial issue of the appropriate judicial function in reviewing the constitutionality of governmental regulations. There is today in the legal literature a renaissance in scholarly and theoretical works on the subject of judicial review.[99] No doubt the Flag Salute cases rival the famous footnote four in *United States v. Carolene Products*[100] as the proper centerpiece for a meaningful theory of judicial review.[101]

Second, the jurisprudence of the freedom of speech clause of the first amendment, while always a popular topic for scholarly endeavor, is presently the subject of uncommonly intense critical analyses.[102] Again,

---

[98] *Barnette*, 319 U.S. at 639-40.

[99] *See, e.g.*, P. Bodditt, Constitutional Fate (1982); J. Choper, Judicial Review and the National Political Process (1980); J. Ely, Democracy and Distrust (1980); M. Perry, The Constitution, The Courts, and Human Rights (1982); Tribe, *The Puzzling Persistence of Process-Based Constitutional Theories*, 89 Yale L.J. 1063 (1980); Tushnet, *Darkness on the Edge of Town: The Contributions of John Hart Ely to Constitutional Theory*, 89 Yale L.J. 1037 (1980); Symposium: *Judicial Review Versus Democracy*, 42 Ohio St. L.J. 1 (1981).

[100] 304 U.S. 144, 152-53 n.4 (1938).

[101] *See supra* Section III.

[102] *See, e.g.*, M. Redish, Freedom of Expression: A Critical Analysis (forthcoming 1983-84); F. Schauer, Free Speech: A Philosophical Enquiry (1982); M. Yudof, When Government Speaks (1982); F. Haiman, Speech and Law in a Free Society (1981); A. Cox, Freedom of Expression (1980).

Barnette and *Gobitis* potentially provide an enlightened starting point for an appropriate theory of the meaning of the constitutionally guaranteed freedom of expression in a democratic society.[103]

Third, Justice Frankfurter's proper place in history has been subjected recently to intense re-evaluation by a new generation of biographers[104] and his disciples have been quick to rise to his defense.[105] No doubt this debate is also destined to be a recurring one. It is equally clear that *Barnette* and *Gobitis*, more than any of Frankfurter's other opinions, will be at the heart of this debate.

Each of these three themes has its own allure as a topic for further exposition. My purpose here, however, is more modest. Professor Hirsch has identified *Barnette* as the turning point of Frankfurter's career on the Supreme Court. His leadership was rejected by the Court and he was relegated to the position of a dissenter for his remaining twenty years on the bench.[106] Joseph Lash's judgment is even more harsh. In his view, the Flag Salute cases "uncoupled [Justice Frankfurter] from the locomotive of history."[107] No doubt Justice Frankfurter served as a foil rather than a guru for the Warren Court. What is less clear, however, is whether Justice Frankfurter's jurisprudence remains in bad odor. Here, the view of Justice Douglas is significant: "Most of Frankfurter's decisions at the constitutional level were eroded within a few years after he retired, in 1962, only to be refurbished when the Nixon appointees arrived."[108] There is thus merit in a brief examination of the stature of *Barnette*, and the opinions of Justices Frankfurter and Jackson in the first amendment jurisprudence of the Burger Court. For this purpose, the recent case of *Wooley v. Maynard*[109] is especially noteworthy.

In 1977, after years of desuetude, the United States Supreme Court rediscovered *Barnette* as a major first amendment freedom of expression precedent. In *Wooley v. Maynard*,[110] the plaintiffs, Jehovah's Witnesses,

---

[103] *See supra* Section II.

[104] *See, e.g.*, B. MURPHY, THE BRANDEIS/FRANKFURTER CONNECTION (1982); H. HIRSCH, THE ENIGMA OF FELIX FRANKFURTER (1981).

[105] *See, e.g.*, Cohen, Book Review, 10 HOFSTRA L. REV. 1327 (1982) (reviewing H. HIRSCH, THE ENIGMA OF FELIX FRANKFURTER (1981)); Danelski, Book Review, 96 HARV. L. REV. 312 (1982) (reviewing H. HIRSCH, THE ENIGMA OF FELIX FRANKFURTER (1981)); French, Book Review, 57 N.Y.U. L. REV. 330 (1982) (reviewing H. HIRSCH, THE ENIGMA OF FELIX FRANKFURTER (1981)); Dorsen, Book Review, 95 HARV. L. REV. 367 (1981) (reviewing H. HIRSCH, THE ENIGMA OF FELIX FRANKFURTER (1981)); Stone, Book Review, 95 HARV. L. REV. 346 (1981) (reviewing H. HIRSCH, THE ENIGMA OF FELIX FRANKFURTER (1981)).

[106] H. HIRSCH, *supra* note 104, at 147-76.

[107] J. LASH, A BRAHMIN OF THE LAW: A BIOGRAPHICAL ESSAY IN FROM THE DIARIES OF FELIX FRANKFURTER 73 (J. Lash ed. 1975).

[108] W. O. DOUGLAS, THE COURT YEARS, 1938-1975: THE AUTOBIOGRAPHY OF WILLIAM O. DOUGLAS 22 (1980).

[109] 430 U.S. 705 (1977).

[110] *Id.*

challenged the constitutionality of New Hampshire statutes which required the display of the state motto "Live Free or Die" on the license plates of privately-owned passenger vehicles and criminalized the obscuring of the motto.[111] The plaintiffs, George and Maxine Maynard, had been thrice arrested and convicted for covering up the state motto on the license plates of their automobiles with red reflective tape.[112] They objected, on religious, political and philosophical grounds, to being coerced by the state into publicly advertising an ideological slogan they found abhorrent.[113] The United States Supreme Court affirmed the federal district court's issuance of an injunction prohibiting further prosecution of the plaintiffs for taping over the state motto on their license plates.[114]

As in *Barnette*, the judicial focus in *Wooley* could have been on either the nature of Maynard's activity or on the character of the governmental regulation. Much of the criticism and confusion surrounding *Wooley* is due to a misguided insistence that first amendment adjudication requires an evaluation of the nature of the individual's activity in order to determine whether it is constitutionally protected.[115] From this perspective the issue in *Wooley* would be framed in one, or both, of two ways: 1) whether the Maynards had been engaged in the exercise of constitutionally protected symbolic expression, or 2) whether the Maynards' first amendment right to be free of any governmentally compelled affirmation of belief had been infringed.[116]

In contrast, Chief Justice Burger's majority opinion after a brief, unfortunate and unnecessary dalliance with an examination of the nature

---

[111] *Id.* at 707, 709.

[112] *Id.* at 708.

[113] *Id.* at 707. Mr. Maynard described his objection in an affidavit:
[B]y religious training and belief, I believe my "government" — Jehovah's Kingdom — offers everlasting life. It would be contrary to that belief to give up my life for the state, even if it meant living in bondage. Although I obey all laws of the State not in conflict with my conscience, this slogan is directly at odds with my deeply held religious convictions. . . . I also disagree with the motto on political grounds. I believe that life is more precious than freedom.
Id. at 707 n.2.

[114] *Id.* at 717, *aff'd*, 406 F. Supp. 1381 (D.N H 1976). The majority opinion was written by Chief Justice Burger. *Id.* at 706. Justices Rehnquist and Blackmun dissented on the merits. *Id.* at 719. Justice White, joined by Justices Rehnquist and Blackmun, dissented on the ground that the issuance of the injunction was barred by principles of equitable restraint. *Id.* at 717. For discussion of this issue, see *Developments in the Law, Section 1983 and Federalism*, 90 HARV. L. REV. 1133 (1977).

[115] *See* Wooley v. Maynard, 430 U.S. at 719 (Rehnquist, J., dissenting). Gaebler, *First Amendment Protection Against Government Compelled Expression and Association*, 23 B.C.L. REV. 995 (1982) is representative of the law review literature.

[116] *See* Wooley v. Maynard, 430 U.S. at 719-22 (Rehnquist, J., dissenting); Maynard v. Wooley, 406 F. Supp. 1381 (D.N.H. 1976).

of the Maynards' activity, ultimately focused properly on the character of the governmental regulation and stated the dispositive issue to be "whether the State may constitutionally require an individual to participate in the dissemination of an ideological message by displaying it on his private property in a manner and for the express purpose that it be observed and read by the public."[117]

It is profitable to focus initially on the analytical problems inherent in the first two phrasings of the issue in *Wooley*, issue characterizations which find their roots in the methodology of Justice Frankfurter's dissent in *Barnette*. First, if the critical inquiry is deemed to be whether the Maynards' activity of obscuring the state motto on their license plates constitutes constitutionally protected symbolic expression then the judiciary necessarily must decide two difficult factual questions: whether the Maynards possessed "[a]n intent to convey a particularized message," and whether, "in the surrounding circumstances the likelihood was great that the message would be understood by those who viewed it."[118] Assuming that there is any intellectual coherence in a distinction between "expression" and "action,"[119] a focus on the nature of the individuals' activity serves only the single purpose of narrowing the scope of constitutional protection, thereby turning the first amendment on its head. Instead of the first amendment fulfilling its proper role as "an impenetrable bulwark against every assumption of [governmental] power,"[120] this methodology places the first amendment as a barrier which the private litigant must hurdle as a condition precedent to judicial consideration of a claim of governmental infringement of the constitutional guarantee.

Furthermore, the application of this approach requires the abandonment of principle in favor of judicial fact-finding of "facts" incapable of objective ascertainment. Before it can be determined whether the particularized message of an activity is understood by those who view it, several value judgments must be made. Thus, it must be judicially decided who constitutes the relevant audience, what proportion of that audience must understand the message and how precisely the message must be understood.[121]

---

[117] 430 U.S. at 713.

[118] Spence v. Washington, 418 U.S. 405, 410-11 (1974).

[119] Professor Kalven, however, demonstrated the analytical futility of this purported distinction many years ago in his seminal essay, *The Concept of the Public Forum: Cox v. Louisiana*, 1965 SUP. CT. REV. 1, 12. For more recent, derivative scholarship criticizing the "expression"-"action" distinction, see L. TRIBE, AMERICAN CONSTITUTIONAL LAW 598-601 (1978); Ely, *Flag Desecration: A Case Study in the Roles of Categorization and Balancing in First Amendment Analysis*, 88 HARV. L. REV. 1482 (1975).

[120] 1 ANNALS OF CONG. 439 (J. Madison ed. 1789).

[121] The built-in bias against new ideas should be noted here. The very requirements of audience understanding necessitates previous audience familiarity with the message and ignores the function of symbols in arousing curiosity about

When the governmental interest supporting a regulation is to burden the expressive content of the individuals' activity, then this focus is distinctly non-neutral. It serves only to expand the power of the government to suppress the ideological message of activities it finds expressive. Moreover, once this barrier is overcome, a judicial focus on the nature of the individuals' activity provides, as Justice Frankfurter's dissenting opinion in *Barnette* demonstrates, no standards or guidance for the resolution of the substantive issue of whether the activity can be regulated consistent with the Constitution. No doubt, then, Chief Justice Burger was wise to refuse to pass on the symbolic expression "issue" which he appropriately considered unnecessary to a principled decision in *Wooley*.[122]

The second possible statement of the issue in *Wooley*, whether the Maynards' first amendment right to be free of any governmentally compelled affirmation of belief had been violated, also mandates a judicial inquiry into the nature of the individuals' activity rather than the character of the governmental regulation. Both the majority opinion and the dissenting opinion devoted attention to this issue. Chief Justice Burger, although asserting that *Barnette* "involved a more serious infringement upon personal liberties"[123] than *Wooley*, had no difficulty in concluding that the New Hampshire statute "invades the sphere of intellect and spirit which it is the purpose of the First Amendment to our Constitution to reserve from all official control."[124] In contrast, Justice Rehnquist reached precisely the opposite conclusion. These two opinions demonstrate the

---

an idea. *See, e.g.*, the testimony of George Maynard:
  A lot of people stop me. And one person says, "You can't do that. That's against the law." I says "Fortunately, I was given permission by the Federal Court in a temporary injunction against the State." And here I was able to converse with him and express my beliefs and my reason for doing so. And so, therefore, I was able to bear witness to the truth of God's Kingdom.
Brief for Appellee at 60-61, Wooley v. Maynard, 430 U.S. 705 (1977).

[122] 430 U.S. at 713. In an unfortunate footnote, however, Chief Justice Burger declared that display of special license plates issued by the state without the state motto would not be "sufficiently communicative to sustain a claim of symbolic expression." *Id.* at 713 n.10. Obviously, if the state issued such license plates to the Maynards, the symbolic expression would never arise. Chief Justice Burger then compounded confusion and demonstrated the intellectual difficulties inherent in a judicial focus on the nature of the individuals' activity by concluding that the Maynards' prayer for issuance of "expurgated" license plates "substantially undermined" their claim that taping over the state motto on the license plates they were issued constituted symbolic expression. *Id.* A more plausible interpretation of the Maynards' position, however, is simply that while they would have preferred to remain silent by displaying "expurgated" license plates, nevertheless if the state insisted on coercing them into entering public debate by displaying the state motto, then they were constitutionally entitled to symbolically express their opposition by covering the motto.

[123] 430 U.S. at 715.

[124] *Id.*, *quoting* West Virginia State Bd. of Educ. v. Barnette, 319 U.S. 624, 642 (1943).

analytical incoherence, originally found in Justice Frankfurter's dissent in *Barnette*, of focusing on the nature of the individuals' activity. Two flaws are particularly striking: 1) such a focus forces the Court to abandon doctrinal principle in favor of artificial line drawing between competing interests, and 2) such a focus erects an improper barrier which the litigant must overcome before the constitutional propriety of the government's conduct can be judicially reviewed.

The first analytical flaw is most apparent in Justice Rehnquist's dissenting opinion. In his view there would be no unconstitutional affirmation of belief unless the individual was placed "in the position of either apparently or actually 'asserting as true' the [government's] message."[125] The doctrinal poverty of this test, despite its facial allure as a statement of constitutional principle, is most clearly demonstrated by an examination of the hypothetical cases suggested by Justice Rehnquist and the subsequent Supreme Court decision in *Prune Yard Shopping Center v. Robins*.[126]

Three examples of unconstitutional governmentally compelled affirmation of belief situations were offered in the dissenting opinion. First, *Barnette* was accepted as correctly decided—the government cannot constitutionally compel an individual to participate in a flag salute ceremony.[127] Additionally, Justice Rehnquist opined that either "wearing a lapel button promoting a political candidate or waving a flag as a symbolic gesture" solely because of governmental coercion would constitute an infringement of constitutionally protected individual liberty.[128]

In contrast, Justice Rehnquist offered two counter-examples which, like the state motto embossed on the New Hampshire license plates, would not constitute an unconstitutional governmentally compelled affirmation of belief in his opinion. One was the mottoes "In God We Trust" and "E Pluribus Unum" which appear on American money.[129] The other example was the erection by the government at taxpayers' expense of "a multitude of billboards, each proclaiming 'Live Free or Die.' "[130] *Prune Yard Shopping Center v. Robins*[131] serves as another such example. In *Robins* the United States Supreme Court held that a state could constitutionally require a privately owned shopping mall to allow third persons to speak, distribute pamphlets and circulate petitions on its premises. The argument of Prune Yard Shopping Center that it was being compelled, in violation of the first amendment to the United States Constitution, to use its property as a forum for the speech of others was rejected.[132]

---

[125] *Id.* at 721.
[126] 447 U.S. 74 (1980).
[127] 430 U.S. at 720-21.
[128] *Id.* at 720.
[129] *Id.* at 722.
[130] *Id.* at 721.
[131] 447 U.S. 74 (1980).
[132] *Id.* at 85-88.

This array of potentially analogous cases offers an excellent opportunity to test whether a judicial focus on the nature of the individuals' activity in order to determine whether there has been either an actual or apparent assertion of the truth of the government's ideological message has a principled doctrinal foundation. Obviously, it must be remembered that it is insufficient to point out hypothetical cases which, if *Wooley* were decided in one fashion, would be inappropriately decided if the Court adhered to the sanctity of precedent as a mandate for doctrinal consistency. The slippery slope always runs in both directions. Jurisprudential soundness requires a principle which, when consistently applied, justifies acceptable results in each of the proffered hypothetical cases. A focus on the nature of the individuals' activity *always* fails this simple standard.

The essential purpose of the proposed judicial inquiry into whether the individual was placed "in the position of either apparently or actually 'asserting as true' the [government's] message"[133] is to reject as insufficient the implication which arises necessarily from the simple display of the message. Thus, Justice Rehnquist denied there was any compelled affirmation of belief in *Wooley* because the Maynards were simply required to display the state motto, not personally endorse it. The difficulty with this proposed standard is that it wholly fails to distinguish the cases in which even Justice Rehnquist would find a first amendment violation. *Barnette* appears, on superficial examination, to meet this test inasmuch as not merely a flag salute but also a pledge of allegiance was required.[134] On closer examination, however, the Jehovah's Witnesses in *Barnette* objected to participating in the flag salute ceremony on religious grounds and, on this basis, the state regulation compelled only the participation in the ceremony and expressly disclaimed any coercion of belief in the message which the flag salute and pledge of allegiance expresses.[135] Furthermore, this standard also fails to distinguish the case of the required wearing of a lapel button promoting a political candidate, offered by Justice Rehnquist as another example of a constitutionally permissible coerced affirmation of belief unless Justice Rehnquist would invalidate such a lapel button only if it read "I support Ken Candidate for President" rather than merely "Ken Candidate for President." The case of the required waving of a flag as an example suffers from the same infirmity. It is difficult to appreciate the wisdom of a constitutional principle which would have the result turn on the redundancy of a requirement that the flag waver also be compelled to add verbally "and I mean it."

Justice Rehnquist also suggested that a relevant factor in applying his

---

[133] 430 U.S. at 721.

[134] West Virginia State Bd. of Educ. v. Barnette, 319 U.S. 624, 628-29 (1943).

[135] The official resolution at issue provided: "the West Virginia State Board of Education honors the broad principle that one's conviction about the ultimate mystery of the universe and man's relation to it is placed beyond the reach of the law . . . ." *Id.* at 626-28 n.2.

proposed standard is whether the audience would perceive the governmentally compelled activity as an affirmation of belief in the government's message.[136] The difficulties inherent in any standard based on the perception of an audience are legion.[137] Here, however, the problem is even more fundamental. Mere compliance with a governmental mandate to display an officially approved message, by whatever means, cannot alone be construed reasonably to be anything other than simple obedience to law. Such compliance says nothing about whether the individuals believe, disbelieve, or even care about the content of the government's message. Unless one accepts the intellectually indefensible position that the touchstone is the notoriety of the governmental regulation, any reliance on audience perception is doomed to failure unless other factors are considered.

Justice Rehnquist would apparently resolve this problem by reference to whether the individuals are free to disavow the government's message.[138] Thus, in his view there was no compelled affirmation of belief in *Wooley* because the Maynards were free to disclaim the state motto by attaching a counter-bumpersticker on their automobiles.[139] No doubt such a bumpersticker would prevent viewers from misperceiving the Maynards' actual beliefs. This factor does not, however, distinguish the hypothetical cases offered by Justice Rehnquist in his dissenting opinion in *Wooley*. For example, the school children in *Barnette*, and their parents, were free to "disavow as publicly as they choose to do so the meaning that others attach to the gesture of salute."[140]

If Justice Rehnquist was not suggesting the overruling of *Barnette*, or at least demonstrating an inability to distinguish it, then he must have been implying that the opportunity for individual disclaimer must be contemporaneous in time and space. In addition to the obvious difficulty of identifying the requisite degree of contemporaneity, subsequent decisions of the United States Supreme Court clearly indicate that students subjected to a compulsory flag salute ceremony could contemporaneously register their dissent by wearing an armband[141] or a jacket emblazoned with the slogan "Down With the Salute," or maybe even "Fuck the Salute."[142]

The freedom to disavow the government's message is also present in

---

[136] 430 U.S. at 720-21.

[137] *See supra* note 121 and accompanying text.

[138] In *Wooley*, 430 U.S. at 722, Justice Rehnquist states: "Since any implication that they affirm the motto can be so easily displaced, I cannot agree that the state [statute] . . . may be invalidated under the fiction that appellees are unconstitutionally forced to affirm, or profess belief in, the state motto."

[139] *Id.*

[140] *Barnette*, 319 U.S. at 664 (Frankfurter, J., dissenting). *Cf.* Taylor v. Mississippi, 319 U.S. 583 (1943).

[141] *Cf.* Tinker v. Des Moines Indep. Community School Dist., 393 U.S. 503 (1969).

[142] *Cf.* Cohen v. California, 403 U.S. 15 (1971).

the other examples of impermissible coerced affirmations of belief suggested by Justice Rehnquist. Individuals required to wear a lapel button supporting a political candidate could easily disclaim affiliation with the government's message by wearing a second lapel button.

Despite these analytical difficulties, Justice Rehnquist expressly relied on the ability of the owners of the shopping center in *Robins* to disassociate themselves from endorsement of the third parties' message to distinguish *Wooley* and *Barnette* and justify the finding of no first amendment violation.[143] As Justice Powell observed in his concurring opinion in *Robins*, Justice Rehnquist's methodology does not alleviate the individuals' dilemma but merely shifts its focus:

> The property owner or proprietor would be faced with a choice: he either could permit his customers to receive a mistaken impression or he could disavow the messages. Should he take the first course, he effectively has been compelled to affirm someone else's belief. Should he choose the second, he has been forced to speak when he would prefer to remain silent. In short, he has lost control over his freedom to speak or not to speak on certain issues. The mere fact that he is free to dissociate himself from the views expressed on his property . . . cannot restore his "right to refrain from speaking at all."[144]

Finally, in *Prune Yard Shopping Center v. Robins*, Justice Rehnquist's majority opinion alluded to yet another factor: whether the governmental views would "likely be identified with those of the owner"[145] of the shopping mall compelled to display the message. In order to avoid the obvious conclusion that the simple fact of official compulsion to display the message negates any reasonable inference that the coerced individuals endorse the message, Justice Rehnquist would focus on whether the display of the message was required to be on property "limited to the personal use"[146] of the owner.

This consideration successfully distinguishes *Robins* and justifies the holding that no violation of any first amendment right was present there since the shopping center was "open to the public to come and go as they

---

[143] 447 U.S. at 87-88.

[144] *Id.* at 99, *quoting Wooley*, 430 U.S. at 714. Justice Powell also noted that requiring the property owner to identify the messages to which he objects would "force him to relinquish his freedom to maintain his own beliefs without public disclosure." *Id.* at 100, *quoting* Abood v. Detroit Bd. of Educ., 431 U.S. 209, 213, 241 (1977).

Moreover, Justice Rehnquist's analysis frequently places on the individuals the financial burden of expending personal funds for a bumpersticker, or lapel button to disavow personal association with the government's message in situations where the individuals' preference is the exercise of the right to remain silent.

[145] *Id.* at 87.

[146] *Id.*

please."[147] Erection by the government of billboards with ideological statements financed at taxpayers' expense would be an even more extreme example of no constitutional violation because there would be no identification of any particular taxpayer with the message. On the other hand, the compulsory flag salute ceremony in *Barnette* involved such direct personal participation that it serves as an appropriate benchmark for clearly unconstitutional infringements of personal liberty under this analysis.

Barnette and *Robins*, however, mark rather obvious extremes at opposite ends of the spectrum of cases. The difficulty with this methodology is that it places the cases on a continuum and then fails to provide any principled standard to distinguish between the myriad cases which occupy the middle of the spectrum. No doctrinal structure exists to aid in the determination of whether the state motto embossed on New Hampshire license plates is sufficiently closely connected to the person of automobile owners to be violative of the first amendment. Nor is it clear what weight should be given to the personal effort required to install the license plate. The mottoes on American money, "In God We Trust" and "E Pluribus Unum," present similar difficulties of analysis. Thus, Chief Justice Burger, writing for the majority in *Wooley* correctly recognized that while the compulsory flag salute was more offensive than the mandatory license plate display of the state motto, "the difference is essentially one of degree."[148] This insight led the Chief Justice to conclude that the first amendment right to be free of a compelled affirmation of belief was implicated, thus necessitating an evaluation of the state's countervailing interests.[149] What remains unclear, however, is the virtue of focusing on the individuals' activity solely for the purpose of erecting an unnecessary barrier to constitutional adjudication.[150]

Chief Justice Burger, after concluding that the interest in being free from any coerced affirmation of belief was implicated to some unstated and unascertainable extent, wisely placed little reliance on that finding in deciding *Wooley*. Rather than focusing on the nature of the individuals' activity, the majority in *Wooley* premised its analysis on an examination of the character of the governmental regulation.

The state of New Hampshire advanced two interests in support of its statute requiring the display of the state motto, "Live Free or Die," on passenger vehicle license plates: 1) the promotion of an appreciation of history, state pride and individualism, and 2) the facilitation of identification of properly licensed vehicles.[151] The challenged New Hampshire statute attempted to achieve the first state purpose of promoting an ap-

---

[147] *Id.*
[148] *Wooley*, 430 U.S. at 715.
[149] *Id.* at 715-16.
[150] *See supra* notes 118-20 and accompanying text.
[151] *Wooley*, 430 U.S. at 716.

preciation of state pride, history and individualism by the mandatory public display of the state motto to all who viewed the passenger vehicle license plates. The evil the governmental regulation was designed to prevent was interference with the public dissemination of the state's message by those who dissented from the government's ideological statement and were thus unwilling to carry the message on their privately owned automobiles. Chief Justice Burger was able to focus the judicial inquiry on the proper question of the compatability of this governmental regulation with the command of the first amendment by phrasing the issue to be "whether the State may constitutionally require an individual to participate in the dissemination of an ideological message by displaying it on his private property in a manner and for the express purpose that it be observed and read by the public."[152] The majority's conclusion in *Wooley* was simply that such an ideologically non-neutral, content-based governmental interest is inconsistent with the command of the first amendment.

In order to fully appreciate the doctrinal significance of the holding in *Wooley* it must be recognized that the government does have a legitimate interest in participating in public debate.[153] As Professor Emerson has explained, such governmental participation in the marketplace of ideas is not merely an evil to be tolerated, but

> is an essential feature of any democratic society. It enables the government to inform, explain and persuade—measures especially crucial in a society that attempts to govern itself with a minimum use of force. Government participation also greatly enriches the system; it provides the facts, ideas, and expertise not available from other sources. In short, government expression is a necessary and healthy part of the system.[154]

The recognition of a legitimate governmental interest in the dissemination of its own ideological message, however, is merely a beginning, not the end, of first amendment analysis.[155] This is especially true given the

---

[152] *Id.* at 713.

[153] *See, e.g., id.* at 717 ("[T]he State is seeking to communicate to others an official view . . . . Of course, the State may legitimately pursue such interests in any number of ways."); Spence v. Washington, 418 U.S. 405, 409 (1974) ("[T]he state or national governments constitutionally may forbid anyone from mishandling in any manner a flag that is public property."); *Barnette*, 319 U.S. 624, 640 (1943) ("National unity as an end which officials may foster by persuasion and example is not in question.").

[154] T. EMERSON, THE SYSTEM OF FREEDOM OF EXPRESSION 698 (1970).

[155] The Supreme Court has addressed this topic of government speech only in dicta. *See supra* note 153 and accompanying text. The recent proliferation of scholarly literature is indicative of the fact that the constitutional contours of this governmental interest are yet to be defined. *See, e.g.,* M. YUDOF, WHEN GOVERNMENT SPEAKS (1982); Kamenshine, *The First Amendment's Implied Political Establishment Clause*, 67 CALIF. L. REV. 1105 (1979); Ziegler, *Government*

potentially limitless reach of this governmental interest. The government's desire to burden individuals' activity on the ground that it is officially deemed to espouse an idea the government believes to be undesirable, unwise, inappropriate or false—an interest which *Barnette* teaches is absolutely impermissible under the first amendment—can easily be rephrased by the government as an interest in preventing interference with a message the government has officially declared to be desirable, wise, appropriate or true. This is so because any individual activity which espouses an idea contrary to the official message competes for public attention and acceptance with the latter and thus reduces to some greater or lesser extent the government's persuasive effectiveness. Thus it would appear that *Wooley* announces an absolute first amendment principle: "[W]here the state's interest is to disseminate an ideology, no matter how acceptable to some, such interest *cannot* outweigh an individual's right to avoid becoming the courier for such message."[156]

Professor David Gaebler, however, has rejected this analysis and has argued:

> While the content-based/content-neutral distinction is appropriate in the affirmative first amendment context, it does not appear applicable to the negative first amendment context. The dangers implicit in government discrimination against particular views do not arise when government discriminates in favor of particular views, at least when it does so either by expressing those views itself or by compelling others to express them. It has been suggested that the "free marketplace of ideas" may be undermined as readily by government protection of particular views. However, this proposition as stated is too broad. Of course special protection of particular views is often tantamount to a restriction upon all other views. Where government protection of particular views works a concomitant restriction on other views, government protection is as injurious to freedom of expression as government restriction. . . . However, when government discrimination in favor of particular views takes the form of the government's merely adding its own voice to the throng on behalf of that view, there is no concomitant restriction on the expression of other views. Government expression does affect the relative quantity of expression of various views but does not restrict any expression on the basis of content. Similarly, government compelled expression does not restrict expression of any specific views but, rather, only affects the relative quantity of all expression. . . . Thus, while compelled expression may infringe upon individual interests it

---

Speech and the Constitution: The Limits of Official Partisanship, 21 B.C.L. REV. 579 (1980).

[156] 430 U.S. at 717 (footnote omitted) (emphasis added).

should not be condemned as an interference with the "free marketplace of ideas."[157]

Professor Gaebler's analysis is severely flawed. It must be remembered that federal, state and local governments occupy a unique position in our society due to the enormous power and influence they wield. As Professor Thomas Emerson has noted, the government controls many of the sources of information in our society, has virtually unlimited access to the means of communication, and the nature of governmental expression is qualitatively different than that of expression by private individuals because "[t]he tendency of government expression to be uniform and repetitive in its message gives it a more concentrated impact than other expression."[158] Most importantly, the government possesses a total monopoly on the legitimate use of force, a factor which alone distinguishes the government from any other participant in the arena of public debate. Indeed, *Wooley* limited its holding to the principle that the first amendment prohibits the government from impermissibly abusing its exclusive control of the legitimate use of force in our society by conscripting unwilling citizens as foot soldiers for the public dissemination of its ideological message.[159]

The content-based/content-neutral distinction, then, has great significance regardless of whether the government is burdening individual activity for the purpose of suppressing the content of private expression or for the purpose of favoring the content of governmental expression. No doubt there are dangers implicit in governmental efforts to regulate on a non-content basis, too. To suggest more rigorous constitutional scrutiny for content-based regulations, however, is not to endorse the abandonment of judicial scrutiny of non-content regulations.[160]

The dangers of ideological discrimination are greater when the government regulates on the basis of the content of expression, regardless of source, than when the government simply encourages pluralist expression without regard to the content of the messages. The danger that the government will be unable to fulfill its role as an "umpire," overseeing the effective functioning of the "marketplace of ideas" in an ideologically neutral manner, is always a matter of grave concern. This concern is heightened whenever the government attempts to regulate on the basis of the content of expression. If the government is acting in the conflicting roles of both umpire and participant in the "marketplace of ideas," in *prima facie* violation of the principle that no one should be permitted

---

[157] Gaebler, *First Amendment Protection Against Government Compelled Expression and Association*, 23 B.C.L. REV. 995, 1008-09 (1982) (footnotes omitted).
[158] T. Emerson, *supra* note 154, at 698.
[159] 430 U.S. at 717.
[160] *See infra* text accompanying notes 183-88.

to be the judge of her own cause,[161] then the vigilance of the judiciary must be very strict indeed.

When the government burdens individual activity in order to favor the content of its own messages and thereby furthers its own ideological self-interest it strikes at the very heart of the first amendment guarantee. Given the pre-existing, natural advantages the government possesses as a participant in the arena of public debate, the danger is enormous that any governmental exercise of its exclusive authority to burden individual activity for the purpose of enhancing its own ideological message will result in the first amendment being uncoupled from its essential function of preserving an open, democratic society.[162] The fundamental principle underlying the constitutional guarantee of free expression embodied in the first amendment was aptly stated by Justice Jackson in *Barnette*: "We set up government by consent of the governed, and the Bill of Rights denies those in power any legal opportunity to coerce that consent. Authority here is to be controlled by public opinion, not public opinion by authority."[163] As James Madison recognized, the very "nature of Republican Government," presupposes and demands that "the censorial power is in the people over the Government, and not in the Government over the people."[164] The danger that governmental expression, especially when artificially enhanced by the government's exercise of its total control over the legitimate use of coercion in our society, will drown out countervailing expression by private individuals thus threatens to turn not only the first amendment but also the democratic premise of our government on its head.

The majority opinion in *Wooley* simply recognized that, as a matter of principle, the government interest in compelling unwilling citizens to assist in the dissemination of the government's ideological message by publicly displaying it for the express purpose that it be viewed by others is so intimately connected to the central concerns of the first amendment as to be deemed constitutionally impermissible. This is true whether the government coerces the display of a slogan on a license plate, a flag salute, or the wearing of a campaign button for the proscribed purpose. On this analysis *Wooley* and *Barnette* are, as a matter of fundamental first amendment principle, not merely analogous, but doctrinal twins. It is simply

---

[161] *See* United States v. Nixon, 418 U.S. 683, 703-05 (1974); Dworkin, *The Jurisprudence of Richard Nixon*, NEW YORK REV. BOOKS, May 4, 1972, at 27.

[162] *See, e.g.*, A. MEIKLEJOHN, FREE SPEECH AND ITS RELATION TO SELF-GOVERNMENT (1948); Gard, *The Absoluteness of the First Amendment*, 58 NEB. L. REV. 1053 (1979); Kalven, *The New York Times Case: A Note on "The Central Meaning of the First Amendment,"* 1964 SUP. CT. REV. 191. *Cf.* BeVier, *The First Amendment and Political Speech: An Inquiry Into the Substance and Limits of Principle*, 30 STAN. L. REV. 299 (1978); Bork, *Neutral Principles and Some First Amendment Problems*, 47 IND. L.J. 1 (1971).

[163] 319 U.S. at 641.

[164] 4 ANNALS OF CONGRESS 934 (1794).

contrary to the democratic premise of the first amendment to allow the government to compel the unconsenting to use their person or privately owned property "as a 'mobile billboard' for the State's ideological message."[165]

The countervailing hypothetical case offered by Justice Rehnquist, in his dissenting opinion in *Wooley*, appears superficially to cast doubt on the doctrinal foundations of this analysis:

> For example, were New Hampshire to erect a multitude of billboards, each proclaiming "Live Free or Die," and tax all citizens for the cost of erection and maintenance, clearly the message would be "fostered" by the individual citizen-taxpayers and just as clearly those individuals would be "instruments" in that communication. Certainly, however, that case would not fall within the ambit of *Barnette*.[166]

Upon closer inspection, however, the appeal of Justice Rehnquist's argument is illusory. Thus, it may be that the prime fallacy of Justice Rehnquist's analysis is his conclusion that "that case would not fall within the ambit of *Barnette*."[167] *Abood v. Detroit Board of Education*[168] is a major precedent suggesting that the first amendment would be violated by any governmentally compelled financial support for ideological governmental expression. In *Abood*, the United States Supreme Court, expressly relying on *Barnette*,[169] held that the governmentally compelled financial support for the ideological activities of a public employees' union, as a condition of government employment, was violative of the first amendment rights of dissenting union members and those required to pay union service charges in lieu of membership dues.[170]

Even if it is true that "the legitimacy of government communication activities, the difficulties in identifying and labeling ideological, noncontroversial, or political speech, and the sheer folly of attempting to calculate how much of an individual's taxes are spent for specific, objectionable government communications"[171] counsel against applying *Abood* to cases involving taxpayers, it does not follow, as Justice Rehnquist argued, that this compels the conclusion that *Wooley* was wrongly decided. In Justice Rehnquist's billboard hypothetical the governmental interest at stake is the government's interest in itself communicating to the populace, not to require individual citizens to unwillingly carry the official message.

---

[165] *Wooley*, 430 U.S. at 715.
[166] *Id.* at 721.
[167] *Id.*
[168] 431 U.S. 209 (1977).
[169] *Id.* at 235.
[170] *Id.* at 233-37.
[171] Yudof, *When Governments Speak: Toward a Theory of Government Expression and the First Amendment*, 57 TEX. L. REV. 863, 893 (1979).

Inasmuch as the government can only express itself or disseminate its message by the expenditure of tax revenues, to hold that the use of such revenues constitutes an impermissible requirement of participation by the unwilling taxpayer would be to wholly defeat the government's asserted claim of a right to express itself.[172]

The majority opinion in *Wooley* sensitively decided only the issue before it, holding simply that an explicit governmental interest in using its exclusive power of legitimate coercion to conscript unwilling persons as foot soldiers to act as amplifying devices for the public dissemination of its ideological message is so closely related to the central concerns of the first amendment that it cannot be constitutionally permitted.[173] Stated in another manner, an explicit governmental purpose of requiring objecting citizens to advertise publicly the government's message constitutes an unfair method of competition in the marketplace of ideas.

The second governmental interest asserted by New Hampshire in support of its requirement that citizens display the motto "Live Free or Die" on the license plates of their passenger vehicles was the facilitation of identification of properly licensed vehicles.[174] This interest, wholly unrelated to the content of the governmentally compelled message, was premised on the notion that since the motto only appeared on license plates issued for non-commercial vehicles the state could easily discover the misuse of a commercial license plate on a non-commercial vehicle, or vice versa, by reference to the presence or absence of the motto on the license plate.[175] Inasmuch as this was a non-content based governmental interest the Supreme Court subjected it to less rigorous scrutiny. Nevertheless, the New Hampshire regulation could not withstand this lessened standard of review.

First, the Supreme Court pointed out that the state's asserted interest was not supported on the factual record because New Hampshire noncommercial license plates normally bore a specific configuration of letters and numbers which adequately distinguished them from commercial license plates.[176] Second, the Court found that the state could achieve its purpose by "less drastic means."[177] The most obvious less drastic alternative would be for New Hampshire to emboss the word "non-commercial" on the appropriate license plates. In other words, there is a gross constitutional impropriety in the official selection of a content-based governmental means to achieve a non-content-based governmental interest.

---

[172] *See* L. TRIBE, *supra* note 17, at 589-91.

[173] 430 U.S. at 717 ("[W]here the state's interest is to disseminate an ideology ... such interest cannot outweigh an individual's First Amendment right to avoid becoming the courier for such message.").

[174] *Id.* at 716.

[175] *Id.* at 716 n.12.

[176] *Id.* at 716.

[177] *Id.* at 716-17.

On first impression it would appear that the mottoes "In God We Trust" and "E Pluribus Unum" on United States currency would succumb to the scrutiny applied in *Wooley*. This, however, is not necessarily true. As the Supreme Court noted: "Currency is generally carried in a purse or pocket and need not be displayed to the public. The bearer of currency is thus not required to publicly advertise the national motto."[178] It is equally true that the traditional use of these mottoes, in a furtherance of the legitimate and indisputably important non-content-based governmental interest in the prevention of counterfeiting, arguably has caused them to lose their ideological character.[179] Most important, however, is the fact that Justice Rehnquist's invocation of this hypothetical is based on a misapprehension of the character of the federal statute at issue. Unlike the New Hampshire statutory scheme, federal law is sensitive to the serious first amendment problem raised by the presence of the national mottoes, "In God We Trust" and "E Pluribus Unum," on United States currency and criminalizes the obliteration of these mottoes only when accompanied by a specific intent to defraud.[180] This may be precisely the sort of a less drastic alternative alluded to in *Wooley*.

In *Prune Yard Shopping Center v. Robins*,[181] the United States Supreme Court upheld a state's non-content-based requirement that a privately owned shopping center open its premises to the speech and petitioning activities of private individuals. In so doing the Court explicitly distinguished *Wooley* as involving a content-based governmental regulation where "the government itself prescribed the message."[182] Consequently, the Supreme Court applied the less rigorous balancing formula traditionally appropriate for the review of non-content-based governmental regulations.[183]

While it is true that the non-content-based regulation at issue in *Robins* served the significant governmental interest and first amendment value of opening a new forum for all speakers and all points of view and presented "no danger of governmental discrimination for or against a particular message,"[184] it cannot be confidently concluded that "[o]pening private property to pluralist expression poses none of the dangers that compelled speech doctrine is designed to prevent."[185] Indeed, this is precisely why judicial review of non-content-based governmental regulations, although properly less rigorous than the scrutiny applied to content-

---

[178] *Id.* at 717 n.15.

[179] *Cf.* School Dist. v. Schempp, 374 U.S. 203, 230 (1963) (Brennan, J., concurring).

[180] *See, e.g.,* United States v. Sheiner, 273 F. Supp. 977 (S.D.N.Y.), *aff'd*, 410 F.2d 337 (2d Cir. 1967); United States v. Lissner, 12 F. 840 (Mass. 1882).

[181] 447 U.S. 74 (1980).

[182] *Id.* at 87.

[183] *Id.*

[184] *Id.*

[185] *The Supreme Court, 1979 Term*, 94 HARV. L. REV. 77, 171 n.23 (1980).

based regulations, is not toothless. On the other hand, Professor Gaebler is simply wrong when he asserts:

> Moreover, the content-based/content-neutral distinction also fails to help identify negative first amendment cases in which the infringement of individual interests is particularly severe. For example, the Court held in *Barnette* that the state may not require school children to recite the pledge of allegiance. Suppose instead a state requirement that school children recite, not the pledge of allegiance per se, but rather, a message to be selected by some non-government entity and that message selected happened to be the pledge of allegiance. Although in this case the government would not have mandated any particular message, the infringement of individual interests would not seem any less severe.[186]

It is inappropriate to criticize the Court's lesser scrutiny of non-content regulations with an example of a content regulation; clearly the government cannot avoid *Barnette* by delegating the choice of the message to a particular private organization and then placing its monopoly police power behind the message selected. Thus, Professor Gaebler is correct, in a perverse sense, when he concludes that "it makes little difference whether it is the government or the nongovernmental entity that chooses the specific message."[187] Unfortunately, the flaw in Professor Gaebler's analysis is that he ignores the central tenet of permissible non-content governmental regulations, expressed most clearly in the Supreme Court's "public forum" cases, that if a forum is open to one person or idea it must be equally open to all.[188]

V. CONCLUSION

Justice Frankfurter, prior to his appointment to the United States Supreme Court, made a comment which later guided his judicial performance in free speech cases: "[W]ith the great men of the Supreme Court constitutional adjudication has always been statecraft. . . . The great judges are those to whom the Constitution is not primarily a text for interpretation but the means of ordering the life of a progressive people."[189]

In contrast to the view of Justice Frankfurter, Justice Jackson did not believe that the only choice of a proper role for a jurist was either deferential or activist Platonic Guardian.[190] The clear import of the majority opinion in *Barnette* was that the members of the Court had a duty to expound

---

[186] Gaebler, *supra* note 115, at 1010.

[187] *Id.*

[188] *See, e.g.,* Kalven, *The Concept of the Public Forum: Cox v. Louisiana,* 1965 SUP. CT. REV. 1.

[189] F. FRANKFURTER, THE PUBLIC AND ITS GOVERNMENT 75-76 (1930).

[190] *See* Griswold v. Connecticut, 381 U.S. 479, 526-27 (1965) (Black, J., dissenting), *quoting* L. HAND, THE BILL OF RIGHTS 73 (1958).

the fundamental law of the Constitution and not to act as statesmen, with or without a sense of modesty, determining as a matter of "personal preference" whether "the legislators" solution is too strong for the "judicial stomach."[191] For Justice Jackson the Constitution was a text for judicial interpretation, and it was the Court's constitutional duty to enforce the first amendment's command that the government is absolutely proscribed from attempting to achieve political orthodoxy by the means of compelling or prohibiting the expression of any statement because of the ideological agreement or disagreement of those who hold political office at that time in history. In the first "balancing"/"absolute" debate, the absolutist, Justice Jackson, had all the better of the argument.

---

[191] L. HAND, THE BILL OF RIGHTS 70:
[J]udges . . . do not, indeed they may not, say that taking all things into consideration, the legislators' solution is too strong for the judicial stomach. On the contrary they wrap up their [decision] in a protective veil of adjectives such as "arbitrary," . . . reasonable, . . . or "essential," whose office usually, though quite innocently, is to disguise what they are doing and impute to it a derivation far more impressive than their personal preferences, which are all that in fact lie behind the decision . . . .

RUSSO v. CENTRAL SCH. DIST. NO. 1, TOWNS OF RUSH, ETC., N. Y.   623
Cite as 469 F.2d 623 (1972)

Mrs. Susan RUSSO, Appellant,

v.

CENTRAL SCHOOL DISTRICT NO. 1, TOWNS OF RUSH, ET AL., COUNTY OF MONROE, STATE OF NEW YORK, et al., Appellees.

No. 26, Docket 72–1303.

United States Court of Appeals, Second Circuit.

Argued Oct. 19, 1972.

Decided Nov. 14, 1972.

Civil rights action brought by probationary teacher who alleged that her dismissal for refusing to pledge allegiance to the flag violated her First Amendment rights. The United States District Court for the Western District of New York, Harold P. Burke, J., dismissed the complaint, and teacher appealed. The Court of Appeals, Irving R. Kaufman, Circuit Judge, held that teacher's First Amendment rights were violated when school officials discharged her for standing silently at attention during daily classroom recitation of the pledge of allegiance in which school regulations required her to participate.

Reversed and remanded.

1. Civil Rights ⟿13.9

Exhaustion of state judicial remedies is not a predicate to a federal court's jurisdiction of a civil action brought for deprivation of rights. 42 U.S.C.A. § 1983.

2. Federal Civil Procedure ⟿2285

Degree of specificity and particularity with which the facts must be found may vary, depending upon the circumstances of each case. Fed.Rules Civ. Proc. rule 52(a), 28 U.S.C.A.

3. Federal Civil Procedure ⟿2282

An important function of findings of fact is to aid an appellate court on review; accordingly, findings that are nothing but cold rhetoric, couched in extraordinarily broad and general terms, and stripped of underlying analysis or justification or an accompanying memorandum or opinion shedding some light on the reasoning employed, invite closer scrutiny, especially when the case concerns fundamental constitutional freedoms.

4. Courts ⟿406.3(6)

Unless due care is given to the process of fact-finding, the reliability of district court's conclusions will be subject to question, thus compelling a reviewing court to scrutinize the findings with a sharper eye than is ordinarily appropriate. Fed.Rules Civ.Proc. rule 52(a), 28 U.S.C.A.

5. Schools and School Districts ⟿133.11

In view of principal's testimony that probationary art teacher who was dismissed was never asked to teach ceramics, and in view of fact that a new teacher, at time of incident in question, had already been hired to serve that function, it simply was not believable that the probationary teacher's statement, at a meeting between the principal and members of the art department, that she would not teach ceramics was meant

7. We caution, however, that our decision is not to be read as holding that Crossroads is required to rent to welfare recipients without regard to their ability to pay the rent. The remedies available when a nonwelfare tenant defaults his rental obligation would be similarly available when a tenant receiving public assistance defaults because of a reduction or elimination of the excess shelter allowance.

325

in any way as a challenge to the principal's authority, or that it could have been construed as such.

6. Constitutional Law ⇐90.1(1)

Probationary art teacher's First Amendment rights were violated when school officials discharged her for standing silently at attention during daily classroom recitation of the pledge of allegiance in which school regulations required her to participate. 28 U.S.C.A. § 1343; 42 U.S.C.A. § 1983; U.S.C.A. Const. Amends. 1, 14.

7. Schools and School Districts ⇐55

Boards of education retain substantial discretion in controlling the educational process in their schools.

8. Schools and School Districts ⇐55

Reasonable regulations designed to effect legitimate purposes are well within the power of a board of education and will be upheld against challenge by the courts.

9. Constitutional Law ⇐82

Children in many instances have more limited First Amendment rights than do adults. U.S.C.A.Const. Amend. 1.

10. Constitutional Law ⇐82

There is little room in the "majestic generalities of the Bill of Rights" for an interpretation of the First Amendment that would be more restrictive with respect to teachers than it is with respect to their students, where there has been no interference with the requirements of appropriate discipline in the operation of the school.

11. Constitutional Law ⇐82
Schools and School Districts ⇐169

Nothing in the First Amendment requires a school administration to wait until disruption has actually occurred before it takes protective action; conduct which leads, or is likely to lead, to violence in the school is not to be tolerated. U.S.C.A.Const. Amend. 1.

12. Schools and School Districts ⇐164

Schools have a substantial interest in maintaining flag salute programs. Education Law N.Y. § 802.

13. Schools and School Districts ⇐172

It is a proper and appropriate function of the educational system to instill in young minds a healthy respect for the symbols of our national government, and school officials may therefore enforce regulations whose purpose is to give effect to this legitimate state aim; but such regulations must be narrowly drawn for precision of regulation must be the touchstone in an area so closely touching our most precious freedoms. U.S.C.A.Const. Amend. 1.

14. Constitutional Law ⇐82

Traditional First Amendment teaching requires that when legitimate state concerns are expressed in a provision which imposes a substantial burden on protected First Amendment activities, the state must achieve its goal by means which have a less drastic impact on the continued vitality of First Amendment freedoms. U.S.C.A.Const. Amend. 1.

15. Schools and School Districts ⇐141(2)

School officials are not limited in their power to dismiss inept or obstreperous instructors, except to the extent they choose to so limit themselves; and public employment is not a sinecure to be retained regardless of merit simply by shouting loudly that any threat of dismissal is motivated by an anti-First Amendment animus; but where in fact a dismissal is directed because a teacher has engaged in constitutionally protected activity, the dismssal may not stand. U.S.C.A.Const. Amend. 1.

16. Constitutional Law ⇐90(1)

Because the First Amendment ranks among the most important of our constitutional rights, it must be recognized that the precious right of free speech requires protection even when the speech is personally obnoxious. U.S.C.A.Const. Amend. 1.

17. Constitutional Law ⇐90(1)

Right to remain silent in the face of an illegitimate demand for speech is as much a part of First Amendment protections as the right to speak out in face of an illegitimate demand for silence. U.S.C.A.Const. Amend. 1.

Richard R. Rowley, Albany, N. Y. (Sneeringer & Rowley, Jeffrey G. Plant, Albany, N. Y., of counsel), for appellant.

William H. Morris, Rochester, N. Y. (Nixon, Hargrave Devans & Doyle, Robert H. Wendt, Rochester, N. Y., of counsel), for appellees.

Before WATERMAN, SMITH and KAUFMAN, Circuit Judges.

IRVING R. KAUFMAN, Circuit Judge:

Events that occur in small towns sometimes have a way of raising large constitutional questions. Henrietta, New York, a town of approximately 6,500 residents, is the geographic setting of this important case, in which we are asked to decide whether the dismissal of Mrs. Susan Russo, a high school art teacher, for what in the end amounts to a silent refusal to participate in her school's daily flag salute ceremonies, violated her constitutional rights under the First Amendment. As in James v. Board of Education, 461 F.2d 566 (2d Cir. 1972), decided by the Court just a few months ago, we must ascertain, and ultimately assess, the sometimes conflicting interests of the state on the one hand, in maintaining and promoting the discipline necessary to the proper functioning of schools, and the interest of a teacher, on the other, freely to exercise fundamental rights of expression and belief guaranteed by the Bill of Rights. There is, however, more to this case than even that difficult balancing test requires, for we are mindful of the fact that the problems associated with the short-hand phrase, "flag salute," bare a complex of deep emotions, calling into question the meaning of patriotism and loyalty, and the different significance those words have for different people. This case, therefore, is made more difficult for us, "not because the principles of decision are obscure but because the flag involved is our own." West Virginia State Board of Education v. Barnette, 319 U.S. 624, 641, 63 S.Ct. 1178, 1187, 87 L.Ed. 1628 (1943).

I.

The facts, which we glean from the trial record below, are as follows. Susan Russo was appointed by the Board of Education for the Rush-Henrietta School District, as a probationary art teacher, and assigned, as of September 1, 1969, to the James E. Sperry High School in Henrietta. As a condition of her employment, Mrs. Russo was required by New York Education Law, McKinney's Consol.Laws, c. 16, § 3002 to sign a loyalty oath affirming her support of the Constitution of the United States and of New York State. She signed that oath, without reservation, on August 27, 1969.

In September, 1969, shortly after the school year began, a notice appeared on the school's bulletin board announcing that the "pledge of allegiance" would be recited each day and that "all students and staff members [were] expected to salute the flag." The practice at the Sperry School was to have the pledge read into the school's intercommunication system by a faculty member or a student. Students and teachers would then stand in their homeroom classes, and recite the pledge along with the voice over the public address system.

Mrs. Russo, in addition to her duties as an art instructor, was assigned to homeroom duty and charged with supervision of between twenty and twenty-five children, ranging from fourteen to sixteen years of age. Mrs. Catherine Adams, a teacher with seven years experience in the Rush-Henrietta school district, was also assigned to supervise the same homeroom, and to exercise senior authority in the classroom.

Although Mrs. Adams saluted the flag and recited the pledge each morning with her class, Mrs. Russo did not.

From her first day in school, when it came time to recite the pledge, Mrs. Russo rose and faced the flag, but neither recited the pledge nor saluted the flag. She simply stood at respectful attention, with her hands at her sides. Significantly, there is no evidence in the record indicating that Mrs. Russo ever tried to influence her students to follow her example, and no evidence disclosing even a trace of disruption in the classroom as a result of her action. The students all knew the pledge and, under Mrs. Adams's guidance, recited it each day, without incident. Mrs. Russo's belief, the sincerity of which is unchallenged in these proceedings, was that the phrase "liberty and justice for all" appearing in the pledge, which to most of us represents the spirit and abiding genius of our institutions, in her mind simply did not reflect the quality of life in America today. For this reason, she felt it to be an act of hypocrisy on her part to mouth the words of the pledge when she lacked a belief in either their accuracy or efficacy.

Although Mrs. Russo had not recited the pledge from the start of the school year in September, her action did not come to the attention of school officials until some time in April, 1970. In fact, as late as April 17, 1970, a teacher's report based on actual observation was prepared by James Bennett, an assistant principal at the Sperry school. He evaluated Mrs. Russo's classroom performance as favorable in all respects.[1]

About that time, in April 1970, certain students and parents reported to the principal, Donald Loughlin, that Mrs. Russo was not saluting the flag. On the morning of April 19, Loughlin entered Mrs. Russo's homeroom class and observed her standing in silence as the pledge was being recited. The following day Mrs. Russo was summoned to Loughlin's office and asked to explain her behavior. Mrs. Russo did so, as we have indicated, adding that her unwillingness to recite the pledge and salute the flag was a matter of personal conscience.

It was hardly coincidence that school officials were informed of Mrs. Russo's behavior in the spring of 1970. During the preceding months the school's flag salute regulations had become a matter of some controversy in Henrietta, and its surrounding towns. A directive of the school Board issued on February 2, reminded school principals that all students were to stand during the pledge. On April 14, the Board reversed itself and announced that students who were unable to participate in the pledge ceremonies because of sincere conscientious belief, would be permitted to remain seated during the pledge if they chose to do so. This Board regulation was the subject of bitter dispute at an open meeting of the school Board. A few

---

1. The portion of Bennett's report, listed as "Summary and Recommendations" appears below:

    I have taken the opportunity to "pass through" several of Mrs. Russo's classes throughout the year and observe her students at work and I have observed her Studio in Art class for an entire period. The current project in that class is a work, preferably in 3-D or a stylistic interpretation, involving social commentary.
    Comments—
    Mrs. Russo has a congenial, relaxed personality and meets students at their level. The pupil-teacher relationship has always appeared quite good.

    Teaching methods and techniques appear to be resourceful and appropriate to individualized instruction in a creative atmosphere. The teacher adopts the role of resource person and helper —guiding individual initiative.
    The teacher plans basic time periods for each project but is flexible in regard to completion time so as to allow for individual differences. Those that finish a project early are encouraged to practice drawing and painting skills.
    Student participation has generally appear to be at a high level—most seem busy at work generally.
    ". . . . . ."
    By this account, Mrs. Russo appears to have been an exemplary teacher.

days later, on May 1, Principal Loughlin visited Mrs. Russo's class for a second time and observed her activity during the pledge. At a subsequent meeting in his office, Loughlin told Mrs. Russo that he intended to recommend that her probationary appointment not be renewed unless she resigned. Mrs. Russo asked Loughlin for the reasons underlying his decision, but he refused to supply any, stating that he was not compelled to explain his action with respect to a probationary teacher.[2] Mrs. Russo refused to resign.

On May 12, Loughlin wrote Superintendent of Schools Richard E. TenHaken, recommending that Mrs. Russo not be reappointed for the coming academic year, and that her employment status be terminated, effective June 30. On the evening of May 12, however, the school board announced new regulations governing student conduct during the pledge. The new regulations modified the policy adopted on April 14 by requiring all students who refused to salute the flag to stand in respectful silence. Finally, at a meeting of the school board, held on June 23, Mrs. Russo was dismissed from service at the Sperry school. No reasons for her dismissal were set forth by the Board. A notice of termination sent to Mrs. Russo by the District Clerk similarly did not provide any statement of the grounds for her dismissal.

II.

[1] This action was brought by Mrs. Russo pursuant to provisions of the Civil Rights Act, 42 U.S.C. § 1983,[3] and 28 U.S.C. § 1343,[4] alleging that her dismissal for refusing to pledge allegiance to the flag violated her First Amendment rights, and that the Board's failure to state reasons for her dismissal denied her the procedural protections safeguarded by the Due Process Clause of the Fourteenth Amendment. Mrs. Russo seeks reinstatement with back pay, and damages. In view of our decision on the merits of the First Amendment

---

2. New York Education Law sec. 3012, Tenure, provides:
   1. Teachers, principals, supervisors and all other members of the teaching and supervising staff shall be appointed by the board of education . . . upon the recommendation of [the] superintendent of schools, for a probationary period of three years. The service of a person appointed to any of such positions may be discontinued at any time during such probationary period, on the recommendation of the superintendent of schools, by a majority vote of the board of education.
   2. At the expiration of the probationary term of a person appointed for such term, subject to the conditions of this section, the superintendent of schools shall make a written report to the board of education recommending for appointment on tenure those persons who have been found competent, efficient and satisfactory. . . .

3. 42 U.S.C. sec. 1983, Civil Action for Deprivation of Rights provides:
   Every person who, under color of any statute, ordinance, regulation, custom, or usage, of any State or Territory, subjects, or causes to be subjected, any citizen of the United States or other person within the jurisdiction thereof to the deprivation of any rights, privileges, or immunities secured by the Constitution and laws, shall be liable to the party injured in an action at law, suit in equity, or other proceeding for redress.

4. 28 U.S.C. sec. 1343. Civil Rights and Elective Franchise, provides:
   The district courts shall have original jurisdiction of any civil action authorized by law to be commenced by any person:
   . . .
   (3) To redress the deprivation, under color of any State law, statute, ordinance, regulation, custom or usage, of any right, privilege or immunity secured by the Constitution of the United States or by any Act of Congress providing for equal rights of citizens or of all persons within the jurisdiction of the United States;
   (4) To recover damages or to secure equitable or other relief under any Act of Congress providing for the protection of civil rights, including the right to vote.

challenge,[5] we do not reach Mrs. Russo's Due Process claim.[6]

As a preliminary matter we are constrained to comment on the cryptic findings filed by the court below. After trial, Judge Burke dismissed Mrs. Russo's complaint on the merits, holding, in a brief series of findings and conclusions unaccompanied by any opinion, that neither First nor Fourteenth Amendment rights were violated in the dismissal of June 30, 1970. Judge Burke recited without explanation that Mrs. Russo's probationary appointment was terminated because of: (1) "her failure to follow school regulations," (2) "her refusal to teach a course in the art department," (3) "her lack of cooperation," (4) "her refusal to participate in the pledge of allegiance," (5) "her failure to perform all her duties," and (6) "her involvement of the student body in her conflict with the school."

[2–4] Ordinarily, of course, Rule 52, F.R.Civ.P., binds us to accept findings of fact made by the district court unless they are "clearly erroneous." But equally compelling is the demand in Rule 52(a) that "in all actions tried upon the facts without a jury . . . the court shall find the facts specially . . . ." The degree of specificity and particularity with which the facts must be found may vary, depending upon the circumstances of each case, see Kelley v. Everglades Drainage District, 319 U.S. 415, 63 S.Ct. 1141, 87 L.Ed. 1485 (1943). But we must remember that an important function of findings of fact is to aid an appellate court on review, see Advisory Committee Note to Rule 52(a) (1946); 5A Moore, Federal Practice ¶ 52.01 [5]. Findings that are nothing but cold rhetoric, couched in extraordinarily broad and general terms, and stripped of underlying analysis or justification or an accompanying memorandum or opinion shedding some light on the reasoning employed, invite closer scrutiny, especially when the case concerns fundamental constitutional freedoms. See, Schneiderman v. United States, 320 U.S. 118, 129–131, 63 S.Ct. 1333, 87 L.Ed. 1796 (1943). The need for precision and clarity in fact-finding and the use of cold conclusory statements as a shield to prevent penetrating the absence of facts is made more significant because of the "clearly errone-

---

5. We reach the merits here because Mrs. Russo did not have any state administrative remedies to exhaust before filing this action under 42 U.S.C. sec. 1983, see Eisen v. Eastman, 421 F.2d 560 (2d Cir. 1969), cert. denied, 400 U.S. 841, 91 S.Ct. 82, 27 L.Ed.2d 75 (1970). Mrs. Russo did file a grievance notice pursuant to the contractual grievance procedure in the district. The Superintendent of Schools informed Mrs. Russo that non-renewal determinations of probationary teachers were not subject to grievance procedures. Of course, exhaustion of state judicial remedies is not a predicate to a federal court's jurisdiction in a sec. 1983 claim, Monroe v. Pape, 365 U.S. 167, 81 S.Ct. 473, 5 L.Ed.2d 492 (1961); Sostre v. McGinnis, 442 F.2d 178 (2d Cir. 1971) (en banc), cert. denied, 404 U.S. 1049, 92 S.Ct. 719, 30 L.Ed.2d 740 (1972).

6. Because we hold that Mrs. Russo was dismissed solely because of the exercise of her first Amendment rights we need not decide what effect the Supreme Court's recent decisions in Board of Regents v. Roth, 408 U.S. 564, 92 S.Ct. 2701, 33 L.Ed.2d 548 (1972) and Perry v. Sindermann, 408 U.S. 593, 92 S.Ct. 2694, 33 L.Ed.2d 570 (1972), might have on future dismissals of probationary teachers in New York. We note only that by statute, probationary teachers in New York are hired for a period of three years. Whether this is a sufficient period to establish the kind of "claim of entitlement" which the Court spoke of in *Sindermann* as being in the nature of a property right in employment that triggers the application of procedural safeguards before such a claim may be taken away is a question we leave for another day. In this context, however, we note the admirable efforts of the New York legislature to afford protection to probationers. A recent 1972 amendment to New York's Education Law specifically requires that teachers who are not recommended for tenure or who are recommended for dismissal henceforth will be entitled to a written statement giving the reasons for such recommendation. New York Education Law § 3031, McKinney's Sessions Laws, c. 866, 1972.

ous" standard, for while errors of law are always correctable by an appellate court, errors of fact rarely are, unless an appellant can scale the high wall which that standard places before him.[7] It stands to reason that unless due care is given to the process of fact finding, the reliability of the district court's conclusions will be subject to question, thus compelling a reviewing court to scrutinize the findings with a sharper eye than is ordinarily appropriate.

"A finding is 'clearly erroneous' when although there is evidence to support it, the reviewing court on the entire evidence is left with the definite and firm conviction that a mistake has been committed." United States v. United States Gypsum Co., 333 U.S. 364, 395, 68 S.Ct. 525, 542, 92 L.Ed. 746 (1948). We are of the view that except with regard to the finding concerning Mrs. Russo's refusal to recite the pledge, the "findings of fact" by the district court with respect to her dismissal are clearly erroneous.

Although Judge Burke lists six grounds for Mrs. Russo's dismissal, his findings discuss only the refusal to salute the flag and the "ceramics incident," a matter about which we shall have more to say in a moment. We are at a loss to understand what Judge Burke meant by his comments upon Mrs. Russo's "failure to follow school regulations," "her lack of cooperation," and her "failure to perform all her duties," unless these "findings" in some way refer to her failure to recite the pledge.[8] Although there was mention in the record of one occasion on which Mrs. Russo, because of some confusion, did not report for hall duty as assigned, we hardly imagine that Judge Burke gave significant factors involved in the decision to dismiss Mrs. Russo. He said: "I stated to the Board, as I had to the Superintendent, that I would not recommend Mrs. Russo because she had been insubordinate in refusing to follow a school regulation. And this coupled with her attitude on the statement she made concerning not teaching ceramics generally was the basis (for non-renewal)."

The extent to which Loughlin was influenced by Mrs. Russo's silent refusal to salute the flag is well-illustrated by a teacher "observation" report he filed concerning Mrs. Russo's classroom performance. The report rates Mrs. Russo's "professional characteristics" as "below average" or "poor" in five of six categories, and concludes with the comment: "Mrs. Russo, a first year teacher, has not met her responsibilities to my satisfaction." The report is dated June, 1970, and appears to refer to the entire 1969–1970 school year. Curiously, Loughlin did not see fit to submit a report about Mrs. Russo's classroom performance until he decided to dismiss her, and he did not decide to dismiss her until he learned of her refusal to participate in the pledge exercise. When Loughlin's report is contrasted with Bennett's glowing evaluation, submitted two months earlier, Loughlin's "observation" clearly appears to have been an after-thought and a mere contrivance to establish non-first amendment grounds to justify Mrs. Russo's dismissal.

---

7. *See,* United States v. Forness, 125 F.2d 928 (2d Cir.) cert. denied, City of Salamanca v. United States, 316 U.S. 694, 62 S.Ct. 1293, 86 L.Ed. 1764 (1942). Judge Frank, for the court wrote:

   Chief Justice Hughes once remarked, "An unscrupulous administrator might be tempted to say 'Let me find the facts for the people of my country, and I care little who lays down the general principles.'" That comment should be extended to include facts found without due care as well as unscrupulous fact-finding: for such lack of due care is less likely to reveal itself than lack of scruples, which, we trust, seldom exists. And Chief Justice Hughes' comment is just as applicable to the careless fact-finding of a judge as to that of an administrative officer. The judiciary properly holds administrative officers to high standards in the discharge of the fact-finding function. The judiciary should at least measure up to the same standards.

   125 F.2d at 942.

8. Loughlin's testimony at trial would appear to indicate that this is indeed the case. He said: "I also told the school board that she [Russo] had failed to comply with school regulations. It happened to be saluting the flag, but it was a school regulation . . . . ." Loughlin also offered testimony that indicated that the failure to salute and the ceramics incident were the only

such weight to this trivial occurrence as to attach to it three separate violations. Finally, the court found that Mrs. Russo had involved the student body in her dispute with the principal. We find no evidence in the record to support such a finding.[9]

[5] The ceramics incident remains an obscure contretemps characterizing the personal relationships at Sperry High School. It is obscure inasmuch as principal Loughlin's account of the occurrence was constantly interrupted by the court, making cogent narration of the event a virtual impossibility. It appears that Loughlin and three members of the school's art department, including Mrs. Russo, met on April 15, 1970 to discuss the qualifications of a teacher who had already been hired to teach ceramics the following year. At that time, Mrs. Russo made the statement that she would not teach ceramics. Loughlin testified quite clearly, however, that he had never asked Mrs. Russo to teach ceramics. Mrs. Russo's version, as she explained to the court, was that she intended her statement as advice to Mr. Loughlin, which she offered in her capacity as one of the three art department teachers present at the meeting. She did not intend to indicate a refusal to teach ceramics, for that issue was not in question. She meant only to say that if she were possessed of the minimal qualifications and training of the replacement ceramics teacher she would not undertake to teach that course. In view of Loughlin's testimony that Mrs. Russo was never asked to teach ceramics, and the fact that a new teacher had already been hired to serve that function, it simply is not believable that Mrs. Russo's statement was meant in any way as a challenge to Loughlin's authority, or that it could have been construed as such.

We are left, then, with the ultimate conclusion that Mrs. Russo's dismissal resulted directly from her refusal to engage in the school's daily flag ceremonies and that all the remaining findings were trimmings to cloak the conduct of the Board and to justify the court's conclusions. We do, however, accept the lower court's findings that school policy required teachers to lead their classes in the pledge exercise and that Mrs. Russo was aware of her responsibility in this respect.

[6] The question, then, is whether dismissal of a high school teacher may be sustained when the sole ground for that dismissal is the teacher's refusal to comply with a school regulation which required her to participate with her class in the pledge of allegiance. To this question we now turn.

III.

If the central character in this drama were one of Mrs. Russo's students, rather than the teacher herself, we might dispose of this case with a simple reference to the Supreme Court's decision in West Virginia State Board of Education v. Barnette, *supra*. There the Court was of the view that "in connection with the pledge, the flag salute is a form of utterance." 319 U.S. at 632, 63 S.Ct. at 1182. "To sustain the compulsory flag salute," the Court said, "we are required to say that a Bill of Rights which guards the individual's right to speak his own mind, left it open to public authorities to compel him to utter what is not in his mind." 319 U.S. at 634, 63 S.Ct. at 1183. The Court declined to do so, and invalidated a West Virginia statute and a Board of Education resolution

---

9. There is some evidence in the record that the school's student body president discussed Mrs. Russo's situation in the school lunchroom, but there is not the slightest hint that Mrs. Russo encouraged him to do so. Indeed, there is evidence indicating that when Mrs. Russo learned of the situation she asked the boy to stop speaking. A petition was circulated by certain students in Mrs. Russo's behalf. Again there is no evidence even tending to show that she encouraged that activity.

promulgated under its authority, that required all students to recite the pledge, or suffer expulsion from school.

[7, 8] Thus, there is no question but that the refusal to recite the pledge and salute the flag is a form of expression, and it matters not that the expression takes the form of silence, see Brown v. Louisiana, 383 U.S. 131, 86 S.Ct. 719, 15 L.Ed.2d 637 (1966). But here we are concerned with a teacher, and we are asked to determine whether the responsibilities which that teacher has voluntarily assumed, to shape and to direct the supple and still impressionable minds of her students in accordance with policies of the school board, somehow lessen the constitutional rights she would otherwise enjoy. In a related context the Supreme Court has said: "To the extent that the [lower] Court's opinion may be read to suggest that teachers may constitutionally be compelled to relinquish the First Amendment rights they would otherwise enjoy as citizens to comment on matters of public interest in connection with the operation of the public schools in which they work, it proceeds on a premise that has been unequivocally rejected in numerous prior decisions of this Court [citations omitted]. 'The theory that public employment which may be denied altogether may be subjected to any conditions, regardless of how unreasonable, has been uniformly rejected.' Keyishian v. Board of Regents [385 U.S. 589 (1970)] at 605–606, 87 S.Ct. [675] at 685, 17 L.Ed. 629." Pickering v. Board of Education, 391 U.S. 563, 568, 88 S.Ct. 1731, 1734, 20 L.Ed.2d 811 (1968); see also Van Alstyne, The Demise of the Right-Privilege Distinction in Constitutional Law, 81 Harv.L.Rev. 1439 (1968). Nevertheless, it is also true that society will not "tolerate undisciplined, coercive, intimidating or disruptive activities on the part of teachers or students which threaten the essential functions of our schools . . . ." James v. Board of Education, supra, 461 F.2d, at 568, and that Boards of Education retain substantial discretion in controlling the educational process in their schools, see generally, Note, Developments in the Law —Academic Freedom, 81 Harv.L.Rev. 1045, 1098 (1968). Reasonable regulations designed to effect legitimate purposes, are well within the Board's power, and will be upheld against challenge, by the courts. See, e. g., Presidents Council, Dist. 25 v. Community School Board, 457 F.2d 289, (2d Cir.) cert. denied, 309 U.S. 998, 93 S.Ct. 308, 34 L.Ed.2d 260 (1972).

[9–11] It has been stated that children, in many instances, have more limited First Amendment rights than do adults. See, e. g., Ginsberg v. New York, 390 U.S. 629, 88 S.Ct. 1274, 20 L.Ed.2d 195 (1968) (obscenity); Emerson, Toward A General Theory of the First Amendment, 72 Yale L.J. 877, 938, 939 (1963); see also, Tinker v. Des Moines Independent School Dist., 393 U.S. 503, 512, 89 S.Ct. 733, 21 L.Ed.2d 731 (1969), (Stewart concurrence). But here, the school board, as it did in James v. Board of Education, supra, would have us decide that the rights enjoyed by school children are broader than the First Amendment rights of their teachers. In James, we declined that invitation. The James case, which called into question the right of a teacher to silently protest America's involvement in the Vietnam war by wearing a black armband in school, was decided after the Supreme Court's decision in Tinker which expressly granted that right to children, where no substantial disruption resulted from the protest. We held that Mr. James could not be dismissed from his employment as a teacher for engaging in protected expression. Similarly, in this instance, the Supreme Court's Barnette decision teaches that school children may not be compelled to utter the pledge of allegiance when it offends their conscientiously held beliefs to do so. There is little room in what Mr. Justice Jackson once called the "majestic generalities of the Bill of Rights," West Virginia State Board of Education v. Barnette, supra, 319 U.S., at 639, 63 S.Ct., at 1186, for an interpretation of the First Amendment that would be more restrictive with respect to teachers than it is with respect to their students, where there has been no interference with the requirements of appropriate discipline in the operation of the school, Tinker v. Des Moines Independent School Dist., *supra*, 393 U.S., at 509, 89 S.Ct. 733. We add, however, as we did in *James*, that nothing in the First Amendment requires a school administration to wait until disruption has actually occurred before it may take protective action. Conduct which leads, or is likely to lead, to violence in the schools is not to be tolerated. James v. Board of Education, *supra*, 461 F.2d, at 572. But such conduct is not involved in this case. We take guidance, instead, from the Supreme Court's instruction in *Tinker*, whose lesson is that neither students nor teachers "shed their constitutional rights to freedom of speech or expression at the schoolhouse gate." 393 U.S. at 506, 89 S.Ct. at 736; *see also* Hanover v. Northrup, 325 F.Supp. 170 (D. Conn.1971).[10]

[12-14] Schools, of course, have a substantial interest in maintaining flag salute programs. New York's Education Law, § 802, imposes a duty upon the Commissioner of Education to prepare a program of flag salute for the public schools, and this duty has been given effect in Regulations of the New York Commissioner of Education, 8 CRRNY §§ 108.5, 108.7.[11] It is a proper, and appropriate function of our educational system to instill in young minds a healthy respect for the symbols of our national government. School officials, therefore, may enforce regulations whose purpose is to give effect to this legitimate state aim. But such regulations must be narrowly drawn for "[p]recision of regulation must be the touchstone in an area so closely touching our most precious freedoms." NAACP v. Button, 371 U.S. 415, 438, 83 S.Ct. 328, 340, 9 L.Ed.2d 405 (1963), quoted in United States v. Robel, 389 U.S. 258, 265, 88 S.Ct. 419, 19 L.Ed.2d 508 (1967). Traditional First Amendment teaching requires that when "legitimate [state] concerns are expressed in a [provision] which imposes a substantial burden on protected First Amendment activities, [the state] must achieve its goal by means which have a 'less drastic' impact on the continued vitality of First Amendment freedoms." (citations omitted). United States v. Robel, *supra*, at 268, 88 S.Ct., at 426; *see* Note, Less Drastic Means and the First Amendment, 78 Yale L.J. 464 (1969). This kind of precision and less restrictive ef-

10. In Hanover v. Northrup, *supra*, a district court, per Blumenfeld, J., applied the test of *Tinker* and held that the refusal of a teacher to lead or recite the pledge was expression which could not be forbidden at the risk of loss of employment.

11. New York Education Law § 802. Instruction Relating to Flag: Holidays
1. It shall be the duty of the commissioner of education to prepare, for the use of the public schools of the state, a program providing for a salute to the flag and a daily pledge of allegiance to the flag, for instruction in its correct use and display and such other patriotic exercises as may be deemed by him to be expedient, under such regulations and instructions as may best meet the varied requirements of the different grades in such schools.
Regulations of the Commissioner of Education.

108.5 Pledge to the Flag. (a) It is recommended that schools use the following pledge to the flag:

"I pledge allegiance to the flag of the United States of America and to the Republic for which it stands, one Nation, under God, indivisible, with liberty and justice for all."

(b) In giving the pledge to the flag, the procedure is to render the pledge by standing with the right hand over the heart.

108.7 Other Instructions. Instruction concerning the flag as a symbol of American life should not be limited to the observance of Flag Day. Before leaving the elementary school each child should come to think of himself as a "maker of the flag" and each pupil who passes through the secondary school should be guided in sober thought as to the meaning of "liberty and justice for all."

fect are noticeably lacking in the Board of Education regulations involved in this case and therefore do not meet the test of constitutional exactness required by the First Amendment.

Mrs. Russo neither disrupted her classes nor attempted to prevent her students from reciting the pledge. The record indicates that the class participated in the flag salute program each day under the capable supervision of the senior instructor, Mrs. Catherine Adams. During the pledge, Mrs. Russo acted in a way that can only be described as respectful: she stood in silence with her hands at her sides. We recall, at this point, that the April 14 action of the Board permitted protesting students to remain seated. We note, moreover, that although the federal statute which treats the pledge of allegiance, 36 U.S.C. § 172, suggests that the pledge be rendered by placing the hand over the heart, it also provides that "civilians will always show full respect to the flag when the pledge is given merely by standing at attention. . . ."

In view of all the circumstances in this case, it is clear that the state's interest in maintaining a flag salute program was well-served in Mrs. Russo's classroom, even without her participation in the pledge ceremonies. We do well to note that her pupils were not fresh out of their cradles: she had charge of a tenth grade homeroom class consisting of students ranging in ages between fourteen and sixteen years. Young men and women at this stage of development are approaching an age when they form their own judgments. They readily perceive the existence of conflicts in the world around them; indeed, unless we are to screen them from all newspapers and television, it will be only a rather isolated teenager who does not have some understanding of the political divisions that exist and have existed in this country. Nor is this knowledge something to be dreaded. As we said in *James*, "schools must play a central role in preparing their students to think and analyze and to recognize the demagogue." Mrs. Russo made no attempt to proselytize her students. Instead, she provided her high school students with a second, but quiet, side of the not altogether new flag-salute debate: one teacher led the class in recitation of the pledge, the other remained standing in respectful silence. There is nothing to indicate that this demonstration had any effect—certainly no evidence of a destructive effect—on Mrs. Russo's students. Indeed, had it not been for the Board's precipitous action in dismissing her, the very fact that Mrs. Russo was permitted to refrain from saluting the flag would clearly have been evidence to her students that the injustice and intolerance against which she was quietly protesting was not merely not well-founded but a demonstrable falsehood at least within the confines of one school's homeroom class.

VI.

[15] By our holding today we do not mean to limit the traditionally broad discretion that has always rested with local school authorities to prescribe curriculum, set classroom standards, and evaluate conduct of teachers and students "in light of the special characteristics of the school environment." James v. Board of Education, *supra*. Nor do we imply that school officials are limited in their power to dismiss inept or obstreperous instructors, except, of course, to the extent they choose to so limit themselves. Public employment is not a sinecure to be retained regardless of merit simply by shouting loudly that any threat of dismissal is motivated by an anti-First Amendment animus. But where in fact, as in this case, a dismissal is directed because a teacher has engaged in constitutionally protected activity, that dismissal may not stand.

[16] We emphasize, too, that despite our holding that Mrs. Russo may not be dismissed for refusing to pledge allegiance to the flag, we do not share her views. But because the First Amendment ranks among the most important of our constitutional rights we must rec-

ognize that the precious right of free speech requires protection even when the speech is personally obnoxious. Freedom of expression, as we said in *James*, requires "breathing room." Patriotism, particularly at a time when that virtuous quality appears much maligned, should not be the object of derision. But patriotism that is forced is a false partriotism just as loyalty that is coerced is the very antithesis of loyalty. We ought not impugn the loyalty of a citizen—especially one whose convictions appear to be as genuine and conscientious as Mrs. Russo's—merely for refusing to pledge allegiance, any more than we ought necessarily to praise the loyalty of a citizen who without conviction or meaning, and with mental reservation, recites the pledge by rote each morning. Surely patriotism and loyalty go deeper than that.

[17] It is our conclusion that the right to remain silent in the face of an illegitimate demand for speech is as much a part of First Amendment protections as the right to speak out in the face of an illegitimate demand for silence, *see* Sweezy v. New Hampshire, 354 U.S. 234, 77 S.Ct. 1203, 1 L.Ed.2d 1311 (1957); West Virginia State Board of Education v. Barnette, *supra*. Beliefs, particularly when they touch on sensitive questions of faith, when they involve not easily articulated intuitions concerning religion, nation, flag, liberty and justice, are most at home in a realm of privacy, and are happiest in that safe and secluded harbour of the mind that protects our innermost thoughts. To compel a person to speak what is not in his mind offends the very principles of tolerance and understanding which for so long have been the foundation of our great land. "If there is any fixed star in our constitutional constellation," Mr. Justice Jackson said in *Barnette*, "it is that no official, high or petty, can prescribe what shall be orthodox in politics, nationalism, religion, or other matters of opinion or force citizens to confess by word or act their faith therein. If there are any circumstances which permit an exception, they do not now occur to us." West Virginia State Board of Education v. Barnette, *supra*, 319 U.S., at 642, 63 S.Ct., at 1187. We believe that to be an accurate and thoughtful statement of the underlying spirit of the First Amendment and we abide by it here.

Accordingly, the judgment is reversed, and the case is remanded to the district court for proceedings not inconsistent with this opinion.

---

* Rule 18, 5 Cir.; see Isbell Enterprises, Inc. v. Citizens Casualty Company of New

OPINIONS OF THE JUSTICES TO THE GOVERNOR.

Supreme Judicial Court of Massachusetts.

May 16, 1977.

Questions were propounded by the Governor to the Justices of the Supreme Judicial Court relating to bill concerning Pledge of Allegiance to the Flag in public schools. A majority of the Justices of the Supreme Judicial Court made answer that as applied to teachers, bill which would require each teacher at the commencement of the first class of each day in all grades in all public schools to lead the class in a group recitation of the Pledge of Allegiance to the Flag would violate the First Amendment of the Federal Constitution, even if under the proposed bill there would be no criminal penalties against noncomplying teachers, since there would still be an element of compulsion on a teacher inherent in the existence of the statutory mandate.

Question answered.

Quirico and Braucher, JJ., filed opinion disagreeing with such answer.

1. Statutes ⟾241(1)

Criminal statute must be construed strictly so that any ambiguity will be resolved in favor of the defendant.

2. Constitutional Law ⟾90(1)

An attempt by a governmental authority to induce belief in an ideological conviction by forcing an individual to identify himself intimately with that conviction through compelled expression of it is prohibited by the First Amendment. U.S.C.A. Const. Amend. 1.

3. Constitutional Law ⟾82

If a statute impinges on First Amendment rights, it may be sustained only if the state has a countervailing interest which is sufficiently compelling to justify its action. U.S.C.A.Const. Amend. 1.

4. Constitutional Law ⟾82

However commendable the legislature's interest may be in imbuing young people with patriotic feelings, that interest can only be implemented through a precise and narrowly drawn provision which achieves the basic purpose without compromising First Amendment rights. U.S.C.A.Const. Amend. 1.

5. Constitutional Law ⟾90.1(1)

Freedom of expression includes the right to remain silent. U.S.C.A.Const. Amend. 1.

---

5. G.L. c. 278, § 33E.

6. Subsequent to the entry of this appeal and to oral argument thereof, the defendant, pro se and without knowledge of his counsel, submitted a letter to the court alleging a conflict of interest by one of the members of the prosecution's appellate team of attorneys. Since such allegations are not a part of this record nor are the facts or significance of such alleged conflict established, we do not reach the issue of whether such conflict, if any, taints this appeal as defendant suggests. Since we have not reached this issue and intimate no opinion thereon, nothing we decide here shall be taken to foreclose whatever remedies, if any, the defendant may seek. Cf. *Commonwealth v. Geraway*, 364 Mass. 168, 301 N.E.2d 814 (1973).

6. Constitutional Law ⚖ 90.1(1)
Schools and School Districts ⚖ 164

As applied to teachers, bill which would require each teacher at the commencement of the first class of each day in all grades in all public schools to lead the class in a group recitation of the Pledge of Allegiance to the Flag would violate the First Amendment of the Federal Constitution, even if under the proposed bill there would be no criminal penalties against noncomplying teachers, since there would still be an element of compulsion on a teacher inherent in the existence of the statutory mandate. M.G.L.A. c. 71 § 69; U.S.C.A.Const. Amend. 1.

7. Schools and School Districts ⚖ 175

No punishment of any kind may be imposed on a student who elects, as a matter of principle, to abstain from participation in Pledge of Allegiance to the Flag. U.S.C.A.Const. Amend. 1.

On May 16, 1977, the Justices submitted the following answer to questions propounded to them by the Governor.

To His Excellency, the Governor of the Commonwealth:

The undersigned Justices of the Supreme Judicial Court respectfully submit their answer to the first of two questions set forth in the request of the Governor dated April 27, 1977, for an advisory opinion relating to a bill, House No. 5627, pending before him.[1] A copy of the bill was transmitted with the request. The bill is entitled, "An Act requiring recitation of the pledge of allegiance to the flag in all public schools at the commencement of class each day." In his request the Governor states that he has grave doubts as to the constitutionality of the bill.

The bill would amend G.L. c. 71, § 69, by striking out the fourth sentence, as appearing in St. 1935, c. 258, and inserting in place thereof the following sentence: "Each teacher at the commencement of the first class of each day in all grades in all public schools shall lead the class in a group recitation of the 'Pledge of Allegiance to the Flag.'"

The questions are:

"1. Would the enactment of H. 5627, coupled with a fine for non-compliance under the sixth sentence of G.L. c. 71, § 69, be an unconstitutional infringement of teachers' rights under either the First Amendment of the Constitution of the United States or Articles 2 or 16, Part the First, of the Massachusetts Constitution?

"2. Would the enactment of H. 5627 be an unconstitutional infringement of students' rights under either the First Amendment of the Constitution of the United States, or Articles 2 or 16, Part the First, of the Massachusetts Constitution?"

General Laws c. 71, § 69, as proposed to be amended would read as follows (with the amending language emphasized): "The school committee shall provide for each schoolhouse under its control, which is not otherwise supplied, flags of the United States of silk or bunting not less than two feet long, such flags or bunting to be manufactured in the United States, and suitable apparatus for their display as hereinafter provided. A flag shall be displayed, weather permitting, on the school building or grounds on every school day and on every legal holiday or day proclaimed by the governor or the president of the United States for especial observance; provided, that on stormy school days, it shall be displayed inside the building. A flag shall be displayed in each assembly hall or other room in each such schoolhouse where the opening exercises on each school day are held. *Each teacher at the commencement of the first class of each day in all grades in all public schools shall lead the class in a group recitation of the 'Pledge of Allegiance to the Flag.'*[2] A flag shall be displayed in each

---

1. House No. 5627 was recalled by the Senate on May 9, 1977, and again laid before the Governor for his approval or disapproval on that day.

2. The fourth sentence of G.L. c. 71, § 69, as appearing in St.1935, c. 258, reads: "Each teacher shall cause the pupils under his charge to salute the flag and recite in unison with him

classroom in each such schoolhouse. Failure for a period of five consecutive days by the principal or teacher in charge of a school equipped as aforesaid to display the flag as above required, or failure for a period of two consecutive weeks by a teacher to salute the flag and recite said pledge as aforesaid, or to cause the pupils under his charge so to do, shall be punished for every such period by a fine of not more than five dollars. Failure of the committee to equip a school as herein provided shall subject the members thereof to a like penalty." [3]

[1] 1. The questions which have been asked arise in a somewhat unusual context because constitutional problems which are apparent in the proposed amendment to G.L. c. 71, § 69, are present in § 69 as it now exists. In fact, the proposed amendment may rectify at least one possible unconstitutional aspect of § 69 as now enacted. If § 69 were to be amended as proposed by House No. 5627, the criminal penalty provided in the sixth sentence of § 69 may be inapplicable to a teacher who does not lead his class in a group recitation of the pledge of allegiance. The sixth sentence of § 69 provides a penalty for a teacher who fails for a period of two consecutive weeks "*to salute the flag* and recite said pledge" (emphasis supplied) or who fails "to cause the pupils under his charge so to do." Because the proposed amendment eliminates the requirement of a salute to the flag, the penalty of the sixth sentence literally would be inapplicable to a teacher who fails to lead his class in a group recitation of the pledge of allegiance to the flag. Such a construction might be warranted because a criminal statute must be construed strictly so that any ambiguity will be resolved in favor of the defendant. See *Commonwealth v. Devlin*, 366 Mass. 132, 137–138, 314 N.E.2d 897 (1974); *Maria v. State Examiners of Electricians*, 365 Mass. 551, 554, 313 N.E.2d 448 (1974).

If, contrary to the assumption of the first question asked us, the proposed amendment removes criminal penalties against noncomplying teachers, the proposed amendment nevertheless contains a direction that each teacher lead the first class of each day in a recitation of the pledge of allegiance to the flag. Failure to adhere to this mandate may threaten the continuance or advancement of a teacher's career. It is difficult to conclude that the Legislature intended House No. 5627 to have no effect. We shall, therefore, answer the first question on the assumption that there is an element of compulsion on a teacher inherent in the mandate of the proposed amendment to § 69. Even if we were to determine that it would be unconstitutional to visit any adverse consequences on a teacher for his failure to comply with the amendment, the very existence of the statutory mandate might inhibit a teacher from exercising whatever constitutional right he may have to refrain from leading his class in the recitation of the pledge of allegiance. Indirect discouragement of the exercise of First Amendment rights has been condemned. The Supreme Court of the United States observed in *Laird v. Tatum*, 408 U.S. 1, 11, 92 S.Ct. 2318, 2324, 33 L.Ed.2d 154 (1972) that "[i]n recent years this Court has found in a number of cases that constitutional violations may arise from the deterrent, or 'chilling,' effect of governmental regulations that fall short of a direct prohibition against the exercise of First Amendment rights. E.g., *Baird v. State Bar of Arizona*, 401 U.S. 1, 91 S.Ct. 702, 27 L.Ed.2d 639 (1971); *Keyishian v. Board of Regents*, 385 U.S. 589, 87 S.Ct. 675, 17 L.Ed.2d 629 (1967); *Lamont v. Postmaster General*, 381 U.S. 301, 85 S.Ct. 1493, 14 L.Ed.2d 398 (1965); *Baggett v. Bullitt*, 377 U.S. 360, 84

---

at said opening exercises at least once each week the 'Pledge of Allegiance to the Flag.'"

3. The Justices did not solicit briefs in this matter because of the shortness of time within which our opinion had to be submitted. We allowed the Attorney General's request to submit a memorandum. That memorandum considered G.L. c. 71, § 69, as now in effect, and concluded that "[i]nsofar as c. 71, § 69 may be read categorically to require teacher participation, it is inconsistent with the First Amendment of the Constitution of the United States and may not be enforced."

S.Ct. 1316, 12 L.Ed.2d 377 (1964)." We, therefore, turn to the question whether a teacher has a constitutional right to decline to comply with a mandate such as is contained in the proposed amendment.

The Supreme Court of the United States has not had an occasion to consider whether a teacher has a constitutional right to decline to participate in the recitation of the pledge of allegiance to the flag in circumstances where a statute or other directive purports to require his participation. In *West Virginia State Bd. of Educ. v. Barnette*, 319 U.S. 624, 63 S.Ct. 1178, 87 L.Ed. 1628 (1943), the Supreme Court held that a requirement that a student recite the pledge of allegiance to the flag and salute the flag, under the threat of expulsion for failure to comply, unconstitutionally violated the rights of a student who objected to the requirement on religious grounds. In reaching its conclusion, the Supreme Court did not express its views solely in terms of persons objecting on religious grounds but rather invalidated the requirement on broad First Amendment principles. That Court said, "If there is any fixed star in our constitutional constellation, it is that no official, high or petty, can prescribe what shall be orthodox in politics, nationalism, religion, or other matters of opinion or force citizens to confess by word or act their faith therein. If there are any circumstances which permit an exception, they do not now occur to us [footnote omitted].

"We think the action of the local authorities in compelling the flag salute and pledge transcends constitutional limitations on their power and invades the sphere of intellect and spirit which it is the purpose of the First Amendment to our Constitution to reserve from all official control." *Id.* at 642, 63 S.Ct. at 1187.

In our view, the rationale of the *Barnette* opinion applies as well to teachers as it does to students. Other courts have relied on the *Barnette* decision in holding that provisions requiring teachers to lead their classes in daily recitations of the pledge of allegiance violate the First Amendment rights of teachers. See *Russo v. Central School Dist. No. 1*, 469 F.2d 623, 630–634 (2d Cir. 1972), cert. denied, 411 U.S. 932, 93 S.Ct. 1899, 36 L.Ed.2d 391 (1973); *Hanover v. Northrup*, 325 F.Supp. 170 (D.Conn. 1970); *State v. Lundquist*, 262 Md. 534, 554–555, 278 A.2d 263 (1971). The Supreme Court of the United States has said that teachers do not "shed their constitutional rights to freedom of speech or expression at the schoolhouse gate." *Tinker v. Des Moines Independent Community School Dist.*, 393 U.S. 503, 506, 89 S.Ct. 733, 736, 21 L.Ed.2d 731 (1969).

[2] The Court's basic reasoning in its decision in the *Barnette* case makes fruitless any attempt to rely on any features of House No. 5627 which may distinguish it from the West Virginia resolution involved in the *Barnette* case. The purpose of fostering expression of patriotic views is apparent in both measures. Although most citizens find affirmation of the patriotic sentiments contained in the pledge of allegiance unobjectionable, the teaching of the *Barnette* decision is clear. Any attempt by a governmental authority to induce belief in an ideological conviction by forcing an individual to identify himself intimately with that conviction through compelled expression of it is prohibited by the First Amendment.[4] *Lathrop v. Donohue*, 367 U.S. 820, 858–859, 81 S.Ct. 1826, 6 L.Ed.2d 1191 (1961) (Harlan, J., concurring).

[3–6] If a statute impinges on First Amendment rights, it may be sustained only if the State has a countervailing interest which is sufficiently compelling to justify its action. See *Wooley v. Maynard*, —— U.S. ——, ——, 97 S.Ct. 1428, 51 L.Ed.2d 752 (1977); *United States v. O'Brien*, 391 U.S. 367, 376–377, 88 S.Ct. 1673, 20 L.Ed.2d

---

4. The viability of the *Barnette* rationale recently has been reaffirmed by the Supreme Court's opinion in *Wooley v. Maynard*, —— U.S. ——, 97 S.Ct. 1428, 51 L.Ed.2d 752 (1977), where the Court held that the State of New Hampshire violated the First Amendment principles articulated in *Barnette* by requiring its citizens to display the State motto "Live Free or Die" on their automobile license plates.

672 (1968). The Legislature's purpose in requiring schoolteachers to lead students in a recitation of the pledge of allegiance is to instill attitudes of patriotism and loyalty in those students. See *Nicholls v. Mayor and School Comm. of Lynn,* 297 Mass. 65, 69, 7 N.E.2d 577 (1937). However commendable the Legislature's interest may be in imbuing young people with patriotic feelings, that interest can only be implemented through a precise and narrowly drawn provision which achieves the basic purpose without compromising First Amendment rights. See *Wooley v. Maynard,* — U.S. ——, ——, 97 S.Ct. 1428, 51 L.Ed.2d 752 (1977); *Sherbert v. Verner,* 374 U.S. 398, 406–407, 83 S.Ct. 1790, 10 L.Ed.2d 965 (1963); *Shelton v. Tucker,* 364 U.S. 479, 488, 81 S.Ct. 247, 5 L.Ed.2d 231 (1960). Freedom of expression, which includes the right to remain silent (*Brown v. Louisiana,* 383 U.S. 131, 86 S.Ct. 719, 15 L.Ed.2d 637 [1966]), is "susceptible of restriction only to prevent grave and immediate danger to interests which the State may lawfully protect." *West Virginia State Bd. of Educ. v. Barnette, supra,* 319 U.S. at 639, 63 S.Ct. at 1186. The views of the Supreme Court of the United States compel us to conclude that the proposed amendment does not meet this standard as to teachers.

Therefore, we answer that as applied to teachers House No. 5627 would violate the First Amendment of the Federal Constitution and for that reason the answer to question 1 is "Yes." [5]

[7] 2. Because we have concluded that H. 5627 unconstitutionally infringes on the First Amendment rights of teachers, we need not consider whether the bill is also an unconstitutional infringement on the rights of students. Section 69 contains no criminal penalty for a student who fails to participate in the recitation of the pledge of allegiance to the flag. See *Nicholls v. Mayor and School Comm. of Lynn, supra,* 297 Mass. at 68, 7 N.E.2d 577. We think it is clear from the opinion of the Supreme Court of the United States in the *Barnette* case that no punishment of any kind may be imposed on a student who elects, as a matter of principle, to abstain from participation.

If the Legislature enacted a statute which permitted a student or teacher to sit quietly without participating in the pledge of allegiance by others in a classroom, different and yet still difficult constitutional questions would be presented, on which our opinion has not and could not be sought by the Governor in the circumstances. See *Goetz v. Ansell,* 477 F.2d 636, 638 (2d Cir. 1973); *Banks v. Board of Pub. Instruction of Dade County,* 314 F.Supp. 285, 294–296 (S.D.Fla. 1970) (three-judge court), aff'd, 450 F.2d 1103 (5th Cir. 1971); *Frain v. Baron,* 307 F.Supp. 27 (E.D.N.Y. 1969).

We answer question 1, "Yes."

We beg to be excused from answering question 2.

EDWARD F. HENNESSEY
BENJAMIN KAPLAN
HERBERT P. WILKINS
PAUL J. LIACOS
RUTH I. ABRAMS

We do not agree with the answer of our colleagues. To answer the questions set forth in the Governor's request, in our opinion, requires a close examination of the prior law and the effect of the amendment proposed by House No. 5627.

Under G.L. c. 71, § 69, fourth sentence, each teacher in a public school must "cause the pupils under his charge to salute the flag and recite in unison with him" at the "opening exercises" in the school "at least once each week the 'Pledge of Allegiance to the Flag.'" Under the sixth sentence of the same section, "failure for a period of two consecutive weeks by a teacher to salute the flag and recite said pledge as aforesaid, or to cause the pupils under his charge so to do, shall be punished for every such

---

5. Because House No. 5627 would violate the First Amendment to the Constitution of the United States, we do not reach that portion of the Governor's first question which asks if the amendment would violate arts. 2 and 16 of the Declaration of Rights of the Massachusetts Constitution.

period by a fine of not more than five dollars."

Long ago this court held that a child who asserted a religious objection to the required salute and recitation could be expelled from the school. *Nicholls v. Mayor and School Comm. of Lynn*, 297 Mass. 65, 69, 7 N.E.2d 577 (1937). For the reasons stated by our colleagues, it is clear that no such decision could be made today. *West Virginia State Bd. of Educ. v. Barnette*, 319 U.S. 624, 63 S.Ct. 1178, 87 L.Ed. 1628 (1943). In our view it is equally clear that teachers who find the salute or pledge "morally objectionable" cannot be required to participate in the salute or pledge. *Wooley v. Maynard*, —— U.S. ——, ——, 97 S.Ct. 1428, 51 L.Ed.2d 752 (1977). See *Russo v. Central School Dist. No. 1*, 469 F.2d 623, 630–634 (2d Cir. 1972), cert. denied, 411 U.S. 932, 93 S.Ct. 1899, 36 L.Ed.2d 391 (1973); *Hanover v. Northrup*, 325 F.Supp. 170, 172 (D.Conn. 1970).

House No. 5627 proposes to substitute a new fourth sentence in G.L. c. 71, § 69: "Each teacher at the commencement of the first class of each day in all grades in all public schools shall lead the class in a group recitation of the 'Pledge of Allegiance to the Flag.'" The effect of this amendment would be (1) to eliminate any requirement that the teacher "cause" his pupils to do anything, (2) to eliminate any reference to a "salute" as distinguished from the "Pledge," (3) to substitute "the commencement of the first class" for the "opening exercises," and (4) to change from a weekly requirement to a daily requirement. No change is proposed in the sixth sentence. In the *Nicholls* case, *supra*, 297 Mass. at 68, 7 N.E.2d at 579, we said that the statute "established no penalty for a disobedient pupil, but is directed to the school committee and to the teacher." After enactment of the proposed amendment, the sixth sentence would be somewhat confusing, but we think it should then be read to impose no fine on teachers either for "failure . . . to salute the flag and recite said pledge as aforesaid," or for failure to "cause" pupils to do anything. A further amendment to strike the two quoted clauses from the sixth sentence would of course make this reading clearer.

There is no constitutional obstacle to a provision for voluntary participation by students and teachers in a pledge of allegiance to the flag. *In re Lewis v. Allen*, 5 Misc.2d 68, 72–73, 159 N.Y.S.2d 807 (N.Y.Sup.Ct. 1957), aff'd, 11 A.D.2d 447, 207 N.Y.S.2d 862 (N.Y. 1960), aff'd, 14 N.Y.2d 867, 252 N.Y.S.2d 80, 200 N.E.2d 767, cert. denied, 379 U.S. 923, 85 S.Ct. 279, 13 L.Ed.2d 336 (1964). Cf. *Gaines v. Anderson*, 421 F.Supp. 337, 346 (D.Mass. 1976) (requirement of moment of silence). We would construe the bill to provide an opportunity for such voluntary participation. So construed, it is not unconstitutional.

We recognize that it is fairly arguable that a daily recitation may be less effective in promoting patriotism and loyalty than a weekly recitation. Any such argument should be addressed to the Legislature, or to the Governor. It is not a constitutional argument. The proposed amendment introduces no constitutional difficulty not found in the present statute.

We would answer both questions "No."

FRANCIS J. QUIRICO
ROBERT BRAUCHER

ACKNOWLEDGMENTS

Grinnell, Frank W. "Children, the Bill of Rights and the American Flag." *Massachusetts Law Quarterly* 24 (1939): 1–7. Courtesy of the Yale University Law Library.

Grinnell, Frank W. "More About the Flag Salute Law." *Massachusetts Law Quarterly* 24 (1939): 1–3. Courtesy of the Yale University Law Library.

Grinnell, Frank W. "More About the Flag Salute: Extracts from the Opinion of the Circuit Court of Appeals for the Third Circuit in Minersville School District v. Gobitis." *Massachusetts Law Quarterly* 24 (1939): 18–20. Courtesy of the Yale University Law Library.

"Minersville School District, Board of Education of Minersville School District, et al. v. Gobitis et al." *United States Reports* 310 (1940): 586–607. Courtesy of the Yale University Law Library.

Andersen, William F. "Constitutional Law—Due Process—Freedom of Religion and Conscience—Compulsory Flag Salute." *Michigan Law Review* 39 (1940–41): 149–52. Courtesy of the Yale University Law Library.

Fennell, William G. "The 'Reconstructed Court' and Religious Freedom: The Gobitis Case in Retrospect." *New York University Law Quarterly Review* 19 (1941): 31–48. Courtesy of the Yale University Law Library.

Rotnem, Victor W. and F.G. Folsom, Jr. "Recent Restrictions Upon Religious Liberty." *American Political Science Review* 36 (1942): 1053–68. Reprinted with the permission of the American Political Science Association. Courtesy of the Yale University Law Library.

Danzig, Richard. "How Questions Begot Answers in Felix Frankfurter's First Flag Salute Opinion." *Supreme Court Review* 1977 (1978): 257–74. Reprinted with the permission of the University of Chicago Press, publisher. Copyright 1978 by the University of Chicago. All rights reserved. Courtesy of the Yale University Law Library.

Commager, Henry Steele. "Civil Liberties and Democracy." *Senior Scholastic* (March 22, 1943): 13. Reprinted with the permission of Henry Steele Commager. Courtesy of Scholastic Inc.

"The West Virginia State Board of Education, etc., et al., Appellants, vs. Walter Barnette, Paul Stull, and Lucy McClure, *Appellees.*" *Brief of the American Legion, Amicus Curiae* 591 (1942): 1–23. Courtesy of the Yale University Law Library.

Amicus Curiae Brief of the Committee on the Bill of Rights, of the American Bar Association, The West Virginia State Board of Education, etc., et al., *Appellants,* vs. Walter Barnette, Paul Stull, and Lucy McClure, *Appellees.* 319 U.S. 624 (No. 591) (1942): 1–26. Courtesy of the Yale University Law Library.

Amicus Curiae Brief for American Civil Liberties Union, The West Virginia State Board of Education, etc., et al., *Defendants-Appellants,* vs. Walter Barnette, Paul Stull, and Lucy McClure.

Amicus Curiae Brief of the American Legion, The West Virginia State Board of Education, etc., et al., *Appellants,* vs. Walter Barnette, Paul Stull, and Lucy McClure, *Appellees.* 319 U.S. 624 (No. 591) (1942). Courtesy of the Yale University Law Library.

"West Virginia State Board of Education et al. v. Barnette et al." United States Reports 319 (1942): 624–71. Courtesy of the Yale University Law Library.

Powell, Thomas Reed. "The Flag-Salute Case." *The New Republic* 109 (1943): 16–18. Reprinted by permission of *The New Republic,* copyright 1943, *The New Republic,* Inc. Courtesy of *The New Republic.*

Boudin, Louis B. "Freedom of Thought and Religious Liberty Under the Constitution." *Lawyers Guild Review* 4 (1944): 9–24. Reprinted with the permission of the National Lawyers Guild. Courtesy of the Yale University Law Library.

Danzig, Richard. "Justice Frankfurter's Opinions in the Flag Salute Cases: Blending Logic and Psychologic in Constitutional Decisionmaking." *Stanford Law Review* 36 (1983–84): 675–723. Reprinted with the permission of the Board of Trustees of the Leland Stanford Junior University. Copyright 1983–1984. Courtesy of the Yale University Law Library.

Gard, Stephen W. "The Flag Salute Cases and the First Amendment." *Cleveland State Law Review* 31 (1982): 419–53. Copyright by Cleveland State University. Courtesy of the *Cleveland State Law Review.*

"Mrs. Susan Russo, Appellant, v. Central School District No. 1, Towns of Rush, et al., County of Monroe, State of New York et al., Appellees." *Federal Reporter* Second Series 469 (1973): 623–34. Reprinted with the permission of West Publishing Company. Courtesy of the Yale University Law Library.

"Opinions of the Justices to the Governor: Supreme Judicial Court of Massachusetts." *North Eastern Reporter* Second Series 363 (1977): 251–56. Reprinted with the permission of West Publishing Company. Courtesy of the Yale University Law Library.

WAKE TECHNICAL COMMUNITY COLLEGE LIBRARY
9101 FAYETTEVILLE ROAD
RALEIGH, NORTH CAROLINA 27603

DATE DUE

APR 2 5 2000			
FEB 14 2001			
FEB 28 2001			
MAR 30			
OCT 2 4 2001			
APR 0 9 02			
NOV - 4 02			
NOV - 4 02			
APR 2 6 2012			
GAYLORD			PRINTED IN U.S.A.